MINORITY
VOTE DILUTION

MINORITY VOTE DILUTION

Edited by
Chandler Davidson

Under the auspices of the
**Joint Center for
    Political Studies**

Howard University Press
Washington, D.C.   *1989*

Printed in the United States of America

Library of Congress Cataloging-in-Publication Data

Minority vote dilution / edited by Chandler Davidson : under the
　auspices of the Joint Center for Political Studies.
　　　p. cm.
　　Contains new postscript by the editor.
　　Includes bibliographical references.
　　ISBN 0–88258–176–7 : $12.95
　　　1. Minorities — Suffrage — United States. 2. Election districts —
　United States. 3. Minorities — Civil rights — United States.
　4. Representative government and representation — United States.
　I. Davidson, Chandler. II. Joint Center for Political Studies
　(U.S.)
　JK1853.M57 1989　　　　　　　　　　　　　　89-39505
　324.6′2′0973 — dc20　　　　　　　　　　　　　　CIP

This book is dedicated to

Alvina Cannon
and
Alice Boston Martin

Texans with Louisiana roots
who by example have taught me
about courage and kindness and love

Contents

PROSPECTS

Foreword

Politics is the new cutting edge of the civil rights movement. The emotional and intellectual excitement that started and sustained the protest movement of the 1960s is today focused on the political arena. More blacks are registering and voting than ever before; more blacks are running for—and winning—elective office at almost every level of government; and more organizations and coalitions are throwing their energies into voter education and registration efforts.

This new-found passion for and commitment to politics has furthered the careers of many black leaders and is expected to pay significant dividends to the black community as a whole. More broadly, this grass roots movement—growing out of local churches, community organizations, and other groups—has enhanced the nation's democratic institutions.

Despite these gains, barriers to minority political participation remain. They take two forms: 1) barriers to actual registration and voting, such as limited hours and locations for registration, dual registration requirements and other unnecessary complexities, and lack of bilingual information and ballots; and 2) vote dilution mechanisms, which make the votes of minority group members less effective than those of whites. This book deals with vote dilution, a subtle—and sometimes not so subtle—form of discrimination.

Even as we approach the twentieth anniversary of the Voting Rights Act, minority vote dilution remains widespread. It is the most common form of electoral discrimination in the United States today, and one that is no less mischievous for being subtle and indirect. As Supreme Court Justice Felix Frankfurter wrote in 1939, "The Constitution nullifies sophisticated as well as simple-minded modes of discrimination."

Jesse Jackson, in his 1984 campaign for the Democratic nomination for president, has focused public attention on the issue of vote dilution through his attacks on runoff primaries. The issue is a controversial one because runoff primaries, like most vote dilution mechanisms, are not discriminatory on the surface. It is only in conjunction with other mechanisms—such as racial gerrymandering and at-large elections—and with white bloc voting that runoff primaries may deprive minorities of equal access to political power.

As a legal matter, the status of various vote dilution systems is currently being tested. Vote dilution systems not covered by Section 5 of the Voting Rights Act can be challenged in court under Section 2, but such court cases were put on hold for two years following the Supreme Court's 1980 *Mobile* decision, which effectively made them impossible to win. (The significance of the *Mobile* decision is discussed in depth by several authors in this volume.) In 1982, however, Congress extended the Voting Rights Act and added a new provision that clarified the standard to be applied in cases brought under Section 2 and restored the section's vitality. Lawsuits are now under way again, as blacks and Hispanics challenge local electoral systems and redistricting decisions based on the 1980 Census.

Perhaps because of the political and legal complexities of the subject there has been relatively little scholarly attention to vote dilution despite the prominence of the issue over the past several years. The Joint Center for Political Studies commissioned Professor Chandler Davidson to compile a volume of essays on all aspects of vote dilution by leading experts on the subject—lawyers, historians, political scientists, and policy makers with extensive experience with voting law. The result is the first book devoted to the subject of vote dilution.

Our deep appreciation goes to four foundations that supported the Joint Center's work on voter law policy and helped make this book possible: the Carnegie Corporation of New York, the Field Foundation, The Ford Foundation, and the Rockefeller Brothers Fund.

Eddie N. Williams
President, Joint Center for Political Studies

Joint Center for Political Studies Board of Governors

Acknowledgments

Many of the essays in this book were written under trying circumstances by people who, because of their expertise on vote dilution, were heavily involved in civil rights litigation and efforts to extend and amend the Voting Rights Act as the manuscript deadlines approached. It is a tribute to their dedication to this project and the larger goal it represents—the abolition of vote dilution—that the deadlines were met. I am grateful to the contributors for this, and also for their good-humored response to my cajolery and threats.

I would like to thank the Joint Center for Political Studies, under whose auspices the book is published, for inviting me to edit this collection of essays, and to its staff for providing help and encouragement along the way. Milton Morris, the center's director of research, deserves special thanks in this regard. Catherine Iino, the center's director of publications, has also been a helpful colleague and friendly critic, as well as an appropriately stern taskmaster when the need arose.

Armand Derfner's advice, criticism, and geniality have been invaluable. I appreciate, as well, conversations over the years on the concept and measurement of vote dilution with Larry Menefee, James Blacksher, Frank R. Parker, J. Morgan Kousser, George Korbel, Jerry Hebert, Laughlin McDonald, Charles Cotrell, and Bill Garrett. The writings of Richard Engstrom, Bernard Grofman, and James Loewin on this subject have also been helpful, as have the seminars and conferences on vote dilution sponsored by the Lawyers' Committee for Civil Rights Under Law, the NAACP Legal Defense and Educational Fund, and the Southern Regional Council.

The copy editing by Howard University Press, and the comments on the manuscripts made by anonymous readers during the review process gave evidence of their concern not only for clarity and accuracy but also the authors' autonomy.

A sabbatical leave provided by Rice University and funding administered by Joseph Cooper, Dean of Social Sciences at Rice, made the final editing chores much easier than would otherwise have been possible.

Manuscript typing by Terri Pallack and Alicia Mikula of Rice's Department of Sociology is gratefully acknowledged, as is my introduction to the mysteries of word processing by Alicia Mikula in the course of preparing this book.

MINORITY VOTE DILUTION

Minority Vote Dilution
An Overview

Chandler Davidson

Taylor, Texas, is a farming town of 10,000 people located near Austin, the state capital. Twenty percent of its population is black. Another 17 percent is Mexican American.

The town is in central Texas, not far enough south toward the Mexican border for its Chicanos to have caught the fever of militancy that radiated from Crystal City through the medium of La Raza Unida party. Nor is it far enough east for its blacks to have shared the hopes of their race, in some of the Texas "black belt" counties, of achieving political power through the mobilization of sheer numbers. Nevertheless, in the 1960s leaders of both groups in Taylor dared hope that the winds of change blowing across the South and Southwest after the passage of the Voting Rights Act would kick up dust in their town, too.

Changes were desperately needed. As in most Texas cities, the minority population was socially and economically deprived. Its status could be traced directly to historical and continuing discrimination by Anglos, including long exclusion from meaningful political participation. The disabilities thus created resulted in special needs that by any defensible theory of justice placed extraordinary obligations on the city government.

Only in 1965 was the first minority person appointed to a municipal board, and he remained the sole minority representative into the 1970s. No blacks or Mexican Americans had been appointed as city election officials. Most minority employees on the city payroll held the least desirable, lowest paying jobs, and none worked at city hall. The town's three housing projects in the 1960s were totally segregated.

Officialdom's neglect of minority neighborhoods was reflected in the poorly maintained streets, the park that was run-down, particularly compared to the Anglos' park, and the city's refusal to heed requests for increased recreational equipment at the housing projects and for refurbishment of a neighborhood center. In 1961, minority spokesmen had asked for a fire station in their area—a request still not acted on by 1982, although a substation was built in an Anglo neighborhood. Serious allegations of police misconduct toward minorities were ignored by city government.[1]

In 1967, minority leaders decided to use the electoral system to help remedy their problems. They got together, black Baptists and brown Catholics, and agreed that the arithmetic of the situation dictated unity in local elections. The newly formed coalition put forward a personable candidate, Paul Sanchez, to campaign for city commissioner. Sanchez was the first minority candidate ever to run for the office. The elections were at large rather than district based. An Anglo candidate defeated Sanchez, although Sanchez received the overwhelming majority of votes cast by blacks and Mexican Americans.

Three years later, another Chicano ventured forth, again with bi-ethnic backing. Gumie Gonzales, who had spent time in the highly politicized climate of nearby Austin, brought the first sophisticated political campaign to Taylor. Gonzales used telephone banks, door-to-door canvassing, and the solicitation of endorsements from most of the ethnic preachers and lay leaders in Taylor. He lost. In 1971, Tommie Rivers, a black, ran and, by prior agreement, no Chicano entered the race. He lost. In 1972 two Chicanos and a black ran. The voter turnout that year was the largest in the city's history up to that point. None of the three was elected.

In 1974, another black ran unsuccessfully. Seven years passed without a minority candidate running for city commissioner. In 1981 Gumie Gonzales ran again. Three posts were to be filled, and there were four candidates—Gonzales and three Anglos. Gonzales came in fourth. Then, a week after the election, an incumbent commissioner resigned, and his post was filled in a special election by another Anglo. Had the incumbent resigned before the earlier election, Gonzales would have won a seat.

Between 1967 and 1974, voter turnout was 50 percent higher in contests where minorities challenged whites than in those where only Anglos contended. By all accounts, the minority community turned out in unprecedented numbers. But Anglos—rallied by the local newspaper, whose special election-day editions hinted ominously of heavy minority turnout—trooped to the polls as well.

After 1974, no Anglo candidates made overtures to the minority community. No campaign promises in return for votes were made to its leaders. Blacks and Chicanos were virtually excluded from the municipal political system. In the late 1970s, minority registration was low, and actual voter turnout, when compared to Anglo rates, even lower. The winds of change seemed to have passed the city by.

Minority leaders, however, had filed a suit in the mid-1970s arguing that Taylor's at-large elections were unconstitutional because they were instrumental in preventing minority voters from electing candidates of their choice. The suit had just been put on the trial docket in the spring of 1980 when the Supreme Court delivered its decision in *City of Mobile v. Bolden*,[2] in which such election systems were declared unconstitutional only if they were intentionally created to discriminate.

The decision presented serious problems to the plaintiffs in Taylor, whose at-large system had been established in 1914. The files of the local newspaper only went back to the 1930s, and official city documents relating to the charter revision shed no light on the motives for the change. After much soul searching, the plaintiffs withdrew the suit, at the cost of three years of trial preparation, dashing the minorities' lingering hopes that the U.S. Constitution might provide them relief.[3]

Minorities in other cities in the South and Southwest were in a comparable situation in the wake of *Bolden*. After having won the franchise at great cost, blacks and Mexican Americans had discovered that it was a useless political tool in many situations. The Supreme Court was now informing them that the Fifteenth Amendment does not guarantee a group the right to cast an effective ballot, and the Fourteenth Amendment does so only when it can be shown that election laws were established purposely to abridge this right.

The story of Taylor illustrates aspects of a phenomenon that scholars and jurists refer to as vote dilution. It is one of three major types of electoral discrimination, in addition to disfranchisement and candidate diminution.

Disfranchisement prevents or discourages people from voting. This may be accomplished directly by prohibiting persons belonging to a particular group from casting a ballot, either by law or extralegally. In the antebellum period, in the North as well as the South, all slaves and the vast majority of free people of color were legally disfranchised. After Reconstruction, blacks were often prevented from voting by force and violence.

Disfranchisement may also be accomplished indirectly by rules and practices that on their face are not discriminatory but in fact discourage a group of potential voters from casting a ballot. For example, around the turn of the century, literacy tests, the poll tax, and similar measures removed most southern blacks from the electorate.

Today several practices still discourage minority groups from voting. They include purges of registration rolls;[4] changing polling places on short notice (or without any notice at all);[5] the establishment of difficult registration procedures;[6] decreasing the number of voting machines in minority areas;[7] and the threat of reprisals.[8]

A continuing pattern of vote dilution may also result in something like disfranchisement. If, after great effort, a minority group decides that the electoral structure prevents it from electing candidates of its choice, as in the case of Taylor, it may cease to vote. This decision may be based on a realistic assessment of the ineffectiveness of the ballot.

A second form of discrimination, *candidate diminution,* occurs when candidates representing the interests of a group of voters are prevented or discouraged from running. Even if a group is enfranchised, therefore, candidate diminution may appreciably affect its voting strength. As with disfranchisement, minority groups have been the major victims of this form of discrimination. Earlier in this century, it was unthinkable for black candidates to run for office in the South. Given the prejudice of whites and the disfranchisement of blacks, a black candidate had no chance of winning. More important, he was likely to encounter violence or threats of violence to himself or his family.

Candidate diminution still exists today. Among the better known methods are the changing of governmental posts from elective to appointive ones when a minority candidate has a chance of winning elective office;[9] setting high filing and bonding fees;[10] increasing the number of signatures required on qualifying petitions; manipulating qualifying deadlines; abolishing party primaries;[11] and intimidating and harassing candidates by threats, violence, cutting off credit, calling in loans and mortgages, and firing them.[12] Candidate diminution, like disfranchisement, is also an indirect result of vote dilution. If electoral rules make it impossible for minority-preferred candidates to win office, their number will gradually decline, as it did in Taylor.

Vote dilution, like the other major forms of vote discrimination, diminishes the political power of a group. Unlike them, however, dilution can operate even when there are no barriers to casting a ballot, and when the group's candidates are able to run for office without hindrance.

The essential characteristics of vote dilution are difficult to specify. In spite of two decades of vote dilution litigation and a number of articles on the subject in law reviews and other scholarly journals, no concise and comprehensive definition has emerged. To be sure, there are several electoral mechanisms, discussed below, that the courts have found to play a role in unlawful dilution under certain circumstances. But because the dilutionary effect of the mechanisms is so closely tied to the context in which they are used, no standard definition has been forthcoming.

What seems to be common to the various types of vote discrimination dealt with by the authors of this book under the label *dilution* is a process whereby election laws or practices, either singly or in concert, combine with systematic bloc voting among an identifiable group to diminish the voting strength of at least one other group. Ethnic or racial minority vote dilution is a special case, in which the voting strength of an ethnic or racial minority group is diminished or cancelled out by the bloc vote of the majority. In extreme cases, minority vote dilution results in the virtual exclusion of one or more groups from meaningful participation in a political system.

Four aspects of vote dilution should be mentioned at this point. First, students of the subject have stressed that the process by which dilution occurs is subtle, compared with some other forms of discrimination. A law stating that a black person's vote must be weighted at half the value of a white person's vote is discriminatory on its face, and if enforced, it would accomplish its discriminatory purpose in a straightforward manner. In the case of "dilutionary laws," on the other hand, there is nothing in their wording to suggest that they are discriminatory and, indeed, they are not in all situations.

Second, dilution as it is discussed in the following pages is a *group* phenomenon. It occurs because the propensity of an identifiable group to vote as a bloc waters down the voting strength of another identifiable group, under certain conditions. One individual acting alone could not dilute the vote of another individual or of a group of individuals.

Third, dilution often operates to diminish a group's potential voting strength that derives from the group's geographic concentration. This is most obviously true for at-large elections and the various forms of dilution that fall under the heading of gerrymandering. The dilutionary process is thus often connected with what the political scientist Andrew Hacker once called "political cartography"—drawing or erasing electoral boundaries in ways that advantage one group at the expense of another.

Fourth, the diminished power resulting from vote dilution is not the result of the behavior of the group whose votes are diluted. It is caused not by apathy, political ineptitude, or ignorance, but by laws or practices that operate in a discriminatory fashion when combined with bloc voting by the majority. Some groups, of course, may suffer diminished voting strength solely as a result of their own shortcomings—their inability to unite behind a candidate, for example. To say that a group's votes are diluted, however, implies that the ineffectiveness of its ballots is beyond its control, and that the causes inhere in the larger political structure.

TYPES OF DILUTIONARY MECHANISMS

At-large Elections

The situation in Taylor illustrates the problem which minorities face in an at-large election system. Most of the city's blacks and Mexican Americans are concentrated in a few neighborhoods, and in the city as a whole they are outnumbered by Anglos. If the city were divided into a number of voting districts, such that the ethnic minorities constituted a majority in their districts, and if people were allowed to vote only for a representative of their district, blacks and Mexican Americans in Taylor would have a fair chance to realize the full potential of their voting strength, measured in this case by their ability to elect candidates of their choice to the city commission. Such an arrangement is called a ward-based or single-member-district system.

But a different election method exists in Taylor. Instead of voting for candidates to represent single-member districts, the way Americans elect their congresspersons, for example, all voters in Taylor vote for all the elective positions. The evidence strongly suggests that the vast majority of the blacks and Mexican Americans usually vote for one of the minority candidates, and that they turn out to vote for them in unusual numbers. During the time period described previously there was enough internal discipline that in most of the races contested by minority candidates, only one such minority candidate ran, so as not to split the minority vote. But the Anglos bloc voted as well. Their votes went overwhelmingly to the Anglo candidates. And as the Anglo electorate was much larger than the minority electorate, their ballots deluged those of the ethnic minorities year after year. This is at-large vote dilution at its most dramatic. The minority communities were effectively denied the presence on city commission of someone whom they had chosen as their representative, and who was answerable to them. Milton Morris, in Chapter 12, assesses the measurable results to minority groups of having their own representatives in elective office. As one might expect, these results can be considerable.

When courts have found illegal vote dilution to exist, they have typically ordered a remedy consisting of the creation of single-member districts, on the assumption that if they are fairly drawn, they will greatly increase the chances of minority groups to elect candidates of their choice. (By examining a wide variety of evidence, George Korbel and I test this assumption in Chapter 4, and find it to be correct. Alternatives to the single-member-district remedy are discussed by Edward Still in Chapter 11.)

The Runoff Requirement

There are a variety of rules which, used in conjunction with the at-large system, add to its dilutionary impact. Because the at-large system is dilutionary under many conditions, and because these auxiliary mechanisms derive most of their discriminatory force from accompanying a dilutionary at-large system, it is logical to classify them as dilutionary, too.

One of these is the runoff requirement. In many locales, particularly in the South and Southwest, candidates are required to obtain an absolute majority of votes (50 percent plus one) in order to win, rather than a mere plurality. If a majority is not obtained, a runoff election is required between the two top vote-getters. This device, on its face, is democratic—for what is more appropriate than requiring a majority of votes to win in a "majoritarian democracy"? As a matter of fact, however, only 20 percent of American cities have a runoff requirement.[13] Nor is a majority of the popular vote required in general elections for the U.S. presidency, Congress, and most state and county offices.

The mandatory runoff precludes the possibility that a minority candidate will win office with a mere plurality if the white vote splits among several other candidates. In that situation, the minority candidate is forced into a runoff against a single white, behind whom the white voters can rally to produce a majority. White officials in numerous instances have changed the election rules to require a runoff after a minority candidate came close to winning—or actually won—under a plurality rule.[14]

The runoff is most often encountered in an at-large system, but it is sometimes used in ward systems as well, where it can have a dilutionary impact. In 1960, a black minister in Slaton, Texas, won election to city council from a ward against five white opponents under a plurality rule. Had a runoff been required, the black minister would probably not have been elected. (Almost immediately afterwards, the council held a referendum on abolishing the ward system. Black and Mexican American voters, the major supporters of the minister, were able to defeat the measure.)[15]

Anti-single-shot Devices

In a pure at-large system without a majority requirement, there are typically several seats on a government body to be filled by an election, and candidates for all the seats compete against each other. Those with the most votes win. For example, if five seats on a school board are up for election, and twenty candidates declare, each voter has five votes, and the top five vote-getters are declared winners. This system enables a minority group to "single-shot." The group decides before the election to vote only for one or a few preferred candidates, and to withhold its remaining votes. This procedure has the effect of a weighted vote system, for it deprives other candidates of votes relative to the group's preferred candidate.

By single-shot voting, minority groups have been able partly to overcome the disadvantages of the at-large system, and elect some candidates of their choice. Responding to this strategy, white lawmakers have passed anti-single-shot or "full slate'' ordinances, invalidating ballots on which the voter has not marked all the choices to which he or she is entitled.

Another device that has the same effect is the place voting system, which also operates to prevent single-shot voting in an at-large context. Place voting requires the candidates to declare for a "place" on the ballot, such as Place 1, 2, 3, and so forth. (An equivalent arrangement is a rule requiring candidates to "represent" a particular geographic area of the city, but to be voted on at large.) The essence of the place system as an anti-single-shot device is that it gives the voter only one vote to cast per candidate per place.

The effectiveness of the single-shot procedure results from the voter's ability not only to cast a vote for his preferred candidate, but to withhold one or more votes from that candidate's competitors. By limiting all voters to one vote per place, the place system destroys the voter's ability to withhold votes from his candidate's competition.

Proponents of the place system justify it as a means of focusing the electorate's attention on individual candidates or issues, by breaking one big contest among all candidates into several smaller contests. It is easier—so their argument goes—for the voters to learn about candidates and issues in these "mini-contests." I know of no scholarly evidence that the place system accomplishes its ostensible purpose. On the other hand, there is ample evidence that it has purposely and successfully been implemented to preclude single-shot voting by minorities.[16] From the viewpoint of racist officials, it also has the advantage of being less obviously discriminatory than the anti-single-shot law.

A third barrier to single-shot voting is staggered terms, which is a variant of the place system. Instead of holding all elections the same year, a jurisdiction may stagger them, usually over a two- or three-year period. In the extreme case, elections can be staggered so that only one position per year is filled, thus eliminating the possibility of a voter's both casting a vote and withholding a vote, inasmuch as he is only allotted one vote to cast.

Decreasing the Size of the Governmental Body

The actual number of seats on a body such as a council or school board affects the possibility of minority electoral success.[17] In a single-member-district system, decreasing the number of seats can decrease the number—and the percentage—of districts that a minority group can elect candidates from. In either single-member-district or at-large systems white voters appear to be more likely to vote for a minority group's candidate when he or she will be one among many on a governmental body than when one among few.

Exclusive Slating Groups

In many areas a dominant nominating or slating group controls access to elective office. When it operates in a system that dilutes the votes of minorities, it can play a role in perpetuating dilution, by contributing to the illusion that dilution no longer exists.

In a number of instances these groups have hand-picked a black or Mexican American candidate as part of their slate, refusing to let minority voters have a fair chance to participate in their decision. When this occurs, the slated minority candidate typically is not popular in the minority community, and is chosen for his docility rather than for his ability to effectively represent minority voters. Once the slating group has installed him in office, he is pointed to as evidence that minority voters are represented by "one of their own," or that they have been able to elect candidates of their choice. In some cases, this ploy seems to have been instituted primarily to discourage threatened vote dilution lawsuits. It has met with varied success on this score. In *Zimmer v. McKeithen* the Fifth Circuit declared,

> [W]e cannot endorse the view that the success of black candidates at the polls necessarily forecloses the possibility of dilution of the black vote. Such success might, on occasion, be attributable to the work of politicians, who, apprehending that the support of a black candidate would be politically expedient, campaign to insure his election. Or such success might be attributable to political support motivated by different considerations—namely that election of a black candidate will thwart successful challenges to electoral schemes on dilution grounds. In either situation, a candidate could be elected despite the relative political backwardness of black residents in the electoral district. Were we to hold that a minority candidate's success at the polls is conclusive proof of a minority group's access to the political process, we would merely be inviting attempts to circumvent the Constitution. This we choose not to do. Instead, we shall continue to require an independent consideration of the record.[18]

The role played by slating groups in four cities using at-large elections is analyzed by Luis Fraga and me in Chapter 6.

Gerrymandering

The boundaries of an entire political jurisdiction can be changed to exclude minority voters. This method is called the "Tuskegee gerrymander," after the city of Tuskegee, Alabama. During the 1950s, when the civil rights movement was raising the political consciousness of blacks throughout the South, the all-white city council of Tuskegee redrew the city's boundaries to exclude almost the entire black population, which had comprised a majority of Tuskegee's citizenry. The Supreme Court held this practice unconstitutional in *Gomillion v. Lightfoot.*[19]

A less extreme method is to deannex racially mixed areas of a city that contain a larger percentage of minority residents than whites. More frequently, cities annex disproportionately white areas or consolidate their population with that of other cities so that the white percentage of the total population will be increased. Although there are legitimate reasons for annexation and consolidation, the effects—often intended—are to water down minority voting strength. This gerrymander can have invidious effects in at-large or district systems.

District gerrymandering consists in changing individual district boundaries to decrease minority voting strength. Its use in the South partially explains why in 1981–82 the southern congressional delegation, consisting of 108 representatives, contained only two blacks although 20 percent of the region's population was black. Mississippi, Alabama, and Georgia, with black populations of 35 percent, 26 percent, and 27 percent, respectively, had *no* black congresspersons among their twenty-two representatives. In the five southwestern states of California, Arizona, New Mexico, Colorado, and Texas, where most Mexican Americans reside, only four of the area's seventy-eight U.S. representatives (5 percent) were Hispanic, although more than 17 percent of the population was.

District gerrymandering can be dilutive if the minority proportion is kept low in all districts. If racially polarized voting exists, this strategy can prevent any minority-backed candidates from winning. An alternative is to "pack" the minority voters in one or a few districts, so they are deprived of the opportunity to elect a larger share of candidates.

Both of these forms of gerrymandering can be accomplished with districts of equal population size. A third form involves creating unequally populated districts in which the one person, one vote requirement is violated. If the overpopulated districts end up containing a disproportionately large number of minorities, their voting strength is diluted. (The complexities of dilutionary gerrymandering are described by Frank Parker in Chapter 5.)

THE THEORY OF THE SWING VOTE

It should now be obvious that a white majority unwilling to share political power with an ethnic minority has a panoply of weapons at its disposal. In many jurisdictions several are used simultaneously. For example, in Houston—the largest municipality so far required to adopt single-member districts for having violated the Voting Rights Act—an at-large system was combined with place voting and a runoff rule until 1979. The city annexed white suburbs in 1977 and 1978, which led to a Justice Department objection. Before 1955, Houston had elected three councilpersons at large and five from districts, but the district boundaries were gerrymandered so that blacks had little chance of election. The simultaneous use of several dilutionary mechanisms decreases the likelihood that a candidate preferred by the minority community will win.

It might be argued, however, that this arrangement does not preclude minorities from exercising significant electoral influence. For is it not possible for a minority bloc to determine election results even when its favored candidate cannot win?

Implicit in this question is the familiar theory of the "swing vote," which goes as follows:

1. The minority vote is often decisive to electoral outcomes; or in other words, the votes cast by the minority community are necessary to the winners' victory.
2. The winners are aware of the decisive role minority votes played in their victory.
3. Out of gratitude for their support, or a desire to win again in the future, the victorious candidates are receptive to the wishes of the minority community.
4. The victorious candidates therefore enact policies, once in office, that benefit the minority community.

The first assumption is by no means necessarily correct. In Houston, blacks in recent years have constituted about a quarter of the population, and in city elections their turnout rate has been similar to that of whites. Yet the margin of victory between 1955 and 1975 among winning council candidates under the at-large system was typically so great that the black vote, even when unified, was able to affect the outcome of only four council races out of eighty-eight. In other words, the black voters could have stayed home in eighty-four races, and if the whites' voting patterns had remained unchanged, the same candidates would still have been elected. Between 1955 and 1981 in Abilene, Texas—a city with a combined black and Mexican American population of about 18 percent during this period, the minority bloc under the most optimistic assumptions could have made the difference in election outcomes for only fifteen of sixty-eight winners. Since 1970, the city's minorities could have affected the outcome in only three of twenty-eight cases.

Further, in many instances, it is impossible for the winners to know precisely the extent of their minority support. In many smaller jurisdictions all voters cast their ballot in a single precinct. A postelection scientific sample survey may be required to determine how the various ethnic groups voted. In other cases, extreme racial heterogeneity of voting precincts may increase the difficulty of determining minority support through an analysis of voting returns.

Even when the first two assumptions about the swing vote are correct, winning candidates do not always pay attention to minority interests after the election. The reason is that white votes also "made a difference," because they, too, were necessary if not sufficient for victory. Indeed, more white votes may have been cast for the winning candidate than black votes. Thus, where there is strong racial polarization, the postelection pressure from white constituents of a winner may be strong enough to minimize or nullify minority pressure on him. In recent city elections in Mobile, Alabama, for example, two commissioners who could not have won without black votes specifically disavowed the notion that blacks had been "decisive" in their election.[20]

In summary, the swing vote theory may sometimes apply. But where minority voters have yet to elect candidates of their choice, and where the racial polarization of attitudes is intense, the swing vote will probably not provide minorities much leverage. Under these circumstances, the minority population is excluded from meaningful political participation. Although its members possess the right to vote, they remain outsiders, unable to use their votes to bargain effectively.

THE GEOGRAPHY OF DILUTION

The history of the adoption of dilutionary practices suggests that they are most often found in the South and Southwest, the areas of the country with the highest proportion of blacks and Hispanics, respectively. (Texas, with its large number of both minorities, is part of both the South—as a former Confederate state—and the Southwest.)

In the postbellum South, as J. Morgan Kousser relates in Chapter 2, at-large city elections "clearly motivated by racial purposes" appeared as early as the first elections in which blacks were allowed to vote. Atlanta adopted them in 1868. Other cities followed suit. Racial gerrymandering was also widespread then, as were numerous other discriminatory devices.

At-large elections and small elective governing bodies were an integral feature of the city commission form of government and usually characterized the city manager form as well. Both types of "reform" government were first implemented in the South and widely adopted elsewhere during the Progressive Era (1893–1917).[21] The place voting system was introduced in Texas as a feature of the Terrell Election Law of 1905—the state's major disfranchising legislation.[22] The Terrell Law, whose ostensible purpose was to "purify the ballot," codified the laws governing the newly instituted poll tax and legalized use of the white primary. It was widely hailed at the time as "progressive" legislation.

Although the Progressive movement is still portrayed in many civics textbooks as motivated by high-minded "good government" reformers, many of the changes in election rules were aimed at diminishing the clout of the working classes and ethnic and political minorities, and they usually had that effect.[23] As C. Vann Woodward has noted, the leaders of Progressivism in the South were also at the forefront of the disfranchising movement.[24]

Although Progressives often adopted dilutionary measures after disfranchising legislation had been passed in the southern states, it would be a mistake to infer, as the Supreme Court did in *Bolden,* that these measures were therefore not racially motivated. "In fact," writes Kousser, "throughout the South, whites in the 'progressive era' feared that their 'solution' to the 'Negro problem' might unravel."

Charles Beard, the noted contemporary historian and political scientist, stated in his 1912 textbook on municipal government that election at large "substantially excludes minority representation."[25] Nonetheless its adoption has continued to the present. The rise of the civil rights movement following World War II, and the increasing enfranchisement of blacks and Mexican Americans in the 1960s, intensified its adoption along with other dilutionary devices. Scholars of southern politics remarked on the shift from wards to districtwide elections at the time, as did the U.S. Commission on Civil Rights.[26] One of the more extreme instances of this response occurred in Georgia. From 1964, on the eve of passage of the Voting Rights Act—which gave blacks in that state the right to vote on a mass scale for the first time since Reconstruction—to 1975, twenty county governments and county boards of education switched from district to at-large elections.[27] Earlier, in 1964, the Georgia legislature had instituted majority vote and place requirements for all at-large county commission elections in the state.[28] In its first session following passage of the Voting Rights Act, the Mississippi legislature enacted laws requiring and allowing members of county boards of supervisors and county school boards, previously elected by wards, to be elected at large.[29] In Texas, legislation passed in the 1950s and 1960s allowed hundreds of school districts to adopt the place system for the first time.[30]

In Alabama, the Justice Department objected to seventy-one proposed changes in election procedures or voting-related matters between 1969 and 1980 on the grounds that they discriminated against minorities. Most involved dilutionary devices. For example, fourteen were attempts to institute the place system, staggered terms, candidate residency requirements, or anti-single-shot laws. Twelve would have created multimember districts; three, runoff elections; fifteen, dilutionary annexations; and two, gerrymanders.[31]

Although numerous discriminatory responses to increased minority voting were successfully countered under the Voting Rights Act, others have succeeded for a variety of reasons. Changes in voting procedures are not always submitted to the Justice Department as required by law.[32] For example, the Alabama legislature passed at least ninety acts dealing with voting in 1975, but thirty-eight were never submitted for preclearance.[33] When submissions are made by white officials, minority voters in some communities are ignorant of their right to voice their concerns about the impact of the proposed changes, and, consequently, the Justice Department may approve them without full knowledge of the facts.[34] Even when submissions are made and objected to, the dilutionary measures are sometimes still implemented. In Mississippi, Georgia, and South Carolina, several jurisdictions whose voting changes were objected to by the Justice Department simply ignored the objections until litigation forced them to obey the law.[35]

In summary, the history of white response to minority enfranchisement—both after the Civil War and World War II—points to the likelihood that dilutionary devices are concentrated in the southern tier of states. Runoff elections seem to be more prevalent in the South.[36] The place system as well is apparently most widespread in that region.[37] While the number of cities with at-large elections has grown nationwide over the past thirty years, the West and the South still have a slightly higher percentage of cities employing this method.[38]

Consequently, it is not surprising to find that blacks are most severely underrepresented on city councils in the South, and Hispanics in the South and West.[39] The evidence is overwhelming that this underrepresentation in the two regions with the highest concentrations of blacks and Mexican Americans, respectively, is primarily the result of dilutionary laws combined with white bloc voting. The abolition of dilutionary laws is almost always accompanied by a sharp increase in elected minority officials.[40]

After hundreds of years of slavery and a century of subordination in a racial caste system, blacks in the southern states covered continuously by the Voting Rights Act since 1965 still account for a miniscule proportion of elected officials. In 1980, of 32,977 elective positions in these seven states (Alabama, Georgia, Louisiana, Mississippi, North Carolina, South Carolina, and Virginia) only 1,830 (5.6 percent) were occupied by blacks, and the proportional increase since 1965 had begun to taper off by the mid-1970s.[41] The total population of these states is 25.8 percent black. In the words of the Joint Center for Political Studies, which tabulates the number of black elected officials, "unfavorable electoral arrangements like at-large elections and some racial gerrymandering are major obstacles to further rapid gains by blacks in winning elective office in the South."[42]

If 5.6 percent of the elected officials in these seven states is black, compared with 25.8 percent of the population, then about one-fifth as many blacks hold office as would be likely in a nonracist society. Suppose that the shoe were on the other foot: the proportion of white officials were reduced to only one-fifth the number

Table 1-1. Blacks as percentage of population and elected officials in southern states covered under the preclearance provisions of the Voting Rights Act, July 1980

State	Population percent black 1980	Elected officials		
			Black officials	
		Total officials	Number	Percent of total
Alabama	25.6	4,151	238	5.7
Georgia	26.8	6,660	249	3.7
Louisiana	29.4	4,710	363	7.7
Mississippi	35.2	5,271	387	7.3
North Carolina[1]	22.4	5,295	247	4.7
South Carolina	30.4	3,225	238	7.4
Texas	12.0	24,728	196	0.8
Virginia	18.9	3,041	124	4.1

[1] Statewide data, including the forty counties subject to preclearance.

Source: U.S. Commission on Civil Rights, *The Voting Rights Act: Unfulfilled Goals* (Typescript edition), Washington, D.C., U.S. Government Printing Office, 1981, p. 31.

that one would expect on the basis of their population percentage. The proportion of white officials would drop from the present 94.4 percent to about 15 percent. Surely whites in that instance would interpret this as massive and intolerable exclusion.

In the eight Southern states now covered under the preclearance provision of the Voting Rights Act, the black population in 1980 ranged from 12.0 percent in Texas to 35.2 percent in Mississippi. (See Table 1-1.) The highest percentage of black officials was 7.7 in Louisiana, which had a total black population of 29.4 percent.

The situation of Mexican Americans in the Southwest is comparable to that of blacks in the South. They have historically been the victims of violence, state-sanctioned segregation in schools and housing, Jim Crow practices, and job discrimination. Today they are still widely excluded from effective political participation. Of all persons who served as members of Texas city councils from 1968 to 1978, less than 6 percent were Mexican Americans, although Texas had a Spanish-origin population of 21 percent in 1980. In South Texas, where Mexican Americans comprise a majority of the population, 31.7 percent of city council members during this period belonged to that ethnic group. In reporting these figures, the Texas Advisory Committee to the U.S. Commission on Civil Rights remarked, "It is significant . . . that even today 179 (83.6 percent) of the 214 larger cities in Texas have at-large elections for city council."[43]

The figures in Table 1-2 reveal the sharp underrepresentation of Hispanics in elective office, compared to their percentage of the population, in 1979–80. Only in Arizona did the percentage of Hispanic officials come anywhere close to the percentage of the Hispanic population. In Texas and California, Hispanics were underrepresented by a factor of about three.

The underrepresentation of blacks and Hispanics is obscured by the occasional election of a minority mayor in a large city, which is often interpreted as a straw in the wind. Reactions to Henry Cisneros' success in San Antonio, Maynard

Table 1-2.   Hispanics as percentage of population and elected officials, by state, 1979–1980

	Population percent Hispanic 1980	Elected officials		
			Hispanic officials	
State		Total officials	Number	Percent of total
Arizona	16.2	1,547	205	13.2
California[1]	19.2	7,550	496	6.6
Colorado[2]	11.7	3,143	172	5.5
Texas	21.0	14,880	933	6.3

[1] Statewide data, including the three counties subject to preclearance.
[2] Statewide data, including one county subject to preclearance.
Source: U.S. Commission on Civil Rights, *The Voting Rights Act: Unfulfilled Goals* (Typescript edition), Washington, D.C., U.S. Government Printing Office, 1981, p. 38.

Jackson's and then Andrew Young's in Atlanta, Ernest Morial's in New Orleans, and Richard Arrington's in Birmingham exemplify this pattern. It is tempting to infer from their election that dilutionary barriers are disappearing.

But these are the exceptions that prove the rule. In each of the cases just mentioned, the city's minority population was near 50 percent, and, consequently, few white votes were needed to put the minority candidate over the top. When Maynard Jackson became mayor of Atlanta in 1974, the city was over 50 percent black. When Ernest Morial, in 1978, and Richard Arrington, a year later, won a mayor's post, New Orleans and Birmingham had black populations of more than 45 and 55 percent, respectively. Henry Cisneros' victory in 1981 occurred in a city whose Hispanic population was 54 percent.

These cases underscore the fact that white bloc voting against minority candidates is so intense in the South and Southwest that an extremely large minority population is typically necessary for the minority community to elect candidates of its choice under at-large conditions. In 1981, for example, twenty Alabama municipalities had black mayors. Except for Birmingham (pop. 284,000) and Prichard (39,541), these were small towns or hamlets, ranging in population from 95 to 11,028. In only one—Franklin, with a population of 133—did blacks make up less than one-half the total. In the remaining nineteen, the average black population was *82 percent*.[44] Of the 147 black elected council members in Alabama municipalities in 1981, two-thirds were in cities with a majority black population,[45] and some of the remaining black council members were elected from wards.

Although most of the elected minority officials in the South and Southwest appear to be from jurisdictions that are heavily black or brown, a minority concentration does not always lead to minority representation. In 1981 there were seventy-six Alabama towns between 25 and 50 percent black in which no blacks sat on city council. There were another twenty-four towns between 50 and 86 percent black without any black council representation whatsoever.[46] In Texas, there were 109 school districts in 1980 with a Chicano population above 50 percent in which no Chicano held an elective school board post.[47] In Mississippi, eight of twenty-two predominantly black counties had no black representation on their county boards of supervisors in 1981; blacks made up a majority on such boards in only two of the twenty-two.[48] While the lower median age of blacks and Mexican

Americans, combined with their typically lower turnout rates, may account for part of this underrepresentation, vote dilution is probably the main culprit.

When minorities are faced with almost total exclusion from the ordinary channels of political participation and deprived of any alternative means of exerting influence, their voter turnout and candidacy rates tend to drop.[49] In Abilene, Texas, minority candidates first ran for municipal office in 1970. In spite of several tries during the decade, none was able to win election without the endorsement of a powerful slating group dominated by the white Anglo business "establishment." By 1979, the black and brown communities had virtually stopped participating in electoral politics. In city council elections that year, only seventy-six Mexican Americans and thirty-one blacks voted, out of a minority population of approximately 19,000.[50]

The case of Abilene points up a particularly disturbing development. In southern and southwestern communities, the passage of the Voting Rights Act brought about an initial surge of political participation by minorities, many of whom were able for the first time in their lives to overcome barriers to the voting and registration process. Dilution, however, has convinced newly enfranchised voters that the old system of racial dominance is still in place. Minorities can now vote—they just cannot cast an effective vote.

PROSPECTS FOR THE FUTURE

The future of vote dilution remains unsettled. While local minority leaders, attorneys, concerned citizens and national civil rights groups have worked diligently since the 1960s to eradicate it, conservative officials have attempted to maintain the status quo.

The three weapons available to minorities before July of 1982, when the Voting Rights Act was significantly amended, were the Fourteenth and Fifteenth Amendments to the Constitution, and Section 5 of the Voting Rights Act. (Section 2 of the act made illegal the denial or abridgement of the right of any United States citizen to vote on account of race, color, or inclusion in a minority language group. It also allowed citizens to challenge discriminatory laws or practices in federal court. However, proving vote dilution under Section 2, modelled after the Fifteenth Amendment, was equivalent to proving it under the Constitution.)

Section 5 was (and remains) by far the cheapest and easiest way to attack dilution. It gives the attorney general or the United States District Court for the District of Columbia the authority to review proposed electoral changes in covered jurisdictions, and either to disallow those which are discriminatory or to require other changes that compensate for their effects. Section 5 is especially important because, in the words of civil rights attorney Barbara Phillips, it provides "a quick, efficient way to halt new efforts in covered jurisdictions to discriminate against minority voters."[51] Its usefulness is analyzed in Chapter 8 by Lani Guinier and former Assistant Attorney General for Civil Rights Drew Days. Problems with its enforcement are addressed in Chapter 9 by Howard Ball, Dale Krane and Thomas P. Lauth.

By 1975 Section 5 applied to all or part of twenty-two states, as it does today. It has been interpreted broadly to cover all proposed changes in election laws, including relatively minor ones. Between 1965 and 1982 approximately 35,000 voting changes were submitted for preclearance, and 815 were found objectionable, many because they were dilutionary.[52] Georgia received the most objections (226), followed by Louisiana (136) and Texas (130), which has been covered by Section 5 only since 1975.[53] These statistics suggest that Section 5 has played a significant role in curtailing attempts at dilution and other forms of vote discrimination.

There are three serious limitations to Section 5 as a weapon for attacking dilution, however. First, it does not apply to the entire United States. Second, voting laws and practices adopted prior to the act, or prior to various jurisdictions' inclusion under Section 5, are not subject to challenge unless they were changed—in ways that render them discriminatory still—after the act went into effect.

For example, suppose that a redistricting in a city diluted minority votes when it was implemented in 1960, and it continues to dilute them today. So long as the boundaries remain in effect, and no attempts are made by local officials to change the current electoral arrangements, minority group members cannot use Section 5 to challenge the dilutionary gerrymander.

The third limitation of Section 5 can be illustrated by carrying the gerrymander example a step further. Suppose that today the city officials decide to redraw the 1960 district boundaries, with the effect that they are still dilutionary. Does Section 5 require that the new districts be drawn so that minority votes are no longer diluted? Or does it just require that the new boundaries not cause greater dilution than the old ones?

The Supreme Court, in *Beer v. United States,* held that a redistricting plan that is not actually "retrogressive" in its impact on minority voting strength does not violate Section 5 unless it otherwise violates the Constitution.[54] According to one student of the law, the retrogression test "has the serious consequence of rewarding those jurisdictions with a history of the worst dilution of black electoral strength."[55] The exact scope of the *Beer* rule is not always clear,[56] especially in light of the 1982 amendments to the Voting Rights Act, but to the extent that remedies to dilutionary changes allowed under Section 5 are subject to the retrogression test, Section 5's cutting edge is blunted.

Because of these limitations, many discriminatory practices could only be challenged prior to 1982 through lawsuits in local jurisdictions as violating the Fourteenth and Fifteenth Amendments. This route was sometimes effective, but as one experienced civil rights lawyer described the situation, "It has also proven to be burdensome and time consuming, and results have often been inconsistent and erratic."[57]

The burden for plaintiffs in these suits was never easy. In *White v. Regester,* decided in 1973, the Supreme Court held that a successful constitutional challenge must provide:

> evidence to support findings that the political processes leading to nomination and election were not equally open to participation by the group in question—that its members had less opportunity than did other residents in the district to participate in the political processes and to elect legislators of their choice.[58]

Zimmer v. McKeithen, a circuit court opinion following *White,* said that unconstitutional dilution could be demonstrated by proving a number of different facts, such as a history of official discrimination, a low proportion of minority group members elected to office, depressed socioeconomic status of minorities, elected officials' lack of responsiveness to the needs of a minority group, a majority vote requirement, lack of access to candidate slating, anti-single-shot requirements, large district size, a tenuous state policy favoring at-large voting, or the absence of places (numbered posts) designated by geographic area.[59] No single factor or specific subgroup could in itself be determinative of a constitutional violation, the court said. Each trial judge would have to assess the "totality of circumstances" and reach a conclusion after considering all evidence.

Obviously, the *Zimmer* ruling gave much discretion to the courts in deciding dilution cases. It also placed a great burden on plaintiffs, who had no way of knowing which of the *"Zimmer* factors" would turn out to be most important; consequently, they had to collect evidence that addressed each one of them. Plaintiffs' lawyers and experts—sociologists, historians, political scientists, and statisticians—were sometimes forced to spend literally thousands of hours accumulating data.

In 1980, the Supreme Court's *Bolden* decision changed what had been a formidable burden of proof for plaintiffs to an impossible one in many instances.

Blacks in Mobile, Alabama, had sued the three-man city commission in 1975, charging that the at-large system in place since 1911 unconstitutionally diluted their vote. In a city that was one-third black, none had been able to win election to the commission, which was perceived by plaintiffs as unresponsive to the needs of the black community. The trial court, applying the *Zimmer* standards, decided in favor of the plaintiffs. The Fifth Circuit Court of Appeals sustained the trial court's decision, but the Supreme Court reversed it. In a sharply divided opinion, a plurality of justices held that the Fifteenth Amendment guarantees only the right to register and vote; it does not protect against dilution. The Fourteenth Amendment, on the other hand, only protects against dilution when it can be shown that the diluting mechanism was adopted for racially discriminatory purposes. The presence of the *Zimmer* factors, the court held, was insufficient to prove such purposes. The case was remanded to the Mobile court, which had the task of ascertaining whether the voting system was adopted or maintained "in part 'because of,' not merely 'in spite of,' " its adverse racial effects.[60] In 1982—seven years after the suit was originally heard—the *Mobile* court once more found in the plaintiffs' favor, after listening to historians discuss events in the nineteenth and twentieth centuries leading to the adoption of the city's commission form of government in 1911.

The new trial alone took 6,000 hours of lawyers' time, along with 7,000 for researchers and expert witnesses; cost $120,000 not counting lawyers' fees; and lasted two and a half weeks, during which the most minute change in city government from 1819 to the present was explored.[61] (The complex racial forces behind Mobile's at-large system are described in Chapter 3 by Peyton McCrary, a historian in the case.)

The Mobile plaintiffs were more fortunate than many. Their efforts were financed in part by the NAACP Legal Defense and Education Fund, which enabled historians to be hired to research in detail the city's past. The Justice Department entered an amicus brief on behalf of plaintiffs, and brought its considerable resources to their aid. In addition, much had been written on Alabama and Mobile by historians, and relevant issues of newspapers and archival material were available.

The problems facing plaintiffs in Taylor, Texas, described at the beginning of this essay, were far more typical of those engendered by the Supreme Court decision in *Bolden*. Their legal aid lawyers were working on a limited budget. No relevant historical writings on the city existed. And the key archival materials—including the back issues of the newspaper—were missing. Frank Parker, a leading voting rights attorney, succinctly assessed the implications of the *Bolden* ruling in such jurisdictions:

> In the absence of a 'smoking gun,' victims of discriminatory laws must resort to evidence producing what courts and legal scholars have called 'inferences,' 'suspicions,' and 'likelihoods' of discriminatory intent. Here, judges frequently disagree, sometimes strenuously, on what constitutes sufficient proof. The nine Justices of the Supreme Court in the Mobile case itself were unable to agree on the proper legal standard for proving discriminatory intent. And if a majority of the Justices can't agree on how discriminatory intent is to be proved, how does anyone know what is required?[62]

Bolden was decided some two years before the Voting Rights Act's nonpermanent features, including Section 5, were scheduled to expire in August of 1982. By early 1981, civil rights forces had begun to lobby for an amendment to Section 2 of the act—a permanent feature—that would overcome the burden of proving intent.

The amendment would render illegal any electoral device whose intent *or result* denied or abridged the voting rights of racial or language minorities. The House of Representatives overwhelmingly passed it in September of 1981. And in spite of strong initial opposition by President Reagan, his attorney general, William French Smith, and Judiciary Committee Chairman Strom Thurmond of South Carolina, a similar bill was passed by the Senate in the summer of 1982, after the civil rights lobby, in a compromise with opponents of the measure, agreed to a twenty-five-year extension of the nonpermanent features of the act instead of making those features permanent, as the House bill had proposed. The result was a strengthened Voting Rights Act that should overcome the difficulties imposed by *Bolden*. (Armand Derfner provides in Chapter 7 an insider's account of events leading up to the passage of the amendment.)

Two days after the president signed the extension of the act, the Supreme Court, in *Rogers v. Lodge*,[63] eased the evidentiary standards in *Bolden* for proving intent to discriminate. In a six to three decision, the court ruled that circumstantial evidence, rather than a so-called smoking gun, was sufficient to prove intentional dilution in cases where unconstitutional abridgement of voting rights was alleged.

While these developments were applauded by foes of dilution, they did not represent a major step forward so much as a return to the status quo before *Bolden* had been rendered, for the language of *White* and *Zimmer* on evidentiary standards had been incorporated into the revision of Section 2 or figured prominently in its legislative history.

To civil rights lawyers familiar with the difficulties of proving dilution even under the the more lenient *Zimmer* standards, this was hardly a cause for rejoicing. The requirement that the courts address the "totality of circumstances" still necessitates collecting and analyzing great quantities of data to prove not only the existence of diminished voting power as a result of dilutionary laws and racial bloc voting—what seems to many observers to be the core elements in a dilution case—but also the local history of race relations in a community, the socioeconomic status of minorities compared with the majority, governmental nonresponsiveness in numerous areas of city services, the existence of unfair slating group practices, and patterns of election finance and campaign practices, among other things. Furthermore, the lack of guidance by the wording of the new Section 2 or by the courts on the relative importance of these complex factors continues to make any court challenge based on Section 2 an arduous, expensive, time-consuming, and ultimately risky enterprise.

What is badly needed, as James Blacksher and Larry Menefee argue in Chapter 10, is a much narrower set of evidentiary standards of dilution, which a) in the name of fairness conform in simplicity to the criteria of proof required in *Reynolds v. Sims*,[64] the major vote dilution case of the 1960s; b) are easily applied; and c) accord far less discretion to trial judges than does the "totality of circumstances" criterion.

This may sound like a tall order, if not a utopian one. But the carefully reasoned and elegant analysis of Blacksher and Menefee, plaintiffs' counsel in *Bolden* and its companion school board case, leads to an alternative standard of proof for unconstitutional dilution in cases that involve at-large elections which, if accepted, might well achieve all three goals. It is impossible to summarize their argument briefly here, but the essence of the proposal is worth quoting in full:

> An at-large election scheme for a state or local multirepresentative body is unconstitutional where jurisdiction-wide elections permit a bloc-voting majority, over a substantial period of time, consistently to defeat candidates publicly identified with the interests of and supported by a politically cohesive, geographically insular racial or ethnic minority group.

It appears unlikely that the Supreme Court will be inclined to give this alternative serious consideration. If, against all odds, it were to do so, it is not clear how it would reconcile its intent standard enunciated in both *Bolden* and *Rogers* with what, in the Blacksher-Menefee formulation, is clearly a results standard. (On the other hand, Blacksher and Menefee demonstrate that the new intent standard, which the court is now requiring of minority plaintiffs, conflicts with the results standard of *Reynolds,* where whites—including suburban Mobilians—were the plaintiffs. So the court's problem is not whether but how to resolve the inconsistencies the intent standard has given rise to.) In the absence of a constitutional solution, Section 2's "totality of circumstances" criterion will continue to render vote dilution litigation expensive and inefficient.

What are the prospects for the future effectiveness of Section 5? Perhaps even more than the courts, the Justice Department is in significant respects a political creature. Its enforcement strategies are inextricably linked to the president's policy priorities. Aggressive enforcement of Section 5, the most efficient way to fight new efforts to dilute votes in covered jurisdictions, depends on the enthusiasm and commitment of those charged with the duty of safeguarding minority voting rights—the Attorney General and the Assistant Attorney General for Civil Rights.

This truth has never been more obvious than during the Reagan administration, whose wide-ranging assault on the institutions created over the past quarter century to secure the rights of minorities in the United States has been devastating. The failure of Assistant Attorney General William Bradford Reynolds to aggressively enforce voting rights is particularly noteworthy. A review by the Washington Council of Lawyers of the Justice Department's Section 5 enforcement during Reagan's first twenty months in office concluded that "the difference in the level of activity is startling. . . . The [Voting] Section has simply not carried out the bipartisan commitment to vigorous enforcement of voting rights which has characterized its own past activities."[65] At this writing, the federal courts have struck down as dilutionary several redistricting plans—including one involving congressional districts—that Reynolds had approved under Section 5.

It would be a mistake to minimize the future potential of Sections 2 and 5 of the Voting Rights Act, as well as the Fourteenth and Fifteenth Amendments, as levers to pry open the tightly shut political systems of the South and Southwest. Yet the history of racial minorities in America, and in those areas in particular, is a troubling reminder of the the the skill, the resourcefulness, the fierce tenacity, and, above all, the patience of privileged groups in fighting to uphold the social and political structures that guarantee their dominance.

NOTES

1. For accounts of similar disparities in city services, see Lawyers' Committee for Civil Rights Under Law, *Voting in Mississippi: A Right Still Denied* (Washington, D.C.: September 1981), 102–111.
2. 446 U.S. 55 (1980).
3. The facts about Taylor were gathered through the author's personal observation and interviews, and material in the files of the Legal Aid Society of Central Texas, Austin, Texas.
4. For recent examples of this in Alabama, see Jane Reed Cox and Abigail Turner, *The Voting Rights Act in Alabama: A Current Legal Assessment* (Mobile, Ala.: Legal Services Corporation of Alabama, 1981), 7–14.
5. On the use of such practices in Mississippi, see Lawyers' Committee, *Voting in Mississippi*, 6–7.
6. Ibid., 14. For example, voter registration for persons living in Sunflower County, Mississippi, involves a round trip journey of one hundred miles to the county courthouse at Indianola, because registration is not allowed at precinct polling places or other locations.
7. The recent use of this practice in Texas is described in Jeannie Stanley, "Cultural Politics in an East Texas Community" (Paper delivered to the annual meeting of the Southwestern Political Science Association, San Antonio, 20 March 1982), 28.
8. For such practices in Mississippi, see Lawyers' Committee, *Voting in Mississippi*, 12–13.

9. Cox and Turner, *Voting Rights Act in Alabama*, 20, document this practice in Alabama. Lawyers' Committee, *Voting in Mississippi*, 82, describes this practice in Mississippi. For its use in Georgia, see Laughlin McDonald, *Voting Rights in the South: Ten Years of Litigation Challenging Continuing Discrimination Against Minorities*, A Special Report from the American Civil Liberties Union (Atlanta, Georgia, 1982), 46–50.

10. McDonald, *Voting Rights*, 111–112.

11. See Lawyers' Committee, *Voting in Mississippi*, 5, regarding the use of these measures in Mississippi.

12. Cox and Turner, *Voting Rights Act in Alabama*, 14, document the use of harassment in Alabama as late as 1981. For instances in Georgia, North Carolina, Mississippi, and South Carolina, see U.S. Commission on Civil Rights, *The Voting Rights Act: Unfulfilled Goals*, Typescript edition (Washington, D.C.: U.S. Government Printing Office, 1981), 146–148.

13. Robert R. Alford and Eugene C. Lee, "Voting Turnout in American Cities," *American Political Science Review* 62 (Sept. 1968): 799.

14. For an account of such a change in Houston, see Chandler Davidson, *Biracial Politics: Conflict and Cooperation in the Metropolitan South* (Baton Rouge: Louisiana State University Press, 1972), 65–66. See also McDonald, *Voting Rights*, 43–46.

15. Herbert H. Werlin, "The Victory at Slaton," *The Texas Observer* (9 September 1960), 5.

16. Roy E. Young, *The Place System in Texas Elections* (Austin: Institute of Public Affairs, the University of Texas, 1965), 21–22. While Young cautions against attributing the adoption of the place system solely to racial motives, he argues that "fear of one-shot voting has caused several Texas communities to adopt the place system." The Supreme Court in *City of Rome v. United States* 446 U.S. 156 (1980) affirmed the lower court's conclusion that numbered posts and residency provisions prevent blacks from electing candidates by single-shot voting.

17. Delbert Taebel, "Minority Representation on City Councils," *Social Science Quarterly* 59 (June 1978): 151.

18. 485 F 2d 1307.

19. 364 U.S. 339 (1960).

20. *Mobile Press*, 17 August 1981, 1, sec. D.

21. Standard accounts of the racial and class overtones of progressivism include James Weinstein, *The Corporate Ideal in the Liberal State, 1900–1918* (Boston: Beacon Press, 1968), chap. 4, and "Organized Business and the City Commission and Manager Movements," *Journal of Southern History* 28 (May 1962): 166–182; Samuel P. Hays, "The Politics of Reform in Municipal Government in the Progressive Era," *Pacific Northwest Quarterly* 55 (October 1964): 152–181; and Bradley Robert Rice, *Progressive Cities* (Austin: University of Texas Press, 1977). For an excellent account of progressive efforts at black disfranchisement in the South, see J. Morgan Kousser, *The Shaping of Southern Politics: Suffrage Restriction and the Establishment of the One-Party South, 1880–1910* (New Haven and London: Yale University Press, 1974), 229–231, 236–237, 260–261.

22. Young, *Place System*, 2–3.

23. Weinstein, "The City Commission and City Manager Movements," and Hays, "Politics of Reform." See J. Morgan Kousser, "Progressivism—For Middle-Class Whites Only: North Carolina Education, 1880–1910," *The Journal of Southern History* 46 (May 1980): 169–194 for an assessment of the effects of Progressivism in North Carolina. His finding is that Progressive disfranchisement of blacks led to greater discrimination against them in school expenditures and tax burdens. Similar findings for Louisiana are reported in Robert R. Margo, "Race Differences in Public School Expenditures," *Social Science History* 61 (Winter 1982): 9–34.

24. *The Strange Career of Jim Crow*, 2nd revised ed. (New York: Oxford University Press,

1966), 91. See also Dewey W. Grantham, "The Progressive Movement and the Negro," *South Atlantic Quarterly* 54 (October 1955): 465.

25. Rice, *Progressive Cities,* 78.

26. Everett Carl Ladd, *Negro Political Leadership in the South* (Ithaca: Cornell University Press, 1966), 103; U.S. Commission on Civil Rights, *Political Participation* (Washington, D.C.: U.S. Government Printing Office, 1968), 21–25.

27. *Election Law Changes in Cities and Counties in Georgia, May 1976.* Voter Education Project Report, Atlanta, Georgia, 1976, 6–8.

28. Georgia Code, Section 34-1513 (1964) and Section 34-1015 (1964).

29. Lawyers' Committee, *Voting in Mississippi,* 32–33.

30. Young, *Place System,* 11-12. For similar trends in North Carolina, see Steve Suitts, "Blacks in the Political Arithmetic after *Mobile:* A Case Study of North Carolina," in National Conference on Voting Rights Issues, *The Right to Vote* (New York: Rockefeller Foundation, 1981), 75.

31. Cox and Turner, *Voting Rights Act in Alabama,* 19–21; for similar data on Mississippi, see Lawyers' Committee, *Voting in Mississippi,* v–vi, and 5.

32. Cox and Turner, *Voting Rights in Alabama,* 21; McDonald, *Voting Rights,* 59–63.

33. Cox and Turner, *Voting Rights in Alabama,* 21.

34. Ibid., 21–22.

35. Lawyers' Committee, *Voting in Mississippi,* 5; McDonald, *Voting Rights,* 58–59.

36. V. O. Key, Jr., *Southern Politics in State and Nation* (New York: Alfred A. Knopf, Inc., Vintage Edition, 1949), 417.

37. Young, *Place System,* 22. Young, whose work is the only systematic treatment of the place voting system, refers to "the apparent concentration of the place system in the South," which "may be partially explained by its concern with attempts to limit the Negroes' political strength." (22) In Texas, "there seems no doubt that the growing political power of Negro and Latin-American citizens . . . has resulted in efforts to dilute or offset it. The place system has been one weapon available to those seeking this aim." (21) Young adds: "An informant well acquainted with Texas school districts believes that the recent trend toward use of the place system is found mostly in East and South Texas districts. In these sections of Texas is found the greatest concentration of Negroes and Latin-Americans. The 1963 statute granting a large number of school districts permission to use this mode of election was also co-sponsored by three South Texas legislators." (21)

38. International City Managers Association, 1974 Survey: "Municipal Elections Systems: GOVT/74" (Washington, D.C.).

39. Albert K. Karnig, "Black Representation on City Councils: The Impact of District Elections and Socio-economic Factors," *Urban Affairs Quarterly* 12 (December 1976): 229; Delbert Taebel, "Minority Representation," 146.

40. U.S. Commission on Civil Rights, *The Voting Rights Act: Unfulfilled Goals,* 107–108; Chandler Davidson and George Korbel, Chapter 4 below.

41. Joint Center for Political Studies, *National Roster of Black Elected Officials 1980* 10 (1981), 7.

42. Ibid.

43. Texas Advisory Committee to the United States Commission on Civil Rights, *Texas: The State of Civil Rights* (Washington, D.C.: U.S. Government Printing Office, 1980), 47.

44. Cox and Turner, *Voting Rights in Alabama,* 39.

45. Ibid., 44–45.

46. Ibid., 46–48.

47. Rolando L. Rios, "The Voting Rights Act: Its Effect in Texas" (Paper prepared under the auspices of the Southwest Voter Education Project, San Antonio, Texas, for delivery to the Special Committee on Election Law and Voter Participation of the American Bar Association, Washington, D.C., 9–10 April 1981), 4.

48. Lawyers' Committee, *Voting in Mississippi,* iv.

49. One study suggests that the obverse is also true: that minority turnout in primaries, though not in general elections, increases when cities change from at-large to district systems. See Peggy Heilig and Robert J. Mundt, "Do Districts Make a Difference?" *The Urban Interest* 3 (Spring 1981), 62–75.

50. Data collected by the author.

51. Barbara Y. Phillips, *How to Use Section 5 of the Voting Rights Act* (Washington, D.C.: Joint Center for Political Studies, Third Edition, 1983), 2.

52. McDonald, *Voting Rights,* 17.

53. Ibid.

54. 425 U.S. 130 (1976). For a discussion of *Beer* see Richard L. Engstrom, "Racial Discrimination in the Electoral Process: The Voting Rights Act and the Vote Dilution Issue," in *Party Politics in the South,* ed. Robert P. Steed, Lawrence W. Moreland, and Tod A. Baker (New York: Praeger Publishers, 1980), 207–209.

55. Gayle Binion quoted in Engstrom, "Racial Discrimination," 209.

56. Hiroshi Motomura, "Preclearance Under Section 5 of the Voting Rights Act," *North Carolina Law Review* 61 (1983).

57. McDonald, *Voting Rights,* 68.

58. 412 U.S. 755, 766 (1973).

59. 485 F. 2d 1297 (5th Cir. 1973) *(en banc).*

60. McDonald, *Voting Rights,* 74.

61. "VRA Extension in the Senate: A Fact Sheet," *Focus* 10 (February 1982), 5.

62. "Op-Ed," *New York Times,* 5 February 1982.

63. 458 U.S. 613 (1982).

64. 377 U.S. 533 (1964).

65. Civil Rights Task Force, "Reagan Civil Rights: The First Twenty Months" (Washington, D.C.: The Washington Council of Lawyers, Mimeographed, 1983), 74, 79.

HISTORICAL
PERSPECTIVES

2

The Undermining of the First Reconstruction
Lessons for the Second

J. Morgan Kousser

It is not only historians who name eras, make analogies, draw lessons from the past. As the Selma March was approaching Montgomery, Alabama, in 1965, and as Congress was pushing House Resolution 6400 toward passage, the *Montgomery Advertiser,* sensing the strong national current, remarked, "It is almost certain that President Johnson's reconstruction bill will be enacted."[1] The President Johnson referred to was not Andrew, but Lyndon; the "reconstruction" alluded to was not the first, but the second; and the bill was not the "Force" or "Ku Klux" laws, but the Voting Rights Act. Renewed in 1970, 1975, and 1982, the Voting Rights Act has been repeatedly attacked as anti-southern, an infringement on matters better left to state and local governments, and, most important, as unnecessary. It is therefore both desirable and safe, according to VRA opponents, to dismantle at least this vestige of the second Reconstruction.

That blacks, despite the guarantee of racially impartial suffrage in the Fifteenth Amendment, gradually lost the right to vote after the end of the first Reconstruction should caution students of policy as well as policymakers against a second abandonment of national regulation of elections. But beyond this obvious parallel, what lessons for the present can be drawn from the earlier period? What were the terms of the national suffrage guarantees passed by Congress in the 1860s and 1870s? What promises did southern white leaders of a century ago make in an attempt to convince northerners that black rights would be safe under "home rule" for Dixie? By what legal and extralegal means was black political power diluted and blacks eventually almost totally disfranchised? How safe is it, if we go by the historical record, to rely on judicial protection of minority political rights? How exact are the parallels, and, therefore, how relevant are the lessons? Have the conditions of blacks and the current and likely actions of whites changed so much that we have little to learn from history?

An earlier version of this paper was presented before The Subcommittee on Civil and Constitutional Rights of the House Judiciary Committee, 24 June 1981, and appears in its *Hearings* (Washington, D.C.: U.S. Government Printing Office, 1982), 2009–2022.

THE FIRST FEDERAL VOTING RIGHTS MACHINERY

During the first Reconstruction, the national government made two attempts by constitutional amendment and four attempts by law to protect black voting rights. Section 2 of the Fourteenth Amendment held out to the states the carrot of increased representation in Congress if they would repeal laws or state constitutional provisions excluding blacks from the right of suffrage. Less than a year after that amendment's ratification, however, Congress passed the more explicit provisions of the Fifteenth Amendment, which absolutely precluded state or national authorities from denying—or *abridging*—the right of citizens to vote on account of race, color, or previous condition of servitude. The Fortieth Congress considered, but, after discussion, rejected broader versions of the Fifteenth Amendment which would have banned literacy and property tests and other similar devices.[2]

Yet Congress recognized that the amendments, as well as the Military Reconstruction Acts which, even before the adoption of the Fifteenth Amendment, had enfranchised blacks in the seceding states, were not self-executing. To preclude official or unofficial violence, intimidation, or election irregularities from robbing citizens of any color of the right to vote and to have their ballots counted as cast, Congress in 1870 and 1871 passed the so-called enforcement, force, and Ku Klux acts, and in 1890 considered the Lodge Fair Elections Bill, but shelved it by one vote in the Senate.[3] Both the enforcement and Ku Klux acts made interfering with the right of citizens to vote a federal crime, and the Force Act went farther, requiring federal courts, upon a petition from two resident citizens, to appoint federal officers to oversee the registration and election process in cities or towns containing 20,000 or more inhabitants. The Lodge Bill in 1890 sought to extend the provisions of the Force Bill to all voters, rural as well as urban.

NINETEENTH-CENTURY SOUTHERN WHITE PROMISES TO RESPECT BLACK VOTING RIGHTS

The first southern white response to threats of Reconstruction was defiance.[4] Believing that the Civil War had settled only the questions of secession and slavery and that those who retained power in the states would be allowed to set the status of the freedmen approximately equal to that of the antebellum free people of color, white southerners virulently and often violently opposed all efforts to guarantee blacks equal rights, notably in the 1866 Civil Rights Bill, the Reconstruction Acts, the Fourteenth and Fifteenth Amendments, the various enforcement acts, and the 1875 Civil Rights Act. That the Republican majority, with substantial support from northern public opinion, continued for a time to insist on equal rights, however, convinced white southern Democrats to alter their tactics. While a "white line" faction continued and even, in the mid-1870s, intensified the forcible intimidation of black voters, a more moderate "New Departure" faction of southern Democrats emerged at the same time, assuring northerners that black rights would be safe if federal protection were withdrawn. The left or moderate hand, the Wade Hampton, L.Q.C. Lamar, and Francis T. Nicholls faction of the party, at least claimed not to know what the right or extreme racist hand, the Martin W. Gary and Ben Tillman faction, was doing. But the combined one-two punch was devastating to black political power in the Deep South.

The moderates' paper pledges were strong, and they persuaded those northerners who, like President Rutherford B. Hayes, were anxious to believe them. The Mississippi state Democratic platform of 1875 affirmed a belief in "the civil and political equality of all men as established by the Constitution of the United States and the amendments thereto." In the words of the authoritative work on Mississippi Reconstruction, however, "the majority of the delegates did not take the document very seriously."[5] Similarly, in Louisiana in 1876, in the words of the leading historical work on Reconstruction in that state, "The Democratic Platform also explicitly recognized the binding effect of the 13th, 14th, and 15th amendments to the United States Constitution, and the party pledged itself to protect every citizen, regardless of race, in the exercise of his rights. Every one of these pledges, except possibly the acknowledgement of the 13th Amendment, would be broken within a few years."[6]

In Virginia in 1873, the state Democratic party platform, again according to the standard scholarly monograph on the subject, "promised to administer equal justice to both races." Nevertheless, the Democrats, including even moderate gubernatorial candidate James L. Kemper, "made much of the color line" during that campaign, and, as we shall see below, the Virginians took action in the 1874 and 1876 legislative sessions to reduce the black vote.[7]

In South Carolina, which had the largest black percentage of any state in the union at the time, the 1876 Democratic state platform announced: "We declare our acceptance, in perfect good faith, of the thirteenth, fourteenth, and fifteenth amendments to the Federal Constitution." The South's best known moderate Redeemer, South Carolina gubernatorial candidate Wade Hampton, promised repeatedly that "not one single right enjoyed by the colored people today shall be taken from them. They shall be the equals, under the law, of any man in South Carolina." Blacks would soon convert to the Democratic party, Hampton prophesied, "because they will find that their rights will be better protected by that party."[8]

Many observers at the time recognized the cynicism which was involved in such pledges and prognostications. As Amos Akerman, who had returned to the South after serving briefly as Attorney General under Grant, remarked at the time, "when speaking for effect at the North" the southern Democrats "say much about accepting the results of the war in good faith, and respecting the rights of everybody," but contradicted those statements by their "drastic policy and unguarded utterances" in the South.[9] Even the oft mentioned moderate policy of appointing blacks to some offices was mostly window dressing. As Gov. Francis T. Nicholls of Louisiana, one of the most prominent New Departure Democrats, noted: "[I] appointed a number of [blacks] to small offices sandwiching them on Boards between white men where . . . they were powerless to do harm."[10]

The southern Democrats' promises had been, in fact, violated even as they were uttered. As U.S. Senate investigations in 1877 and 1878 documented, widespread Ku Klux and Red Shirt violence kept many blacks from the polls, racially discriminatory voting restrictions and facially neutral laws administered in a discriminatory fashion discouraged others, and blatant ballot box stuffing and fraudulent counting negated the votes of many who managed to overcome other obstacles to voting.[11] By 1880, even President Rutherford B. Hayes, whose southern policy was built on the assumption that white moderates would live up to their promises, hold the more openly racist whites in check, and join a Whiggish alliance with Republicans, recognized the southern violations and asked Congress to pass more legislation to protect black rights effectively.[12]

FOUR STAGES IN THE ATTACK ON BLACK VOTING RIGHTS AFTER THE FIRST RECONSTRUCTION

There were four overlapping stages, four sets of distinct tactics in the late nineteenth and early twentieth century attacks on black voting rights: the *Klan stage,* the *dilution stage,* the *disfranchisement stage,* and the *lily-white stage.* In the first era, which is the best known, the basic tactics were violence, intimidation, and fraud. These methods continued to be used in later periods, as they were needed, to reinforce other, subtler devices, and that they were always available often deterred blacks from organizing challenges to white political domination. Coordinated and deftly targeted white violence and fraud in the South from 1870 to 1876 gradually overthrew every southern Republican government.

Much less well known or understood, the second or "dilution" phase was much more subtle. It aimed at reducing the threat of black political power efficaciously but quietly, so as to decrease the possibility that the national government would again intervene to protect blacks from white southerners.

The third or "disfranchisement" phase is familiar to every student of the South. Beginning as early as the 1870s and culminating in the constitutional conventions from 1890 on, white Democrats passed literacy and property tests and poll taxes with the expressed intent and demonstrated effect of disfranchising the vast majority of blacks. Though they provided loopholes for poor or illiterate whites—the grandfather and "fighting grandfather" clauses and the "understanding" clause—they also meant to and did disfranchise large numbers of lower status white people. Nonetheless, the prime object of all these attacks on universal or impartial suffrage was the black man.[13]

The final or "lily-white" stage generally succeeded the disfranchisement of most blacks. Its aim was to crush any elevation of blacks above the distinctly secondary political status into which the disfranchisement measures had forced them, and to reduce, from very slim to none, any chances of blacks being elected or appointed to office or exercising any political muscle whatsoever. Some blacks remained on the voter rolls even after the turn of the century constitutions and amendments went into effect, and had the registration procedures been at all fair, many more could have registered. According to the U.S. Census of 1900, for instance, close to half of the adult black males in the South were literate, and others were direct descendants either of whites or of the more than 200,000 blacks who had served in the Civil War or earlier wars. Republican and even Democratic administrations in the late nineteenth century had appointed blacks to federal offices—postmasterships, tariff and other tax collection posts, as well as many positions in the justice system. Yet during the so-called "Progressive Era," white southern politicians considered the prospect of any black at or near an office of responsibility as an impudent and intolerable attack on the newly established racial status quo, and they tried to ensure, through further "reforms" of local government, that never again could a black be elected to even a minor office within the South.[14]

NINETEENTH CENTURY DILUTION OF
BLACK POLITICAL POWER—LESSONS FOR THE 1980s

Black economic status is sufficiently secure and national public opinion committed enough to racially impartial suffrage in the 1980s that it is improbable to expect a return to the days when widespread violence, intimidation, or fraud, literacy tests, or poll taxes could be reimposed in order to *deny* black voting rights altogether. Nevertheless, more sophisticated means of *abridging* black political power are presently in use in numerous areas, and, if the federal check provided by the Voting Rights Act were repealed or its administration relaxed, such means might well be employed much more in the future than they are today. But the abridgement as well as the denial of impartial suffrage is against the Fifteenth Amendment, and subtle as well as blatant discrimination can undermine the effective exercise of citizens' rights. It is therefore appropriate to take a closer look at the historical record in the two less well-known of the four stages, particularly at the second stage. By what means was black political power diluted in the post-Reconstruction South?

Reconstruction and post-Reconstruction southern Democrats used at least sixteen different techniques to hamper black political power without actually denying the franchise to sufficient numbers of voters to invite a strengthening of federal intervention. Many of these devices were facially neutral and might possibly be upheld by courts even today. Indeed, some of them, adopted as long as a century ago, are still in effect and *have* recently been ruled not to violate the Constitution or laws of the United States.[15] Thus, by looking at the past, we see also a possible future, a future which may well come about if continuous federal supervision of election practices is withdrawn from areas where racial bloc voting is still prevalent, a future of relatively subtle, but nonetheless effective racially discriminatory electoral procedures.

Although they all had the same purpose—the minimization of officeholding by black or black-influenced white officeholders—the specific schemes varied because of differences in the black percentage of the population and its geographic distribution. If the blacks were geographically concentrated within the politically relevant area, judicious *gerrymandering* could minimize the number of seats they could hope to win, but single-member districts, always preferred by most whites, could be maintained. If Afro-Americans were in the minority, *at-large elections* could deny them any representation at all, especially when combined with *white primaries*, which minimized defections by disgruntled white factions in the general elections. If they had clear, but not substantial majorities, *registration* acts, *poll taxes, secret ballot* or *multiple-box* laws or *petty crimes* provisions could cut those majorities down, so that the previously mentioned tactics could be used. For temporarily white-controlled cities in such binds, *annexation,* or, in suitable circumstances, the strikingly inventive device of *deannexation or retrocession* of territory was available. If the majorities were too large to be overcome, *bonds* for officeholders could be set so high as to deter from running any but the extremely affluent or those with rich and brave friends, or the authorities might arbitrarily *refuse to accept the bonds* as valid, or election officials might *consolidate polling places* to such an extent as to make the trip to the polls or the line at the polls intolerably long, or they might just *fail to open the polls* altogether. In extremes, the legislatures could *impeach or otherwise displace* elected officials or *do away with local elections* altogether and vest the power to choose local officials in the legislature or governor or their appointees. Since many areas still lack detailed political histories, this list and historians' current knowledge of the incidence of all these practices are necessarily incomplete. Nonetheless, some illustrations are useful to lend concreteness to the catalogue.

Racially motivated gerrymandering was widely employed in cities as well as states, for legislatures as well as Congress. Although more than 60 percent of South Carolina's people were black in the 1880s, only one of her seven congressional districts had a secure black majority. Known at the time as the "black district," the South Carolina Seventh sliced through county lines and ducked around Charleston back alleys picking up every possible black, while avoiding as many whites as it could; was contiguous at one point only by considering the Atlantic Ocean a land mass; contained nearly a third more people than another of the state's districts; and was shaped, the *New York Times* said, like a boa constrictor, the color of its intended victim clear.[16] Similarly, partisan and racial considerations—the two correlated almost perfectly in the Deep South at the time—gave North Carolina its "Black Second" Congressional District, Alabama its "Black Fourth," and Mississippi its notorious "Shoestring District," which tracked the Mississippi River down the whole length of the state in order to concentrate as much of the Negro vote as possible in one seat.[17] In the Texas legislature, the boundaries of all the black belt multicounty "floater" districts, in the words of the standard work on race relations in that state, "were gerrymandered in order to create a white majority."[18] Similar racially tainted gerrymanders "whitened" state legislatures all across the South, as well as in the cities of Richmond, Nashville, Montgomery, Raleigh, Chattanooga, Jackson (Mississippi), and doubtless others which have not yet received intensive study.[19]

At-large city elections, clearly motivated by racial purposes, appeared in the South as early as the first elections in which blacks were allowed to vote. "To guard against the possibility of the election of black city officials," white Atlanta Democrats in 1868 "secured from the legislature the general ticket system."[20] Two years later, after a temporarily Republican Georgia legislature restored the ward system, two of the ten candidates elected were black. But when the G.O.P. lost control of the legislature in 1871, the Democrats went back to the at-large system, and no more blacks were elected to the Atlanta city government until 1953.[21] In

Mobile, Alabama, the rabidly racist 1874 and 1876 Redeemer legislatures mandated explicit at-large systems for the election of school board and city government officials. In the case of the school board, this replaced a system which had been designed to guarantee "minority representation," and in the instance of the city government, it was a substitute for a vague 1870 law which a local racist faction of white Republicans had interpreted, under Democratic pressure, to require at-large elections. No black has ever been elected to either governmental body under these at-large systems, which persist in Alabama law to this day.[22] Chattanooga, Memphis, and Nashville "reformers," too, introduced and at times succeeded in getting the Tennessee legislature to pass at-large election statutes for their cities. "Their efforts stemmed from partisan and racial motives," says the leading authority on the subject, who titles his chapter on the topic: "Urban Reform: The Nemesis of Black Power."[23]

The Democratic primary was not at first principally a disfranchising device, for the vast majority of blacks wished only to cast Republican or independent votes and have them counted as cast; and, in fact, a few blacks were often allowed to vote in such primaries, in return for pledges of allegiance to the Democrats, in order to cut down the Republican totals in the general elections. But the local primary soon became the real election in many areas, and it was restricted to whites only in certain Texas counties from 1874 on, in Edgefield and Charleston counties in South Carolina from 1878 on, in Birmingham from 1888 on, and in Atlanta for various periods before 1895 and from that date until at least the *Smith v. Allwright* decision in 1944.[24]

By lengthening residency requirements, by requiring periodic voter registration at centrally located places during working hours and presentation of registration receipts at the polls (which burdened lower-class voters who were not accustomed, in those prebureaucratic days, to keeping records), by demanding copiously detailed information, which sometimes had to be vouched for by witnesses, before a voter could register, by allowing registration boards sufficient discretion to enable them to pad or unfairly to purge the rolls, by not guaranteeing equal party representation on such boards, and by permitting widespread challenges to voters at the polls, nineteenth century southern Democrats could keep the black vote under control.

Speaking for local Democrats in February 1875, for instance, the *Montgomery Daily Advertiser* pleaded that "if the Legislature does not come to the aid of the negro [sic] dominated communities then there is no help for this portion of Alabama." The legislature responded with a strict local registration law.[25] In Mississippi in the same year, according to a leading modern scholar, "the new registration law provided an excellent means for local Democrats to reduce Negro voters to a manageable proportion—an opportunity many seized upon immediately."[26] Texas in 1874 gave city councils the right to delete "ineligibles" from the rolls after the close of registration, a measure "undoubtedly motivated," in the words of Lawrence D. Rice, "by the mobility of certain portions of the population—principally the Negroes."[27] In Tennessee, a municipal registration act was beaten in 1885 only when the Republicans in the state senate walked out, breaking the quorum. When it passed, along with a secret ballot act (which served as a de facto literacy test, since illiterates were not allowed assistance in voting) in 1889, registration devastated the black vote in the four major Tennessee cities, as it was intended to.[28]

The South Carolina registration and eight-box law was one of the most clever stratagems, and its provisions illustrate better than any other instance how ingenious southern authors could twist seemingly neutral devices for partisan and racist purposes. As first introduced, the bill took the "neutral principle" of voter registration and turned it into a literacy test by requiring potential registrants to sign their names. Its author, the "patrician" Edward McCrady, Jr., estimated that this would disfranchise a majority of the blacks. To those who pointed out that a literacy test would also affect many whites, McCrady proposed as an escape mechanism the first form of the grandfather clause. Massachusetts in 1857 had required literacy of all future voters, but allowed those already on the rolls to stay. McCrady simply adopted the principle of the Massachusetts provision, along with its 1857 date, which, as everyone realized, predated black suffrage. As the bill finally passed, the literacy test was shifted into a new section of the law which provided for separate ballot boxes for each of eight offices, required election officials to shift the boxes around during the voting to make it impossible for a literate friend to put an illiterate's tickets in the correct order before he entered the polling place, and prohibited anyone but the election officers (all but one or two of whom in the entire state seem to have been Democrats) from assisting unlettered voters. In place of the grandfather clause, the registration provision which finally passed allowed the registrar at the close of the registration period to add to the list any voter who had failed to register if the official, to quote the law, "upon such evidence as he may think necessary, in his discretion" judged that the voter should be on the rolls. This open invitation to fraud and discrimination was designed to let registrars enfranchise all whites. Black turnout in South Carolina in the presidential election of 1884 dropped by an estimated 50 percent from its 1880 level.[29]

Although some scholars have doubted the effect of the poll tax on black voting, contemporaries knew better. It was "the most effective instrumentality of Negro disfranchisement," according to a member of the 1890 Mississippi Constitutional Convention's Franchise Committee, and "practically disfranchised the Negroes" in Georgia, according to a prominent North Carolina disfranchiser. And it was adopted early in some states. Georgia Republicans suspended the tax as a suffrage prerequisite in 1870, but the Democratic Redeemer legislature promptly restored it in 1871, and the 1877 Georgia Constitutional Convention not only fixed it in the fundamental law, but made it cumulative—that is, taxes for all previous years had to be paid before one could vote. Tennessee Democrats in 1870 and Virginia Democrats in 1876 followed Georgia's lead, but anti-Democratic "independent" movements, which were allied with the heavily black Republican parties in each state, made poll tax repeal one of their first orders of business during the 1870s. As is well known, by 1908, all eleven ex-Confederate states had made the poll tax a suffrage prerequisite, and the Afro-American was always its chief intended victim.[30]

Less well known were laws and constitutional provisions disfranchising people for having committed various crimes. While the effect of such provisions is unclear, since many were apparently adopted primarily as insurance if courts struck down more blatantly unconstitutional clauses or mandated fair implementation of those clauses, their intent is obvious. According to the *Richmond State* and the *Petersburg Index and Appeal,* Virginia's petty crimes provision, along with the poll tax, effected "almost . . . a political revolution" in cutting down the black vote.[31] Mississippi's infamous 1875 "pig law" defined the theft of property valued at ten dollars or more, or of any cattle or swine, whatever their value, as grand larceny, thus bringing those convicted of such minor offenses under the previous state constitutional suffrage ban.[32] During debate in the 1895 South Carolina Constitutional Convention, a delegate moved to add to the list of disfranchising crimes housebreaking, receiving stolen goods, breach of trust with a fraudulent intention, fornication, sodomy, assault with intent to ravish, miscegenation, incest, and larceny, and to strike out theft and the middle-class crime of embezzlement. The conventioneers agreed, as they did to another member's proposal to include wife beating. Murderers, however, were allowed to vote.[33] The framer of the crimes provision in the Alabama Constitutional Convention of 1901 thought that its wife-beating provision alone would disqualify 66 percent of the black males.[34] Recent attempts to have the South Carolina and Alabama petty crimes provisions declared unconstitutional have failed in federal courts.[35]

To reduce a black majority in 1877, Montgomery deannexed a predominantly black section, even though the area contained enough valuable industrial property that its retrocession noticeably reduced the city's tax base. Whites in Selma convinced the legislature to reduce that city's size, too, as a Dallas County Democratic state senator later recalled, "in order to cut the [N]egroes out of the city."[36]

To discourage black candidates, the town of Huntsville, Texas, raised the required bond for constables during the 1880s to twenty thousand dollars.[37] In Vance County, North Carolina, in 1887, a sheriff's bond was fixed at fifty-three thousand dollars and a treasurer's, at eighteen thousand dollars. Since few Republicans were wealthy enough to sign such bonds, only those acceptable to rich Democrats could serve. Even if they had affluent friends, successful candidates sometimes had their bonds arbitrarily refused by the county commissioners in North Carolina who were all appointed by the Democrats. In Warren County in 1886, the commissioners turned down a candidate because he "was a colored man." His white opponent, rejected by the voters, was given the office.[38]

Fraud, notorious and ubiquitous in the postbellum South, was supplemented by somewhat less blatant polling place irregularities, which are best illustrated by one scholar's description of the 1876 election in the Alabama "Black Belt": "On election day some polls opened and closed at the whim of election officials while other polls moved several times during the day. Some election officials refused to open the polls at all, and others announced that they were not going to remain at the polls all day to permit blacks to make 'radical majorities.' The failure to open polls in Republican strongholds in Hale, Perry, Marengo, Bullock, Barbour, Greene, Pickens, Wilcox, and Sumter counties undermined Republican strength as effectively as the earlier terror of the Ku Klux Klan, and it involved no bloodshed."[39]

If all else failed, officials could be impeached or forced from office, often on trumped-up charges, and local governments could be made appointive. Thus, North

Carolina Governor William W. Holden was impeached in 1870 for trying to put down the Klan, and Mississippi Governor Adelbert Ames, whom no one credibly charged with any illegal act, was pressured out of office during impeachment proceedings, which also led to resignations by other statewide executive and judicial officials, as well as circuit judges, in that state and in South Carolina.[40] In Tennessee in 1869 and in Virginia in 1870, conservative state legislatures summarily ousted the Nashville and Richmond city governments and replaced Republicans with Democrats. The Alabama legislature abolished the Dallas county criminal court because the elected black Republican judge refused to resign, and did away with the elective office of county commissioner in at least five black belt counties during the 1870s, substituting officers appointed by the Governor. The purpose of Alabama's action was later openly avowed by state legislator James Jefferson Robinson:

> Montgomery county came before us and asked us to give them protection of life, liberty and property by abolishing the offices that the electors in that county had elected. Dallas asked us to strike down the officials they had elected in that county, one of them a Negro that had the right to try a white man for his life, liberty and property. Mr. Chairman, that was a grave question to the Democrats who had always believed in the right of the people to select their own officers, but when we saw the life, liberty and property of the Caucasians were at stake, we struck down in Dallas county the Negro and his cohorts. We put men of the Caucasian race there to try them.[41]

In North Carolina, the state legislature first divested the voters of the right to elect county commissioners and justices of the peace, then arrogated to itself the power to name justices of the peace, then gave the justices of the peace the responsibility of choosing the commissioners. The complexion of county government in Wake and other Republican counties changed immediately and irredeemably.[42]

What policy conclusions can we draw from this review of the nineteenth century dilution phase? First, since politics is often a matter of small margins and any change in the rules potentially can make a large difference in outcomes, it follows that even minor alterations in election structures can be extremely important. Many of the nineteenth century dilutive devices had no impact or only a marginal impact on blacks' ability to vote per se, but they very often made the difference between winning and losing—that is to say, between having some political influence and little or none. Second, many of the schemes were ingenious and their exact form could not have readily been predicted in advance. Any attempt to prohibit discriminatory voting devices must have built into it sufficient administrative flexibility to be able to deal with schemes which cannot all be precisely anticipated. Third, many of the means of abridgement depended largely on discriminatory administration of seemingly fair laws. Since such practices are particularly difficult for courts to evaluate, and since litigation tends to drag on for many years, perhaps allowing the discrimination to continue while lawyers delay and judges make up their minds, it is preferable to vest oversight power in an executive administrative agency, if one really wants to prohibit this type of discrimination. Fourth, many of the existing practices and structures which were in effect grandfathered in, at least by the current legal interpretation of Section 2 of the Voting Rights Act, were adopted as long as a century ago for purposes which historians would probably be willing to conclude were discriminatory. Although it is difficult and extremely time consuming to uncover evidence of their exact intent which would convince an unsympathetic judge, and nearly impossible to find guns still merrily smoking after so long a time, it is possible to discover quite a lot about motives in many instances.

But variations in judges' opinions on whether a discriminatory motive on the part of the original framers of a particular law has been proved—the crucial constitutional question for the plurality in the Supreme Court's *Bolden* decision—have been extremely wide. Thus in four post-*Bolden* cases, one appeals court panel in *Lodge v. Buxton* doubted that such intent could ever be established; another panel, in *Kirksey v. Jackson,* denied that the voters' intent in a referendum could even be inquired into; Federal District Judge Frank McFadden, in *Underwood v. Hunter,* dismissed all evidence of intent and returned to the effect standard of *Palmer v. Thompson;* and Federal District Judge Virgil Pittman believed the plaintiffs' evidence in two Mobile cases, declaring in *Brown v. Board of School Commissioners* that "Given the relatively limited indicia of legislative intent available in this era, it is difficult to imagine a case of discriminatory intent more precisely or convincingly made out." [43] In directing minorities to enter the political thicket of determining the intent of ancient legislatures and recent voters in order to challenge political structures they allege to be discriminatory, Mr. Justice Stewart in *Bolden* in effect established a lottery. As *Lodge, Underwood,* and the Mobile cases show, the *Bolden* intent standard is so vague that the outcome depends almost entirely on the luck of the judicial draw.

MUNICIPAL "REFORM" AND THE LILY-WHITE STAGE

In his plurality opinion in *Mobile v. Bolden,* Mr. Justice Stewart contended that "It is noteworthy that a system of at-large city elections in place of elections of city officials by the voters of small geographic wards was universally heralded not many years ago as a praiseworthy and progressive reform of corrupt municipal government." In support of this view, Justice Stewart cited only one pertinent source, Banfield and Wilson's *City Politics,* blatantly misread the relevant sentence on the page he cited, and failed to note that Banfield and Wilson elsewhere in the book devoted a full page to the deleterious effect of at-large systems on black representation.[44] Moreover, Justice Stewart's summary is at least a generation out of date, and the view he expressed no longer commands the respect of the community of professional historians, if it ever did. In the nation as a whole, it is clear that commission government and at-large elections had as one of their prime purposes the strengthening of upper-class influence and the corresponding weakening of lower-class influence in politics. In the South, a large part of that lower-class was black. Municipal reform in the region was often part and parcel of the movement to ensure that government would remain lily-white.

The recent historiography of municipal political reform during the early part of the twentieth century has been dominated by the so-called "Weinstein-Hays Thesis." In seminal articles in 1962 and 1964, James Weinstein and Samuel P. Hays examined the social origins and consequences of the city commission and manager movements. Their conclusions, now widely accepted by historians, were summarized by Weinstein:

> The heart of the [commission] plan, that of electing only a few men on a citywide vote, made election of minority or labor candidates more difficult and less likely. Before the widespread adoption of commission and manager government it was common for workingmen to enter politics and serve as aldermen, or even mayor . . . But once the commission plan was in effect this became rare. Working-class aldermen were hard hit because the resources needed to conduct a citywide campaign were much greater than those needed for a ward election, and because minorities—political, racial, or national—were usually concentrated in specific wards . . . The nonpartisan ballot, a feature of most commission-manager plans and widely heralded as a great advance in democracy, also tended to operate against minority groups. . . . The end result of the movements was to place city government firmly in the hands of the business-class.[45]

Hays's description of the origins of the municipal reform movement makes clear that these consequences were foreseen and intended: "The movement for reform in municipal government, therefore, constituted an attempt by upper-class, advanced professional, and large-business groups to take formal political power from the previously dominant lower- and middle-class elements so that they might advance their own conceptions of desirable public policy."[46]

Historical works written since the Weinstein and Hays articles have broadened and deepened their research, but have left their conclusions essentially unchanged. In Galveston, fount of the twentieth century commission idea, businessmen led the drive for both at-large elections (which preceded commission government in that city) and the abolition of the mayor-council structure. But the movement was damaging to blacks, as Bradley Rice noted in his recent book: "As some black leaders had anticipated, the at-large feature of the 1895 charter effectively terminated Negro office-holding in Galveston despite the fact the race comprised twenty-two percent of the city's population in 1900. The black incumbent whom the People's Ticket endorsed carried his district but fell victim to city-wide prejudice in the total vote."[47] All across the nation, Rice finds, minority and lower-status groups opposed at-large elections during this era: "The lower classes correctly perceived that the at-large election of a small board would make it difficult for people of limited means to be elected. They expected that governmental schemes devised and promoted by business interests would be run for the benefit of those same interests."[48] Appealing for black votes against the commission in Des Moines, Iowa, in 1908, for instance, an orator told the Trades and Labor Assembly that "This is the Galveston system pure and simple to keep the so-called white trash and colored vote of the south from exerting itself in participation of [sic] the affairs of the city."[49]

But why, after the passage of constitutional disfranchisement measures had devastated the black vote in the South, was further "reform" necessary? Whatever the impetus of "reform" electoral structures elsewhere in the nation or before "hard" suffrage restriction laws went into effect in the South, weren't most of the post-1900 changes passed in "race-proof" situations? To understand why the implications of this question are misleading requires a deeper look at both disfranchisement and at the lily-white "progressive" impulse.

Never after the passage of the Fifteenth Amendment were all southern blacks disfranchised. In every state, and particularly in southern cities, where the literate, and, relative to sharecroppers, comparatively wealthy black middle class congregated, thousands of Afro-Americans remained on the voting rolls.[50] In close elections, especially in the often desultory municipal election contests, geographically concentrated minority votes might hold the balance of power. In Mobile in 1908, for instance, nearly 200 blacks were registered, in an era when the normal turnout was about 3,000 in municipal campaigns. When the legislature temporarily shifted to a scheme in which the members of one part of the bicameral city governing body would be selected on a ward basis, there was a real fear that blacks might influence the selection of a member from one or two wards. The answer to this threat was first, to ban blacks altogether from the local Democratic primary—some had previously been allowed to vote, and others then apparently desired to—and second, to return to totally at-large elections, which the legislature ordered in 1911.

In fact, throughout the South, whites in the "Progressive Era" feared that their "solution" to the "Negro problem" might unravel. To counter the possibility that blacks might be able to take advantage of splits within the white community, the Democrats sought to impede the growth of any potential opposition party by legalizing the direct primary and banning defeated primary candidates from running in the general election. All whites, they hoped, would come to consider the primary the real election, and organized party opposition would fade. As we know, the scheme succeeded. Increasingly completely excluded from what became known at that time as the "white primary," blacks could thereafter no longer cherish even the slightest hope that they could ally with a disgruntled white faction or party and thereby regain some political influence.[51]

Two famous incidents underscore the extent to which southerners in the early part of this century insisted upon absolutely lily-white government. They help us understand the pervasiveness and depth of racial motives, the lengths to which white southerners of the time were willing to go to eliminate even the least vestige of black political power, and therefore the improbability that any political change which affected blacks could have been devoid of a racial purpose.

The first incident involved Mrs. Minnie Cox, who had been postmistress at Indianola, Mississippi, during the Harrison and McKinley administrations and had been continued in her job when McKinley's assassination brought Theodore Roosevelt to the presidency. Wealthy and college educated, Mrs. Cox was widely respected in the white community in Sunflower County, and there was never any question of her competence or probity. In 1902, however, a complicated series of maneuvers by opportunistic local, state, and national politicians led to such loud demands for her replacement that the unoffending third-class postmistress in the tiny Mississippi town became the subject of numerous editorials in national newspapers, cabinet meetings, a U.S. Senate debate, and a formal congressional investigation! Mrs. Cox was eventually replaced by a white man.[52]

In the second black cause célèbre of the Theodore Roosevelt administration, the U.S. Senate, responding to southern white protests, held up for two years, solely on racial grounds, the appointment of an affluent, college-educated black doctor, William D. Crum, for the collectorship of the Port of Charleston. The prolonged struggle and agitation over the issue of appointing an Afro-American to this comparatively unimportant post was enough to win Roosevelt the virtually unanimous support of Negroes throughout the country at the same time that it helped scotch any hopes the president, previously immensely popular in the South, had for reviving the Republican party in the region.[53]

Along with the Cox affair, the Crum controversy reinforces the findings of other studies which document the pervasiveness of racism and the centrality of racial concerns in the so-called Progressive Era, and establishes a prima facie case of discriminatory intent against laws which affected blacks and which date from that period.[54] Would people who had been about the job of manipulating electoral structures to reduce black influence for over a generation, people who would openly and repeatedly defy a charismatic president in an attempt to keep political offices pure white, be likely to have been unconscious that one of the most widely noted effects of a particular change in the political rules, such as a shift from ward to at-large elections, would be to make it virtually impossible for the foreseeable future to elect a black to office?

THE SUPREME COURT THEN AND NOW

Sanguine nineteenth century supporters of black rights sometimes contented themselves after Reconstruction with the idea that the constitutional protections of those rights would be enforced by the courts, even if Congress and the states reneged. That those hopes proved ill-founded by the turn of the century is well known. And the parallels between past and current judicial language and decisions are close enough to give pause to any who would counsel relaxation of administrative protections of voting rights by offering the hope that the courts will still be around to protect constitutional rights.

The Supreme Court's retreat in such major cases as *Slaughter House, The Civil Rights Cases,* and *Plessy v. Ferguson* is common textbook knowledge. Rather less widely known, often mistakenly interpreted, and more closely analogous to more recent decisions is the Court's series of turn of the century opinions on black voting rights and the intent to discriminate.

In *Yick Wo v. Hopkins,* 118 U.S. 356 (1886), an attorney for Chinese laundrymen in San Francisco had presented an extensive factual brief detailing both the open avowal of an intent to disadvantage Chinese laundrymen during the San Francisco Board of Supervisors' debate over adoption of the facially neutral ordinance at issue, and the discriminatory effect on the Chinese of the ordinance as administered. In a rather expansive opinion, parts of which it later in effect declared dicta, the Supreme Court found an equal protection violation. Reading *Yick Wo* too broadly, Cornelius J. Jones, a clever but inexperienced black lawyer from Greenville, Mississippi, challenged a client's murder conviction on the grounds that the jury panel had been drawn from the voting rolls, from which blacks had been effectively excluded by the 1890 Mississippi constitution. Quoting extensively from newspaper reports of the debates at the Mississippi disfranchising convention, but offering no direct evidence of the notorious fact that the intent of the delegates had been carried out, Jones asked the Court to declare the Mississippi voting rules unconstitutional and to let his client go free.[55] The Court easily side-stepped Jones, declaring that proof of intent was insufficient, that one had to prove effect as well.[56]

In the next case after the *Williams* debacle, a more savvy black lawyer, Wilford H. Smith of New York, was secretly hired by Booker T. Washington to plug the loopholes in Jones' case. Challenging the 1901 Alabama Constitution's suffrage provisions directly, Smith's brief charged that the state constitution's "fighting grandfather" clause was a blatant attempt to subvert the Fifteenth Amendment, that the debates provided plentiful evidence that the whole scheme was designed to disfranchise blacks both through provisions which the delegates knew would have a disproportionate impact upon them and through preplanned discrimination in the administration of provisions which appeared neutral on their face, and finally, that the plot had been carried out, since Mr. Giles and other literate Negroes had been denied the right to register.[57] Since it could no longer use the impact/intent ploy, the Court turned to another classic dodge in the equal protection game, the question of relief. Smith had contended that the suffrage provisions of the Alabama constitution were so tainted with racist intent that the Court should declare the whole package unconstitutional, but also that it should order the Montgomery registrar to add Mr. Giles to the rolls. But, responded Mr. Justice Holmes, suppose the Court attacked administrative discrimination by ordering Giles and other literate blacks registered, but left the suffrage provisions otherwise intact. Wouldn't the discrimination complained of still persist for most Negroes? Conversely, suppose the Court threw out the provisions altogether. Then if it ordered Giles registered, the Court would become a party to a purportedly unlawful scheme. Anyway, Holmes concluded, grasping either horn of the dilemma would involve the courts too deeply in "political questions," which were best left to Congress and the state legislatures. It was a constitutional violation which the judiciary could not relieve.

Interestingly enough, Congress was considering the same question simultaneously. At the same time that he brought the *Williams* case to court, Cornelius J. Jones had challenged the seating of three congressmen from Mississippi before the quasi-judicial House Elections Committee on the grounds that blacks had been unconstitutionally excluded from the electorate and that therefore the elections were illegal per se. While he had not presented a full-fledged case, other lawyers who followed Jones's lead later did, and the committee had put off ruling on the issue until the *Dantzler* challenge from South Carolina in 1903. In that case, decided within six months of *Giles,* the house committee invoked what might be called, in analogy to the "political questions" doctrine, a "judicial questions" doctrine, ruling that such charges of discrimination were best left to the courts. The Alphonse-Gaston routine of Congress and the Supreme Court in *Dantzler* and *Giles* left blacks with no rights that the white men of the national government were bound to protect.[58]

In another turn of the century case, the Supreme Court used an extremely stringent intent criterion to slam the door on efforts to mandate as much equality as was possible in a segregated system. (I use "equality" here, of course, only in the very restricted sense of schools in which the expenditures per child, the physical facilities, and the teacher qualifications are roughly the same for children of every race.) If Mr. Justice Harlan's opinion in *Cumming v. Richmond County School Board*,[59] had been precisely followed, it would have made it practically impossible to prove a constitutional violation against a prudent discriminator. In 1897, the Augusta, Georgia school board, claiming financial stringency and a desire to use available moneys for black elementary education, had cut off funds for a black high school, while continuing to subsidize two high schools for whites. Pointing out that the school board had just received a very large increase in appropriations from the state government and that, if more money was needed for black elementary schools, it could come from the state supplement or from funds previously devoted to white as well as black schools, black parents charged that the school board's action was unconstitutional. But since school board members had not openly said that they acted because they wished to disadvantage black children, Justice Harlan treated their economic distress excuse as a "rational basis" and disregarded the view, strenuously pressed by one of the great constitutional lawyers of the day, former U.S. Senator George F. Edmunds, that the discriminatory impact of the law should be considered dispositive as to its real intent.[60]

The trend in recent cases on voting rights discrimination poses disturbing parallels to the Supreme Court's post-Reconstruction restriction of constitutional protection of minority rights. Although it denied the requested relief in the first multimember districting case, *Fortson v. Dorsey*,[61] the Court did proclaim a generous and perhaps even workable standard for proving a violation. Those who claimed that a multimember scheme disadvantaged "racial or political elements" of the population could prevail if they could show that the scheme "designedly *or otherwise*" discriminated against them.[62] In *Whitcomb v. Chavis*,[63] the Court denied that the lawyers for the Indianapolis blacks had proved either discriminatory intent or effect, but did not foreclose an attack on either ground. A general history of "bias and franchise dilution in the State's drawing of lines" was sufficient evidence of intent to convince the Supreme Court in *Taylor v. McKeithen*[64] to overturn a southern redistricting scheme. *White v. Regester*[65] held a Texas multimember scheme invalid on the basis of a "totality of the circumstances" approach which blended both "design and impact." And in *Connor v. Johnson*,[66] the Court directed a federal district court to devise a reapportionment scheme which did not include multimember districts, presumably because it recognized the unfairness of such districts to minorities.

In related areas of equal protection law, the Court zigzagged. *Palmer v. Thompson*[67] held that the decision of Jackson, Mississippi, to close its swimming pools could not be reversed on the grounds of discriminatory motive alone, which was established in the record. Impact became the key element.[68] Yet in a series of cases beginning with *Washington v. Davis*,[69] the Court applied an ever stricter "motive test." Although he held that an equal protection violation "must ultimately be traced to a racially discriminatory purpose" in *Washington*, Mr. Justice White did rule that a disproportionate effect on minorities was "not irrelevant" to an inquiry into purpose and that intent was to be assessed by looking at the "totality of the relevant facts."[70] In *Village of Arlington Heights v. Metropolitan*

Housing Development Corp.,[71] the Court appears to have dismissed the discriminatory impact of the Chicago suburb's zoning ordinance on racial minorities as irrelevant to a determination of motive, and it readily accepted the Village's explanation that its actions were not motivated by issues of race. And in *Personnel Administrator of Massachusetts v. Feeney,* impact became even less relevant to motive, since the Court held that the challenged action had to be shown to have been taken "at least in part 'because of,' not merely 'in spite of,' its adverse effects upon an identifiable group." [72]

These two streams flow together in *Mobile v. Bolden,* a confusing hodgepodge of opinions headed by Mr. Justice Stewart's for a four-person plurality. Pushing *Feeney* further, Justice Stewart found impact largely irrelevant, dismissed the view that the failure of the state of Alabama to take positive steps to remedy the historical pattern of past discrimination by itself constituted a violation of the Constitution, and, according to one reading of the opinion, limited "the constitutional inquiry to a search for a smoking gun." [73] Like *Cumming* before it, *Bolden* was both a seal of approval on an unjust status quo and an invitation to engage in soft-pedaled discrimination, an announcement that a credulous Court is ready to defer to any state and local authorities who can offer plausible reasons besides race for their actions. (It is interesting to note that Mr. Justice Blackmun concurred in Bolden upon the same grounds that Justice Holmes toyed with in *Giles*—relief.) If Congress were to take away the preclearance section of the Voting Rights Act or relax its heretofore fairly stringent controls, *Bolden* would open the door to widespread electoral changes, aimed at reducing minority political power, but adopted either so quietly or accompanied by such heated denials of any discriminatory purpose as to make the true motives difficult if not impossible to prove in court.

NOTES

1. 17 March 1965, quoted in Steven F. Lawson, *Black Ballots: Voting Rights in the South, 1944–1969* (New York: Columbia University Press, 1965), 314.
2. A convenient source on these matters is Bernard Schwartz, ed., *Statutory History of the United States: Civil Rights,* 2 vols. (New York: Chelsea House Publishers, 1970), I, 184, 371–74, 385–87, 392–95, 408–20.
3. Ibid., 445–53, 548–58, 593–96 give provisions of the first three laws. On the Lodge Bill, see J. Morgan Kousser, *The Shaping of Southern Politics: Suffrage Restriction and the Establishment of the One-Party South, 1880–1910* (New Haven, Conn.: Yale University Press, 1974), 29–31, and the sources cited there.
4. See Michael Perman, *Reunion Without Compromise: The South and Reconstruction, 1865–1868* (Cambridge, Eng.: Cambridge University Press, 1973).
5. William C. Harris, *The Day of the Carpetbagger: Republican Reconstruction in Mississippi* (Baton Rouge & London: Louisiana State University Press, 1979), 654–55.
6. Joe Gray Taylor, *Louisiana Reconstructed, 1863–1877* (Baton Rouge: Louisiana State University Press, 1974), 483–84.
7. Jack P. Maddex, Jr., *The Virginia Conservatives, 1867–1879* (Chapel Hill, N.C.: University of North Carolina Press, 1970), 108, 195.
8. All quoted in George B. Tindall, *South Carolina Negroes, 1877–1900* (Columbia, S.C.: University of South Carolina Press, 1952), 12.

9. Quoted in William Gillette, *Retreat From Reconstruction, 1869–1879* (Baton Rouge & London: Louisiana State University Press, 1979), 313.

10. Quoted in William J. Hair, *Bourbonism & Agrarian Protest: Louisiana Politics, 1877–1900* (Baton Rouge: Louisiana State University Press, 1969), 22.

11. *Senate Reports*, No. 855, 45th Cong., 3d Sess.; *Senate Reports*, No. 704, 44th Cong., 2d Sess.

12. Rayford W. Logan, *The Betrayal of the Negro: From Rutherford B. Hayes to Woodrow Wilson* (New York: Collier Books, 1965), 45.

13. See, in general, Kousser, *Shaping of Southern Politics*.

14. It should be noted that the various disfranchisement measures were. generally described as "reforms" during this period and that suffrage restriction was a central part of southern "Progressivism." See e.g., ibid., 257–61.

15. *Mobile v. Bolden*, 100 S. Ct. 1490 (1980). But see Federal District Court Judge Virgil Pittman's reversal of this outcome in his decision in *Bolden v. Mobile*, on remand from the Supreme Court, 15 April 1982. See also *Rogers v. Lodge*, 458 U.S. 613 (1982) for the court's clarification of the *Bolden* intent standard.

16. *New York Times*, 13 July 1882, 5.

17. Eric Anderson, *Race and Politics in North Carolina, 1872–1901: The Black Second* (Baton Rouge & London: Louisiana State University Press, 1981); Sarah Woolfolk Wiggins, "Alabama: Democratic Bulldozing & Republican Folly," in Otto H. Olsen, ed., *Reconstruction and Redemption in the South* (Baton Rouge & London: Louisiana State University Press, 1980), 68–69; *New York Times*, 27 July 1882, 5.

18. Lawrence D. Rice, *The Negro in Texas, 1874–1900* (Baton Rouge: Louisiana State University Press, 1971), 101, 132.

19. Howard N. Rabinowitz, *Race Relations in the Urban South, 1865–1890* (New York: Oxford University Press, 1978), 270–73, 323; Joseph H. Cartwright, *The Triumph of Jim Crow: Tennessee Race Relations in the 1880s* (Knoxville: University of Tennessee Press, 1976), 158.

20. Eugene J. Watts, "Black Political Progress in Atlanta, 1868–1895," *Journal of Negro History*, 59 (1974): 273.

21. Watts, "Black Political Progress," 273; Rabinowitz, *Race Relations in the Urban South*, 269.

22. See the federal court decisions in *Bolden v. City of Mobile* 542 F.Supp. 1050 (S.D. Ala. 1982), and *Brown v. Board of School Commissioners of Mobile County*, 542 F.Supp. 1078 (S.D. Ala. 1982).

23. Cartwright, *Triumph of Jim Crow*, 119–160, quote at 159.

24. Rice, *Negro in Texas*, 113–27; Tindall, *South Carolina Negroes*, 26, 33; Carl V. Harris, *Political Power in Birmingham, 1871–1921* (Knoxville: University of Tennessee Press, 1977), 58; Eugene J. Watts, *The Social Bases of City Politics: Atlanta, 1865–1903* (Westport, Conn.: Greenwood Press, 1978), 24, 30, 31.

25. *Advertiser*, 6 February 1875, quoted in Rabinowitz, *Race Relations in the Urban South*, 274.

26. Harris, *Day of the Carpetbagger*, 701.

27. Rice, *Negro in Texas*, 130.

28. Cartwright, *Triumph of Jim Crow*, 134–35, 223–254; J. Morgan Kousser, "Post-Reconstruction Suffrage Restrictions in Tennessee: A New Look at the V. O. Key Thesis," *Political Science Quarterly*, 88 (1973), 655–83.

29. Kousser, *Shaping of Southern Politics*, 84–92.

30. Ibid., 63–72 and passim.

31. Quoted in Maddex, Jr., *Virginia Conservatives*, 198. Similarly, see Paul Lewinson, *Race, Class, and Party: A History of Negro Suffrage and White Politics in the South* (New York: Russell and Russell, Inc. 1963), 66.

32. C. Vann Woodward, *Origins of the New South, 1877–1913* (Baton Rouge, La.: Louisiana State University Press, 1951), 212–13.

33. South Carolina Constitutional Convention of 1895, *Journal of the Proceedings* (Co-

lumbia, South Carolina: Charles A. Calvo, Jr., 1895), 298, 487; Tindall, *South Carolina Negroes*, 82.

34. Jimmie Frank Gross, "Alabama Politics and The Negro, 1874–1901" (Ph.D. thesis, University of Georgia, 1969), 244; Malcolm Cook McMillan, *Constitutional Development in Alabama, 1798–1901: A Study in Politics, The Negro, and Sectionalism* (Chapel Hill, North Carolina: University of North Carolina Press, 1955), 275. That this delegate, John Fielding Burns, was undoubtedly grossly exaggerating only strengthens the case for the racist motivation behind the provision.

35. *Allen v. Ellisor*, No. 79-1539, Fourth Circuit Court of Appeals (en banc) 6 January 1981; *Underwood v. Hunter*, No. 80-7084, Fifth Circuit Court of Appeals, 15 July 1980, and, on remand, 23 December 1981. *Underwood* is currently being appealed for the third time.

36. Rabinowitz, *Race Relations in the Urban South*, 323; *Montgomery Advertiser*, 9 October, 24 November 1900.

37. Rice, *Negro in Texas*, 88–89.

38. Anderson, *Race and Politics in North Carolina*, 162–65. For other examples, see Wiggins, "Democratic Bulldozing," 67; Allen J. Going, *Bourbon Democracy in Alabama, 1874–1890* (University, Alabama: University of Alabama Press, 1951), 33; Cartwright, *Triumph of Jim Crow*, 152–53.

39. Wiggins, "Democratic Bulldozing," 71–72. For examples of such tactics in South Carolina, see Tindall, *South Carolina Negroes*, 72; in Mississippi, see the contested congressional election cases of *Buchanan v. Manning* and *Chalmers v. Morgan*, in Chester H. Rowell, comp., *Digest of Contested Election Cases, 1789–1901* (Washington, D.C.: Government Printing Office, 1901), 373–75, 457–58; in Virginia, see *Stovell v. Cabell*, *Waddill v. Wise*, and *Langston v. Venable*, in Rowell, *Digest*, 393, 452–54, 457–60.

40. Anderson, *Race and Politics in North Carolina*, 3; Harris, *Day of the Carpetbagger*, 694–98; Tindall, *South Carolina Negroes*, 15–18.

41. Rabinowitz, *Race Relations in the Urban South*, 267–69; Wiggins, "Democratic Bulldozing," 68; *Montgomery Advertiser*, 23 April 1899. For a similar, earlier avowal of the racist intent of the Dallas County judgeship abolition, see *Selma Southern Argus*, 24 December 1875.

42. Rabinowitz, *Race Relations in the Urban South*, 269–70; Anderson, *Race and Politics in North Carolina*, 56–57.

43. *Lodge v. Buxton*, 639 F. 2d 1358 (1981); *Kirksey v. City of Jackson* (Former Fifth Circuit, 11 December 1981); *Underwood v. Hunter* (23 December 1981 decision); *Palmer v. Thompson*, 403 U.S. 217; *Brown v. Board* (15 April 1982 decision).

44. 100 S.Ct. 1490 at footnote 15 of Mr. Justice Stewart's opinion; Edward C. Banfield and James Q. Wilson, *City Politics* (Cambridge, Mass.: Harvard University Press and Massachusetts Institute of Technology Press, 1963), 151, 307–08. What Banfield and Wilson actually say on p. 151 is merely that "nonpartisanship, the council-manager plan, and at-large election are all expressions of the reform ideal and of the middle-class political ethos." That they are not uncritical of that ideal and that ethos is one of the signal features of their book.

45. Weinstein's "Organized Business and The Commission and Manager Movements" first appeared in *The Journal of Southern History*, 28 (1962), and was reprinted in his book, *The Corporate Ideal and The Liberal State, 1900–1918* (Boston: Beacon Press, 1968), in which the quoted passage appears on 109–10, 115.

46. Hays' "The Politics of Reform in Municipal Government in The Progressive Era" first appeared in *Pacific Northwest Quarterly*, 55 (1964), and was reprinted in his book, *American Political History as Social Analysis* (Knoxville: University of Tennessee Press, 1980), in which the quoted passage appears on 215–16.

47. Bradley Robert Rice, *Progressive Cities: The Commission Government Movement in America, 1901–1920* (Austin and London: University of Texas Press, 1977), 5.

48. Ibid., 29. For a similar treatment, see Martin J. Schiesl, *The Politics of Efficiency:*

Municipal Administration and Reform in America, 1800–1920 (Berkeley, Los Angeles, and London: University of California Press, 1977), 133–48.

49. Quoted in Rice, *Progressive Cities*, 47.
50. For figures on postdisfranchisement black registration, see Kousser, *Shaping of Southern Politics*, 61.
51. See ibid., 72–82.
52. Willard B. Gatewood, Jr., *Theodore Roosevelt and the Art of Controversy* (Baton Rouge: Louisiana State University Press, 1970), 62–89.
53. Ibid., 90–134.
54. On this point, virtually all modern scholarship follows the Woodward thesis expressed in a chapter title in his *Origins of The New South:* "Progressivism—For Whites Only." Similarly, see his testimony before the House Judiciary Committee in its 1981 hearings, p. 2024.
55. National Archives file on *Williams v. Mississippi,* 170 U.S. 213 (1898).
56. As Justice McKenna noted for a unanimous court, the laws "do not on their face discriminate between the races, and it has not been shown that their actual administration was evil; only that evil was possible under them." Ibid.
57. *Giles v. Harris,* 189 U.S. 475 (1903).
58. See the House Elections Committee cases of *Brown v. Allen, Newman v. Spencer, Ratliff v. Williams, Carter Glass, Dantzler v. Lever, Prioleau v. Legare,* and *Myers v. Patterson* in Rowell, *Digest of Contested Election Cases,* 540–41, and Merrill Moores, *A Historical and Legal Digest of All the Contested Election Cases in the House of Representatives . . . 1901–1917* (Washington, D.C.: Government Printing Office, 1917), 3, 16, 25–28. See also H.R. 2915, 57th Cong., 2 Sess.; and H.R. 1638, 1639, and 1640, 60th Cong.
59. 175 U.S. 528 (1899).
60. See J. Morgan Kousser, "Separate But *Not* Equal: The Supreme Court's First Decision on Racial Discrimination in Schools," *Journal of Southern History,* 46 (1980), 17–44.
61. 379 U.S. 433 (1965).
62. Italics supplied. See the discussion in Lawrence H. Tribe, *American Constitutional Law* (Mineola, N.Y.: The Foundation Press, Inc., 1978), 750–55.
63. 403 U.S. 124 (1971).
64. 407 U.S. 191 (1972).
65. 412 U.S. 755 (1973).
66. 402 U.S. 690 (1971).
67. 403 U.S. 217 (1971).
68. Tribe, *American Constitutional Law,* 1025–28.
69. 426. U.S. 229 (1976)
70. Tribe, *American Constitutional Law,* 1028–32; Aviam Soifer, "Complacency and Constitutional Law," *Ohio State Law Journal,* 42 (1981): 388.
71. 97 S Ct. 555 (1977).
72. 442 U.S. 256, 279 (1979).
73. Soifer, "Complacency and Constitutional Law," 404.

3

History in the Courts
The Significance of
The City of Mobile v. Bolden

Peyton McCrary

The wine-red carpet, rich mahogany furnishings, Sienna marble columns, and dark velour hangings of its courtroom provide the United States Supreme Court a regal setting for its pronouncements on constitutional issues. Against this backdrop it has granted many a victory to the cause of racial justice since outlawing the white primary in *Smith v. Allwright* in 1944. When Justice Potter Stewart read the Court's decision in *City of Mobile v. Bolden* on 22 April 1980, however, many observers concluded that the cause of black voting rights had suffered a major defeat. The central thrust of the opinion was to erect a new, more difficult standard of proof in cases such as this where black plaintiffs challenged the constitutionality of at-large election laws. During the 1970s the lower federal courts in the South had frequently ruled in favor of such claims, if plaintiffs demonstrated that citywide or countywide elections "diluted" the vote of a racial minority and thus minimized the chances for black candidates to win public office. Now the Court ruled that, in addition to proving that an at-large election system had this discriminatory effect, plaintiffs must show that the system was created or maintained for a racial purpose. Thus, it remanded the case (and a companion suit challenging at-large school board elections in Mobile County) to the lower courts for a new trial to consider evidence of discriminatory intent.[1]

Bolden did not, in truth, rank among the Court's great opinions. Justice Stewart spoke only for a plurality of four, with two other justices concurring in the decision to remand but disagreeing about the issue of intent. The three surviving liberals filed dissenting opinions. The result was an ambiguous, if not downright confused, new standard that left civil rights lawyers scratching their heads in dismay. Over the next year at numerous conferences, both formal and informal, they debated what the justices were trying to say and how to prove discriminatory intent.[2]

Most immediately affected were James U. Blacksher and Larry T. Menefee, principal attorneys for the black plaintiffs in Mobile. Edward Still was an associate counsel who practiced in Birmingham. Meeting the new standard, they decided, would require a dramatic departure from earlier cases. Under the old "effect" standard associated with *Zimmer v. McKeithen*, they had used political scientists, sociologists, and economists to present primarily statistical evidence documenting racial polarization in voting patterns and discrimination in the delivery of municipal services or education, focusing on the years following large-scale enfranchisement of blacks under the Voting Rights Act of 1965. Under the new requirements, they would need to hire historians to do research and testify as expert witnesses. Now the focus would be the purposes underlying the creation of the at-large election system in the half century preceding 1911.[3]

For years the federal courts had given some consideration to the question of intent; as a result, Blacksher and Menefee had used historians in several cases. Jerrell Shofner, a specialist in the Reconstruction period, had played a key role in their successful challenge to the at-large system in nearby Pensacola, Florida.[4] Another Reconstruction scholar, Peyton McCrary, had already agreed to do research for future vote dilution cases, and expressed willingness to work on the new trials in *Bolden* and *Brown v. Board of School Commissioners of Mobile County, Alabama*. Because McCrary taught at the University of South Alabama and thus lived in Mobile, he was the logical person to undertake the bulk of documentary research in the two cases.[5] Blacksher and Menefee wanted the insurance policy of a more experienced hand, however, and asked Shofner to testify as well.

In order to draw on as wide a range of academic talent as possible, the two attorneys decided to organize an ad hoc conference on the at-large election controversy. They asked McCrary to draw up a list of historians and political scientists whose expertise might be useful in exploring the evolution of this form of electoral discrimination. McCrary noticed that, as he himself was, many of the scholars on his list were already scheduled to deliver papers at the Southern Historical Association convention at the Atlanta Biltmore Hotel in November 1980. Fifteen of the persons contacted were able to remain in Atlanta for an extra day. Civil rights lawyers Armand Derfner and Frank Parker flew in from Charleston, South Carolina, and Jackson, Mississippi, to join Blacksher, Menefee, and Still. Laughlin McDonald and his associates came over from the Atlanta office of the American Civil Liberties Union. The attorneys explained the new *Bolden* standard and the professors pooled their knowledge of the evidence that might be relevant to the analysis of discriminatory intent. There was some discussion of a combined research effort, but the most immediate fruit of the conference was the addition of two new expert witnesses for the Mobile cases, historian J. Morgan Kousser and sociologist Chandler Davidson.[6]

Menefee jokingly dubbed this "the Biltmore School" of interpretation, but the opposing counsel in *Bolden* saw nothing humorous about it. During the trial, lawyers for the City of Mobile required each expert witness to "name names" of those present at the Biltmore Hotel and tried to picture the conference as a cabal designed to prostitute the muse of history to the cause of civil rights.

In January 1981, the United States government entered the school board suit on the side of the plaintiffs. Two Justice Department lawyers, Gerald Hebert and Ellen Weber, joined the research team in Mobile and found the key documents that broke open that case. McCrary employed two graduate students, Dianne Thompson and Joseph Roe, as research assistants. Reading newspapers on microfilm, poring over the records of the school board and the city government, going to the state archives in Montgomery to examine personal correspondence, everyone pitched in to piece together the complex patterns of electoral manipulation in Mobile in the 115 years since the Civil War. In the end, Blacksher and McCrary drafted the basic narrative and interpretation, pacing back and forth through the xerox copies of documents and notes spread all over Blacksher's livingroom and screened front porch.[7] Throughout the months of preparation, the lawyers emphasized that the historians were to lay out the evidence as they saw it. When dealing with the relationship between race and southern politics, as Blacksher told Mc-Crary, the truth is almost always sufficient for black plaintiffs to win their case.

In order to demonstrate that at-large elections continued to have the discriminatory effects documented in the first trials, the Justice Department put Chandler Davidson of Rice University on the stand. He had written on the dilutive effects of at-large elections and had testified in several court cases. Briefly he summarized the research of political scientists and sociologists, the vast bulk of which agrees that an at-large system minimizes the chance of victory by minority candidates.[8] Using a standard measure of residential segregation, Davidson then showed that housing patterns in Mobile were among the most rigidly segregated in the country. His analysis of recent election returns and census data revealed unmistakable and overwhelming racial polarization. Under these conditions, he concluded, it was unlikely that blacks—or white candidates publicly identified as sympathetic to black interests—could win office.[9]

The crux of the case, however, was the historical evidence concerning the origins of at-large elections. Shofner presented a general assessment of the evolution of southern racial attitudes. Kousser's special role in the school board case was to present statistical evidence of the discriminatory impact on educational expenditures for blacks of the shift to at-large elections in 1876. In both cases, he served the added function of reviewing and assessing the validity of McCrary's approach.

McCrary's job was to present a detailed narrative of the facts and to offer an assessment of "the intent of the framers" of each significant election statute. Like his colleagues, McCrary delighted in the label applied by the Mobile *Register,* which denounced the four expert witnesses as "pointy-headed perfessers."[10]

THE HISTORY OF VOTE DILUTION IN MOBILE

McCrary's account in *Bolden* began with the antebellum political system. Before the Civil War no blacks could vote in Mobile, and it was safe for whites to employ ward elections. In a referendum held in 1826, the city's white voters indicated a preference for a ward system; as a result, the mayor and aldermen divided Mobile into three wards, each of which was to elect two aldermen.[11] This system of district voting, first put into effect in 1828, continued with various modifications for forty years.[12] The most important change was the creation of a bicameral municipal government in 1840; a new board of common councilmen was to be chosen on an at-large basis, but each ward was still to elect its own aldermen. This pattern prevailed even under the Confederacy.[13]

At the end of the Civil War, the Union occupation authorized the Confederate city government to continue in office until new elections could be held. President Andrew Johnson appointed Lewis Parsons, a native white Unionist, as provisional governor of Alabama. In accordance with Johnson's conservative Reconstruction policy, Governor Parsons held elections for delegates to a state constitutional convention in the summer of 1865, and only white males were allowed to vote, as before the war. The conservative whites elected to this convention had supported the Confederacy in varying degrees. The 1865 constitution retained the traditional prohibition against the vote for blacks. Thus, when new elections took place that fall for governor, state officers, a legislature, and the congressional delegation, conservative whites—who were shortly to form the Alabama Democratic Party on a white supremacy platform—won most of the offices. The first postwar legislature enacted a series of proscriptive "black codes," such as the vagrancy statute that authorized the sheriff to arrest anyone who could not prove he was employed. In order to defray the expense of incarceration, the sheriff could then hire out the person's services to local employers. Whites perceived this law as a useful weapon to compel blacks to sign sharecrop contracts with local landowners.[14] The same legislature continued in effect, with slight modification, the antebellum system of electing municipal officeholders in Mobile under which a new city government was chosen in December 1865.[15]

In March 1867, the Congress passed the first of several Reconstruction acts which brought an end to the conservative policies of President Johnson. The Congress required each former Confederate state to hold new elections for constitutional conventions; southern blacks were to cast ballots for the first time. The constitutions drafted by these conventions were to be ratified by a majority of the registered voters. Alabama whites hoped to sabotage the congressional program by registering and then refusing to go to the polls, but the boycott strategy failed when the Congress altered its requirement to a majority of the votes cast. By refusing to participate, the conservatives allowed Republicans to win most of the convention seats; in Mobile, all of the delegates were Republicans, several of them black. The 1867 constitution provided for universal suffrage, civil equality for blacks, and free public education for both races. Under its authority a new legislature was elected in 1868.[16]

This legislature was the only one in the Reconstruction period in which the Mobile delegation included black representatives; three of the four house members were black Republicans during the first session.[17] The 1868 legislature immediately passed a Mobile municipal government act which provided for gubernatorial appointment of city councilmen, aldermen, and mayor. A subsequent statute, designed to alter the personnel of city government, required the governor to make new appointments. The only blacks ever to serve as aldermen or councilmen in the history of Mobile were those chosen under the authority of these two acts.[18]

The Republicans thought that an appointive system was necessary in Mobile because Democrats—who had switched from the hapless boycott strategy to the use of violence and intimidation—could win control of a majority of seats if elections were held. The first local election took place on August 3, 1869, to replace a black house member who resigned his seat. The white Democratic candidate, a former Confederate major named Adolph Proskauer, defeated the black Republican candidate, Allen Alexander, by a margin of 5,167 to 3,721; but Alexander contested the results on the grounds that Democratic intimidation and fraud had turned the tide in the balloting. The most sensational example occurred when the Democrats wheeled a piece of field artillery from a firehouse and trained it on a crowd of perhaps one thousand blacks waiting to cast their votes. "As may be expected, especially from the timid," observed a conservative Republican newspaper, "hundreds left the place as fast as possible." [19]

Alabama's Republican party was more conservative on the race question than any other in the South, according to most historians. Thus, it should be no surprise to learn that the house accepted the validity of Alexander's charges but seated the white Democrat anyway. The mayor, a conservative white Republican named Caleb Price, responded to the violence by appointing a "Committee of Public Safety" made up of white Democrats to assist in maintaining order. [20]

Understandably, blacks in Mobile were upset at the course of events in the fall of 1869. At their request, a senator from Dallas County, a white Iowan named Datus Coon, introduced a new Mobile municipal government bill calling for a third slate of appointments (removing the Price regime). The senator from Mobile, Frederick Bromberg, was a conservative Republican ally of Mayor Price and refused to introduce the bill. [21] Like the Democrats, Bromberg favored the immediate election of city officeholders (as a concession to "public opinion"), and he fought the "Coon bill" at virtually every step. The legislature amended the bill to provide an election for city government, as Bromberg demanded, but the date was set for December 1870—a year away, *after* the gubernatorial and legislative elections to be held in the fall. [22] The Democrats charged, apparently with some accuracy, that the Republicans planned to repeal this election provision if their party retained control of both houses for another two years. [23] When the votes were counted in November 1870, however, the Democrats won the governorship and control of the house. As a result, the elections provided by the statute were held on schedule.

The election of mayor, councilmen, and aldermen in December 1870—the first occasion on which the city's voters were able to cast their ballots for municipal officeholders since the enfranchisement of blacks—was held on an at-large basis. Unfortunately, the surviving historical evidence is quite vague about the reasons why this Republican legislature eliminated the ward system by which aldermen had been elected for decades. Despite extensive debate over the bill, legislative journals and newspaper accounts record absolutely no mention of this particular feature of the statute. Indeed, it is not clear that the wording of the election provision required the change. The law merely stated that "the qualified electors of said city" should cast their ballots for all city officeholders. Legislators may have assumed that the electoral procedures set down in the 1866 act would be in effect. [24]

Before the election could be held, of course, *someone* had to decide how the wording of the statute should be interpreted. Under the law, that decision was in the hands of Sheriff Almon Granger, a conservative Republican ally of Price and Bromberg on the "old school board." [25] His reasons for interpreting the law as requiring at-large election of aldermen as well as councilmen have not come to light, but may be inferred from the context of events. We know that lawyers for

the Democratic party studied the election laws shortly before the December balloting and concluded that the statute established at-large voting for all offices.[26]
On the basis of the trends in recent elections, the Democrats had every right to
expect an across-the-board victory for their white supremacy ticket in at-large
elections. Sheriff Granger may have followed the reasoning of the Democratic
lawyers as part of an "understanding" that conceded local control in Mobile to
Democrats in exchange for Democratic support of conservative Republicans like
Bromberg for higher office. Bromberg did not have Democratic opposition when
he ran for Congress as an independent in 1872, and as a result he won a term in
the U.S. House of Representatives by beating a black Republican.

Another possible explanation is that Mobile's Republican leadership gambled
on the possibility of winning at-large elections. The existence of a gerrymandered
ward system which concentrated the overwhelming majority of Republican voters
in the seventh ward (almost 80 percent black) could not have escaped their attention.

A careful reconstruction of 1870 census data and election returns from the
period 1869 to 1873 indicates that the black population, and thus the Republican
vote, approached 50 percent in only three wards; only in the Seventh Ward did
the Republicans ever obtain an actual majority of the votes cast. Ward elections
would undeniably have guaranteed black representation in public office, but probably would have given the Democrats a majority of the seats, and thus partisan
control of municipal government. Mobile's population was approximately 40 percent black; solid black support coupled with a significant white vote might conceivably have given the Republicans a citywide majority in an at-large system.

Either of these two explanations indicates that conservative white Republicans in Mobile sacrificed the principle of black representation in office in order to
advance their own political self-interest. No other hypothesis fits the surviving evidence concerning the decision to eliminate ward elections for aldermen in Mobile
in 1870. A continuation of the traditional system that had prevailed for forty years
before the enfranchisement of blacks would have meant the election of at least
some black aldermen as long as blacks exercised the right to vote. Under the all
at-large system no blacks were ever elected to municipal office in Mobile.

In November 1874, the Democrats won complete control of Alabama state
government as a result of a white supremacy campaign in which violence played
a key role. In the streets of Mobile white horsemen shot down black voters on
their way to the polls, killing one, wounding four, and frightening countless others
from the polls. "White supremacy sustained," declared the Mobile *Register* jubi-
lantly, because "the white men [functioned] as a unit."[27] Immediately after this
"redemption" of the state from Republican rule, the Democratic legislature convened and before the month was out passed a new Mobile city government act.
The effectiveness of at-large elections in assuring complete victory for Democrats
was so evident that they retained the system, adding a new procedure for re-
registering voters. Election officials used the new law to purge approximately 40
percent of the previous voters in the three weeks before municipal officeholders
were chosen.[28] Clearly, the 1874 statute was motivated by invidious racial discrimination.

Although a number of laws were passed during the ensuing decades that modified Mobile's form of government in one way or another, this at-large mode of elections was not altered—at least not for the general election—until 1907.[29] The city's whites were able to vote for municipal candidates by wards, however, because the Democratic party conducted primary elections in that fashion.

Mobile Democrats held what was apparently the state's first primary election on 25 November 1872. The purpose of this "municipal reform," as the *Register* characterized the new procedure, was white supremacy: "the election of Mayor and city officers will be virtually decided, so far as the white people are considered, at the primary polls." Not only aldermen but council members were chosen by ward in the primary. Only whites who had voted against the regular Republican ticket—a test which explicitly allowed Bromberg's conservative Republican supporters to qualify—were able to cast ballots in the primary.[30]

In subsequent years, the Democrats alternated between primary elections and the traditional caucus or convention system, until the passage of a Mobile primary election statute in 1885. This was the first primary law passed in Alabama and applied only to Mobile.[31] The need for a formal process of state supervision arose because of a split in the local Democratic organization in 1884. Dissenters angered by fraudulent activities in the party convention formed a separate "Citizen's Party" ticket and won the municipal elections with Republican support. A Republican described in the *Register* as a "carpetbagger" won a seat on the school board as a member of the Citizen ticket. Subsequently, the dissenting Democrats supported the Republican presidential candidate James G. Blaine, who lost Mobile County by only a handful of votes, together with the Republican congressional nominee, a black man named Frank Threat, who lost the county by less than 100 votes.[32] With the Democrats in such disarray, the primary law provided a useful means of re-creating party unity.

Thereafter, Mobile elected approximately half its municipal officeholders by ward in the Democratic primaries, where only a few Negroes considered trustworthy by party officials were allowed to cast ballots. In the general election, where most blacks voted as Republicans, the at-large requirement for all offices prevented the victory of blacks or unsuitable whites. This pattern closely parallels the arrangement in twentieth-century Pensacola, Florida, which the Fifth Circuit Court of Appeals has recently viewed as clear evidence of discriminatory purpose.[33]

The 1901 Constitutional Convention disfranchised most blacks in Alabama through such devices as a cumulative poll tax and a literacy test administered by local registrars. Yet, in Mobile, close to two hundred Negroes retained the right to vote. The precise number, 193, remained unchanged from 1903 to 1911, although in other counties the number of registered blacks increased; thus more than 193 blacks may have been registered voters in Mobile.)[34] Apparently many of this select group were persons called "Creoles," a term used in Mobile (unlike other areas of the Gulf coast) to designate light-skinned Negroes whose ancestors had been free at the time the city became part of the United States in 1819. Most of the remaining voters were concentrated in the traditional black stronghold, the Seventh Ward, still 79 percent black in 1910. Their ballots may have accounted for half the votes cast for aldermen in that ward in the Democratic primaries, even after disfranchisement.

By 1907, the disfranchisement process in the state as a whole had been so effective, however, that the legislature felt confident in returning to a system of ward elections. Thus it adopted a comprehensive municipal reorganization act that applied to all larger cities, including Mobile. Under the act, aldermen were to be chosen by single-member districts in the general election; each ward had one alderman, with additional aldermen elected at large, as was the mayor. The backers of the bill were mostly from Birmingham and Montgomery, and Mobile's political leadership merely acquiesced in its passage.[35]

The first elections under this statute were conducted in 1908, and in Mobile this unsolicited change in the electoral structure triggered a dramatic return to racial politics. The incumbent mayor was a businessman named Pat Lyons, whose start in politics had come ten years earlier with his election as alderman from a downtown ward with a large black minority. Lyons enjoyed Negro support as alderman and, despite the general increase in racial antagonism in Alabama after 1900, he did not indulge in race-baiting campaign tactics. The opponents of his "machine" in 1908 accused the mayor of trying to manipulate the black vote in order to determine the outcome of the Democratic primary and demanded a ruling from the Democratic State Executive Committee outlawing all Negro participation.[36]

The state party instructed the Mobile County Executive Committee that under the 1903 primary law "only WHITE Democrats will be allowed to participate," explained the Mobile *Daily Item,* which supported Mayor Lyons. In an editorial it expressed regret that "this primary, contrary to a long established custom in the party, will only be participated in by white Democrats," and complained that "this drawing tightly of the color-line" would eliminate "a considerable vote of Creoles and negroes who have from days of long ago voted with the Democratic Party."[37]

At the next meeting of the county executive committee, a prominent Lyons supporter moved that "Creoles" be allowed to vote in the primary despite the state party's ruling, because unlike some whites who voted for Republican presidential candidates, these men of color were loyal to the Democrats. The motion was ruled out of order, but opponents continued to charge that "the Lyons campaign committee is making an effort to make a black and tan party out of the Democratic Party in this city." In the May primary, the Lyons ticket won, as usual. Lyons' ally, Thomas S. Kaver, defeated his opponent in the Seventh Ward by a margin of 229 to 115, while the mayor carried the ward easily against the candidate of the Better Businessmen's Club. That there was no significant decline in the number of votes cast in the predominantly black Seventh Ward raises the possibility that the mayor's "machine" ignored the state party ruling.[38]

The racially charged municipal elections of 1908 were followed in the next legislative session by the first attempt to enact a city commission bill to replace the existing system with nonpartisan, at-large elections in which black political influence would be minimized. The 1909 bill was sponsored by political leaders in Mobile, Birmingham, and Montgomery; it would authorize all three cities to adopt commission government. The bill failed to win passage because of opposition from the lieutenant-governor, who was from Birmingham, but the *Register* declared that the adoption of the commission form was inevitable for Mobile.[39] In the next session, indeed, the legislature passed separate bills for each city, authorizing the shift to commission government. Under the authority of this 1911 act, Mobile held a referendum in which supporters of a city commission won a majority, and, as a result, single-member districts were eliminated from municipal elections.[40] Not surprisingly, there was a strong correlation (.78, significant at the .01 level) between opposition to the commission and the percentage of a ward's population that was black.

Curiously, there is little evidence concerning racial attitudes in the public debate concerning commission government in Mobile. As was true of cities throughout the country, the leaders of the Chamber of Commerce orchestrated a public relations campaign on behalf of the idea: the city commission would place municipal government in the hands of the right sort of men—businessmen or lawyers who could operate the city on the same efficient, cost-conscious basis as they conducted their own firms. The new form of government would also eliminate the corruption and "ward-heeling" produced by partisan "machines," according to the rhetoric of its supporters. As in the rest of the nation, however, the result of placing government in the hands of a small elite of businessmen or lawyers was to eliminate the election of working class people, particularly in the case of ethnic or racial minorities. This aspect was clearly recognized at the time, and historians now emphasize that this was a central purpose behind the adoption of the commission form of government.[41]

The leaders of the business community do not always express their full intentions publicly, of course, but in the southern cities of this day racial concerns were as a rule discussed openly. The advocates of commission government in Mobile, however, had a specific reason for ignoring the race issue. The city had gained great notoriety in preceding years as a result of a double lynching in 1906, which the *New York Times* covered, another lynching in 1907, and yet a third in 1909. The last episode, also reported in the *New York Times,* was particularly embarrassing because a mob took the prisoner from the county jail and lynched him two blocks away in the middle of the city. One advocate of the commission form observed in the *Register* that public identification of Mobile with racial hostilities was driving bright young men from the city.[42] Concern over Mobile's reputation, in short, lay behind the movement's reliance on the "good government" rationale to sell the city commission concept.

Black votes could, under some circumstances, still determine which whites in Mobile were elected to office, as the municipal elections of 1908 revealed. Obviously there was little immediate threat of blacks themselves being elected to office, but political leaders were aware that the disfranchising mechanisms of 1901 might be open to legal challenge in the federal courts at any time.

The most explicit expression of this concern among white Mobilians was an "open letter" to the Alabama legislature published by the *Register* and other newspapers in the state in 1909. The author was Frederick Bromberg, the same conservative Republican leader who represented Mobile in the state senate during the Reconstruction period and won a term in the Congress through an "understanding" with white supremacy Democrats. Most recently he had served as president of the state bar association. Bromberg urged the Mobile legislative delegation to support a proposed constitutional amendment banning Negroes from holding office. A member of the state senate had introduced the amendment at Bromberg's request. The disfranchising devices established in 1901 were not constitutionally sound, he warned, because they were dishonest. "We have always, as you know, falsely pretended that our main purpose was to exclude the ignorant vote, when, in fact, we were trying to exclude, not the ignorant vote, but the negro vote." Bromberg predicted pessimistically that "sooner or later, probably sooner, a case will be made up having back of it competent counsel, which will go to the supreme court of the United States." Citing the precedent of *Yick Wo v. Hopkins*, he argued that in such a case the Supreme Court "will overturn the present methods of applying the registration laws."[43]

Why did Bromberg believe an amendment outlawing black officeholding would be constitutional if the existing barriers to Negro voting were not? The shrewd old lawyer anticipated judicial views in 1980 when he declared that the Fifteenth Amendment to the U.S. Constitution merely protects the right to cast one's ballot without racial discrimination, but offers no constitutional security for the right to hold office. Thus the procedure he suggested would bear legal scrutiny, not just in the short run but permanently. Bromberg was also among the most ardent backers of the commission form of government with its at-large election feature.[44] This barrier to black officeholding was also designed to stand the test of time.

Indeed, the form of government established in Mobile in 1911 has enabled whites to control all elective municipal offices until the present, despite the enfranchisement of most blacks under the provisions of the Voting Rights Act. In 1964, it is true, Mayor Joseph Langan appointed a blue-ribbon committee of respected private citizens, including some older black leaders, to investigate the possibility of altering the existing commission system or changing to another form of government. This "charter commission" reported in February 1965 in favor of a modified mayor-council form with single-member districts for the election of most councilmen. This recommendation was ignored by the Mobile legislative delegation, which offered its own bill instead.[45]

The statute that passed the legislature in 1965 did allow voters to petition for a referendum on the change of government, but unlike the plan of the charter commission it included only two options. The citizens were to choose between the existing commission system and the mayor-council form with exclusive use of at-large elections. The single-member-district alternative was never given serious consideration, according to the testimony of the two legislators who drafted the final version of the bill. The reason was simple: any legislator who seemed to advocate single-member districts would have been labeled a friend of black political rights and that, in Mobile, Alabama, in 1965—in the midst of the Selma demonstrations and the passage of the Voting Rights Act—would have been tantamount to political suicide.[46]

The legislators who made this decision to exclude any mode of elections that would make black officeholding possible understood clearly the consequences of their action, and they made their choice because of, not in spite of, its discriminatory effects on blacks. This was the last act regarding Mobile's form of government to pass the legislature before the *Bolden* trial began, and it preserved the system of at-large elections that had served the cause of white supremacy so well since 1870.

THE SCHOOL BOARD CASE

Compared with the complicated electoral history of municipal government in Mobile, the research for the school board case proved relatively straightforward, dealing almost entirely with the Reconstruction period. Until the ratification of the 1868 Alabama Constitution, the school board members were elected at-large in Mobile, under the terms of an 1852 statute.[47] The new Republican constitution established an elective state board of education and gave it full legislative authority over educational matters. The board was headed by an elected state superintendent of public instruction; the first person to fill this office was a native Alabamian named Noah B. Cloud. In August 1868, Cloud appointed a member of the state board, George L. Putnam, to serve as county school superintendent for Mobile. Putnam was a northern Republican who had come to the city after the war to administer the freedmen's schools set up by the American Missionary Association.[48]

At that point, the existing school board initiated a two-year war against Putnam and the Republican state board of education, whose authority to end the "special status" of the Mobile school system the conservatives challenged. Probate Judge Gustavus Horton, a conservative Republican ally of Frederick Bromberg, was, like Bromberg, a member of the "old board." He refused to accept Putnam's bond as county superintendent, thus preventing him from assuming control of the city's schools. The old board continued to run the schools, collecting tuition in violation of state law and refusing to incorporate the American Missionary Association schools into the public system.[49]

In an effort to work out a compromise with the old board, Cloud came to Mobile in January 1869. His primary goal was to establish schools for both races on a sound footing. He agreed to replace Putnam with conservative spokesman Allen H. Rylands, if the board members would agree to accept Putnam as superintendent of "colored schools" and to incorporate the AMA schools and teachers into the public school system. Despite apparent agreement, the old board ultimately refused to carry out its side of the bargain. In the summer of 1869, Cloud removed Rylands, reappointed Putnam as county superintendent, and helped him post bond so that he could assume office. Putnam then appointed a new board of school commissioners, three of whom were black.[50]

Because the old board refused even now to give up its authority over the school funds, Putnam brought suit in state court and won. The recalcitrant commissioners refused to obey the court order, so the judge jailed them for contempt. The old board included several conservative Republicans, who had, said the Democratic Mobile *Register*, "been tried and found faithful," and after all "on the new board are to be found three Negroes. Tried white men are safer than untried Negroes." Following this reasoning, the conservative public lionized the jailed board members, both Republican and Democratic, for their principled defense of white supremacy. The old board even held an official meeting in the county jail, finally agreeing to stop the collection of tuition for attendance at public schools. Released after two days by order of a state supreme court justice, the old board continued to operate the Mobile school system for the remainder of the academic year. In the June term of 1870, however, the state supreme court upheld Putnam's authority and the old board finally relinquished its control.[51]

The fall elections of 1870 altered the political situation in Alabama, however, by giving the Democrats control of the governorship, the state superintendent of public instruction, and the lower house of the legislature. This increase in power gave the Democrats enough leverage to exact from the state board of education—which still had a two-thirds Republican majority—a compromise statute for the election of Mobile school commissioners. Board members were to be elected at large, which would give the Democrats the advantage, but voters could cast ballots for a maximum of nine out of twelve seats. The purpose of this limited-vote provision, said the *Register,* was "to secure to the minority a representation in affairs wherein they are interested." (The term "minority" clearly referred in this context to blacks, not merely to a political minority.) The elections in March 1871 gave the Democrats the county superintendent and nine of twelve commissioners, as might be expected, but the limited-vote procedure also allowed three Republicans, one of whom may have been black, to win seats.[52]

The Democrats replaced this system at the first opportunity by a return to an all at-large mode of electing school commissioners. The crucial phase in this process was, of course, the total victory of white supremacy Democrats in the state elections of 1874. "Race was the issue of the 1874 campaign," according to a prominent Alabama historian.[53] Their triumph allowed the Democrats to call a new constitutional convention in 1875, and among their most important actions at the convention was the elimination of the state board of education. Educational matters were once again entirely in the hands of the legislature, which immediately eliminated without debate the limited-vote provisions of school board elections. As a direct outgrowth of the Redeemer campaign, the 1876 statute was indisputably a product of an invidious intent to eliminate black representation on the Mobile County Board of School Commissioners.[54]

The effect of the elimination of minority representation was graphically documented in Kousser's testimony, based on a quantitative analysis of educational expenditures from Mobile County between 1870 and 1963. During the first six years, while there was still Republican representation, per pupil expenditures for blacks and whites were substantially equal. By 1882, black students were receiving little more than half the support of white pupils, and the ratio continued to decline thereafter, reaching a low point of 27 percent of the per pupil expenditure for whites in 1940. Kousser's hard data evidently made a forceful impression on Judge Pittman, who incorporated his statistics in the final opinion.[55]

Although the legislature reduced the number of seats in 1919, the at-large election of school board commissioners remained in effect at the time plaintiffs brought suit in 1975.[56] After the initiation of the lawsuit, a bill proposing a single-member district system for the school board was introduced in the Alabama legislature by Cain Kennedy, a black lawyer elected under a court-ordered single-member district plan the previous year. As a "local bill" it had to be advertised publicly prior to introduction. The school board offered to support the Kennedy bill if amended in certain details, and its legal counsel helped draft the changes. When the bill was signed into law, however, the school board instituted a suit in state court attacking the constitutionality of the act on the grounds that it differed significantly from the bill as originally advertised. Judge Pittman appropriately regarded this course of action as a sign of bad faith on the part of the school board, similar to its dilatory tactics over the years in resisting full integration of the public school system. As a result, he ordered the creation of a single-member district plan, to be implemented gradually so that no member's term of office was cut short. In 1978, the first two blacks were elected to the board.[57]

Throughout Mobile's history, in short, at-large elections have functioned as part of a conscious pattern of excluding blacks both from municipal office and from the school board. In the years since 1965, blacks have obtained the right to vote, by means of the intervention of the federal government through the Voting Rights Act. Because of the at-large system, however, the effects of enfranchisement have been minimal. Only in legislative elections, conducted on a single-member-district basis under court order, have blacks been able to win public office. Racial polarization has been the overwhelming characteristic of Mobile voting behavior since 1965, according to the most advanced statistical analysis. Nor have recent elections shown any diminution of this polarization. In Mobile single-member-district elections—or, if one wishes to borrow from history, at-large elections with a limited-vote provision—provide the only reasonable avenue by which black voters can secure effective representation in public office.

POST SCRIPT

Judge Pittman ordered a return to single-member districts, finding in favor of the plaintiffs once again in both *Brown* and *Bolden* on 15 April 1982. To an overwhelming degree his opinions reflected the evidence presented in court by the expert witnesses for the plaintiffs and the Justice Department.[58] Blacksher, Menefee, and Still had succeeded, with the help of the Justice Department in the Brown case, in meeting the new "intent" standard set forth by the Supreme Court. The extraordinary cost of this effort meant, however, that few could afford to seek protection of their constitutional rights. The question remained, moreover, whether the most relevant issue in deciding a vote dilution case in the 1980s should be the purposes of legislators who sat in southern state capitals seventy-five to one hundred years ago.

In the summer of 1981, hearings began before the Subcommittee on Civil and Constitutional Rights of the House Judiciary Committee on the renewal and strengthening of the Voting Rights Act. A central issue throughout two months of hearings and the months of subsequent debate on Capitol Hill was the need to amend Section 2 of the act to indicate that it was the will of Congress to outlaw state and local election laws that have a discriminatory effect on minority voters, without inquiring specifically into the original legislative intent of the statute. It was known on the Hill as "the *Bolden* amendment."

The Voting Rights Act, as amended, passed the House by an overwhelming margin in October 1981 (even securing the support, on the final roll call, of Mobile's conservative Republican congressman). A slightly amended version passed the Senate and was signed by President Reagan in June 1982. Passage of the strengthened Voting Rights Act vindicated *Bolden*'s many critics, including the plaintiffs' expert historians, by making history less crucial, ironically, to the achievement of justice.[59]

NOTES

1. *City of Mobile v. Bolden*, 446 U.S. 55 (1980). For a detailed analysis of the legal issues involved in this and earlier vote dilution cases, see the essay in this volume by James U. Blacksher and Larry Menefee, "At Large Elections and One Person, One Vote."
2. The most extensive of those conferences resulted in the publication of a volume of essays assessing the impact of the *Bolden* decision: *The Right to Vote: A Rockefeller Foundation Conference, April 22–23, 1981* (New York, 1981).
3. Judge Virgil Pittman's decision in the first trial is reported in *Bolden v. City of Mobile*, 423 F.Supp. 384 (1976), and the opinion of the U.S. Fifth Circuit Court of Appeals in 571 F.2d 238 (1978). For the school board case, see *Brown v. Moore*, 428 F.Supp.1123 (1976).
4. *McMillan v. Escambia County, Florida*, Civil Action No. 77-0432 (N.D. Fla.) (Order of 10 July 1978). His major work is Jerrell H. Shofner, *Nor Is It Over Yet: Florida in the Era of Reconstruction, 1863–1877* (Gainesville, Fla., 1974), but he has also published a large number of articles in scholarly journals.
5. Peyton McCrary, *Abraham Lincoln and Reconstruction: The Louisiana Experiment* (Princeton, N.J., 1978), is his major work, but he has also produced several articles and papers. McCrary found Richard Kluger, *Simple Justice: The History of Brown v. Board of Education* (New York, 1975), enormously suggestive concerning the role of expert witnesses in a civil rights case, and re-read it twice during preparation for *Bolden* and *Brown*.
6. Although each has produced numerous articles in scholarly periodicals, they are best known for: J. Morgan Kousser, *The Shaping of Southern Politics: Suffrage of Restriction and the Establishment of the One-Party South, 1880–1910* (New Haven, Conn., 1974) and Chandler Davidson, *Biracial Politics: Conflict and Coalition in the Metropolitan South* (Baton Rouge, La., 1972).
7. See Proposed Findings of Fact and Conclusions of Law of Plaintiffs in *Wiley L. Bolden, et al. v. City of Mobile*, Civil Action No. 75-297-P (S.D. Ala. 1982), pp. 19–59.
8. Among the most persuasive analyses are Davidson, *Biracial Politics*, 59–67; Clinton B. Jones, "The Impact of Local Election Systems on Black Political Participation," *Urban Affairs Quarterly*, 11 (March 1976): 345–56; Albert K. Karnig, "Black Representation on City Councils," *Urban Affairs Quarterly*, 12 (Dec. 1976): 223–42; Theodore P. Robinson and Thomas R. Dye, "Reformism and Black Representation on City Councils," *Social Science Quarterly*, 59 (June 1978): 133–41; Delbert Taebel, "Minority Representation on City Councils: The Impact of Structure on Blacks and Hispanics," *Social Science Quarterly*, 59 (June 1978): 143–52; Margaret K. Latimer, "Black Political Representation in Southern Cities: Election Systems and Other Causal Variables," *Urban Affairs Quarterly*, 15 (Sept. 1979): 65–86; Richard L.

Engstrom and Michael D. McDonald, "The Election of Blacks to City Councils: Clarifying the Impact of Electoral Arrangements on the Seats/Population Relationship," *American Political Science Review,* 75 (June 1981): 344–54; and Chandler Davidson and George Korbel, "At-large Elections and Minority-Group Representation: A Re-Examination of Historical and Contemporary Evidence," *Journal of Politics,* 43 (Dec. 1981): 982–1004. The study by Susan A. MacManus, "City Council Election Procedures and Minority Representation: Are They Related?" *Social Science Quarterly,* 59 (June 1978): 153–61, appears to offer evidence that at-large procedures do not exercise a discriminatory effect, but I share the methodological objections raised by Chandler Davidson, "At-Large Elections and Minority Representation," *Social Science Quarterly,* 60 (Sept. 1979): 336–38. For additional documentation of southern jurisdictions, both rural and urban, see *The Voting Rights Act: Unfulfilled Goals: A Report of the U.S. Commission on Civil Rights* (Washington, D.C., 1981), 101–180; and June Reed Cox and Abigail Turner, *The Voting Rights Act in Alabama: A Current Legal Assessment* (Mobile, 1981), 24–34.

9. The index of residential segregation Davidson employed is that set forth in Karl C. and Alma F. Taeuber, *Negroes in Cities: Residential Segregation and Neighborhood Change* (Chicago, 1965). The census data was provided by the Department of Justice in advance of publication and the electoral returns by Dianne Thompson, whose statistical analysis of the 1980 elections (in a graduate research paper for McCrary) Davidson also used. The same results for an earlier period are presented in detail in Dianne Thompson, "The Strange Career of Racial Polarization: Electoral Behavior in Mobile, Alabama After the 1965 Voting Rights Act," (M.A. thesis, University of South Alabama, 1982).

10. Mobile *Register,* 19 April 1981.

11. *Alabama Acts,* 1825–26 (9 January 1826), 33–34. In investigating every change of election laws, I have examined not merely the wording of the statute in question but also the manner in which the election returns were reported in the newspapers. This is the only way to determine whether elections were actually conducted on an at-large or district basis. The returns are gathered in Plaintiffs' Exhibit No. 68 in the Bolden case.

12. An 1833 statute required the election of a special commission to divide the city into four wards: *Alabama Acts,* 1833, No. 68 (9 January 1833), 106.

13. *Alabama Acts,* 1840, No. 70 (5 February 1840), 53–58; ibid., 1844, No. 221 (15 January 1844), 175–92; ibid., 1852, No. 199 (19 February 1852), 324–27.

14. *Alabama Acts,* 1865–66, 119–21; Sarah W. Wiggins, *The Scalawag in Alabama Politics, 1865–1881* (University, Alabama, 1977), 1–32; Jonathan M. Wiener, *Social Origins of the New South: Alabama, 1860–1885* (Baton Rouge, Louisiana, 1978), 3–108.

15. *Alabama Acts,* 1865–66, No. 165 (2 February 1866), 202–36.

16. Malcolm C. McMillan, *Constitutional Development in Alabama, 1798–1901: A Study in Politics, the Negro, and Sectionalism* (Chapel Hill, North Carolina, 1955), 110–74. An illustration of the sentiments behind the boycott strategy is the pamphlet listing the "collaborators" who cast ballots in this "illegal" election: *Roll of the Black Dupes and White Renegades Who Voted in Mobile City and County for the Menagerie Constitution for the State of Alabama* (Mobile, 1868).

17. Wiggins, *Scalawag in Alabama Politics,* 148–49; "Officers and Members of General Assembly of Alabama (1868–1870)" (Plaintiffs' Exhibit No. 47).

18. *Alabama Acts,* 1868, No. 8 (18 July 1868), 4–5; ibid., No. 71 (21 December 1868), 421. I have compiled a complete list of municipal officeholders (by race) from 1865 to the present, drawing on newspapers, city directories, and the minutes of the city's governing bodies.

19. *Alabama State Journal,* 4 December 1869. This quotation comes from a lengthy account of the Proskauer-Alexander election challenge (Plaintiffs' Exhibit No. 69).

20. *Alabama State Journal,* 4 December 1869; Allen Alexander to House of Representa-

tives, 17 November 1869, Legislative Correspondence, Drawer 17, Civil Archives Division, Alabama State Library and Archives (ASLA), and Congressman A. E. Buck to Gov. William H. Smith, 13 August 1869, Smith Papers, Civil Archives, ASLA (Plaintiffs' Exhibit Nos. 77, 74).

21. The views of Mobile blacks are presented in a letter from James Bragg to Frederick G. Bromberg, 20 November 1869, Bromberg Papers, Southern Historical Collection, University of North Carolina (Plaintiffs' Exhibit No. 80), and in a Memorial read to the state senate by Datus Coon on 19 November 1869, *Senate Journal, 1869–70,* 57–58.

22. *Alabama Acts, 1869–70,* No. 97 (8 February 1870), 451–54. The statute, together with the entire legislative history of the bill from the house and senate journals, constitutes Plaintiffs' Exhibit No. 14.

23. Mobile *Register,* 20 January and 6 November 1870.

24. *Alabama Acts, 1869–70,* No. 97, section 11. The ward-election provision of the 1866 statute (section 6) was repealed along with nine other sections by section 2 of the 18 July 1868 act.

25. See Allen Alexander, et. al., to Gov. William H. Smith, 29 June 1868, Smith Papers, ASLA.

26. Mobile *Register,* 6 December 1870.

27. Mobile *Register,* 4 November 1874; Wiggins, *Scalawag in Alabama Politics,* 97.

28. *Alabama Acts, 1874–75,* No. 365 (28 November 1874), 532–38; Mobile *Register,* 13, 16 December 1874.

29. *Alabama Acts, 1878–79,* No. 308 (11 February 1879); ibid., 1886, (10 December 1886); ibid., 1896–97, No. 214.

30. Mobile *Register,* 21 November 1872; see also 9, 15 November 1872.

31. *Alabama Acts, 1884–85,* 480–83; McMillan, *Constitutional Development,* 244.

32. Mobile *Register,* 10, 11, 12, 18, and 24 June; 6, 15, and 20, July:3, 6, and 12 August; and 12 November 1884; W. Dean Burnham, *Presidential Ballots, 1836–1892* (Baltimore, 1955), 270.

33. *McMillan v. Escambia County, Florida,* 638 F.2d 1239 (5th Cir. 1981).

34. *Alabama Official and Statistical Register* (Montgomery, 1911).

35. *Alabama Acts,* 1907, No. 797 (15 August 1907).

36. Mobile *Register,* 24 Apr. 12 May 1908; Mobile *Daily Item,* 24 April 1908. My understanding of the Lyons regime owes much to David E. Alsobrook, "Alabama's Port City: Mobile During The Progressive Era, 1896–1917," Ph.D. Dissertation, Auburn University, 1983, which I read in penultimate draft.

37. Mobile *Daily Item,* 24 April 1908.

38. Mobile *Daily Item,* 3 May 1908; Mobile *Register,* 12–17, 24 May 1908.

39. Mobile *Register,* 20 August 1909.

40. *Alabama Acts,* 1911, No. 281 (8 April 1911); Official Returns, Referendum Election, 5 June 1911, in Mobile City Council Minutes, June 1911, p. 15, Mobile Public Library.

41. James Weinstein, "Organized Business and the Commission and Manager Movements," *Journal of Southern History,* 28 (May 1962): 166–82; Samuel P. Hays, "The Politics of Reform in Municipal Government in the Progressive Era," *Pacific Northwest Quarterly* 55 (1964), reprinted in his book, *American Political History as Social Analysis* (Knoxville, Tennessee, 1980), 204–32; Martin J. Schiesl, *The Politics of Efficiency: Municipal Administration and Reform, 1880–1920* (Berkeley, California, 1977); Bradley R. Rice, *Progressive Cities: The Commission Government Movement in America, 1901–1920* (Austin, Texas, 1977). Charles A. Beard, *American City Government* (New York, 1912), 95–97, commented that the commission form of government "concentrates too great a power in the hands of a few men." Beard disliked the fact that "its members do not represent single districts, but are elected at large by the voters of an entire city—a practice which, of course, substantially ex-

cludes minority representation, and is so highly undesirable as to constitute a serious objection to the adoption of the scheme in large cities."

42. Mobile *Register*, 24 and 31 January 1909.

43. Mobile *Register*, 25 July 1909.

44. Mobile *Register*, 25 July 1909.

45. The final report of the charter commission, together with its minutes, were obtained from the personal files of its secretary, Dr. Howard Mahan, who testified for the plaintiffs: see Plaintiffs' Exhibit No. 119.

46. *Alabama Acts*, 1965, No. 823 (2 September 1965), 1539–1546; interviews with Robert Edington and William McDermott.

47. *Alabama Acts*, 1851–52, No. 378 (9 February 1852), 463–64.

48. *Alabama Constitution of 1868*, Article VI, Section 5; *Alabama Acts*, 1868, (11 August 1868), 148–49; Noah B. Cloud, *Report of the State Superintendent of Public Instruction to Governor William H. Smith* (Montgomery, 1869), 3–7, 11.

49. Minutes, Mobile County Board of School Commissioners, 24, 27 August, 9 September 1868 (Barton Academy, Mobile); Cloud, *Report*, 35–36; Willis G. Clark, *History of Education in Alabama* (Washington, D. C., 1889), 230–32. Clark was himself a member of the "old board" and thus his account has the character of a participant's memoir.

50. Cloud, *Report*, 36–48; *Journal of the Board of Education of the State of Alabama. . . .* (Montgomery, 1869), 7–9; Mobile *Register*, 8 September 1869.

51. *Mobile School Commissioners v. Putnam, et al.*, 44 *Ala.* 506 (1870); Mobile *Register*, 8, 23, 25 September, 1–3 October 1869. I have also examined the school board minutes for the entire period of controversy.

52. The act, passed by the State Board of Education on 14 December 1870, does not appear in *Alabama Acts* but in Joseph Hodgson, comp., *Laws Relating to the Public Schools of Alabama. . . .* (Montgomery, 1871), 43–44; Mobile *Register*, 15 December 1870, 3, 4, 10 March 1871.

53. Wiggins, *Scalawag in Alabama Politics*, 97.

54. McMillan, *Constitutional Development*, 175–210; *Alabama Acts*, 1875–76, No. 242 (15 February 1876), 363–67; see also *Alabama Acts*, 1919, No. 229, p. 273.

55. *Brown v. Board of School Commissioners of Mobile County*, Civil Action No. 75-298-P (S.D. Ala. 1982), (Order of 15 April 1982), 35–37.

56. *Alabama Acts*, 1919, No. 229, p. 273. In the first trial this was assumed to be the relevant statute creating at-large elections for the school board.

57. Judge Pittman's opinion in *Brown v. Board of School Commissioners*, reviews this episode on pp. 37–42. Blacksher, Menefee, and McCrary examined the correspondence in the school board files at Barton Academy in Mobile, and confirmed the story in great detail.

58. *Brown v. Board of School Commissioners of Mobile County*, Civil Action No. 75-298-P (S. D. Ala. 1982), (Order of 15 April 1982); *Bolden v. City of Mobile*, Civil Action No. 75-297-P (S. D. Ala. 1982), (Order of 15 April 1982).

59. See written testimony of C. Vann Woodward, J. Morgan Kousser, and Peyton McCrary, prepared for the hearing on renewal of the Voting Rights Act Before the Subcommittee on Civil and Constitutional Rights of the U. S. House Judiciary Committee, 24 June 1981; *House Reports*, 97 Cong., 1 Sess., No. 97-227, "Voting Rights Extension," esp. pp. 1–2, 28–32.

4

At-Large Elections and Minority Group Representation
A Reexamination of Historical and Contemporary Evidence

Chandler Davidson and George Korbel

The effects of at-large or multimember-district elections on the opportunities of ethnic minority groups to participate effectively in the political process is a question of great practical importance. This paper attempts to clarify both the history and present effects of such elections and to situate this device within the context of developments that are reshaping local governments in the South and Southwest.

The use of at-large elections is widespread nationally. In 1960, 60 percent of cities with a population of more than 10,000 elected their councilmen at large, while only 23 percent elected them solely from districts.[1] In cities of at least 5,000 population, most councilmen in 1971 were chosen at large and over twice as many cities elected some councilmen by this method rather than entirely by ward. Less than 1 percent of council members were black, American Indian, Oriental, or Hispanic.[2]

Is there a causal relation between the small proportion of minority officials and the use of at-large elections? Scholars have long believed so:

> The municipal reform ideal of non-partisan, efficient, apolitical politics is certain to seem attractive to white, native, Protestant, middle-class citizens. By abolishing party labels, the lower-status groups are disoriented and become unwitting clients of the upper-status press. By doing away with 'peanut politics' (which apparently got its name from a political row over an Italian peanut vendor's stand), abolishing the small constituencies, and making the election of councilmen citywide, ethnic solidarity is weakened.[3]

Citing Myrdal's[4] observation that "Negro apathy" in Detroit was partially the result of at-large elections, Lane concludes,

> Municipal reforms of this nature: nonpartisanship, smaller city councils, the replacement of mayors by city-managers, may serve admirable technical purposes and in the long run be in the best interests of most groups in the community—but they weaken

Originally published in *The Journal of Politics* 43 (1981), 982–1005.

the political ties of the disorganized and depressed groups in the community. And, in doing this, they serve a strong, but usually repressed interest of the community's 'power elite,' whose focus is ostensibly upon the gains in efficiency and honesty brought about by the reforms, but who profit from the political apathy of the underdog.[5]

Where accepted generalizations are concerned, however, one is entitled to ask for supporting evidence. One important source is the historical context in which at-large elections have developed. Associated with a self-described reform movement in the early twentieth century, this method was introduced widely in the name of "good government." An inquiry into the situations in which it was typically implemented will shed light on the extent to which the reformers were motivated solely by such abstract civic concerns, as well as on the effects this reform was known to have had on citizen participation in that era.

A second source of evidence is the legal and political events of the 1970s. In this period several court decisions reflected a widespread belief among social scientists and jurists that at-large elections under certain conditions result in the unconstitutional dilution of minority group votes. The landmark U.S. Supreme Court case *White v. Regester* (1973) and its progeny have defined the situations under which at-large elections operate in an impermissible manner.[6] The court has held that the at-large construct is not unconstitutional *per se* but may be so if it operates to limit minority access to the electoral process or, in other words, dilutes or minimizes their vote.

The full judicial examination of an at-large electoral system involves a number of additional factors including historical discrimination; the existence of electoral devices which magnify the objectionable features of the at-large system (that is, place voting, anti-single-shot laws, the majority requirement); the size of the electoral unit; the cost of campaigning; and the public policy behind at-large elections. More recently, the Supreme Court in *City of Mobile v. Bolden* (1980) has ruled that a demonstration of unconstitutional vote dilution must include proof of discriminatory intent in the adoption or maintenance of the at-large system.[7]

Electoral changes in the wake of *White* have been extensive. In Texas, for example, almost one-half of the state legislature in 1970 was elected from multimember districts, and virtually all city councilmen and school district trustees were so chosen. By 1976 all legislators were chosen from single-member districts. In 1980 about one-third of the state's urban inhabitants elected at least some of their council from wards and several of the larger school districts also had changed to single-member districts. These modifications came about largely through federal court intervention. Even when jurisdictions "voluntarily" changed their election methods, litigation was usually either in progress or threatened. While no systematic assessment of the scope of reform has been made, other southern states—particularly Louisiana—may have undergone even more extensive transformations.

It therefore is very likely that at-large elections presently render the election of minority candidates much more difficult than ward-based systems, which have been ordered as remedies in vote dilution cases. At the very least, minority plaintiffs and numerous federal judges hold this opinion, as the results of extensive litigation show.

However, a few academic studies have challenged this opinion. Inasmuch as they are based on statistical analysis of sizable samples of American cities, it might appear that a confidently held hypothesis is collapsing under the assault of systematic evidence.

Such is not the case. We shall review the statistical research on this issue over the past decade in order to reconcile the disparate findings. Then, in the final section of the paper, we present original data on the effects of at-large elections in Texas, using a research design that enables us to overcome problems of measurement and covariance that in other studies obscure the independent effects of several factors on the success rate of minority candidates.

AT-LARGE ELECTIONS AND PROGRESSIVISM

Change took many paths during the Progressive Era. Holli distinguishes between two dominant tendencies. The "social reformers" located corruption among businessmen, whom they criticized for benefitting unfairly and often illegally from favors in franchises, taxes, and public services. Social reformers "accepted a traditional, democratic faith in the ability of the masses to participate in the process of ruling themselves."[8] To be sure, some were themselves businessmen. But, like most successful reform mayors or governors of the day, they encouraged popular participation in municipal politics. Their advocacy of cheaper utility rates, more equitable taxation, a wider distribution of urban services, and better working conditions benefitted ordinary people.[9]

The "structural reformers," on the other hand, believed the enfranchisement of recent immigrants was a major factor in corrupt city government. Businessmen and experts were suited best to govern. "The inferior moral fiber of foreign-born and lower-class electorates and their representatives, and the dereliction of upper classes," writes Holli, "was one of the most pervasive themes in the early Conferences for Good City Government" sponsored by the National Municipal League.[10]

Radical demographic changes activated structural reform. Between 1815 and 1914 approximately thirty-five million newcomers entered the United States, most of them settling in the Northeast, especially in cities. By 1910 first and second generation immigrants comprised at least two-thirds of the population of most of the major northeastern cities, and more than three-fourths in New York, Boston, and Chicago. (Presumably structural reformers did not favor at-large elections in cities where immigrants constituted an effective electoral majority. Assuming low turnout among recent immigrants, however, reformers may have been tempted to abolish ward elections where the ethnic population only slightly exceeded 50 percent.)[11]

Structural reform, however, was hardly limited to the Northeast. Two important vehicles for this brand of municipal reformism, the commission and city manager plans, both originated in the South. The first city in the nation to install a commission was Galveston, Texas, in 1901, and it spread rapidly to other Texas and southern cities. By 1913 most of the larger cities in the South and many smaller ones had adopted it. The city manager model was inaugurated in Staunton, Virginia, in 1908.[12] The initiative for both plans came from business groups who argued that a municipality was essentially a business corporation and should be run according to business principles.[13] The at-large election and the nonpartisan ballot were associated with both the commission and city-manager forms of government.[14] A study of fifty cities that had adopted the manager system by 1938 showed that forty had at-large elections. Some had had such elections before adoption of the manager form. Of the seventeen which changed their method of election at the time of adoption of manager government, however, sixteen changed from ward-based elections. The tendency also was to decrease council size upon adoption of the city manager form.[15]

The association between commission and city-manager governments and at-large elections is still obvious today. In cities that by 1930 had a population of 30,000 or more, Gordon found that in 1960 councilmen were elected at large in 100 percent of the commission cities, in 76 percent of the manager cities, but in only 22 percent of the "unreformed" cities.[16] At-large elections also remain concentrated in the South (and in the West, though possibly for a different reason).[17] Karnig has shown that 75 percent of southern cities elect councilmen at large, compared with 47 percent elsewhere.[18] Among Texas' 185 home-rule cities in 1968 all but six elected councils at large.[19]

While a major purpose of structural reform was to take city government out of the hands of neighborhood and ethnic leaders, thus centralizing it under the control of businessmen, the ostensible reasons were the lofty goals of abolishing corrupt machines and bringing efficiency and businesslike principles to local government.[20] While proponents spoke in the name of "the people," their statements sometimes revealed a peculiar concept of popular representation. As a Des Moines capitalist told a labor audience during the debate over commission government, the businessmen's slate represented labor "better than you do yourself."[21]

In the South, Progressivism coincided with the peak of racial reaction. The introduction of the party primary system, a key item on the reform agenda, was facilitated by its exclusion of blacks from the nominating process. "Racism," writes Woodward, "was conceived of by some as the very foundation of Southern progressivism." Edgar Gardner Murphy, one of the most articulate and cultured of southern progressives, thought of "the conscious unity of race" as "the broader ground of the new democracy."[22] Southern progressive leaders made the race issue their chief stock-in-trade and were among the principal advocates of disfranchisement. "The Vardamans and Hoke Smiths might have represented 'a genuine movement for a more democratic government in the south,' as Ray Stannard Baker contended, but their democracy was for whites only and did great harm to the cause of the Negro and to good relations between blacks and whites."[23]

In Texas, for example, racism clearly was intertwined with Progressive reform. The poll tax as a prerequisite for voting and the so-called Terrell Election Law, both enacted before 1910, were advertised as progressive measures—the poll tax because it ostensibly made ballot fraud less likely, the election law because it paved the way for "fair" party primaries. But the poll tax was intended clearly to disfranchise blacks and the white poor, and it was opposed by spokesmen of both groups and by labor unionists.[24] The Terrell Law made poll tax payment a requirement for voting in party primaries and conventions, gave county executive committees discretion to exclude blacks from primaries, and instituted the place voting system in Texas for the first time.[25]

Ethnic minorities and laboring people were well aware of the structural reformers' intentions. Hays cites numerous instances of opposition to progressive charter changes by the lower-middle and working classes.[26] Rice concludes that early commission governments in Texas were consistently endorsed by businessmen and only slightly less consistently opposed by the working class, especially organized labor, a pattern manifested in cities elsewhere.[27] "The lower classes correctly perceived that the at-large election of a small board would make it difficult for people of limited means to be elected."[28] Undoubtedly for the same reason a bank president in Sherman, Texas, one of the early commission cities, reported that "those who pay taxes are generally satisfied with the commission system."[29]

Galveston, the birthplace of the commission movement, provides an instructive example of the forces leading to an at-large council. In its early years, the commission model popularly was referred to as the Galveston plan. It was characterized by a five-man governing body elected at large, each member of which was a city department head.

In the standard account of the Galveston commission's creation, a hurricane devastated the island city in September 1900 and, during the crisis that followed, the need for a "modern," honest, efficient government adequate to the task of recovery suddenly was recognized and acted on, leading to the adoption of a commission. Rice has demonstrated recently that, in reality, the famous hurricane simply provided a rationale for a charter change already favored by leading businessmen who had been locked in a struggle with laboring people—including blacks—for council control during the 1890s.[30]

A change to at-large elections actually occurred in 1895. Prior to 1891 the city had operated under a mayor-council charter with twelve aldermen elected from wards. New charter amendments initiated by businessmen and effective in 1891 and 1893 added four at-large seats. The Chamber of Commerce in 1895 proposed a completely at-large council of twelve members. The amendment passed, and the businessmen's group behind it organized the Good Government Club which offered a slate of "typical middle-class businessmen and a physician," in sharp contrast to the incumbent council of longshoremen, bartenders, small businessmen, and a drayman, which included a black. Opponents of the Good Government Club formed a slate dubbed the People's Ticket, appealing to the city's laboring classes. Spokesmen for the People's Ticket pointed out that the Good Government Club had no blacks on its slate, in contrast to their own, which included the black incumbent.

Ten of the twelve members of the Good Government Club won, including two who had also been endorsed by the People's Ticket. Five winners citywide lost their own wards. Conversely, the black incumbent carried his ward, but was defeated citywide as black leaders had predicted, leaving an all-white council in a town that was 22 percent black.[31] Even then the Good Government Club subsequently had trouble controlling the council. By the summer before the 1900 storm, the business elite was casting around for a different plan that would ensure its control. The city's shaky financial situation at this point—including a large debt and a failure to meet city payrolls two months in a row—fuelled popular discontent on which the business elite based its case for a new charter.)[32] When the storm provided the catalyst for change, the elite ensured that the at-large device was incorporated into the commission model.

In the first third of the twentieth century the impact of at-large elections on the socioeconomic makeup of councils nationwide in many instances was similar to its effect in Galveston.[33] Elsewhere, racial gerrymandering was sometimes the remedy of choice, when at-large elections were impossible to implement because of the strong popular support for wards.

In the South, disfranchising measures such as the poll tax, literacy test, and grandfather clause—delicately spoken of by apostles of reform as a means of "purifying" the ballot—as well as intimidation through economic sanction and violence accomplished the same end. The white primary, gerrymander, place system, and runoff requirement also were used.

Consequently, in cities that already had dealt with the threat of blacks in electoral politics, the advent of at-large elections probably did not signal as dramatic a change in the racial makeup of councils as it did in their social class composition. Galveston's 1895 change is especially useful, therefore, as a before-and-after study of its impact on racial representation.

By 1905, when the Galveston plan had begun to catch on throughout the South, the ranks of black voters had been reduced sharply. Even so, the at-large mechanism became a formidable barrier to effective political participation after the decline of Progressivism, with the massive influx of blacks and Hispanics into the cities of the North and West. The at-large system was in place in the South and Southwest when the blacks and Mexican Americans of those regions began their political resurgence in the 1940s; and where it was not yet in effect, city fathers often inaugurated it to deal with the new threat.

Research in the post-Progressive era demonstrates that at-large systems diminish minority representation. Banfield and Wilson conclude that Boston's at-large councilmen were generally less responsive to voters' wishes than were ward-based ones.[34] Wilson attributes the speed with which blacks won office in Chicago to high-density black areas and the fact that councilmen were elected from a large number of small wards. He observes that large districts, as in New York, were not as effective because racial gerrymandering was easier in them.[35] This conclusion corroborates Myrdal's observation a generation earlier that, "Negroes in Chicago were more favored than Negroes in any other city," with regard to officeholding. Speaking of the North as a whole, circa 1939, Myrdal pointed out that with the exception of a few minor offices, "No Negro has attained a city-wide elective position."[36]

Salter found that ward-based elections of Philadelphia committeemen in the 1930s enabled ethnic minorities, including blacks, to choose their own representatives.[37] Dahl's study of New Haven supports this view.[38] Williams and Adrian stress the advantages that accrue to working-class people generally under the ward system.[39]

Black electoral failure in Florida between 1944 and 1954 has been linked to at-large elections.[40] Ladd points out that many southern cities switched to at-large elections when confronted with a growing black vote.[41] Significantly, the first black elected to public office in competition with white candidates in the South since the turn of the century—an alderman in Winston-Salem in 1947—was elected from a ward. He was assisted by a partisan ballot and the backing of CIO-PAC leaders.[42] Instead of changing to at-large elections, as many cities did under similar circumstances, the city's Democratic leadership gerrymandered the ward boundaries to limit blacks to a majority status in only one of the city's eight districts.[43] Events in Waco, Texas, were perhaps more typical. After a black almost won election to council from a ward in 1950, the newly elected council enacted a resolution abolishing districts.[44] This action conforms to a general pattern in the South, noted by Hamilton, in which multimember legislative districts have been tailored to minimize Republican and black membership.[45] Studies by the U.S. Commission on Civil Rights in southern states lend added weight to this point.[46]

RECENT EMPIRICAL EVIDENCE

In spite of the overwhelming evidence for the dilutionary impact of at-large elections, the accepted view has lacked broad-based statistical corroboration until recently. This situation has now changed. Table 1 presents a summary of the findings of research on the subject in which samples of sixteen or more electoral systems were used. In some cases, we have extracted the necessary data from information published in other formats.

In every study but one, the independent variable is the election method.[47] The classification is usually three-fold: (1) all members elected at large; (2) some members chosen at large; and (3) all members chosen from districts. The dependent variable consists of a measure of minority representation, typically a comparison between the proportion of minority members on a governing body and the proportion of the same minority population residing in the jurisdiction. In some cases this comparison is a *ratio*—the minority proportion on council divided by the minority proportion in the community. In others, it is the *difference* between the proportion on council and the proportion in the community. In the case of ratios, a score of 1.0 indicates exact proportional minority representation, and a smaller score indicates underrepresentation. Where differences are used, a score of zero indicates proportional representation and a negative score indicates underrepresentation.

The thirteen studies allow sixteen comparisons of the effects of electoral systems on minority representation. (Two studies examine black and Hispanic representation separately. Another, besides comparing effects among cities, compares minority representation in at-large seats and ward seats within mixed systems.) We describe a study as confirming the conventional hypothesis if the authors conclude that at-large elections, independent of other factors, depress minority representation. In twelve comparisons the conventional hypothesis is confirmed. The findings in the remaining four are dubious, for reasons explained below.

Welch and Karnig find a slight overrepresentation of blacks in at-large systems, underrepresentation in ward-based ones, and a sharper underrepresentation in mixed systems.[48] This is the only study in Table 4-1 focusing on school boards

Table 4-1.   Results of studies of the effects of at-large elections on blacks and Hispanics, 1969–1981

	Investigator	N	Population size	Percent minority[p]	Region	Was conventional hypothesis confirmed?
1.	Sloan (1969)[a]	19	500,000+	15+	U.S.	Yes
2.	Cole (1974)[b]	16	25,000+	15+	N.J.	No
3.	Jones (1976)[c]	136	50,000+	5+	U.S.	Yes
4.	Karnig (1976)[d]	139	25,000+	15+	U.S.	Yes
5.	Robinson-Dye[e] (1978)	105	50,000+	15+	U.S.	Yes
6.	Taebel (1978)[f]					
	Blacks	166	50,000+	q	U.S.	Yes
	Hispanics	60	50,000+	q	U.S.	Yes
7.	MacManus (1978)[g]					
	Blacks	243	50,000+	0+	U.S.	No
	Hispanics	243	50,000+	0+	U.S.	No
8.	Welch-Karnig[h] (1978)	33	278,000+	5+	U.S.	No
9.	Karnig-Welch[i] (1978)					
	Comparison #1[n]	200	25,000+	10+	U.S.	Yes
	Comparison #2[n]	56	25,000+	10+	U.S.	Yes
10.	Karnig (1979)[j]	126	25,000+	15+	U.S.	Yes
11.	Latimer (1979)[k]	80	10,000+	7.3+	Ala., La., S.C.	Yes
12.	Engstrom-McDonald (1981)	239	50,000+	0+	U.S.	Yes
13.	Vedlitz-Johnson[m] (forthcoming)	70	50,000+	q	U.S.	Yes

[a] Lee Sloan, " 'Good Government' and the Politics of Race," *Social Problems* 17 (Fall 1969): 161–75.

[b] Leonard A. Cole, "Electing Blacks to Municipal Office: Structural and Social Determinants," *Urban Affairs Quarterly* 10 (September 1974): 17–39.

[c] Clinton B. Jones, "The Impact of Local Election Systems on Black Political Representation," *Urban Affairs Quarterly* 11 (March 1976): 345–356.

[d] Albert K. Karnig, "Black Representation on City Councils," *Urban Affairs Quarterly* 12 (December 1976): 223–242.

[e] Theodore P. Robinson and Thomas R. Dye, "Reformism and Black Representation on City Councils," *Social Science Quarterly* 59 (June 1978): 133–141.

[f] Delbert Taebel, "Minority Representation on City Councils," *Social Science Quarterly* 59 (June 1978): 143–152.

[g] Susan MacManus, "City Council Election Procedures and Minority Representation: Are They Related?," *Social Science Quarterly* 59 (June 1978): 153–161.

[h] Susan Welch and Albert K. Karnig, "Representation of Blacks on Big City School Boards," *Social Science Quarterly* 59 (June 1978): 162–172.

[i] Albert K. Karnig and Susan Welch, "Electoral Structure and Black Representation: An Updated Examination," (Revision of paper presented at the annual meeting of the Midwest Political Science Association, Chicago, Ill., 20–22 April 1978).

[j] Albert K. Karnig, "Black Resources and City Council Representation," *Journal of Politics* 41 (February 1979): 134–149.

rather than city councils; and the authors acknowledge that their unpublished data on councils in the same cities as the school boards in fact do confirm the conventional hypothesis. The score for ward-based systems is based on a sample of only two school districts.[49]

Cole finds no appreciable differences in black representation between at-large cities and other types. But two problems render the findings doubtful. The black officeholders are not simply council members, as in the other studies of municipalities, but rather "the maximum number of Black elected officials at any one time in 1972,"[50] which would include everyone from mayor on down. As whites vote more readily for blacks in lower positions, this method may exaggerate the proportion of blacks on council. A more crucial difficulty stems from Cole's classifying the cities as ward cities when council is actually elected by a mixed plan.[51] (This classification procedure is also used by Latimer in her study which confirms the conventional hypothesis.)[52] If mixed systems are more unrepresentative than ward systems, this fact would exaggerate the unrepresentativeness of Cole's "ward" systems in comparison with at-large ones.

Suspecting that the sixteen New Jersey cities which Cole analyzed were atypical, Karnig replicated his study using a national sample of 139. He limited his research to councilmen and correctly classified cities by election method, thus improving on Cole's procedure. Karnig's findings confirm the conventional view.[53]

MacManus's analysis leaves much to be desired in terms of method and interpretation.[54] She does not report an average representation score for at-large systems as a group. Instead, she separates at-large systems into various kinds, depending not only on the type of residency and place requirements but on governmental type as well, such as strong versus weak mayoral systems. She then calculates representation scores for each subtype. Because she finds a wide range of scores for both blacks and Mexican Americans among the subtypes of at-large systems, she concludes that her data "reveal the lack of marked variation in equity of minority representation by council election plan."[55] MacManus's data are unavailable for reanalysis, and it therefore is impossible to calculate the mean score for all at-large systems combined. However, the only subcategory of at-large cities with a mean score indicating less black underrepresentation than the average in ward cities contains only 13 cases out of a total of 136 at-large cities, implying that the mean score for all 136 cities indicates less equitable black representation

---

[k] Margaret K. Latimer, "Black Political Representation in Southern Cities," *Urban Affairs Quarterly* 15 (September 1979): 65–86.

[l] Richard L. Engstrom and Michael D. McDonald, "The Election of Blacks to City Councils: Clarifying the Impact of Electoral Arrangements on the Seats/Population Relationship," *American Political Science Review* 75 (June 1981): 344–354.

[m] Arnold Vedlitz and Charles Johnson, "Community Racial Divisions, Electoral Structure, and Minority Representation," forthcoming.

[n] Comparison #1 is between types of cities. Comparison #2 is an analysis of cities with mixed systems, comparing within each city the representation of minorities elected to at-large seats and that of minorities elected to ward seats.

[p] Blacks, unless otherwise noted.

[q] Minority threshold varies according to council size.

than in ward cities.[56] Essentially the same is true for her analysis of Mexican Americans.

Another serious problem stems from the fact that MacManus's sample includes numerous cases that have virtually no minority population. Assuming no minorities were elected to office, each of these cities consequently has a score of zero indicating perfect proportional representation. If the percentage of such cities is not distributed equally among the various election systems, the mean scores could be distorted seriously. MacManus's study is the only one in Table 4-1 employing her mode of analysis in which cities without minority populations were included.

Robinson and Dye use an almost identically generated data base of 243 cities collected within a year of MacManus's research, but employ a 15 percent cutoff point for minority percentages in the cities analyzed.[57] This study comes to conclusions very similar to those of Taebel, who used MacManus's data, but excluded cities with low or nonexistent minority percentages.[58] Robinson and Dye, as well as Taebel, reach opposite conclusions from those of MacManus.

In summary, the studies by Cole, MacManus, and Welch and Karnig, because of the previously mentioned problems, do not constitute convincing counterevidence for the conventional hypothesis. The other ten studies have been done carefully enough to meet acceptable standards, although Latimer should have separated mixed from at-large systems. Each confirms the hypothesis that single-member districts afford minority groups a better chance for representation than at-large elections.

Even these studies, however, may actually understate the relation between minority underrepresentation and at-large elections. The reason is that several other factors are known to affect adversely minority chances, including gerrymandering, the nonpartisan ballot, place voting (or its functional equivalent, the anti-single-shot rule), small council size combined with small minority percentages, low minority geographical concentration, and the runoff requirement. The problem of isolating their effects is formidable when the research design specifies the collection of cross-sectional data. The procedure would entail, for example, constructing a measure of ward boundary fairness that could easily be applied to a sample of cities. The use of regression techniques to arrive at "percentage of variance explained" depends upon the dubious scalability of variables such as election systems, place rules, and partisanship.

CHANGE FROM AT-LARGE SYSTEMS IN TEXAS

To overcome these difficulties, we employed a before-and-after design. The sample consists of all known political entities in Texas changing from at-large elections to mixed or pure ward systems between 1970 and 1979, which have had sufficient time to elect a full complement of officeholders under the new system. Changes usually resulted from vote dilution litigation initiated by minority plaintiffs or from Justice Department intervention under Section 5 of the 1965 Voting Rights Act as amended. In all, forty-one cases are analyzed, consisting of twenty-one cities, twelve state legislative districts, and eight educational districts.

Jurisdiction population size ranged from 4,719 to 1.74 million. The minority population in the forty-one units (blacks and Chicanos combined) ranged from 7.8 percent to 79.1 percent. All but four, however, contained a minority population of at least 20 percent. The mean minority percentage was 32.4.

The jurisdictions are widely dispersed geographically across the face of Texas, thereby representing various subcultures. Some are located in deep East Texas, the traditional black belt area with relatively high black concentrations. Others are located on the rim of East Texas, in a north-south corridor that contains the state's largest and most cosmopolitan urban areas. Still others are located in the southern or western part of the state, where Mexican Americans are concentrated heavily.

The structural change, as noted, involved abolishing pure at-large systems. In thirty-three cases a pure ward scheme was substituted. A mixed plan was adopted in the remaining eight, with the at-large seats averaging 30 percent of the total seats in the jurisdiction.

There were virtually no other changes in electoral procedure that accompanied the change from at-large elections, and therefore the confounding effects of other variables are minimized. The most important effect, we believe, stems from racial gerrymandering. Under the Voting Rights Act, any change in an electoral scheme (including annexation) in covered jurisdictions must be precleared by the Justice Department. When such changes are judged dilutionary, and a single-member-district remedy is required, the Justice Department reviews the newly drawn boundaries to prevent blatant racial gerrymandering. When a court orders the remedy, the court itself has the responsibility to ensure fairly drawn boundaries.

There are no rigid criteria of boundary fairness, which means that there is still some discretion allowed in drawing them. Even so, the extent of gerrymandering to dilute minority votes is now more narrowly delimited. It is therefore only a slight exaggeration to say that our design enables us to separate the effects of at-large elections from those of racial gerrymandering.

It might be argued that our sample is biased because in most cases the change to ward-based elections resulted from a finding of minority vote dilution. Are not these cases the ones most likely to reveal a dramatic change in minority representation?

The answer is affirmative. But this is exactly the point that needs to be made, because it is sometimes overlooked in discussions of the effects of at-large elections. Surely no one wishes to argue that at-large systems dilute the votes of ethnic minorities under all circumstances. On the contrary, it is those instances where racially polarized voting exists that one would expect at-large elections most seriously to underrepresent minorities. Consequently, our data demonstrate the effects of at-large elections in such jurisdictions. That they are not isolated cases, however, is indicated by the size and number of Texas and other southern jurisdictions in which vote dilution has been proven, according to legal criteria, and by the finding of Murray and Vedlitz of a sharp increase in racially polarized elections in major southern cities since the early 1960s.[59]

The findings appear in Table 4-2. Minority representation is measured (a) as the difference between the percentage of elected officials (legislators, councilmen, or educational board members) who are black and/or Mexican American in a po-

Table 4-2.   Minority representation on Texas governmental bodies before and after change from at-large systems

Type of jurisdiction	N	Mean representation scores		
		Before	After	Change
Legislative District	12	−23.6	+0.9	+24.5
		(0.38)	(0.97)	(0.59)
City Council	21	−18.7	−3.3	+15.4
		(0.28)	(0.86)	(0.58)
School Board/ Jr. College Board	8	−21.5	−0.1	+21.4
		(0.18)	(1.04)	(0.86)
Total	41	−21.2	−1.4	+19.8
		(0.29)	(0.93)	(0.64)

Superior scores are differences; scores in parentheses are quotients.

litical unit and their percentage in the unit's population; and (b) as the quotient of the minority percentage of officials divided by their percentage in the population. Minority officials are not always the choice of the minority electorate, of course. In comparative studies, however, their presence in office is a rough measure of the ability of the minority community to elect candidates of its choice. Before the changes, only 10 percent of the 259 officials were blacks or Mexican Americans. After the changes occurred, 29 percent of the 283 were. This increase resulted in near parity of representation overall.

Ward-based elections benefited both groups. Black officials increased from 6 to 17 percent and Mexican Americans from 5 to 12 percent. Although Taebel doubts that wards remedy discrimination against Mexican American voters, who are less geographically concentrated than blacks, our findings indicate that their concentration in many cases is sufficient to warrant a ward-based remedy.[60]

The figures in Table 4-2 are means, and scores vary a great deal around them. Our sample is too small to explore systematically the reasons for this variation. A few common-sense observations are appropriate, however.

Generally speaking, there are four reasons why wards did not increase minority representation. In two kinds of circumstances proportional representation was possible before the at-large system was dismantled: (1) when "minorities" constituted a sizeable majority of the electorate; or (2) when minority candidates received the endorsement of a powerful Anglo slating group. Once wards were implemented, two factors sometimes rendered them ineffective: (1) gerrymandered boundaries; or (2) a small minority ratio.

A Large Minority Population

In Hidalgo County, the Mexican American population was 79 percent. In spite of their lower turnout rate they were able to elect Hispanics to both of the county's legislative seats under the at-large system. In jurisdictions where the socioeconomic characteristics of minorities and whites are similar, an even smaller percentage will suffice to allow equitable representation.

Slating

Some cities anticipated judicial challenges to their at-large system by slating minority candidates who were able to win at large with the imprimatur of white political dominants. Among cities in which the change to wards did not result in increased minority representation, both the Dallas municipality and Houston Independent School District had already elected minorities to office by means of a conservative slating group. (But in two other cities, Waco and San Antonio, the advent of single-member districts doubled the number of minorities previously elected when a conservative slate-making system was operative.)

Gerrymandering

As explained earlier, our design enabled us partially to control for the influence of racial gerrymanders, given the narrower limits within which political cartographers were forced to operate in the 1970s. Yet, some room for maneuvering remained. We were able to identify fourteen cases in which districts were drawn either by minority groups or the Department of Justice, and five in which they were drawn by defendants or individuals hostile to minority group interests. In the remaining twenty-two cases, the identity of the cartographers was unknown. Table 4-3 demonstrates the results of authorship. Where the change to wards was accompanied by a *decrease* in minority representation on city council (Dallas and El Paso), plans were drawn by "hostile" groups. (The city of Dallas has redrawn its eight districts since our analysis was completed; and a Mexican American was elected, thus placing Dallas in the "no change in minority representation" category. It was only under this condition of reapportionment that the city was able to obtain preclearance under the Voting Rights Act.) In a third case, Houston Independent School District, no change in minority representation occurred. In the case of H.I.S.D. the slating of black candidates by a conservative white group under the at-large system was also a contributing factor. In a fourth case, Houston city council, the adoption of the council's plan over one advocated by a minority coalition probably shaved ten points off the elected minority proportion, in part because of gerrymandered districts, and in part because of a mixed plan instead of a pure ward one.

Table 4-3.   Is change in minority representation affected by who draws district boundaries?

Authorship of boundaries	N	Mean score change[a]
Minority groups or Justice Department	14	+34.3 (1.0)
Authorship unknown	22	+13.3 (0.51)
Groups hostile to minorities	5	+3.8 (0.18)

[a]Superior scores are differences; scores in parentheses are quotients.

Small Minority Population

In some cities, the small number of seats on a governmental body results in a large average district population. Thus, even if geographically concentrated, the minorities may have difficulty mustering 51 percent of the district's vote, especially when their turnout is low. This is true in the city of Gainesville, and in two legislative districts where no change in minority percentages resulted from wards. Gainesville has a minority population of 8 percent. With six councilmen elected from districts, the mean district size was 17 percent. Assuming high voter polarization, a minority candidate will have difficulty winning under those circumstances.

Galveston and McLennan County legislative districts both have fairly large minority percentages, but only two legislative seats apiece, which means that the minority electorate has to constitute more than 25 percent of the total in a highly polarized situation. However, the Waco (McLennan County) city council and school board have a larger number of seats available than in the McLennan County legislative district. Thus, single-member districts in council and school board elections resulted in an increase in elected minority officials.

As eight of the forty-one cases involved changes to mixed rather than pure ward systems, it is possible to compare postchange representation in the two types of remedies. Surprisingly, minority representation is slightly greater in mixed systems than in wards. When cities and legislative districts with small minority populations are eliminated, however, the pure ward systems are the most representative. Moreover, in several of the mixed systems, notably the Houston and Dallas city councils, and the Waco school board, the elimination of at-large seats would undoubtedly increase the proportion of minority office holders.

SUMMARY AND CONCLUSIONS

An examination of the history of reform during the Progressive Era demonstrates that many reformers, belonging to the business classes, introduced at-large elections to wrest control of municipalities from the laboring classes and ethnic minorities. Research on the use of at-large elections since the 1920s indicates that they continued to be introduced or maintained as barriers to minority office holding, especially when disfranchising measures began to come under challenge.

Persuasive as the evidence is for intent, the statistical evidence for effect is also strong. Research reveals that the accepted view on the subject is firmly grounded in empirical fact, which is especially significant because it applies to cities in the 1960s and 1970s. There has been a popular conceit, predicated more on hope than fact, that voter polarization has declined. Our before-and-after study demonstrates dramatically, however, that recent changes from at-large to single-member-district elections increase minority representation in different kinds of political subdivisions, suggesting that bloc voting in at-large systems is still widespread.

In conclusion, a word of caution is necessary regarding future attempts to measure the impact of structure on minority representation. The mere presence of minority officials does not ensure minority groups representation. Racial or ethnic head counting is a somewhat limited and misleading measure of representation, partly because dominant white groups tend to co-opt "safe" minority candidates by including them on a ticket or slate which guarantees their election citywide. The minority candidates selected seldom are supported actively by the ethnic community they ostensibly represent. This pattern has been observed in a current study of Texas cities by one of the present authors. For example, in Houston, an incumbent black councilman who had won at large with the imprimatur of the city's informal business establishment ran a poor third against two other black candidates in a primary race for the congressional seat vacated by Barbara Jordan, which represents the heart of Houston's black ghetto. In Waco, the black elected at large to city council was unable to carry the black area of town. If co-optation through slating groups in citywide elections is more probable than in single-member-district systems, where voters in minority wards usually are better able to provide a counter-balance to the blandishments of the white political dominants, then a relative increase in the "representation scores" of at-large systems compared to ward systems could understate the differences in actual representation offered by the two types of electoral structures.

NOTES

1. Edward C. Banfield and James Q. Wilson, *City Politics* (Cambridge: Harvard University Press, 1964), 88.
2. Alan Klevit, "City Councils and their Functions in Local Government," in *The Municipal Yearbook* (Washington, D.C.: International City Managers' Association, 1972), 19, 25.
3. Robert E. Lane, *Political Life: Why People Get Involved in Politics* (Glencoe, Ill.: The Free Press, 1959), 270.
4. Gunnar Myrdal, *An American Dilemma* (New York: Harper, 1944), 493.
5. Lane, *Political Life,* 270.
6. 412 U.S. 755 (1973).
7. 446 U.S. 55 (1980)
8. Melvin G. Holli, "Urban Reform," in *The Progressive Era,* ed. Lewis L. Gould (Syracuse: Syracuse University Press, 1974), 140.
9. John D. Buenker, *Urban Liberalism and Progressive Reform* (New York: Charles Scribner's Sons, 1973), 28.
10. Holli, "Urban Reform," 137.
11. Buenker, *Urban Liberalism,* 1–2.
12. C. Vann Woodward, *Origins of the New South 1877–1913* (Baton Rouge: Louisiana State University Press, 1951), 388–389.
13. James Weinstein, "Organized Business and the City Commission and Manager Movements," *Journal of Southern History* 28 (May 1962): 168–170. Weinstein (166) and Hays identify structural reform supporters as persons primarily from the upper class. See Samuel P. Hays, "The Politics of Reform in Municipal Government in the Progressive Era," *Pacific Northwest Quarterly* 55 (October 1964): 160.
14. As of 1966, three-fourths of southern cities of more than 25,000 population elected councilmen or commissioners with nonpartisan ballots. James Q. Wilson, "The Negro in American Politics: The Present," in *The American Negro Reference Book,* ed. John P. Davis (Englewood Cliffs, N.J.: Prentice-Hall, 1966), 449.
15. Harold A. Stone, Don K. Price, and Kathryn H. Stone, *City Manager Government in*

the United States: A Review After Twenty-Five Years (Chicago: Public Administration Service, 1940), 269.

16. Daniel N. Gordon, "Immigrants and Urban Governmental Form in American Cities 1933–60," *American Journal of Sociology* 74 (September 1968): 161.

17. Raymond E. Wolfinger and John Osgood Field, "Political Ethos and the Structure of City Government," *American Political Science Review* 60 (June 1966): 326.

18. Albert K. Karnig, "Black Representation on City Councils," *Urban Affairs Quarterly* 12 (December 1976): 235. This finding is based on a sample of cities with 25,000 population and larger.

19. Philip W. Barnes, "Alternative Methods of Electing City Councils in Texas Home Rule Cities," *Public Affairs Comment* 16 (May 1970): 1.

20. The founder and guiding genius of the city manager movement, multimillionaire businessman Richard S. Childs, was influenced by the ideas of Frederick Winslow Taylor, whose theory of "scientific management" was intended to provide capitalists with a tool for crushing labor control of the workplace. For a description of the social context of Taylor's theory, see Harry Braverman, *Labor and Monopoly Capital* (New York: Monthly Review Press, 1974), 85–123.

21. Hays, "The Politics of Reform," 162.

22. C. Vann Woodward, *The Strange Career of Jim Crow,* 2nd revised ed. (New York: Oxford University Press, 1966), 91.

23. Dewey W. Grantham, "The Progressive Movement and the Negro," *South Atlantic Quarterly* 54 (October 1955): 465.

24. Darlene Clark Hine, *Black Victory: The Rise and Fall of the White Primary in Texas* (Millwood, N.Y.: KTO Press, 1979), 37.

25. Roy E. Young, *The Place System in Texas Elections* (Austin: Institute of Public Affairs, The University of Texas, 1965), 2; Charles Chamberlain, "Alexander Watkins Terrell: Citizen, Statesman," Ph.D. Diss., University of Texas, 1956), 494; Ralph W. Steen, *Twentieth Century Texas* (Austin: The Steck Company, 1942), 332.

26. Hays, "The Politics of Reform," 162–163.

27. Bradley Robert Rice, *Progressive Cities* (Austin: University of Texas Press, 1977), 110. However, Rice notes that "a full understanding of the commission movement must go beyond a pure class interpretation."

28. Ibid., 29.

29. Weinstein, "Organized Business," 174.

30. Rice, *Progressive Cities,* 3–4.

31. Ibid., 4–5.

32. Ibid., 6.

33. Weinstein, "Organized Business," 173; Hays, "The Politics of Reform," 162–163.

34. Banfield and Wilson, *City Politics,* 95.

35. James Q. Wilson, *Negro Politics* (Glencoe, Ill: The Free Press of Glencoe, 1960), 26.

36. Myrdal, *An American Dilemma,* 501.

37. J.T. Slater, *Boss Rule* (New York: McGraw-Hill, 1935), 41.

38. Robert Dahl, *Who Governs?* (New Haven: Yale University Press, 1959), 36.

39. Oliver P. Williams and Charles R. Adrian, *Four Cities* (Philadelphia: University of Pennsylvania Press, 1963), 73–76, 86, 145–146.

40. Hugh Douglas Price, "The Negro and Florida Politics, 1944–1954," in *Negro Politics in America,* ed. Harry A. Bailey, Jr. (Columbus, Oh: Charles E. Merrill Books, 1967), 272–273.

41. Everett Carll Ladd, *Negro Political Leadership in the South* (Ithaca: Cornell University Press, 1966), 103.

42. Henry Lee Moon, *Balance of Power* (Garden City, N.Y.: Doubleday and Company, 1949), 188.

43. Ladd, *Negro Political Leadership,* 102–103.

44. *Graves v. Barnes,* 378 Federal Supplement 640, 651 (Western District of Texas 1974).

45. Howard Hamilton, "Legislative Constituencies: Single-Member Districts, Multi-Member Districts, and Floterial Districts," *Western Political Quarterly* 20 (June 1967): 331.
46. U.S. Commission on Civil Rights, *Political Participation,* III, Washington, D.C.: U.S. Government Printing Office, 1968), 21–25.
47. The one exception is the study by Engstrom and McDonald. Instead of measuring proportional representation as the difference or ratio between the minority population and minority seats on council, as in the other studies, the authors treat proportionality as a relation across elections, rather than as a variable itself. See Richard L. Engstrom and Michael D. McDonald, "The Election of Blacks to City Councils: Clarifying the Impact of Electoral Arrangements on the Seats/Population Relationship," *American Political Science Review* 75 (June 1981): 346–347. In using this measure, the absence of a threshold for minority population in the sampled cities is not the problem that it is in the MacManus study described below. Susan MacManus, "City Council Election Procedures and Minority Representation: Are They Related?," *Social Science Quarterly* 59 (June 1978): 153–161.
48. Susan Welch and Albert K. Karnig, "Representation of Blacks on Big City School Boards," *Social Science Quarterly* 59 (June 1978): 164–165.
49. Ibid., 166. In a subsequent paper the authors note that their "limited sample of district cities makes confident generalization impossible." Albert K. Karnig and Susan Welch, "Electoral Structure and Black Representation in City Councils: An Updated Examination," (revision of a paper presented at the annual meeting of the Midwest Political Science Association, Chicago, April 20–22, 1978), 2.
50. Leonard A. Cole, "Electing Blacks to Municipal Office: Structural and Social Determinants," *Urban Affairs Quarterly* 10 (September 1974): 19.
51. Ibid., 20.
52. Margaret K. Latimer, "Black Political Representation in Southern Cities," *Urban Affairs Quarterly* 15 (September 1979): 65–86.
53. Karnig, "Black Representation on City Councils," 223–242.
54. MacManus, "City Council Election Procedures." 153–161.
55. Ibid., 158.
56. Ibid., 157.
57. Theodore P. Robinson and Thomas R. Dye, "Reformism and Black Representation on City Councils," *Social Science Quarterly* 59 (June 1978): 133–141.
58. Delbert Taebel, "Minority Representation on City Councils," *Social Science Quarterly,* 59 (June 1978): 143–152.
59. Richard Murray and Arnold Vedlitz, "Racial Voting Patterns in the South," *The Annals of the American Academy of Political and Social Sciences* (September 1978): 29–39.
60. Taebel, "Minority Representation," 151.

CURRENT STRATEGIES OF VOTE DILUTION

5

RACIAL GERRYMANDERING AND LEGISLATIVE REAPPORTIONMENT

By Frank R. Parker

THE HISTORY OF GERRYMANDERING

The practice of gerrymandering in America dates from the founding of the Republic. Patrick Henry has been credited with leading an effort to gerrymander the congressional district containing James Madison's home county to prevent Madison's election to Congress because of his alleged opposition to the Bill of Rights.[1] The term "gerrymander" was coined in 1812 by Gilbert Stuart, the portrait painter, after looking at a map of the redistricting of Essex County, Massachusetts, signed into law by Governor Elbridge Gerry. When Stuart sketched a head, wings, and claws on the distorted district, Stuart thought it looked like a dragon, but his companion thought it looked more like a salamander. "Better call it a 'Gerrymander,' " Stuart is alleged to have replied.[2]

Gerrymandering covers any redistricting practice which maximizes the political advantage or votes of one group, and minimizes the political advantage or votes of another. Historic examples include the Mississippi congressional "shoestring district" of 1876–1882, five hundred miles long and forty miles wide, which was designed to make difficult the reelection of black Mississippi congressman John R. Lynch; the Pennsylvania district resembling a dumbbell; the "saddlebag" and "belt line" districts in Illinois; and the district in Missouri which was longer, if measured by its windings, than the state itself.[3]

In response to these abuses, legislative efforts have been made to check excessive gerrymandering. In 1842, for example, Congress passed a reapportionment act requiring the election of members of the House of Representatives from single-member districts composed of compact and contiguous territory.[4] Many states have adopted similar requirements and have added the criterion that districts have equal population. Nevertheless, as political scientist Robert Luce aptly put it in his 1930 study, "Gerrymandering has become so general and familiar a procedure that it may fairly be called a characteristic of American politics."[5]

The author is grateful for the assistance of Rose Nathan and Samuel Issacharoff.

The Supreme Court's landmark "one person, one vote" decision, *Reynolds v. Sims,*[6] was designed to check a particular kind of gerrymandering—legislative districts which, because of large population deviations, discriminated against heavily populated urban areas in favor of rural areas and small towns. The goal of that decision was "full and effective participation by all citizens in state government."[7] Although *Reynolds* and subsequent Supreme Court decisions have dealt effectively with the mathematical issue of population disparities among districts, the constitutional requirement that state legislatures and other governing bodies redistrict themselves every ten years has created new opportunities for racial and political gerrymandering. This is not to say that the one person, one vote rule should be abandoned, but rather that the courts must also develop strict standards to ensure that the *Reynolds* goal of "full and effective representation" is not circumvented by other, equally invidious forms of gerrymandering. As the late Prof. Robert G. Dixon has noted:

> A mathematically equal vote which is politically worthless because of gerrymandering or winner-take-all districting is as deceiving as "emperor's clothes."[8]

Even before the *Reynolds* decision, the Supreme Court in the Tuskegee, Alabama, gerrymandering case, *Gomillion v. Lightfoot,*[9] held that racial gerrymandering violated constitutional guarantees and that aggrieved voters could sue for judicial relief. After *Reynolds* and the enactment of the Voting Rights Act of 1965, the United States Commission on Civil Rights reported to Congress, in supporting an extension of the Act, that "gerrymandering and boundary changes had become prime weapons for discriminating against Negro voters."[10]

Racial gerrymandering in legislative reapportionment has implications which extend far beyond the immediate issue of the effective use of the electoral franchise. Almost a century ago, the Supreme Court described the right to vote as "preservative of all rights."[11] Voting rights were a cornerstone of the Court's definition of fundamental rights, the abridgment of which could only be justified by a compelling state interest. Underlying the elevated status of voting rights claims is the realization that voting discrimination not only results in disfranchisement of the victims, but also is closely correlated with racial discrimination in state policy, allocation of state funds, and provision of municipal services.[12] When minorities are deprived of an effective voice in the policy-making bodies of their states or localities, state and local officials are free to disregard their needs and concerns. This combination of political powerlessness and racist victimization has devastated poor black, Hispanic, and other minority communities throughout this country. Thus, the terrain upon which the struggle for voting rights is waged symbolizes the struggle for social justice for America's embattled minorities.

THE TECHNIQUES OF RACIAL GERRYMANDERING

Racial gerrymandering includes any redistricting scheme which minimizes or dilutes the voting strength of racial minorities.[13] Traditionally, gerrymandering has been defined in terms of irregularities in the boundaries and shapes of districts and lack of contiguity.[14] There is some merit in the traditional view in the sense that odd-shaped districts may be indicative of an intent to discriminate. However, more recent research and experience have revealed that discriminatory racial gerrymandering can be effectuated in regularly shaped districts as well, including districts which are based on political subdivision lines and which follow traditional and natural geographic boundaries.[15]

Rather than concentrating on the shape of the district, the better approach is to examine the impact of a particular districting scheme on the minority community, that is, where the lines are drawn in relation to concentrations of black, Hispanic, and other minority populations. Any districting scheme necessarily involves a political decision concerning the allocation of political power and influence within a given state or community. At stake is the determination of which groups in the political community will elect candidates of their choice to public office, and which will not; who will be elected to public office, and who will not. Reapportionment decisions, therefore, are directly reflected in the resulting distribution of electoral power.

Generally, in legislative reapportionment, there are four categories of racial gerrymandering: at-large voting, "cracking," "stacking," and "packing."[16] Because the focus of this essay is on legislative reapportionment, municipal gerrymandering, such as discriminatory annexations, deannexations (as in *Gomillion v. Lightfoot*), and separate incorporation of predominantly white enclaves are not included. Also not included is county consolidation, which can be used as a gerrymandering device. Legislative reapportionment, as used herein, does include redistricting at the congressional, state legislative, county, and municipal levels.

At-Large Voting

At-large voting constitutes a form of racially discriminatory districting when it submerges minority voting strength in a districtwide white voting majority. Minority voters might constitute a substantial majority in a particular area of the district, or in particular wards or precincts, but a decided minority in the district as a whole. At-large voting schemes discriminate because of their "winner-take-all" feature, permitting the white districtwide majority to elect all the representatives from the district and denying to minority voters representation of their choice.

For example, in Mississippi during the late 1960s and early 1970s, 84,000 black citizens in Hinds County, where Jackson is located, were sufficiently concentrated in particular precincts to permit the creation of five majority black single-member House districts and two majority black single-member Senate districts. Blacks constituted only 40 percent of the population countywide, however. Black citizens were completely shut out of the political process and denied representation of their choice by successive state legislative reapportionment plans which required the election of all twelve Hinds County representatives and all five Hinds County senators in at-large, countywide voting. As a result, black voters in Mississippi's most populous county were denied legislative representation in the Mississippi legislature until 1975, when single-member districts were created in a court-ordered plan and black legislators were elected.[17]

Discriminatory at-large voting can occur at all levels of government. It includes multimember legislative districts, in which more than one legislator is selected from a single legislative district in at-large voting, at-large county elections, and citywide municipal elections. It encompasses retaining discriminatory at-large voting schemes, as well as switches from district to at-large elections.

After the Voting Rights Act was passed in 1965, multimember legislative districts with at-large voting were the primary barrier to black voters gaining representation of their choice in southern state legislatures. Almost every such legislature, from Texas to Virginia, employed multimember districts in both houses (although Georgia and Texas have no multimember senate districts) [18] which consequently remained virtually all white despite dramatic increases in black voting strength. (See Table 5-1.) Even though blacks were now permitted to register and vote, voting was, by and large, a futile exercise when black voting strength was cancelled out in multimember legislative districts.

During the 1970s, multimember legislative districts were eliminated by Voting Rights Act Section 5 objections or by federal court reapportionment litigation in all southern states covered by the Voting Rights Act, except Virginia, North Carolina, South Carolina (state senate), and Florida. [19] Once these discriminatory multimember districtings were replaced by single-member district legislative re-

Table 5-1.   Increase in black representation in southern legislatures resulting from elimination of multimember districts

States	Total 1980 population (% black)	Legislature (% black)					
		1971		1976		1981	
		House	Senate	House	Senate	House	Senate
Alabama	24.5	1.9	0.0	12.4	5.7	12.4	8.6
		(2)	(0)	(13)	(2)	(13)	(3)
Georgia[a]	26.2	7.2	3.6	11.1	3.6	11.7	3.6
		(13)	(2)	(20)	(12)	(21)	(2)
Louisiana	29.6	1.0	0.0	8.6	2.6	9.5	5.9
		(1)	(0)	(9)	(1)	(10)	(2)
Mississippi	35.1	0.8	0.0	3.3	0.0	12.3	3.8
		(1)	(0)	(4)	(0)	(15)	(2)
South Carolina[b]	31.0	2.4	0.0	10.5	0.0	12.1	0.0
		(3)	(0)	(13)	(0)	(15)	(0)
Texas	12.5	1.3	3.2	6.0	0.0	8.7	0.0
		(2)	(1)	(9)	(0)	(13)	(0)

[a]The Attorney General's 1972 objections to Georgia's legislative reapportionment plan for the state house of representatives objected to discriminatory multimember districts in areas which at that time had black population concentrations. Multimember districts in then predominantly white areas, where they had no discriminatory impact, were also to be retained. Some of these multimember districts, nondiscriminatory in 1972, may now be discriminatory as a result of population changes.

[b]Multimember districts were eliminated in the state house of representatives only; multimember state senate districts were retained.

Source: Joint Center for Political Studies, *National Roster of Black Elected Officials,* vols. 1 (1971), 6 (1976), and 11 (1981).

apportionment plans, black representation in southern state legislatures increased dramatically.

Numerous empirical studies based on data collected from throughout the nation have found a direct causal relationship between at-large elections and underrepresentation of minorities.[20] Discriminatory at-large voting schemes are still widespread at the county and municipal levels in many parts of the South and Southwest. Currently, for example, in Georgia most counties continue to elect county commissioners on an at-large countywide basis,[21] and most school board members in Texas are elected at large.[22] A majority of cities nationwide with populations 25,000 and over elect city council members on an at-large basis, but at-large municipal elections predominate in the South, where 76 percent of cities 25,000 and over have at-large city council elections.[23] In Virginia, for example, all but nine of the state's forty-one independent cities elect all city council members on an at-large basis.[24]

Cracking

Minority voting strength is diluted and cancelled out when a minority population concentration, large enough for separate representation, is broken up (cracked) by district lines, fragmented and dispersed throughout two or more districts with white voting majorities.

Cracking is illustrated by the history of Mississippi congressional redistricting. (See Figure 5-1.) The black population in Mississippi has been concentrated historically in the northwest area of the state commonly known as the Delta, and today, thirteen of the state's twenty-one majority-black counties are located there. A unique geopolitical entity, the economy of which is based primarily on agriculture, particularly cotton and soybeans, the Delta is noted for its large plantations and oppressive social structure. From 1882 to 1966—when black citizens were denied the right to register and vote—the Mississippi legislature drew congressional district lines so that the Delta was always contained within one congressional district. In 1960 the population of this district (District 3) was 66 percent black. Mississippi lost one congressional seat under the 1960 Census, and, in 1962, the legislature combined the Second and Third Districts. But the Delta was kept intact within the new Second District, which was 59 percent black.

In 1965, Congress enacted the Voting Rights Act, and just as blacks were beginning to register and vote, the Mississippi legislature in 1966 redrew the congressional district lines horizontally along an east-west configuration, dismembered the heavy black population concentration in the Delta, and split it up among four of the five congressional districts. All five districts were majority-white in voting age population, and this scheme was preserved in the Mississippi redistricting plans of 1972 and 1981.[25]

Cracking also occurs when majority-black counties, previously put together in a legislative district, are split up and placed in separate majority-white districts. Prior to 1981, four of the five majority-black counties in Southside Virginia—Charles City (70 percent black), Surry (63 percent black), Sussex (61 percent black),

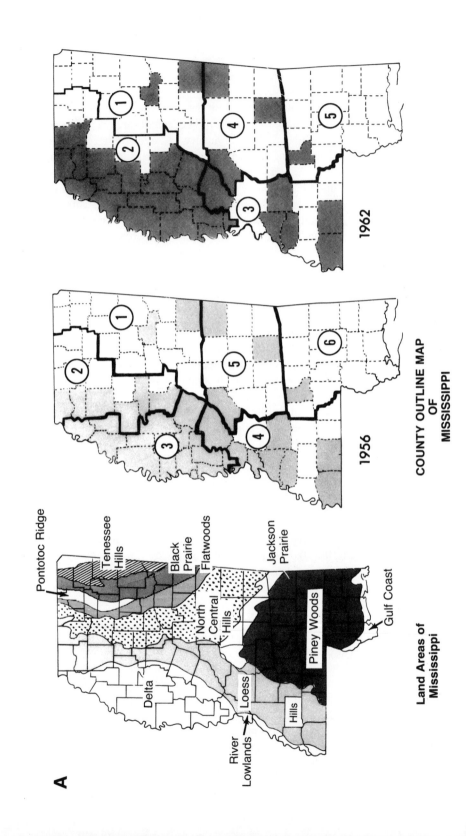

COUNTY OUTLINE MAP
OF
MISSISSIPPI

1956

1962

Land Areas of
Mississippi

A

Pontotoc Ridge

Tenessee
Hills

Black
Prairie

Flatwoods

North
Central
Hills

Jackson
Prairie

Delta

Loess

River
Lowlands

Hills

Piney Woods

Gulf Coast

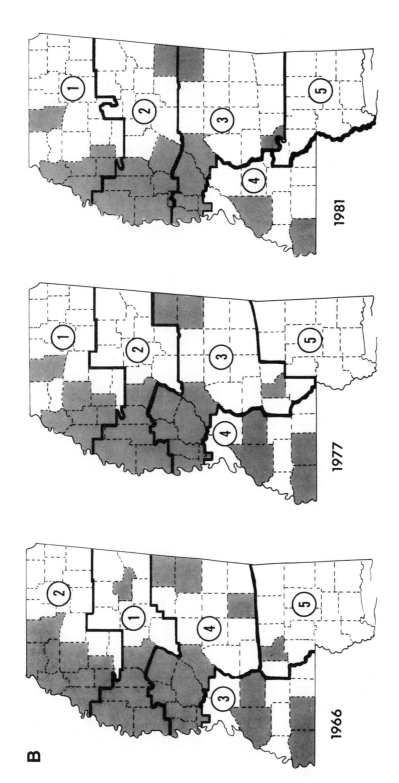

Figure 5-1. Cracking in Mississippi Congressional redistricting. A. Prior to the passage of the Voting Rights Act, the heavily black Delta, in the northwest part of the state, was preserved intact from 1882 to 1962. B. After the Voting Rights Act became law, the Delta area was split up among Mississippi's congressional districts, diluting black voting strength. Majority-black counties are shaded.

and Greensville (57 percent black)—were contained within a single House of Delegates' district, which was majority-black in population. (See Figure 5-2.) In the Virginia General Assembly's 1981 legislative reapportionment plan, these four majority-black counties were split up and distributed among five separate legislative districts, all majority-white.[26]

Cracking can also take place in large urban areas. In Norfolk, Virginia's largest city, the black population—which constitutes 32 percent of the city's total—is concentrated in a number of contiguous, majority-black precincts in the southern part of the city. (See Figure 5-3.) In its 1981 legislative reapportionment plan for Norfolk's two senate districts, the Virginia General Assembly bisected the black area, creating two districts which were 62 percent and 60 percent white. The assembly rejected an alternative plan proposed by Douglas Wilder, the only black member of the Virginia senate, which would have kept this black population intact and created a majority-black senatorial district.[27]

Cracking can occur in county and municipal redistricting as well. In Warren County, Mississippi, the black population is concentrated in the county seat of Vicksburg. (See Figure 5-4.) Prior to redistricting, three of the county's five supervisors' districts were entirely within the Vicksburg city limits, and all three were majority-black in population. In three successive county redistricting plans, in 1970, 1975, and 1978, the Warren County Board of Supervisors redrew the boundaries of the five supervisors' districts so that each district, like spokes of a wheel, converged on Vicksburg, and split the black population concentration up among the districts.[28]

Racial gerrymandering such as this can occur on a large scale. Between 1968 and 1980, more than half of Mississippi's eighty-two counties redrew the boundaries of their supervisors' districts to incorporate urban and rural areas in each of the five districts and split up the municipal population center—which frequently contained more than half of the county's black population—among the districts. In each of the litigated cases, the county proffered a nonracial justification contending that it was necessary to equalize each county supervisor's road and bridge maintenance responsibilities among the districts.[29] In at least twenty-two cases this type of gerrymandering was challenged in Section 5 objections or in federal district court litigation.[30] However, in some counties, such district alignments were put into effect in court-ordered plans, which are immune from Voting Rights Act scrutiny,[31] or were never challenged in court.

Stacking

Stacking is the racial gerrymandering technique in which a large minority population concentration is put together with a larger white population with the purpose or effect of depriving minority voters of a voting majority. Stacking can occur in multimember districts or single-member districts.

A classic instance of stacking was the Alabama House of Representatives redistricting plan enacted by the Alabama legislature just six weeks after the Voting Rights Act became law. In *Sims v. Baggett*,[32] an early decision in the Alabama reapportionment case, the district court declared the House plan unconstitutional

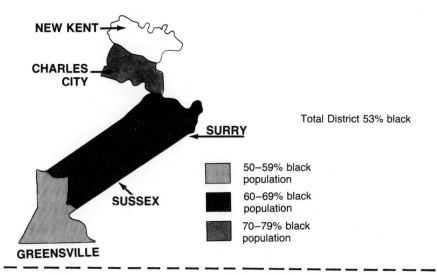

NEW KENT →

CHARLES
CITY

← SURRY

Total District 53% black

SUSSEX

GREENSVILLE

■ 50–59% black
population

■ 60–69% black
population

■ 70–79% black
population

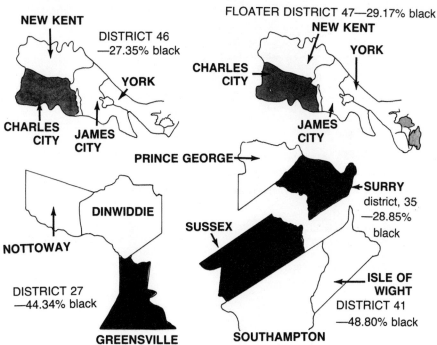

NEW KENT

DISTRICT 46
—27.35% black

YORK

CHARLES
CITY

JAMES
CITY

FLOATER DISTRICT 47—29.17% black

NEW KENT

YORK

CHARLES
CITY

JAMES
CITY

PRINCE GEORGE →

SURRY

district, 35
—28.85%
black

DINWIDDIE

SUSSEX

NOTTOWAY

ISLE OF
WIGHT

DISTRICT 27
—44.34% black

GREENSVILLE

SOUTHAMPTON

DISTRICT 41
—48.80% black

*Figure 5-2. Cracking in Virginia House of Delegates redistricting. Before redistricting
(top map), Virginia House District 45 combined four majority-black counties, and was majority-black in population. After redistricting (bottom map), District 45 was broken up, and
the majority-black counties all were placed in separate majority-white districts.*

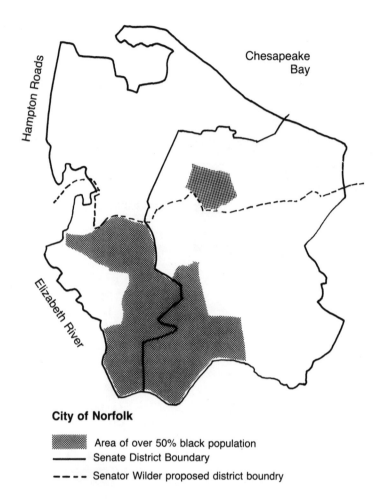

Chesapeake
Bay

Hampton Roads

Elizabeth River

City of Norfolk

Area of over 50% black population

Senate District Boundary

Senator Wilder proposed district boundry

Figure 5-3.   Cracking in Virginia State redistricting. Norfolk, Virginia senate redistrict-
ing. The black population concentration in south Norfolk was divided between two districts
in the Virginia Senate's plan (solid line). Sen. Douglas Wilder's plan, which kept this black
population concentration intact (broken line), was voted down.

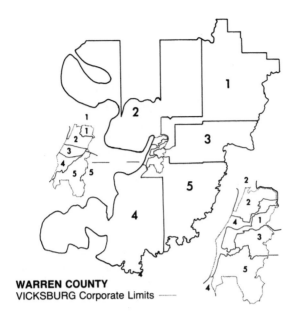

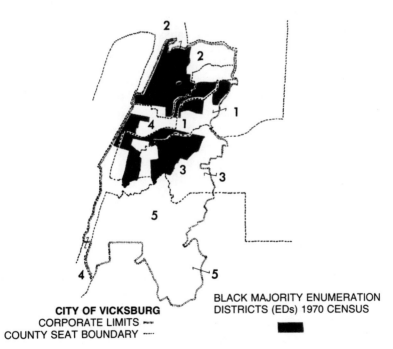

WARREN COUNTY
VICKSBURG Corporate Limits ········

CITY OF VICKSBURG
CORPORATE LIMITS ▬▬
COUNTY SEAT BOUNDARY ╍╍

BLACK MAJORITY ENUMERATION
DISTRICTS (EDs) 1970 CENSUS

*Figure 5-4. Cracking in Mississippi county redistricting. Warren County, Mississippi re-
districting. Before redistricting, there were three majority-black districts in Vicksburg (top
left). After redistricting, all five districts converged on Vicksburg (top middle and right) and
fragmented the black population concentration (bottom map).*

for one person, one vote violations, but found racial gerrymandering as well. The district court noted that Macon County (Tuskegee), a predominantly black county east of Montgomery, had almost enough population to meet the norm for an equi-populous House district. Instead of giving Macon County separate representation, the legislature combined Macon with two predominantly white counties to create a majority-white, three-member House district. Similarly, the legislature linked Bullock County, which was 71.9 percent nonwhite, with three predominantly white counties to create another multimember House district.[33] "Systematic and inten-tional dilution of Negro voting power by racial gerrymandering," the district court held," is just as discriminatory as complete disfranchisement or total segrega-tion."[34] It continued:

> In the present case, we have a situation where nonwhites have long been denied the right to vote and historically have not been represented by nonwhites in the councils of state. Historically, counties have been the voting unit, but suddenly we find without any apparent reason a number of counties that are entitled to their own representatives on a population basis aggregated, turning Negro majorities into minorities. It would be unfortunate if Alabama's Negroes were to find, just as they were about to achieve the right to vote, that that right had been abridged by racial gerrymandering.[35]

Similarly, in Mississippi, until 1979, majority-black counties were combined with predominantly white counties throughout the state in successive legislative reapportionment plans, both court ordered and legislatively enacted, to create majority-white multimember districts which denied black voters the opportunity to elect senators and representatives of their choice. (See Figure 5-5.)[36]

A more recent example involves Petersburg, Virginia, which is 61 percent black—the highest black percentage of any city in the state. (See Figure 5-6.) Be-fore legislative reapportionment in 1981, the city constituted a single House of Delegates' district. Under the 1980 Census, however, Petersburg lacked sufficient population to remain a correctly apportioned House district. Instead of combining Petersburg with adjoining majority-black areas, the Virginia legislature combined the black population concentration in Petersburg with the almost totally white ad-jacent city of Colonial Heights, turning a black majority into a black minority and creating a 56 percent white single-member House district.[37]

Packing

Packing occurs when minority populations are overconcentrated in a single dis-trict, generally at the 80 percent level and above, in excess of the percentage needed for minority voters to elect candidates of their choice. The purpose of packing is to deprive minority voters of the opportunity to obtain a voting majority (or to influence the outcome of elections) in adjoining districts. Politically, each minor-ity vote packed into the discriminatory district above the number needed to elect a minority candidate is a wasted vote.

The classic case of packing is the 1961 New York congressional redistricting plan challenged (unsuccessfully) in *Wright v. Rockefeller*.[38] The New York legis-lature packed black and Puerto Rican voters into one of four Manhattan congres-sional districts, where, combined, they comprised 86 percent of the population,

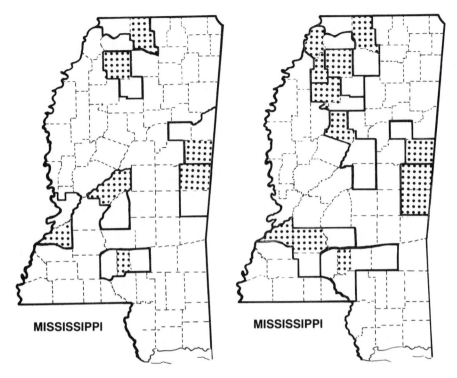

Figure 5-5. Stacking in Mississippi legislative reapportionment. 1975 Mississippi legislative reapportionment plan. Majority-black counties throughout the state were combined with majority white counties in multimember districts in both the House (left map) and Senate (right map) plans. The attorney general objected to this plan in 1975.

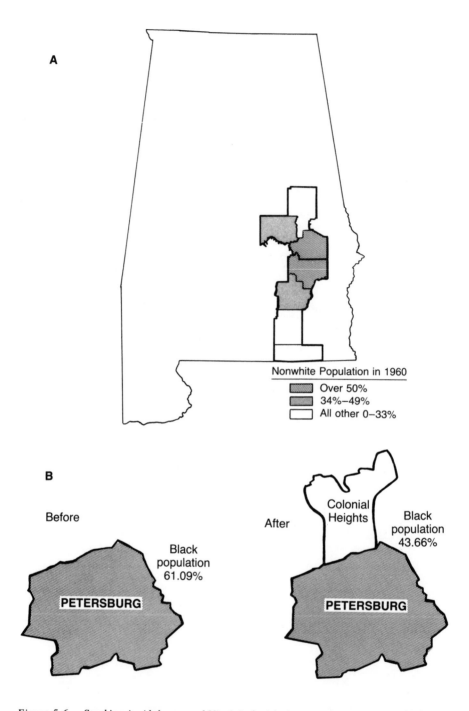

Figure 5-6. Stacking in Alabama and Virginia legislative reapportionment. A. 1965 Alabama legislative reapportionment. Heavily black counties were combined in large multi-member districts with predominantly white counties to create majority white house districts. B. 1981 Virginia legislative reapportionment. The city of Petersburg, which prior to redistricting made a complete house district which was 61 percent black, was combined with the almost all-white city of Colonial Heights, to create a new 56 percent white, single-member house district.

leaving minority voters only 29 percent, 28 percent, and 5 percent of the population in the adjoining districts. Justice Douglas, in a dissenting opinion, described the districts as follows:

> [Z]ig zag tortuous lines are drawn to concentrate Negroes and Puerto Ricans in Manhattan's Eighteenth Congressional District and practically to exclude them from the Seventeenth Congressional District. . . . The record strongly suggests that these twists and turns producing an 11-sided, step-shaped boundary between the Seventeenth and Eighteenth Districts were made to bring into the Eighteenth District and keep out of the Seventeenth as many Negroes and Puerto Ricans as possible.[39]

Packing continues to be used as a racial gerrymandering device, as the 1981 Texas congressional redistricting plan illustrates. South Texas, which includes the counties along the Rio Grande Valley and the Gulf of Mexico, experienced a substantial population growth between 1970 and 1980, and, according to the 1980 Census, the area is now 67 percent Mexican American. Because of this substantial population growth, the area, which had six congressional districts, was entitled to an additional one. Under the preexisting scheme, Mexican Americans comprised more than 65 percent of the population in two districts, and elected two Mexican American members of Congress from them.

Because of the extensive population growth, the Texas legislature could have created a third district with a substantial Mexican American majority. Instead, however, in its 1981 plan it packed Mexican Americans into new District 15, which was 80 percent Mexican American, in order to prevent them from having a substantial majority in the new District 27, which was only 53 percent Mexican American and which actually had an Anglo majority in the voting age population. The legislature rejected alternative plans which would have avoided this dilution of Mexican American voting strength. After the attorney general objected, a three-judge district court ordered into effect a plan creating three districts in South Texas with substantial Mexican American majorities of 72 percent (District 15), 71 percent (District 20), and 64 percent (District 27).[40]

Packing can also occur below 80 percent. In Virginia, there is a contiguous black population concentration in two Tidewater cities in southeast Virginia, Hampton and Newport News. The ACLU of Virginia proposed to the Virginia House of Delegates a legislative reapportionment plan which would have created two majority-black districts in these two cities. But instead, the House in January 1982 adopted a plan which packed the black concentration into one single-member district which combined portions of Hampton and Newport News and which was 75 percent black. In lodging a Section 5 objection to the plan, the attorney general found:

> Chapter 16 "packs" most of the concentrated black population of Hampton and Newport News into one 75% black district, a level which appears to be well in excess of that necessary to give black voters a fair opportunity to elect a candidate of their choice, while the remainder of the black concentration is divided among three other districts, all of which have substantial white majorities.[41]

JUDICIAL ENFORCEMENT OF
RACIAL GERRYMANDERING PROTECTIONS

At-Large Voting

Racial gerrymandering of district lines violates the Fourteenth and Fifteenth Amendments to the United States Constitution and Sections 2 and 5 of the Voting Rights Act of 1965. In court challenges to at-large elections, the Supreme Court has flip-flopped on whether proof of discriminatory intent is required to demonstrate a constitutional violation and what kind of evidence shows discriminatory intent.[42] When the issue first arose in the context of the first legislative reapportionment cases in the mid-1960s, the Supreme Court indicated that an "invidious result"[43] would be sufficient, and that multimember legislative districts could be struck down if it could be shown that

> designedly or otherwise, a multi-member constituency apportionment scheme, under the circumstances of a particular case, would operate to minimize or cancel out the voting strength of racial or political elements of the voting population.[44]

Then in two cases challenging multimember legislative districting,[45] the Court held that the mere fact that minorities were not proportionately represented does not prove a constitutional violation.

> The plaintiffs' burden is to produce evidence to support findings that the political processes leading to nomination and election were not equally open to participation by the group in question—that its members had less opportunity than did other residents in the district to participate in the political processes and to elect legislators of their choice.[46]

Utilizing this standard, the Court in *White v. Regester* held unconstitutional at-large voting for state legislators in two multimember districts in Dallas and Bexar (San Antonio) counties in Texas for dilution of black and Mexican American voting strength, respectively. The Court held that plaintiffs satisfied their burden of proving a denial of equal access to the political process on the "totality of circumstances" which showed a prior history of racial discrimination in voting, electoral mechanisms such as majority vote requirement and a "place" or post requirement which enhanced discrimination at the polls, underrepresentation of minorities, racial bloc voting, discrimination in slating, unresponsiveness of white elected officials, and the continued effects of past discrimination in education, employment, economics, health, politics, and other areas.[47]

In 1980 in *City of Mobile v. Bolden*,[48] a challenge to at-large, citywide city council elections in Mobile, Alabama, a sharply divided court held that proof of discriminatory purpose was required to prove a violation under the Constitution and Section 2 of the Voting Rights Act. In reversing two lower courts which had upheld the black voters' challenge, the Court rejected as "far from proof that the at-large electoral scheme represents purposeful discrimination,"[49] the same evidentiary factors which proved unconstitutional discrimination in *White v. Regester*.[50]

The *Bolden* decision evoked a firestorm of criticism and protest in the legal community.[51] Under *Bolden,* the burden of proving that a voting law which dilutes minority voting strength was adopted or retained for a specific discriminatory purpose is an extremely difficult, frequently impossible task. Evidence of why a particular at-large voting scheme was adopted may be lacking or inconclusive. If, as in the *Bolden* case, the system was adopted many years ago, there may be little documentary evidence showing motivation, and, as the *Birmingham* (Ala.) *Post-Herald* succinctly put it,

> many discriminatory voting and registration rules were adopted years ago by persons who are now dead. It would be a neat trick to subpoena them from their graves for testimony about their racial motivations.[52]

In most cases, legislators are unlikely to admit any racial motivations, and thus the true intent is likely to be concealed. In the absence of a "smoking gun," courts must resort to circumstantial or indirect evidence of intent. But in *Bolden,* a majority of the Court was unable to agree on the proper legal standard for determining discriminatory intent. And if a majority of the justices of the Supreme Court cannot agree on a proper legal standard for proving discriminatory intent, how is anyone to know what is required? The obligation to prove a specific discriminatory intent also maximizes judicial intrusion into the legislative process, puts state legislatures and local governing bodies on trial, and requires federal judges to label public officials "racist" in order to find a constitutional violation.

After extensive hearings, in October 1981 and June 1982, both houses of Congress, by overwhelming majorities, amended Section 2 of the Voting Rights Act of 1965 to eliminate the discriminatory intent requirement engrafted onto the statute by the *Bolden* decision. The new Section 2 of the Voting Rights Act prohibits any voting practice "imposed or applied . . . in a manner which results in a denial or abridgement of the right . . . to vote" on account of race, color, or language-minority status.[53] The Section 2 amendment did not alter the constitutional standard, however.

Two days after President Reagan signed into law the new Voting Rights Act extension bill, in July 1982, the Supreme Court in *Rogers v. Lodge,*[54] in effect reversed itself once again, ruling that "discriminatory intent need not be proven by direct evidence,"[55] and held unconstitutional at-large, countywide elections for county commissioners in Burke County, Georgia. The evidence in that case, which, according to the Court, showed intent in retaining at-large voting, was very similar to the evidence accepted by the Court in *White v. Regester,* but rejected in the *Mobile* case: blacks were a minority of the county's registered voters; "overwhelming evidence of bloc voting along racial lines"; a past history of discrimination in voting, education, political party participation, and other areas which "restricted the present opportunity of blacks effectively to participate in the political process"; evidence that "elected officials of Burke County have been unresponsive and insensitive to the needs of the black community"; "the depressed socio-economic status of Burke County blacks"; the large geographic size of the county; and a majority vote requirement, a post requirement, and lack of any district residency requirement, which enhanced "the tendency of multi-member districts to minimize the voting strength of racial minorities."[56]

The *Rogers v. Lodge* decision considerably eased the burden of proving discriminatory purpose by accepting as probative circumstantial evidence showing that minority voters are denied equal access to the political process. This eliminates the need for direct evidence showing the subjective motivation of legislators which the *City of Mobile v. Bolden* decision appeared to require. However, the *Rogers* ruling did not do away with the requirement of proving discriminatory intent to make out a constitutional violation.

The new Section 2 "results" test, on the other hand, is much more expansive in that it focuses on the results and impact of the discriminatory practice, rather than on the intent of the lawmakers. Not only is proof of discriminatory intent no longer necessary for a statutory violation, but evidence of such objective factors as a past history of official discrimination, racially polarized voting, the existence of voting practices such as majority vote and anti-single-shot requirements which discriminate against minorities, and depressed socioeconomic conditions in the minority community, in and of themselves, are sufficient to prove a Section 2 violation.[57] Whether the white elected officials are responsive to minority needs is not critical.[58]

Section 5 of the Voting Rights Act also provides a remedy for switches to at-large elections in states and localities covered by that section. In the earliest Supreme Court case interpreting the scope of the Section 5 preclearance requirement, *Allen v. State Board of Elections,*[59] the Court held that a Mississippi statute permitting county boards of supervisors to switch from district to at-large elections was a voting law change for which federal preclearance must be obtained because of its potential for diluting black voting strength:

> The right to vote can be affected by a dilution of voting power as well as by an absolute prohibition on casting a ballot. See *Reynolds* v. *Sims,* 377 U.S. 533, 555. Voters who are members of a racial minority might well be in the majority in one district, but in a decided minority in the county as a whole. This type of change could therefore nullify their ability to elect the candidate of their choice just as would prohibiting some of them from voting.

In no case subsequently has the District Court for the District of Columbia or the Supreme Court approved a change from district to at-large voting in a jurisdiction covered by Section 5. The federal courts and the Justice Department also have forced cities with at-large municipal elections to implement ward plans by refusing to preclear, under Section 5, discriminatory municipal annexations until single-member-district ward plans have been adopted.[60]

Discriminatory Line-Drawing

To date, since *Wright v. Rockefeller* in 1964, the Supreme Court has not given plenary consideration to a case alleging unconstitutional racial line-drawing in a legislatively enacted single-member redistricting plan. However, in *Connor v. Finch*[61] the Court did apply constitutional cases prohibiting dilution of minority voting strength to condemn cracking and stacking in a reapportionment plan ordered by a Mississippi district court. In addressing plaintiffs' charges that the plan impermissibly diluted black voting strength, the Court censured unexplained departures from the district court's own neutral guidelines which had "the apparent effect of scattering Negro voting concentrations among a number of white majority districts." [62]

The Court first held that the district court's plan impermissibly diluted black voting strength in Hinds County, Mississippi, by unnecessarily fragmenting a black population concentration in the city of Jackson. In Hinds County, 69 percent of the county's black population (1970 Census) was concentrated in forty-eight contiguous, majority-black Census enumeration districts in the central-city portion of Jackson. In 1969, and again in 1975, the county board of supervisors drew five supervisors' districts for the election of county officials which split up this heavy black population concentration, and the Mississippi district court decided to use these five county supervisors' districts (sometimes called "beats") as senatorial districts in its state senate plan.

The Supreme Court criticized this cracking of black votes through

> five oddly shaped beats that extend from the far corners of the county in long corridors that fragment the City of Jackson, where much of the Negro population is concentrated.

The Court indicated that although the supervisors' districts were assertedly drawn to equalize the responsibilities of the county supervisors in road and bridge construction and maintenance, those justifications were "irrelevant to the problem of apportioning State Senate seats." Given that there was no state policy of beat representation in the state legislature, there was no justification for the district court's decision to use the discriminatory Hinds County supervisors' districts for state senatorial districting.

The Supreme Court also criticized stacking, which unnecessarily combined black population concentrations with more populous white concentrations to create legislative districts with white voting majorities. Claiborne County, majority-black, was combined with Lincoln County, majority-white, and Beat 3 of Copiah County, also majority-white, "to make a white majority senatorial district." Similarly, majority-black Jefferson County, which is contiguous with Claiborne, was combined with four supervisors' districts in an adjoining majority-white county, Adams, "to make an irregularly shaped senatorial district with a slight Negro voting-age majority." The plaintiffs' alternative plan, which would have placed Claiborne and Jefferson together in a single district with Copiah County to create a compact senate district with 55 percent black voting age population, was rejected without explanation.

The Court held that all these elements—unexplained departures from the district court's own neutral guidelines, the fragmentation and dilution of black voting strength, the distorted shapes of the districts, and the rejection of alternative plans which would have avoided this dilution—were probative of intentional racial discrimination and led "to a charge that the departures are explicable only in terms of a purpose to minimize the voting strength of a minority group."

Connor v. Finch is the leading Supreme Court case invalidating a legislative reapportionment plan for racial gerrymandering of single-member legislative districts. In a number of cases, lower federal courts have held redistricting plans unconstitutional for cracking[63] and stacking.[64]

Cases brought pursuant to Section 5 of the Voting Rights Act differ from cases alleging unconstitutional discrimination in several important respects. In constitutional cases, states or local jurisdictions have enacted and already implemented the redistricting plan challenged by aggrieved minority voters. Under Section 5, however, redistricting plans enacted by states or localities cannot be implemented until federal preclearance already has been obtained. Hence, Section 5 cases are filed by states or other political subdivisions as plaintiffs against the United States or the attorney general, and aggrieved minority voters may intervene in these actions to protect their right to a nondiscriminatory plan. In cases alleging a constitutional deprivation, the minority voter plaintiffs have the burden of proving that the challenged plan was enacted or maintained for a racially discriminatory purpose; discriminatory effect alone is not sufficient. But in Section 5 lawsuits, the state or political subdivision has the burden of proving that its proposed reapportionment plan does not have a racially discriminatory purpose or effect.[65] Federal court jurisdiction for Section 5 preclearance cases is limited by the Voting Rights Act to the District Court for the District of Columbia, with a direct appeal to the Supreme Court.

In Section 5 cases, the District Court for the District of Columbia has refused to approve reapportionment plans which unnecessarily combine black population concentrations with more populous white concentrations or which split up black population concentrations with the purpose or effect of diluting black voting strength. In the most recent decision, *Busbee v. Smith,*[66] involving the 1981 Georgia congressional redistricting plan, the district court found that the black population in the Atlanta area was concentrated in one contiguous band stretching across the southern portion of Atlanta and Fulton County to south central DeKalb County, south of an east-west racial boundary line formed by the Southern Railroad line in Fulton and North Avenue in Atlanta. The Georgia General Assembly rejected proposed districts which corresponded to this racial boundary, and instead, enacted a plan with districts running north and south, combining portions of the black concentration with predominantly white areas of north Fulton and DeKalb counties. The District Court ruled:

> In this case, the state fragmented the large and contiguous black population that exists in the metropolitan area of Atlanta between two Congressional districts, thus minimizing the possibility of electing a black to the Congress in the Fifth Congressional District.

On the basis of this effect, together with statements of the chairman of the House Reapportionment Committee that ''I'm not for drawing a nigger district,'' the district court concluded that the plan was drawn for a racially discriminatory purpose.

In the Warren County, Mississippi, county redistricting case, *Donnell v. United States,*[67] the Supreme Court summarily affirmed a district court decision denying Section 5 preclearance to a plan which split up and dispersed the black population concentration at Vicksburg, which formerly was contained intact within majority-black districts.

In only one Section 5 case, *Beer v. United States,*[68] has the Supreme Court allowed preclearance of a plan which split up black population concentration. In the *Beer* case, the attorney general objected to a New Orleans city redistricting plan that split up black neighborhoods—which form a curving east-west band through central New Orleans—among five districts. The district court also disapproved the plan, but the Supreme Court reversed by a vote of five to three, the majority interpreting the Section 5 "effect" standard as merely protecting minority voters from voting changes which would diminish their voting strength:

> In other words, the purpose of § 5 has always been to insure that no voting-procedure changes would be made that would lead to a retrogression in the position of racial minorities with respect to their effective exercise of the electoral franchise.[69]

Under the prior 1961 plan, none of the five districts had a clear black registered majority, while the proposed plan, despite this slicing up of black neighborhoods, gave blacks a registered majority in one district and a population majority—but not a registered majority—in another. Thus, the Supreme Court reasoned, the plan offered the opportunity for the election of one and possibly two blacks to the city council, and could not be considered to have a discriminatory effect under this retrogression standard.

The Supreme Court's *Beer* decision dealt minority voting rights a severe setback. Under the *Beer* retrogression standard, if the prior plan is 90 percent discriminatory, and the new plan is only 80 percent discriminatory, the new plan must be precleared (in the absence of evidence of discriminatory purpose) because it constitutes a 10 percent enhancement of black voting strength and is not retrogressive. The apparent basis of this retrogression holding may have been the Court's fear that Section 5 could be interpreted to require racial quotas or proportional representation. The district court, having established a numerical test for judging redistricting plans, calculated that blacks, on the basis of their percentage of the registered voters, should be able to elect 2.42 of the city's seven council members, and on the basis of their percentage of the city's population, 3.15 council members.[70]

In subsequent cases, however, the Supreme Court has summarily affirmed district court decisions which have ameliorated a strict application of this *Beer* retrogression standard. In *Wilkes County v. United States,* the district court with the approval of the Supreme Court held that if the prior plan is severely malapportioned, it should not be used as a benchmark for measuring retrogression and

> it is appropriate, in measuring the effect of the voting changes, to compare the voting changes with options for properly apportioned single-member districts.[71]

In *Mississippi v. United States,*[72] the district court, again with Supreme Court endorsement, held that the discriminatory effect of a new single-member-district plan cannot be measured by comparing it with a prior, racially discriminatory multimember district plan which diluted black voting strength. Instead, the district court used as the benchmark for measuring retrogression a nondiscriminatory court-ordered single-member-district legislative reapportionment plan.

Recently, the district court in the Mississippi Section 5 congressional redistricting case held that any prior plan not subjected to Section 5 preclearance on the merits would probably not be an adequate benchmark for measuring whether a new, proposed plan diminished existing levels of minority voting strength:

> It is very doubtful that an apportionment plan never reviewed on the merits under Section 5 and which in fact is retrogressive compared to the districting scheme in effect on the effective date of the Voting Rights Act can ever serve as a firm benchmark for the purpose of measuring the possible discriminatory effect of subsequent plans.[73]

Supreme Court and lower court decisions generally have recognized the discriminatory impact of the racial gerrymandering techniques of at-large elections, cracking, and stacking, and have struck down voting schemes and reapportionment plans which diluted minority voting strength, both in constitutional and Section 5 cases. In each of these cases submergence of minority voting strength in at-large districts, and cracking and stacking characteristics, were an essential element of the court's holding, although these factors were not entirely sufficient, in and of themselves, to invalidate the plan. In voting rights litigation, more has to be proven than simply the discriminatory effect of the challenged plan. However, in constitutional cases, as the Supreme Court's recent decision in *Rogers v. Lodge* demonstrates, the discriminatory impact of a challenged plan "bear[s] heavily on the issue of purposeful discrimination."[74] While the Supreme Court has not recently addressed the "packing" issue, several reapportionment plans have been objected to by the attorney general under Section 5 which have employed packing to dilute minority voting strength, and those Section 5 objections provide important precedents for the courts to use in future litigation.

CURRENT ISSUES IN RACIAL
GERRYMANDERING LITIGATION

The increased use of computers has brought about a technological revolution in the legislative reapportionment process. With computers, it is now possible in any state or locality to draw numerous, even hundreds, of legislative reapportionment plans which meet the one person, one vote standard with total deviations of less than 5 percent or even 1 percent. Given the large number of plans to choose from, the challenge in the 1980s for the courts and persons involved in legislative reapportionment is to develop objective and nondiscriminatory standards for selection of the "best" plan among the wide range of choices. The courts will now be compelled, more than ever before, to develop strict antidiscrimination guidelines governing legislative reapportionment.

The reapportionment litigation of the 1980s is likely to raise several fundamental issues for definitive resolution: What is dilution of minority voting strength? Are minorities better off spread around and having a significant influence in the election of a number of white officials, or concentrated in a few districts where they can elect candidates of their choice? Is it sufficient to create districts in which minority voters are 50 percent or more in a district, or does the minority population percentage have to be higher to give minorities a chance to elect their own officials? What remedial action is required in vote dilution cases, and what restrictions limit the remedies available?

The Vote Dilution Principle

Increasingly, states and political subdivisions have attempted to justify their racial gerrymandering efforts—whether at-large voting or discriminatory line drawing—with the rationalization that minorities are better off having influence in several white majority districts in the election of white officials than having one or a few black- or Hispanic-majority districts in which minorities can elect candidates of their choice. For example, in the Mississippi congressional redistricting case, described before, state legislators justified fragmentation of black voting strength in the majority-black Delta area with the argument that a congressional redistricting plan with two districts which were at least 40 percent or more black was preferable to a plan which created one district with a significant black majority, because the former plan would give black voters significant influence in at least two districts, while the latter plan would give them influence in only one.[75] Similarly, state officials in Virginia in the 1981 legislative reapportionment litigation attempted to defend discriminatory multimember districts for the Virginia House of Delegates by arguing that in two-member or four-member districts, black voters would have influence over the entire legislative delegation, while in single-member, majority-black districts, black voter influence would be less.[76]

The history of legislative gerrymandering, and the racial gerrymandering examples previously discussed in which legislative redistricting plans have been struck down by the courts or objected to under the Voting Rights Act, show that such explanations generally are after-the-fact rationalizations for dilution of minority voting strength. Submerging minority voting strength by spreading minority voters around among several majority-white districts or by at-large voting schemes is, in fact, the hallmark of racial gerrymandering.

However, there have been instances in which minority voters have requested legislative officials, for strategic reasons, to create two or more high-influence districts, rather than a district in which minorities would be a substantial majority. This apparently happened in the recent Texas congressional redistricting in order to preserve the reelection chances of two white liberal members of Congress from the Dallas area.[77] The question then arises, how can one distinguish when such redistricting is discriminatory, and when it is benign? The preferences of the minority community may not always be controlling, since in some instances opinions in the minority community may be mixed, and the desires of minorities may not always be determinative of a constitutional violation.

An important test is whether or not racial bloc voting exists. This test is wholly objective and can be determined by the voting statistics. Racial bloc voting shows the degree to which the minority community is politically isolated and unable to elect candidates of its choice to public office. If there is racial bloc voting, at-large election schemes and redistricting plans which dilute and fragment minority voting strength in majority-white districts render minority voters politically powerless.

Minorities are both unable to elect their choices to office and unable to form coalitions with whites for the election of candidates favored by the minority community. Further, white officials are free to ignore the needs and interests of the minority community, since white voters control the elections. Minority voters, as one court put it, are "frozen into permanent political minorities destined for constant defeat at the hands of the controlling political majorities."[78]

The importance of racial bloc voting proof in determining whether a given districting scheme is unconstitutionally discriminatory has been recognized by the Supreme Court. In *Rogers v. Lodge,*[79] in which the Supreme Court struck down at-large, countywide voting in Burke County, Georgia, Justice White, writing for the majority, held:

> Voting along racial lines allows those elected to ignore black interests without fear of political consequences, and without bloc voting the minority candidates would not lose elections solely because of their race.[80]

The 65 Percent Rule

Another technique legislators have attempted to utilize to discriminate against minority voters is the disguised majority-white district. Legislators will enact a plan with a district which is 53 percent or 54 percent minority, and then contend that they have not discriminated because they have devised a majority-black or majority-Hispanic district.

The statistical reality in most parts of the country is that such a district is simply not sufficient to give minority voters an opportunity to elect candidates of their choice to office. The facts of the Hinds County (Jackson), Mississippi, redistricting case are illustrative.[81] Prior to county redistricting, blacks—who constituted almost 40 percent of the county's population—had substantial majorities of 76 percent and 68 percent in two of the five supervisors' districts. The county board of supervisors redistricted itself in 1969, sliced up the black concentration in the Jackson central city, and created five districts, all of which were majority-white. This plan was held unconstitutional for excessive malapportionment based on 1970 Census data, and the board of supervisors drew a new plan in 1973 in which blacks had slight population majorities of 54 percent and 53 percent in two of the five districts. (See Table 5-2.) The board argued that this plan could not be considered discriminatory because it provided two majority-black supervisors' districts.

Although total population statistics are the proper measure of numerical malapportionment in the one person, one vote cases, other vote dilution cases must measure actual minority voting strength to determine whether minority voters have been discriminated against.[82] The board's argument failed to account for white-black disparities between total population, on the one hand, and voting-age population, registered voters, and turnout, on the other.

Census statistics showed that 68 percent of the total white population—two out of every three white persons—were of voting age, compared with only 55 percent of the total black population, or slightly more than one out of every two. Consequently, the black voting-age population for each of the five districts was

approximately five percentage points less than the total black percentage, and the white voting-age population was approximately five percentage points more than the total white percentage. The two districts which were 54 percent and 53 percent black in total population were actually majority-white in voting-age population.

Further, registration statistics showed that 63 percent of the white voting-age population was registered to vote, compared with only 49 percent for blacks. Also, historically, turnout among black voters had been disproportionately lower than white turnout. Some have argued that voter registration and turnout disparities should not be considered because, as a result of the Voting Rights Act, there are no current barriers to black registration, and therefore these disparities can only be due to apathy. However, as the testimony in this case and others has indicated, these disparities are directly attributable to the extensive history of past discrimination, including purposeful denial to blacks of the opportunity to register and vote, and depressed socioeconomic conditions in the black community which limit electoral participation and are also the direct result of past discrimination.[83] In addition, low turnout may result from alienation of eligible black voters caused by past exclusion and racial gerrymandering, giving rise to the perception that these official, continuing barriers and continued racial bloc voting have made black political participation futile. As a result of registration disparities, the percentage of black registered voters in these two majority-black supervisors' districts was approximately five to six points lower than the black voting-age population percentages, and the reverse was true for the white voter registration percentages.

Altogether, the differences between the black population percentage and the black registered-voter percentage of these five districts ranged from 8 points to 12 points. Generally, the blacker the district, the greater the difference. The result was that District 2, whose total population was 53 percent black, was actually 58 percent white in registered voters, and District 5, whose total population was 54 percent black, was 58 percent white in registered voters.

The turnout differences were difficult to quantify in the same way because there were no reliable turnout statistics by race. The expert witnesses who testified in this case estimated that black turnout was at least 3 to 4 percent lower than white turnout.

Accordingly, as a result of these factors, the expert witnesses for the black voter plaintiffs estimated that in order for black voters to have an equal opportunity, or a fifty-fifty chance to elect candidates of their choice, the districts would have to be at least 65 percent black in total population or 60 percent black in voting age population. These estimates were actually confirmed in this case. The 1973 plan was struck down by the Court of Appeals for the Fifth Circuit for unconstitutional discrimination, and the board of supervisors was ordered to devise a new plan. This new plan provided two districts in which black persons were more than 65 percent of the population, and in the 1979 county elections two black county supervisors, two black justices of the peace, and two black constables were elected to county office, the first elected black officials in Hinds County since Reconstruction.

The principles embodied in this case have come to be known as the "65 percent rule." In areas with a past history of racial discrimination affecting the right to vote, and with strict patterns of racial bloc voting, minorities frequently must constitute at least 65 percent of the population or 60 percent of the voting age population of districts in order to have an equal opportunity to elect candidates of their choice. This 65 percent rule has been endorsed by the courts,[84] and accepted by the Justice Department as a rule of thumb in reviewing Section 5 submissions.[85] Contrary to what some have charged, it is not overreaching and does not embody any form of racial preference for minority voters. Rather, it is empirically based and confirmed by the statistical data in case after case.

The Remedy Issue

Having found a constitutional or statutory violation in a particular at-large voting scheme or redistricting plan, or faced with a Section 5 objection and imminent elections, what is a court supposed to do by way of providing a remedy? Some have argued that courts should limit themselves to ordering redistricting authorities to devise a new racially neutral, color-blind redistricting plan. This argument derives from the view that all the Constitution and laws require is racially neutral, color-blind election systems and that any race-conscious remedy violates basic societal values.

The fundamental defect in this argument is that a racially neutral remedy may be no remedy at all. Any redistricting plan drawn without regard to the location of minority population concentrations—whether by legislative bodies or by the courts themselves—may be just as discriminatory as a conscious gerrymander. For example, the 1973 Hinds County, Mississippi, county redistricting plan, described previously, was ordered into effect by the district court as a judicial remedy for a prior, unconstitutionally malapportioned plan and had all the characteristics of an intentional racial gerrymander. Yet both the district court and the court of appeals concluded that the plan was "racially neutral" in intent,[86] drawn to equalize the county supervisors' road and bridge construction and maintenance responsibilities among the districts, and not to discriminate. Nevertheless, the Fifth Circuit held it unconstitutional because, by fragmenting black voting strength, it perpetuated a past intentional denial to blacks of equal access to the political process.[87]

Furthermore, court orders directing state or local political bodies to produce a race-neutral plan may simply be unrealistic. Any politician who has campaigned for political office knows exactly where the minority population in his or her district lives. He or she doesn't have to have racial census data to know this. To expect these politicians to close their eyes to the important fact of minority population locations is like asking someone not to think of a pink elephant.

In *Connor v. Finch*,[88] the leading Supreme Court decision establishing judicial guidelines governing court-ordered legislative redistricting plans, the Court specifically directed district courts to devise remedial plans which avoid vote dilution through cracking and stacking of black population concentrations. This cannot be accomplished without first identifying the areas of minority vote concentrations, and by drawing district lines in such a manner to avoid fragmenting these concentrations or unnecessarily combining them with white concentrations.

In most instances, to remedy vote dilution, courts must create election districts in which minorities constitute 65 percent or more of the population, or 60 percent or more of the voting age population, to give minority voters the opportunity to elect representatives of their choice. Many federal judges, particularly conservative district judges in the South, are reluctant to do this, and call it reverse gerrymandering.

However, in *United Jewish Organizations v. Carey,*[89] the Supreme Court, by a vote of seven to one, with only Chief Justice Burger dissenting, held that devising 65 percent nonwhite majority districts to remedy a Section 5 objection to a legislative reapportionment plan does not violate Fourteenth or Fifteenth Amendment guarantees. Although that case directly involved remedial action of the New York State legislature to satisfy the Justice Department's Section 5 objection, the Court's reasoning also is applicable to court-ordered remedial redistricting plans as well.

Compliance with the Voting Rights Act itself often necessitates the use of racial criteria in drawing district lines. Once a state or local jurisdiction has been found guilty of diminishing existing levels of minority voting strength, regardless of motivation, the covered jurisdiction must carve out large enough nonwhite-majority districts and increase the percentage of black voters in those districts to satisfy the act's requirements.

Further, in devising such districts, the court or legislative body must determine how large the minority percentage must be in order to satisfy the Voting Rights Act, or in the constitutional case, the constitutional requirements. If the district court determines that a challenged plan is unconstitutional because it denies minority voters the opportunity to elect candidates of their choice, then in order to provide an effective remedy, it must devise a plan which does allow minorities to elect their choices to office. In most instances, this requires the creation of 65 percent nonwhite districts. Otherwise, the court will supplant a plan which denies minorities the opportunity to elect candidates with another one which does the same thing. If the creation of 65 percent nonwhite districts were barred, on grounds of reverse gerrymandering or for some other reason, the minority voters would be left without any effective remedy for unlawful dilution of their voting strength.

Using race conscious remedies in redistricting does not stigmatize the minority community in the same way as does the use of racial criteria in other contexts, as when minorities are fenced out of particular districts because of race. In this instance the use of racial criteria is benign and beneficial to the minority community because it enhances their voting strength. Furthermore, the creation of 65 percent minority districts does not discriminate against whites or unfairly dilute their voting strength as a group so long as the percentage of white-majority districts approximates the percentage of whites in the population.

The critics of the *United Jewish Organizations* decision frequently overlook that the creation of three Brooklyn senate districts and six assembly districts which were over 65 percent nonwhite still left whites, who constituted 65 percent of the Kings County population, in the majority in 70 percent of the county's legislative districts.[90] Thus, the Supreme Court concluded that even if there was racial bloc voting, "whites would not be underrepresented relative to their share of the population."[91]

In individual districts where non-white majorities were increased to approximately 65%, it became more likely, given racial bloc voting, that black candidates would be elected instead of their white opponents, and it became less likely that white voters would be represented by a member of their own race; but as long as whites in Kings County, as a group, were provided with fair representation, we cannot conclude that there was a cognizable discrimination against whites or an abridgement of their right to vote on grounds of race.[92]

White voters in 65 percent nonwhite districts are in no worse position than minority voters in majority-white districts.

CONCLUSION

Mere access to the ballot does not ensure that minorities will be accorded the opportunity to participate effectively in the electoral processes. At-large election schemes and discriminatory redistricting remain prime weapons for minimizing and cancelling out the voting strength of minority voters. By extending the Voting Rights Act, and by enacting the new Section 2 "results" test, Congress has preserved and expanded the statutory protections against dilution of minority voting strength.

Enforcement of these protections, however, remains a problem. In some instances, the courts have been insensitive to vote dilution claims. The Reagan Administration's retreats from active enforcement of voting rights guarantees[93] mean that most lawsuits to enforce these protections will have to be brought by disadvantaged minority voters, who frequently are not able to bear the financial costs of expensive voting rights litigation. Racial gerrymandering strikes at the heart of our electoral processes and must be eliminated on all fronts if the democratic goal of full and effective participation by all citizens in government is to be achieved.

NOTES

1. Robert Luce, *Legislative Principles* (DaCapo Press: New York, 1971), 396.
2. Ibid., 397–398.
3. Ibid., 399; see also *Encyclopedia of Social Sciences* (Macmillan Co.: New York, 1931), 6: 638.
4. *Encyclopedia of Social Sciences*, 638.
5. Luce, *Legislative Principles*, 398.
6. 377 U.S. 533 (1964).
7. 377 U.S. at 565.
8. Robert G. Dixon, Jr., *Democratic Representation: Reapportionment in Law and Politics* (Oxford University Press: New York, 1968), 22.
9. 364 U.S. 339 (1960).
10. Quoted in *Perkins v. Matthews*, 400 U.S. 379, 389 (1971).
11. *Yick Wo v. Hopkins*, 118 U.S. 356, 370 (1886).
12. See, e.g., *Bolden v. City of Mobile*, 423 F. Supp. 384, 389–92 (S.D. Ala. 1976); Lawyers' Committee for Civil Rights Under Law, *Voting in Mississippi* (Washington, D.C.: 1981), 28–31, 102–111.
13. Dixon, *Democratic Representation*, 460.
14. See, e.g., *Encyclopedia of Social Sciences*, 638; *Reynolds v. Sims*, 377 U.S. at 578–79.

15. Dixon, *Democratic Representation*, 460–461.
16. Frank R. Parker, "County Redistricting in Mississippi: Case Studies in Racial Gerrymandering," *Mississippi Law Journal* 44 (1973): 391 ff. The terms "cracking," "stacking," and "packing" were first coined in a nonracial context of population malapportionment and urban gerrymandering by Gus Tyler in "Court versus Legislature: The Socio-Politics of Malapportionment," *Law and Contemporary Problems* 27 (1962): 390, 400.
17. *Voting in Mississippi*, 27.
18. Council of State Governments, "Apportionment of the Legislatures," *The Book of the States, 1968–69*, vol. 17 (Chicago, Ill.: 1969), 66–67.
19. See *White v. Regester*, 412 U.S. 755, 765–70 (1973) (Texas); *Sims v. Amos*, 336 F. Supp. 924, 936 (M.D. Ala.) (1972) (three-judge court), *aff'd mem.*, 409 U.S. 942 (1972) (Alabama); *Bussie v. Governor of Louisiana*, 333 F. Supp. 452, 454 (E.D. La.) (1971), *modif'd and aff'd*, 457 F.2d 796 (5th Cir. 1972), *vac'd and remanded on other grounds sub nom.* McKeithen 407 F. Supp. 191 (1972) (Louisiana); *Mississippi v. United States*, 490 F. Supp. 569 (D.D.C. 1979) (three-judge court), *aff'd*, 444 U.S. 1050 (1980). Multimember district schemes were objected to by the Attorney General under Section 5 of the Voting Rights Act for racial discrimination in Georgia (see *Georgia v. United States*, 411 U.S. 526 (1973)), Louisiana, Mississippi, and South Carolina (*but see Morris v. Gressette*, 432 U.S. 491 (1977). U.S. Department of Justice, *Complete Listing of Objections Pursuant to Section 5 of the Voting Rights Act of 1965*, February, 1981.
20. Chandler Davidson and George Korbel, "At Large Elections and Minority Group Representation: A Reexamination of Historical and Contemporary Evidence," *Journal of Politics* 43 (1981): 982-1,005; Richard L. Engstrom and Michael D. McDonald, "The Election of Blacks to City Councils: Clarifying the Impact of Electoral Arrangements on the Seats/Population Relationship," *American Political Science Review* 75 (1981): 344–54; Delbert Taebel, "Minority Representation on City Councils," *Social Science Quarterly* 59 (1978): 143–52; Theodore P. Robinson and Thomas R. Dye, "Reformism and Black Representation on City Councils," *Social Science Quarterly* 59 (1978): 133–41; Albert K. Karnig, "Black Representation on City Councils," *Urban Affairs Quarterly* 12 (1976): 223–43; Clinton B. Jones, "The Impact of Local Election Systems on Black Political Representation," *Urban Affairs Quarterly* 11 (1976): 345–56.
21. Laughlin McDonald, *Voting Rights in the South* (American Civil Liberties Union: Atlanta, 1982), 40–43.
22. Southwest Voter Registration Education Project, *Survey of Chicano Representation in 361 Texas Public School Boards, 1979–80* (San Antonio, 1981), 7.
23. Heywood T. Sanders, "Government Structure in American Cities," *The Municipal Year Book 1979* (Washington, D.C.: International City Management Association, 1979), 99.
24. Michael S. Deeb, *Election and Composition of City and Town Councils in Virginia* (Virginia Municipal League: Richmond, 1977), 36.
25. Section 5 objection letter from William Bradford Reynolds, Assistant Attorney General in charge of the Civil Rights Division, U.S. Department of Justice to Jerris Leonard, attorney for the State of Mississippi, 20 March 1982; briefs filed on behalf of Henry J. Kirksey, et al., defendants-intervenors, in opposition to state's motion for partial summary judgment, *Mississippi v. Smith*, 541 F. Supp. 1329 (D.D.C. 1982) (three-judge court), *appeal dism'd*, 103 S. Ct. 1888 (1983).
26. Section 5 objection letter from Reynolds to Perkins Wilson, Virginia Assistant Attorney General 31 July 1981; Plaintiffs' Trial Memorandum of Law, *Elam v. Dalton* consolidated with *Cosner v. Dalton*, 522 F. Supp. 350 (E.D. Va. 1981) (three-judge court).
27. Section 5 objection letter from James P. Turner, Acting Assistant Attorney General, U.S. Department of Justice, to Perkins Wilson, 17 July 1981; Plaintiffs' Trial Memorandum of Law, *Elam v. Dalton*.

28. *Donnell v. United States,* Civil No. 78-0392 (D.D.C. 31 July 1979) (three-judge court) *aff'd,* 444 U.S. 1059 (1980).
29. E.g., *Donnell v. United States.*
30. Lawyers' Committee, *Voting in Mississippi,* 49–50.
31. *Connor v. Johnson,* 402 U.S. 690 (1971).
32. 247 F. Supp. 96 (M.D. Ala. 1965) (three-judge court).
33. 247 F. Supp. at 107, 109.
34. 247 F. Supp. at 109.
35. Ibid.
36. Lawyers' Committee, *Voting in Mississippi,* 19–27.
37. Section 5 objection letter from Reynolds to Perkins Wilson, 31 July 1981; Plaintiffs' Trial Memorandum of Law, *Elam v. Dalton.*
38. 376 U.S. 52 (1964).
39. 376 U.S. at 60–61 (dissenting opinion).
40. Section 5 objection letter from Reynolds to David Dean, Texas Secretary of State, 29 January 1982; *Seamon v. Upham,* 536 F. Supp. 931 (E.D. Tex. 1982) (three-judge court), *rev'd on other grounds sub nom. Upham v. Seamon,* 456 U.S. 37, 71 L.Ed.2d 725 (1982), *on remand,* 536 F. Supp. 1030 (E.D. Tex. 1982).
41. Section 5 objection letter from Reynolds to Gerald L. Baliles, Virginia Attorney General, 12 March 1982.
42. See, e.g., S. Rep. No. 97-417, 97th Cong., 2d Sess., 19–27 (1982) (Senate Judiciary Committee Report on the extension of the Voting Rights Act); Frank R. Parker, "The Impact of *City of Mobile v. Bolden* and Strategies and Legal Arguments for Voting Rights Cases in Its Wake," in Rockefeller Foundation, *The Right to Vote* (Rockefeller Foundation: New York, 1981), 98–125.
43. *Burns v. Richardson,* 384 U.S. 73, 88 (1966).
44. 384 U.S. at 88; *Fortson v. Dorsey,* 379 U.S. 433, 439 (1965).
45. *Whitcomb v. Chavis,* 403 U.S. 124 (1971); *White v. Regester,* 412 U.S. 755 (1973).
46. 412 U.S. at 766–67.
47. 412 U.S. at 767–69.
48. 466 U.S. 55 (1980).
49. 466 U.S. at 74.
50. 466 U.S. at 73–74.
51. See, e.g., "The Supreme Court, 1980 Term," *Harvard Law Review* 95 (1980): 91, 138; Comment, "*City of Mobile v. Bolden:* A Setback in the Fight Against Discrimination," *Brooklyn Law Review* 47 (1980): 169; Note, "*City of Mobile v. Bolden:* Voter Dilution and New Intent Requirements under the Fifteenth and Fourteenth Amendments, *Houston Law Review* 18 (1981): 611; Hearings on the Extension of the Voting Rights Act of 1965 Before the Subcomm. on the Constitution of the Senate Comm. on the Judiciary, 97th Cong., 2d Sess. (1982).
52. Editorial, 13 November 1981, *Birmingham Post-Herald.*
53. Public Law No. 97-205, §3, 96 Stat. 134 (29 June 1982) (to be codified at 42 U.S.C. § 1973).
54. 458 U.S. 613 (1982).
55. 458 U.S. at 618.
56. 458 U.S. at 623–27.
57. S. Rep. No. 97-417, 97th Cong., 2d Sess., pp. 29–29 (1982).
58. Ibid., 29 n. 116.
59. 393 U.S. 544, 569 (1969).
60. *City of Petersburg, Virginia v. United States,* 354 F. Supp. 1021 (D.D.C. 1972), *aff'd mem.,* 410 U.S. 962 (1973); *City of Richmond, Virginia v. United States,* 422 U.S. 358 (1975).
61. 431 U.S. 407 (1977).
62. 431 U.S. at 421–26.
63. See, e.g., *Kirksey v. Board of Supervisors of Hinds County, Mississippi,* 554 F.2d 139, 151 (5th Cir. 1977) *(en banc), cert. denied,* 434 U.S. 968 (1977) ("By frag-

menting a geographically concentrated but substantial black minority in a community where bloc voting has been a way of political life, the plan will cancel or minimize the voting strength of the black minority and will tend to submerge the interests of the black community.''); *Robinson v. Commissioners Court, Anderson County,* 505 F.2d 674, 676 (5th Cir. 1974) ''Here we are confronted with a county Commissioners Court which has cut the county's black community into three illogical parts in order to dilute the black vote in precinct elections, acting as a modern Caesar dissecting its private Gaul. Such apportionment poisons our representatives democracy at its roots. Our constitution cannot abide it.''); *Moore v. Leflore County Bd. of Election Comm'rs,* 361 F. Supp. 603, 604 (N.D. Miss. 1972), *aff'd* 502 F.2d 621 (5th Cir. 1974) (invalidated plan ''utilized narrow corridors to bring into southwest Greenwood the lines of four districts (Beats 1, 2, 3 and 5), whereby the concentrations of black residents heretofore in Beat 3 were borken up and placed in those several districts'').

64. E.g., *Sims v. Baggett.*
65. *City of Rome v. United States* 446 U.S. 156, 172 (1980).
66. 549 F. Supp. 494 (D.D.C. 1982) (three-judge court). *Aff'd mem.,* 103 S. Ct. 809 (1983).
67. Civil No. 78-0392 (D.D.C. 31 July 1979) (three-judge court), *aff'd mem.,* 444 U.S. 1059 (1980).
68. 425 U.S. 130 (1976).
69. 425 U.S. at 141.
70. 374 F. Supp. 363 (D.D.C. 1974), *rev'd,* 425 U.S. 130 (1976).
71. 450 F. Supp. 1171, 1178 (D.D.C. 1978) (three-judge court), *aff'd mem.,* 439 U.S. 99 (1978).
72. 490 F. Supp. 569, 582 (D.D.C. 1979) (three-judge court), *aff'd mem.,* 444 U.S. 1050 (1980).
73. *Mississippi v. Smith,* 541 F. Supp. 1329, 1332 (D.D.C. 1982) (three-judge court), *appeal dism'd,* 103 S. Ct. 1888 (1983).
74. 458 U.S. at 623.
75. See *Jordan v. Winter,* 541 F. Supp. 1135, 1143 (N.D. Miss. 1982) (three-judge court), *vacated and remanded,* 103 S. Ct. 2077 (1983).
76. Frank R. Parker, ''The Virginia Legislative Reapportionment Case: Reapportionment Issues of the 1980s,'' *George Mason University Law Review* 5 (1982): 43.
77. *Upham v. Seamon,* 456 U.S. at 39–40.
78. *Graves v. Barnes,* 373 F. Supp. 704, 732 (W.D. Tex. 1972) *aff'd sub nom. White v. Regester,* 412 U.S. 755 (1973).
79. 458 U.S. 613 (1982).
80. 458 U.S. at 623.
81. *Kirksey v. Board of Supervisors of Hinds County, Mississippi,* 402 F. Supp. 658 (S.D. Miss. 1975), *rev'd,* 554 F.2d 139 (5th Cir. 1977) *(en banc), cert. denied,* 434 U.S. 968 (1977).
82. *City of Rome v. United States,* 446 U.S. 156, 186–87 and n. 22 (1980); *Kirksey v. Board of Supervisors,* 554 F.2d at 149–50; *Moore v. Leflore County Board of Election Commissioners,* 502 F.2d 621, 624 (5th Cir. 1974); *Zimmer v. McKeithen,* 485 F.2d 1297, 1303 (5th Cir. 1973) *(en banc), aff'd on other grounds sub nom. East Carroll Parish School Board v. Marshall,* 424 U.S. 636 (1975).
83. The principle that low socioeconomic status and deprivations in education, income, employment and other areas have a negative impact on opportunities for political participation is firmly established in the social science literature, e.g., Raymond E. Wolfinger and Steven J. Rosenstone, *Who Votes?* (New Haven and London: Yale University Press, 1980), 91–93; Lester Milbraith, *Political Participation* (Chicago: Rand McNally, 1965), chap. V; William Erbe, ''Social Involvement and Political Activity: Replication and Elaboration,'' *American Sociological Review* 29 (1964): 198–215; Angus Campbell, et al., *The American Voter* (New York: John Wiley & Sons, 1960), chap. 17; Angus Campbell, Gerald Gurin, and Warren E. Miller, *The Voter Decides* (Evanston, Ill.: Row, Peterson & Co., 1954), 187–99. (Footnote continued.)

84. See, e.g., *Mississippi v. United States,* 490 F. Supp. 569, 575 (D.D.C. 1969) (three-judge court), *aff'd mem.*, 444 U.S. 1050 (1980); *Donnell v. United States,* Civil No. 78-0392 (D.D.C. 31 July 1979) (three-judge court), *aff'd mem.*, 444 U.S. 1059 (1980).
85. See, e.g., *United Jewish Organizations v. Carey,* 430 U.S. 144 (1977).
86. 554 F.2d at 141, 146.
87. 554 F.2d at 148–51.
88. 431 U.S. 407, 421–26 (1977).
89. 430 U.S. 144 (1977).
90. 430 U.S. at 166.
91. Ibid.
92. Ibid (footnote omitted).
93. Washington Council of Lawyers, *Reagan Civil Rights: The First Twenty Months* (Washington, D.C.: 1982), 57–59.

6

Nonpartisan Slating Groups in an At-Large Setting

Chandler Davidson and Luis Ricardo Fraga

The development of minority voting strength in the South and Southwest can be understood as a series of stages. Alfred B. Clubok and his associates have set forth a stair-step model of black political participation in southern towns that is useful in this regard.[1] At the extremes are "nonvoting towns," in which blacks are disfranchised; and "office-holding towns," where a highly mobilized black vote is responsible for the election or appointment of black officials. Between these extremes are "low-voting unorganized towns," in which for one reason or another few blacks vote; "manipulative towns," where "the electoral activists—those responsible for turning out the Negro vote—are primarily agents of members of the white political structure"; and the "independent bargaining towns," where the electoral activists are black and have some independent leverage with white dominants.

Since the battle for the minority franchise has largely been won, the nonvoting town is a thing of the past. Yet office-holding towns are not nearly as numerous in the Sunbelt as one might have expected almost two decades after passage of the Voting Rights Act of 1965. The foremost reason for this is vote dilution, whereby election rules and practices combine with white bloc voting to diminish the political strength of blacks and Hispanics, even when there are no formal impediments to their voting or running for office. (See Chandler Davidson's more extensive discussion of vote dilution in Chapter 1.)

A phenomenon that often accompanies vote dilution which has so far received scant attention by scholars is the nonpartisan slating group. Such organizations are apparently widespread and operate most effectively in jurisdictions with at-large elections. Our analysis of its operation in four Texas cities suggests that it may play an important role in preventing low-voting and manipulative towns from becoming independent bargaining and office-holding ones.

A nonpartisan slating group is defined as an organization whose purpose is to recruit candidates, nominate them, and campaign for their election to office in a nonpartisan election system. However, it should be said at the outset that the term *nonpartisan* in this context is misleading. Students of nonpartisanship have long been aware of its ambiguous meaning.[2] On the one hand, it refers to a system in which candidates' party affiliation is absent from the ballot. "Ballot nonpartisanship'' in this sense must be distinguished from systems of ''participatory nonpartisanship'' in which political parties are not involved in campaigns. Obviously, ballot nonpartisanship is entirely compatible with participatory partisanship, as when the Democratic and Republican county committees either formally or informally work in behalf of a local candidate whose party affiliation is not on the ballot. In other words, it is possible to have ''party politics'' in a system of ballot nonpartisanship.

It is also possible to have party politics of this sort even though the parties involved are not national but local. Sometimes the participants are straightforward in calling their organizations parties; and at other times, because of a curious but widespread American belief that parties at the local level are evil, they are called citizens' associations, good government leagues, or nonpartisan slating groups. They conform, however, to Leon Epstein's definition of a party as ''any group, however loosely organized, seeking to elect governmental officeholders under a given label.'' Epstein adds, ''Having a label (which may or may not be on the ballot) rather than an organization is the crucial defining element.''[3] So if the group operates under a specific label, even if the word *party* is absent, it is in fact one. Thus, paradoxically, a local party operating in a system of ballot nonpartisanship is a ''nonpartisan party.''

The significance of this fact can be understood by keeping in mind that local politics, like politics generally, is a struggle over the distribution of scarce resources, which determines who gets the benefits local government is expected to provide, including fire and police services, street paving, flood control, legal and health services, and so forth. In the United States this struggle is manifested both as class conflict and racial and ethnic competition. Who gets elected to city council influences how these struggles are resolved. In a town with a continuing history of racial discrimination, for example, the failure of a minority race to elect its choice of candidates to council affects its ability to get a fair share of public goods.

By calling nonpartisan slating groups local parties, we wish to debunk their image, often advanced by proponents, as high-minded citizens' groups that are above politics. As a party, the slating group's purpose is to affect the outcome of municipal elections and, by so doing, to influence the way in which public goods are allocated to different categories of citizens. The political nature of slating groups takes on even greater significance when they are the only party in a local system. Given their power to mobilize votes, slating groups in one-party systems often arrogate to themselves the role of gatekeeper to public office. In this situation, one must ask how open or accessible is the slating group's internal process for selecting nominees. If it is the only party in town and its nominees almost always win, do all groups of citizens have reasonable access to the slating mechanism? Or, as in the ''white primary'' of the Southern Democrats that was declared unconstitutional in 1944, is access open to a certain class of voters but denied to others? The answer to this question, as the following case studies suggest, points to some striking parallels between the white primary and the nonpartisan slating group in a local one-party system.

The studies are of Texas cities—somewhat larger than Clubok's ''towns''— in which nonpartisan slating groups operated in the 1970s. All had a considerable minority population, containing both blacks and Mexican Americans. The cities are not a scientifically chosen sample, and we do not wish to suggest that they are necessarily representative of all cities with such slating groups. However, research on other cities, and our conversations with city officials, scholars, and civil rights lawyers lead us to believe that the dilutionary processes exemplified in these cases is today widespread, especially in areas with appreciable minority populations.

ABILENE

Abilene is a city of about 100,000 population in West Texas. In 1980, 7 percent of its people were black and another 22 percent were Mexican American. A century-long pattern of overt discrimination and the occasional use of violence by Anglos has kept both ethnic groups "in their place." They consequently suffer from low income, inferior jobs, inadequate housing, and poor education. As late as 1981, the city's municipal work force contained only seven blacks or Mexican Americans in the upper echelons of management compared with eighty-six whites.[4] Minority leaders have long criticized city government for its failure to meet the needs of the minority community, especially regarding public transportation, park facilities, street repair, flood control, and adequate housing.[5]

Government consists of a city manager and seven councilpersons, including a mayor. Throughout the twentieth century the council (earlier a commission) has been elected at large on a nonpartisan ballot, and for most of that period the numbered place system and residency requirements have been in effect. Since World War II, at least, staggered elections have been held. In 1962, as the civil rights protest movement was gathering momentum, a new charter was adopted which included a runoff requirement. Although the council was enlarged from four to six members that year, it is still relatively small. In summary, Abilene's political system contains five features that have been identified as potentially dilutionary: at-large elections, the place system, the runoff requirement, a small council, and staggered elections.

Since 1966 the slating group in Abilene has called itself Citizens for Better Government (CBG). In a slightly altered form, it can be traced back to 1963, when the town's businessmen who supported the revised city charter the previous year first ran a slate of candidates for council, capturing the mayor's post and three of the four contested council seats.

The electoral success of CBG between 1966 and 1982, the period under analysis, has been remarkable. Only twice—in 1966 and again in 1980—did a rival slate attempt to defeat its candidates. The former slate had the active support of a far-right element in the city, including local members of the John Birch Society. The CBG, on the other hand, represented the business establishment, which was portrayed by its opponents as "king makers." The election that year saw the highest turnout for council elections in the city's history—10,001 voters, approximately 20 percent of the voting-age population—and the far-right element was decisively defeated.[6] In 1980, a group urging higher salaries for police and firemen endorsed two candidates, neither of whom won.[7]

Election results after 1966 demonstrate that CBG holds a virtual monopoly on elective office. Between 1966 and 1982 there were forty council or mayoral positions filled by election. CBG fielded candidates for every post and won thirty-seven, for a success rate of 93 percent. The magnitude of CBG's success is enhanced by the fact that only six of its winning nominees had the advantage of incumbency.

All three non-CBG victories involved unusual circumstances. One victor had been a popular TV weathercaster who had appeared daily on a local station for several years preceding his campaign. Another faced a CBG nominee who had previously run on an anti-CBG ticket, earning the ire of his erstwhile supporters who labeled him a turncoat. The other CBG candidate that year also lost, perhaps because he received some of the hostility directed at his running mate.

Of the councilpersons and mayors elected between 1966 and 1979, 94 percent were professionals or businessmen—usually the presidents or chief executives of their firms. One of the three non-CBG candidates to win says that CBG picks "the kind they can depend on without question—mainly established businessmen." This, he believes, results in an extraordinarily tightly knit council. "When a maverick occasionally wins," he continues, "he would probably be looked on as an outsider, just as I was. I set out to bring an independent voice to city hall, and my main problem was in getting along with the other councilmen."[8]

The power of the organization to assure victory to its nominees stems from three facts: 1) CBG mobilizes friendship networks that are highly concentrated among the city's business and social elite. 2) The organization collects and spends money effectively, so that its candidates almost always outspend rivals. 3) Its success discourages serious opposition from potential candidates and discourages turnout among those who would be most likely to vote for the opposition.

Networks

The addresses of contributors to CBG of ten dollars or more in 1975 and 1976 were plotted on a city map. The majority (126 out of 210) were located in a small section of the southwestern suburbs, contained in the two census tracts with the highest median family income in 1970. Few contributions came from the nonsuburban core of the city, and none came from predominantly black and Hispanic neighborhoods, in which more than half of the minority population lives.

Money

In council elections between 1966 and 1978, the linear relation between a candidate's proportional expenditure of "efficient dollars" (explained below) in a contested race and his percentage of the vote was 0.86 ($p<.001$). The average efficient dollars spent by the winning candidates during that period was $3,434, compared to $985 spent by the runners-up. Of the twenty-four winning candidates in these same races, twenty were also the biggest spenders. Given the fact that the winners were almost entirely CBG candidates, money probably played a role in CBG's success. The costs of running for office at large are greater than from single-member districts. Had Abilene had six single-member districts of equal size, "shoe leather"—door-to-door canvassing by candidates—could have substituted for the costs of TV, radio, and newspaper ads.

Slating of multiple candidates is more efficient than individual candidates running alone. Suppose a group slates three candidates, and that three candidates running individually oppose them. Suppose further that a half-page newspaper ad costs $500. If each independent candidate buys a half-page ad, it will cost collectively $1,500. The slating group, however, can purchase one $500 ad and include pictures of all three of their candidates. Its dollars are therefore three times as efficient as those of the candidates running singly.

Discouraging the Opposition

Nothing succeeds like success, and CBG's won-lost record—combined with its reputation for being able to raise large sums of money quickly—reportedly has discouraged many voters from going to the polls. CBG's money-raising capacity is formidable. While it may not spend more than a few thousand dollars in a given election year, it can spend two or three times as much in another, if it believes it faces strong opposition. For example, in 1979 CBG spent $7,844 on its two candidates. The next year it spent $18,656.[9] A potential opposition candidate knows that if he raises a large sum, CBG can probably exceed it. The result is a widespread view that CBG is something of a juggernaut. A scientific poll of voters in the 1979 council races asked if respondents had ever heard of CBG. Ninety-one percent said they had. These were then asked: "Some people believe that if Citizens for Better Government endorses a candidate for city government, that candidate is almost certain to win. Do you believe this is true or false?" Sixty-one percent agreed with the statement.[10] This perception of CBG's power undoubtedly discourages opposition. Indeed, the group's chairman in 1978 expressed the view that CBG's success dampened voter turnout in city elections.[11]

How open is CBG's nominating process to blacks and Hispanics? This is a matter of controversy. In 1973 the group slated a Mexican American, Joe Alcorta, who easily won, serving two three-year terms. His last year in office CBG slated a black, Leo Scott, who ran unopposed. When Scott's term expired in 1981, CBG slated yet a third minority candidate—Carlos Rodriguez. Thus at least one-seventh of the council has been black or Hispanic for almost a decade, a fact emphasized by the city as a defendant in a 1982 vote dilution trial brought by minority plaintiffs.[12] How could CBG's slating process be closed to Abilene's minorities, the city argued, if it had slated minority candidates in 1973, 1976, 1978, and 1981?

Plaintiffs countered that as a result of CBG's internal nominating procedure, minority voters had not been able to slate candidates of their choice. The CBG candidates were hand-picked by the Anglo dominants in the organization. Neither Alcorta nor Scott had been active in minority causes before or during his stint on council, unlike some of the independent minority candidates who lost. Rodriguez, plaintiffs argued, had been somewhat more active before his election in 1981, but he was nominated only after the vote dilution suit had been filed and plaintiffs' experts had begun an extensive study of the CBG nominating process.

Between 1970 and 1982, six minority candidates ran (one of them twice) opposing CBG candidates. None received as much as a third of the vote, although evidence suggests that at least two had the enthusiastic and overwhelming support of both minority communities. However, by the late 1970s it appeared that minority voter turnout had diminished almost to the vanishing point. In 1979, when the last independent minority candidate ran, only 76 Mexican Americans and 31 blacks went to the polls, out of an estimated adult minority population that year of around 10,000.

In brief—so the plaintiffs argued—independent minority candidates in Abilene cannot win office, in part because of the white bloc vote and in part because of minority vote discouragement, itself a function of CBG's successes. On the other hand, the minority candidates elected under CBG's aegis were not generally the kind of councilpersons that the city's minority community would have chosen, had they had equal access to the slating process.

The claim that minority voters did not have equal access rests on evidence collected in a three-year study of the internal nominating process of CBG.[13] The findings can be summarized as follows:

1. Three of the city's best-known and most active minority group leaders, the Rev. T. G. Oliphant, Ken Deckard (head of the city's Community Action Program), and Robert English—all blacks—had participated, by invitation, on the CBG nominating committee which presents the names of possible CBG candidates to the organization's board of directors. The independently obtained description each leader gave of his attempts to secure the nomination of strong minority candidates indicates that the board of directors was biased against them. All three men refused to participate in CBG again, charging that the board favored "token" minorities.

2. The core of CBG consists of Anglo businessmen who dominate the organization. The chairman, always an Anglo male, is not popularly elected at the CBG annual meeting, open to the public, but automatically accedes to the post after having been elected vice-chairman the previous year by the board of directors, a small group some of whom are elected at the annual meeting and some of whom are appointed by the chairman. The group's structure is very loose, in that no standard parliamentary guide such as *Robert's Rules of Order* is used. The vice-chairman is typically nominated by the chairman without discussion or opposition—in clear violation of *Robert's Rules* if it were used.[14] Thus the line of succession of the chairman, who pretty much runs the organization when the entirely appointive nominating committee is considering candidates, is tightly controlled by a small group composed of the town's business elite. The suggestions of the nominating committee are just that—suggestions—and the board of directors, or a subgroup, has formal authority to reject the nominating committee's suggestions, which it has sometimes done in the past. One such rejection involved a black woman school principal whom minority participants on the nominating committee had apparently gotten the committee to approve.[15]

3. The vulnerability of the slating process to manipulation by the chairman and

the board of directors is great, given the fact that parliamentary rules are not followed, meetings are not open to the press, minutes of meetings are not kept, procedures are not consistent from year to year, and hardly anyone—including members of the board of directors—can describe even the formal procedures of the nominating process spelled out in the group's bylaws, copies of which are difficult to obtain. A past chairman of CBG admitted that "only the rough sediment" of the bylaws is followed in practice.[16]

4. An unspoken rule of the organization is that anyone who asks for the endorsement of CBG will not receive it. As several leaders of CBG explained—in almost identical terms—the organization does not want candidates "who have an axe to grind," that is, candidates who are self-starters, in the sense that they have issues or programs on which they want to base their campaigns.[17] In announcing their candidacy, some CBG nominees have told reporters that they would not have run for council had they not been asked to do so by CBG, and that they had no idea of what their platform would be.[18] Although the "no controversy" or "no axe to grind" rule applies generally, its effect on potential minority nominees who might wish to mount a campaign around issues of special minority concern, such as flood control, is to skew the process of selecting minority CBG nominees in the direction of safe, cautious, and generally quiet candidates.

In an interview after six years on city council, Joe Alcorta was asked what difference his presence on council had made, so far as the interests of the minority community were concerned. He said that he was instrumental in getting minorities appointed to "all the boards and commissions."[19] Yet evidence submitted by the city at trial indicated that half of all the city's boards and commissions had *never* had a minority member.[20] In 1979, Alcorta's last year on council, sixteen of twenty-four boards had no minorities.[21] He admitted that minority parks were grossly inferior to those in majority areas,[22] although he had not spoken out on the issue during the previous six years. He stated that he had never seen a copy of the city's affirmative action program, and was not even sure it had one.[23] He did not live in a minority neighborhood. Indeed, at the time he was first asked to be CBG's nominee in 1973, he was working on his Ph.D. degree at Texas Tech, a university in Lubbock, sixty miles away.[24]

In late 1982 the district judge found in favor of the city of Abilene. A year and a half later the Fifth Circuit remanded the case for reconsideration, in part because the trial judge had ignored in his opinion the plaintiffs' claims concerning CBG's lack of access to minorities. CBG continues to operate as the only slating group in the city. Participation in city elections has gradually decreased since CBG's inception in 1966. In the decade of the 1970s, the average turnout in the annual council elections was 4,513, a mere 7 percent of the voting-age population. Although cities with "reform" structures typically have lower voting rates than "unreformed" cities, CBG's invincibility may also play a role in voter apathy. As an unsuccessful anti-CBG candidate expressed it in a letter to the newspaper, "One person told me, 'With all that money they could elect Smokey the Bear.' "[25]

WICHITA FALLS

Wichita Falls is located on the northern border of Texas, across the Red River from Oklahoma. Its population grew from less than 5,000 at the turn of the century to 94,000 in 1980; 11 percent of its inhabitants are black, 8 percent Mexican American.

The city has a "reform" government: a city manager answers to a council of six aldermen and a mayor, who are elected to two-year staggered terms in nonpartisan elections using the place system. All are elected at large by a plurality vote. The city also has a slating group, Citizens Committee for Good Government (CCGG), which between its formation in 1962 and 1982 endorsed seventy-six candidacies for every council post up for election but two. Sixty-eight (89 percent) were successful.

The first minority candidate ran unsuccessfully for city office in 1956, before CCGG was formed. A second black ran in 1964, and a third was appointed in 1967 to fill an unexpired term, but died in office. Altogether, ten separate minority persons—eight blacks and two Mexican Americans—ran for office between 1964 and 1982, for a total of twenty candidacies. Two blacks, Harrison Taylor and Horace Boston, and one Mexican American, Guillermo "Bill" Garcia, were elected: Taylor, four times in a row (1968, 1969, 1971 and 1973); Boston, twice (1980, 1982); and Garcia once (1975). All three had CCGG endorsements. None of the independent minority candidates won.

Thus, as in Abilene, the slating group has a near monopoly on elective office, and any minority who wins must consequently have its backing. Even the "won-lost" record of the CCGG-endorsed minority candidates does not tell the full story of the group's clout, however. The thirteen candidacies of the seven independent minorities garnered a mean of 21 percent of the total vote; the seven candidacies of the three slated minorities yielded a mean of 65 percent.

Taylor, the successful black, received overwhelming support from the one identifiable black precinct every time he ran for office. He was first appointed to fill the unexpired term of another black appointee who had died in office. This was the year of Martin Luther King's assassination, and Taylor's presence on council was obviously seen as important to blacks in that context. (It was also seen as important to whites. Disturbances by Wichita Falls' blacks at the time seem to have been a factor in Taylor's election, once he had the sanction of CCGG.)

Whatever may be said about Taylor's actual popularity among blacks, he was described as a "safe" candidate by whites. One chairman of CCGG described him as "very quiet—quite a gentleman. He conducted himself very well at city council meetings."[26] Given this interviewee's hostility to racial minorities in general, expressed several times in the course of his conversation, it seems fair to say that Taylor won the approval of the more racially conservative members of the city's business structure.[27]

Garcia was widely perceived as one who was inactive on behalf of minority issues. A Spanish teacher at Midwestern University, a local college, Garcia was born in Mexico, where he received his Ph.D., and only became a U.S. citizen in the mid-1960s. He does not call himself a minority person ("I detest the term," he says), and he specifically disavowed any intent to run as a representative of minority interests in 1975.[28] Once in office, he turned down the request of a delegation of Mexican Americans who came to his office, lecturing them on the fact that "I'm not representing you, but the people of Wichita Falls."[29]

Events surrounding CCGG's endorsement of Garcia shed light on the group's approach to minority candidates. When Taylor, the black councilman, decided not to run for office in 1975, a group of black leaders, hoping that a tradition had been established of having a black councilman, approached a newspaper editor they identified with CCGG and asked him if they could have the right to name a black candidate for CCGG's endorsement. According to one report, the editor said yes. The name the black group came up with, after some controversy among themselves, was James Esther, an outspoken "race man."[30] CCGG found him unacceptable, but he and another black independent announced for office. Garcia also announced. No Anglos had yet entered the race, and about two weeks later CCGG approached Garcia and asked if he would run with their endorsement.[31] He agreed to do so, and in the subsequent election narrowly edged out the black contenders, who received 96 percent of the black vote.

However, once in office Garcia quickly made himself unpopular with CCGG by pursuing issues of his own, although none apparently directly involved ethnic minorities. "I was seen as somebody who wasn't looking out after the interests of banking and industry," he later complained bitterly.[32]

After he had publicly advocated firing a city employee whose friends included influential businessmen, Garcia was invited to the Wichita Club by the president of Midwestern University to have lunch with "a person who wants to meet you." The person turned out to be a wealthy individual who was a backer of the controversial city employee. He got right to the point.

"Why do you want to get rid of Col. Yaeger?" he asked. "I think he's a very good person to be in city government—a good PR person for the city."

"Well," Garcia responded, "if so, we should pay him for that reason instead of calling him Commissioner of Public Safety."

The man turned to the president and snapped, "If I was in your place, that is a man I would get rid of."

He told the president that he had been instrumental in getting Midwestern its status as a university rather than a college. "And now this man [Garcia] is doing things harmful to Midwestern. He should be fired."

"I beg your pardon," the president said, "but Professor Garcia wasn't elected by Midwestern, he was elected by the city of Wichita Falls."[33]

Garcia was at the center of other controversies as well. While he was trying to decide whether to run for reelection in 1977, the CCGG chairman came to see him and informed him that the group would not endorse him again. " 'The CCGG tries not to put the same candidate up for reelection,' he said. That was a lie. The other incumbents had already been told they would be nominated," Garcia said.

He was not completely without friends on council, however, and they offered to contribute money to his campaign. Garcia went to the mayor. "I'm so mad at what CCGG did," Garcia said, "I'm thinking of running against their candidate."

"I wouldn't run against them," the mayor said. "They can make your life miserable."

He thought about his job. He decided not to throw his hat in the ring.[34]

Boston, a black dentist elected on the CCGG slate, is variously described as a "don't make waves type," "unrepresentative" of minorities, and a "low profile" councilperson. Tommy Robinson, a black who ran unsuccessfully for council three times without CCGG endorsement, said Boston is "in the same ballpark with Harrison Taylor. He is never prepared for council. At many council meetings he says nothing—then votes with the majority."[35] Boston does not live in a minority area. Prior to his election, he had not been active in community minority affairs or in the NAACP.[36] He had not been active in CCGG when they approached him and asked him to run.[37] The Wichita Falls *Times* endorsed Robinson instead of Boston in 1982, but incumbent Boston was reelected with a plurality of 42 percent.[38]

As informal as the nominating process is in Abilene's CBG, the one in CCGG is even more so. "Many persons have remained almost totally in the dark about the operations and membership of CCGG," an article in the Wichita Falls *Times* said in 1976. "Many stories about the group have evolved—most of them, according to CCGG leaders, untrue."[39]

The article attempted to clarify the organization's structure and function based on comments made by two CCGG leaders, a lawyer and a banker. Among the "apparent misunderstandings" which the leaders denied was that "the committee is a closed group, made up of a handful of powerful businessmen, who operate in secret." Although such a popular misconception may have been technically incorrect, it was not so far off the mark.

As in the Abilene case, an annual meeting is held, which "anyone can attend," according to the above newspaper story. Before this, however, the chairman on his own appoints a nominating committee which proposes names for the steering committee for the following year. When the annual meeting is held, the steering committee is formally elected. The number in attendance usually ranges from fifteen to forty-five.[40]

It is hardly surprising that the meeting is so small, given the policy of CCGG not to advertise it publicly in advance. Indeed, attendance is by invitation only, limited primarily to those who have contributed funds to CCGG in the past. (One estimate is that this pool of contributors, most of whom typically donate fifty dollars, consists of from 175 to 200 people.)[41] And while in theory any person will be admitted who takes the trouble to find out when the annual meeting is held and turns up at the appointed time, he would hardly receive a warm reception. The 1979 CCGG chairman, in describing the invitations, said, "We're selective in who we put on the list. We stay away from people who might use CCGG as an entering wedge."[42]

The steering committee, whose membership is ratified at the annual meeting, then begins considering endorsements. Its meetings are not open to the public.[43] And the procedure that governs deliberation is completely informal inasmuch as there is no constitution or set of by-laws. There are also no records or minutes kept of the deliberations.[44]

While two CCGG chairmen stressed that blacks (though not Mexican Americans) had sat on the steering committee in the past, they agreed that minority participation was typically minimal.[45] When asked how minorities might attempt to take part, one former chairman said, "I can't answer that question."[46] Another, after admitting that there were no minorities currently in the organization, said, "[They could] just call me, and I'd send 'em a letter."[47] As this individual referred to the black residential areas as "colored town," and used the term "Meskin" to designate Mexican Americans, it seems unlikely that he would be the recipient of many such requests. He went on to opine why so few minority candidates were slated by CCGG.

> You have a city manager here who is a professional—he hires top-notch professional assistants. They often come from outside Wichita Falls. So you have to have councilmen geared to do business with these bureaucrats. You can't have lightweights dealing with the professional bureaucracy. This is why you run into a situation that limits black participation.[48]

As in Abilene, the slating group has an unofficial policy of refusing to nominate a candidate who solicits its nomination. Neither CCGG chairmen interviewed could think of a case to the contrary. One said, "Two or three people came up to me after the last elections and said, 'Would you select me next year?' We *consider* them, of course, but when we look into the matter more closely, we usually find that they have an axe to grind."

When asked for an example of such an "axe," he replied, "We looked into this one fellow's background, and we found that a while back he had been left waiting two hours in the waiting room at a local hospital, and he wanted on the council to make some changes here."[49]

This policy tends to create homogeneous councils. The CCGG claims that once they have nominated a candidate, they put no pressure on him to vote a certain way. But as a local observer remarked, "I'm not sure how much pressure they *need* to bring on them. They're their kind of people to start with."[50] And a former councilwoman—one of the few non-CCGG candidates to win—put the matter as follows: "The council is so packed when it's run by a self-appointed group like CCGG. I bitterly resent that." Amplifying her point, she said, "Almost all the councilmen I served with were of the conservative Democratic or Republican variety."[51]

One might assume, of course, that the CCGG slating process simply facilitates a result that would naturally occur anyway. Yet one of the most interesting aspects of the political system in Wichita Falls is that, in statewide politics, the county has long had a liberal reputation. In the past twenty-five years, its liberal-labor faction has fairly regularly controlled the county's delegation to the state convention. Texas's last moderate-to-liberal governor, James Allred, was a native of the city, and his son, a liberal legislator, was for a time the county Democratic chairman. The Wichita Falls delegation was one of handful at the 1968 state convention that voted against John Connally's favorite-son candidacy. Liberal U.S. Senator Ralph Yarborough usually did quite well there during his campaigns.

Part of the reason for this was that liberal and conservative factions of Democrats had long been organized around economic issues, and the resultant polarization roughly approximated two-party competition. The "liberal" and "conservative" tags were the functional equivalents of national Democratic and Republican party labels. Such a system provided two foci of competing ideologies, which surfaced in Democratic primary campaigns, rallied adherents, and provided cues for voters. This organizational base provided the less affluent classes—including minorities—the wherewithal to prevail in many instances.

In municipal politics, however, the situation is different. CCGG's own policy rigidly adhered to, of ignoring issues—and characterizing those who do not as "having an ax to grind"—apparently has convinced its opponents that speaking out on issues is an unseemly reflection of self-interest. CCGG leaders also espouse a view, essential to the ideology of Progressive era reform, that in municipal politics there are no divergent group interests. Policy is made through "administration" rather than "politics." The very expression of a point of view implying that one group or class may have special needs is taken as an attack on community solidarity. Only under extraordinary circumstances, therefore, does anyone feel comfortable in espousing controversial issues, for that would imply that this (largely mythical) community of interest did not exist.

In Willis Hawley's terms, the city's politics illustrates the conservative bias of nonpartisanship—the tendency of the nonpartisan ballot to push political outcomes in a more conservative direction than would ordinarily be true in a genuine two-party system.[52] This effect of nonpartisanship is strengthened in an at-large setting. Yet CCGG, by occasionally slating "acceptable" minority candidates, fosters the illusion that minorities participate fully and effectively in the electoral process.

DALLAS

Dallas, the state's second largest city, is located slightly to the west of the East Texas "black belt." In 1980, 25 percent of its population of 844,000 was black, and another 8 percent was Hispanic. Despite its lack of heavy industry, it has been a central location of major oil, finance, and insurance firms. The city's commercial success is due in large measure to the existence of a very close working relation between business interests and city government.

The development of this relationship, in turn, is the result of the Citizens' Charter Association (CCA), Dallas's most noted, and unquestionably its most successful, nonpartisan slating group, which was one of the major factors in city electoral politics from 1930 to 1975. The business-dominated CCA maintained a clear voting majority in twenty-one of twenty-three city councils elected during this forty-five-year period.

The origin of the CCA is linked to the adoption of council-manager government in 1930 by the city's voters. However, the connection between organized business and Dallas government goes back at least to 1907. Under the leadership of the publisher of the *Dallas Morning News* and the Civic Improvement League, a commission plan was adopted that year, changing a fifteen-member aldermanic council to a system of government where four commissioners and a mayor were elected at large.[53] Those behind the change hoped that the subsequently elected commission would adopt a program of municipal public works which the previous council had refused to enact, and which the Chamber of Commerce and other major business interests felt was necessary if the city was to prosper.[54]

During the commissioners' election campaign of 1907, and again in 1927, nonpartisan slating groups ran entire slates of candidates for city elective office. The interests behind these organizations, the Citizens Association in 1907 and the Nonpartisan Association in 1927, were the same as those which advocated the commission plan.[55]

The operation of commission government in Dallas did not have the anticipated consequences. It was characterized by "buck passing," infighting, the use of public jobs as patronage, and the lack of a unified policy due to the "private political ambitions" of each commissioner. In the end, no program of public works was enacted, and by 1930 the city was in debt and provision of city services was far from adequate.[56]

As a result of disenchantment with the commission, the CCA was organized to ensure the adoption of city manager government. Consistent with the rhetoric of municipal "reform," the proponents of the Dallas plan hoped to rid government decision-making of "politics," that is, "patronage and selfish intrigue."[57] A city manager, it was argued, would help develop the kind of policy which business interests had desired since 1907. Public works programs, the removal of railroad tracks from the central business district, flood control programs, the creation of a new industrial area, and the dredging of a canal to the Gulf of Mexico were all to be made possible under city management government.[58]

To achieve its goals, the CCA organized itself hierarchically. In addition to a president and vice president, a campaign manager and a clerical staff of five were hired. Separate divisions were established for men and women. A lieutenant was assigned to each of the city's fifty-nine voting precincts.[59]

The business community gave enthusiastic support to the adoption of the city manager plan. The Chamber of Commerce and the Dallas Advertising League publicly endorsed it. All industrial plants and large business firms allowed the CCA's "flying squadron" of speakers to address their employees during business hours. Service clubs, the Pastor's Association, and women's organizations also supported CCA efforts.[60]

The planning and organization proved effective. On October 10, 1930, the voters of the city adopted manager government, with all nine at-large council seats (including the mayor) to be filled by the place system with a majority requirement. Six of the seats, in addition, had residency requirements.[61] To guarantee that the newly elected council-members would be imbued with the same spirit as that of the reformers, the CCA in 1931 drafted a slate of candidates who would not fall prey to the same "vices" that the commissioners had. All nine were proprietors and/or top executives of major Dallas business firms.[62] With only token opposition, the entire CCA slate won.

A slate drawn from the same pool was fielded by CCA in 1933, but this time it encountered opposition from three other slates—the Home Government Association, the Progressive Voters League, and the Socialist Party. All CCA candidates won without a runoff.[63]

Opposition to CCA-dominated government developed fairly quickly. Central business district interests conflicted with those of neighborhoods in East Dallas over the creation of a levee district. Disgruntled municipal employees became extremely critical of the CCA and its city manager as a result of layoffs caused by budget cuts. For different reasons, so did the local utility company. Lower-income groups resented the imposition of a sewer tax.[64]

The three groups which ran separate slates in 1933 coalesced two years later into the Citizens' Civic Association. Its candidates were not members of the corporate elite, but were "merely substantial citizens, prominent in church, lodge, and service club activities."[65] Its platform advocated the maintenance of manager government, repeal of the sewer tax, a new city manager, and better cooperation with the Dallas Centennial program.[66] The Citizens' Civic Association won all council seats in 1935. But the CCA made a respectable comeback in 1937 by winning four places, and in 1939, it won all nine seats without a runoff.[67]

Thus, for all intents and purposes, CCA had established its reputation as the dominant slating group in Dallas by the end of the 1930s, much as the CBG in Abilene and the CCGG in Wichita Falls had done by the middle 1960s. (Founders of both the latter organizations mentioned Dallas' CCA as a model, albeit with modifications suited to their own locales.)

By any standards, CCA's success since 1939 was phenomenal. Of 179 council seats up for election between 1939 and 1975, it entered candidates for all but four; and it won 159 of these seats (89 percent). While a systematic analysis of the twenty losses is not available, several seem to have resulted from challenges by temporary rival slates. In addition, four—all occurring in 1975—came about as a result of court-ordered single-member districts.

The structure of CCA differs in one important respect from the other slating groups described so far. By 1937 it was no longer an autonomous political group. In that year, the Dallas Citizens Council (DCC) was organized, and in its goals it resembled, in Marxian terms, an executive committee of the ruling class. The DCC was formed to bring the one hundred major Dallas business firms together to promote unity of action regarding major local and statewide issues of public policy.[68] Membership today is by invitation only, and one must be either the chief executive officer or the chairman of the board of a major company to be considered for voting membership.[69] No lawyers, doctors, ministers, or educators are allowed entry—it is for businessmen only.[70] In 1980, all ten members of its executive committee lived in the affluent section of Far North Dallas.[71]

The CCA became the political arm of the DCC.[72] Thus, while the CCA has been characterized as "an election-year phenomenon" whose only year-round functioning officer was a president,[73] the DCC—an ongoing organization with regular meetings—provided it with a formal continuity that is lacking in Abilene and Wichita Falls.

Meaningful decisions on CCA nominees were probably made by the DCC leadership.[74] The vast majority of CCA candidates from 1931 to 1975 were proprietors or upper-level executives in prominent Dallas firms. Of 211 candidates slated, the occupations of 195 were determined. Seventy-five percent were proprietors or upper-level executives and 22 percent were high-prestige professionals. As Mayor Erik Jonsson stated in 1975,

> With one or two exceptions, the CCA candidates have all been successful in some kind of business. They are proven decisionmakers. And a large part of the job of running this city is a business job, it's just management. The city budget is now up to a quarter of a billion dollars, and that ain't hay. If you were in charge of picking a candidate to manage that kind of money, would you pick one who'd never even managed $100,000 successfully?[75]

CCA slates had very limited racial and ethnic diversity. The first black and Mexican American were slated in 1969. Up through 1975 one member of each group was on each slate. However, a federal court concluded that year that in spite of this fact, minorities did not have equitable access to the CCA's nominating process.[76]

Domination of Dallas electoral politics by the CCA was partly the result of its ability to provide nominees with a centralized system of campaigning and financing. Campaigning was generally not conducted independently by the candidates, but by the organization as a whole.[77] Each CCA advertisement pictured all its candidates, and campaign literature advocated support of the entire slate. Thus, as in Abilene, funds collected by the group benefitted all its candidates. The significance of this multiplier effect is obvious in a year like 1971, when the CCA spent nearly $130,000 on its slate of eleven candidates.[78]

The at-large election system in Dallas was essential for CCA success, and it operated as well to dilute the votes of blacks. A study of the 1931 to 1937 elections revealed a substantial racial vote polarization.[79] Elections in 1959, 1961, 1965, and 1971 in which non-CCA black candidates ran reflected a similar pattern.[80] Through 1975, only those minority candidates who were slated by the CCA won office.

A federal court in 1975 ruled that Dallas's at-large system of electing council members unconstitutionally diluted black votes. The city's history of racial discrimination, housing segregation, and racial vote polarization, and the limited access of minorities to the slating process were cited by the court as evidence.[81]

The remedy was an enlarged council consisting of eight single-member district seats and three at-large ones, including that of the mayor. Although the CCA ran a slate of candidates in 1975 under the 8-3 plan, it was able to win only six seats. Two were filled by CCA-supported blacks elected from predominantly black districts.

Since 1975 the CCA has not run a slate in Dallas city elections, although there has been talk of revitalizing its organization through the creation of miniature CCAs in each single-member district.[82] As things now stand, there is more diversity of interests represented on council than at any time since the 1930s.

SAN ANTONIO

Located in south central Texas, San Antonio is unique among the state's large cities in having long had a proportionally high Mexican American ratio, which has increased substantially in recent years—from 41 percent in 1960 to 52 percent in 1970 and to 54 percent ten years later. Blacks constituted 7 percent in 1980. The city as a whole contained 785,000 people that year.

Despite its overwhelming cultural presence, the Hispanic community had very little municipal political influence until the late 1970s. This was in large measure the result of the Good Government League (GGL), a nonpartisan slating group which manipulated minority participation and dominated San Antonio politics from 1955 to the 1970s.

As in Dallas, the slating group was connected with structural "reform." From 1837 to 1913, San Antonio elected aldermen on a ward basis. Unhappy with the policies of the political machine of Bryan Callaghan II, businessmen in 1914 led a successful move to install commission government, hoping that the newly elected commissioners would commit the city's resources to rapid residential and commercial expansion.[83]

However, as in the Dallas case, business interests soon found that many of the vestiges of ward politics remained in commission government. "Professional politicians" who regained control of city government seemed more interested in perpetuating themselves in office through patronage than in encouraging the city's economic growth.[84]

Similar motives led prominent businessmen, along with liberal mayor Maury Maverick, to urge the adoption of the council manager plan in the late 1930s.[85] But it was only in 1951 that this goal was achieved through popular referendum.[86] Nine councilmen (including the mayor) were to be elected to two-year terms, running for numbered posts in a system requiring a majority of the votes to win. The mayor was elected by the council. San Antonio continued to operate on a nonpartisan basis as it had at least since 1914.

City manager government got off to a shaky start when the new mayor, Jack White, attempted to increase the mayor's powers at the expense of the city manager's, contrary to the essential idea behind the council-manager model.[87] Conflict between White and his critics led to a confrontation between rival slates in the 1953 election. White's "San Antonio Ticket" campaigned for a return to commission government and resoundingly defeated the "Citizens Committee" slate.[88]

Businessmen behind the charter revision responded by establishing the GGL the following year to recruit, nominate, and elect slates of candidates for municipal office. On December 7, 1954, Tom L. Powell, president of the Chamber of Commerce, asked sixty influential San Antonians to his home to discuss the establishment of a slating group.[89] Of those invited, 43 percent were business proprietors, 17 percent attorneys, and 14 percent other professionals and clergymen. Three were heads of local business associations. Most lived in affluent North Side neighborhoods.[90] From this meeting, the GGL quickly expanded its membership to 3,000, and although it was more diverse than the original leadership, it still came primarily from the North Side and from beyond San Antonio's city limits in the affluent "bedroom" municipalities of Olmos Park, Alamo Heights, and Terrell Hills.[91]

The GGL enunciated two goals: eliminate unnecessary conflict on council, thereby solving common problems; and facilitate growth and economic expansion.[92] To the businessmen who founded GGL, writes Luther L. Sanders,

> the GGL was simply a logical step in making council manager government work. One interviewee stated: 'We realized that you just couldn't run anyone and expect council manager government to work. That was our mistake in 1951 and 1953.'[93]

The GGL ran its first slate in 1955, filing candidates for eight of the nine positions available. All won election, an augury of the organization's future success. Between 1955 and 1975 the GGL won eighty-five of ninety-nine (86 percent) council positions available. It failed to file a candidate in only two races. Three of GGL's losses occurred in the late 1960s, when a loosely formed liberal coalition was able to elect Peter Torres (1967 and 1969), a Chicano activist, and Mary Baker (1969). Most of the remaining losses resulted from a split in the business establishment during the 1970s, when the diverging interests of the "downtown group" and the "northside group" ultimately led to GGL's demise.

In its internal structure the GGL was similar to Abilene's CBG, whose founders borrowed a copy of GGL's by-laws in establishing their own charter.[94] Anyone who paid five dollars could belong. The president each year appointed a nominating committee to submit names of candidates for the 100 to 125-member board of directors, of whom only a majority had to be qualified voters of San Antonio.[95] Thus, sizeable numbers of nonresidents from surrounding silk-stocking suburbs played a major role in the nominating process that was denied most San Antonio voters.

The general membership was then mailed a ballot with the candidates' names. Once the board was elected, it met at least twice a year. But an elected executive committee of ten to twenty persons made the important routine decisions. This committee met once a month at a minimum, and usually once a week. (Blacks and Mexican Americans sat on both the board and the executive committee.)[96]

After receiving suggestions from the board and other individuals and groups, the executive committee appointed a second nominating committee, this one to come up with names of potential council candidates.[97] The nominating committee was sheltered from public scrutiny. Its membership was kept secret, as were its deliberations, on the grounds that meaningful debate of controversial issues and personalities was only possible under such conditions.[98] Once the committee had agreed on a list of potential nominees, it was submitted to the board for approval.[99]

Likely candidates' names came from three sources. The major one was the GGL board itself. The other two generated only minority candidates' names. Citizens for Community Progress, composed of Mexican American businessmen, civic leaders, and professionals, submitted Hispanic names. An informal group of prominent blacks submitted its list as well.[100]

Once their names were in the hopper, potential candidates were intensively screened. Such things as police records, credit ratings, political involvement, civic club participation, and professional reputation were considered. Those who made the grade were then interviewed. Finally, the committee circulated the names of potential candidates among several groups and individuals to measure their reaction. This "test group" was heavily larded with bankers, builders, manufacturers, real estate brokers, and religious leaders.[101] After GGL formed an advisory finance committee of about two hundred business leaders in the late 1960s, the opinions of this group, too, were sought regarding likely candidates.[102]

Nominees were expected to be financially secure enough to devote sufficient time to council matters. Their public prominence and "civic mindedness" were important. It was hoped that they would have no future political ambitions. And they were expected to represent the "entire community."[103]

Of GGL's eighty-five winning candidates, 71 percent were Anglo, 24 percent were Mexican American, and 6 percent were black.[104] Almost all were business proprietors, real estate brokers, bankers, or professionals. Sixty-five percent—including some of the Hispanics—resided in North Side neighborhoods.[105] The GGL's preference for affluent suburbanites was expressed in an interview by one of its chairmen, who deemed it "unfortunate" that so many "really qualified people" lived in the satellite cities. It was a real problem, he said, to find good men who wanted to run for public office among San Antonio residents.[106]

All of the GGL candidates ran as a slate on a single platform prepared by the organization. Most of their speaking arrangements were also coordinated by GGL. Media activities were centralized.[107] Campaign expenditures always exceeded $100,000, and between 1971 and 1975 GGL spent an average of $170,466 in each election.[108] Opposition candidates and slates were seldom able to come close to matching the GGL war chest.

In San Antonio, as in each of the cities studied, the election of councilpersons at large, when coupled with racially polarized voting, disadvantaged minority voters. Although Mexican Americans since 1970 have comprised more than half of San Antonio's population, they have yet to constitute 50 percent of the actual electorate in a municipal race, given their lower median age and lower registration and turnout rates.[109] Indeed, even when blacks are included with Hispanics, Anglos comprised the majority of voters between 1955 and 1975.[110]

Overall, heaviest GGL support came from Anglo upper-class North Side precincts that were most strongly Republican in partisan contests.[111] Weakest support came from the Mexican American precincts on the West Side. Between 1971 and 1975, the West Side supported only four of twenty-six GGL candidates.[112] Thus in spite of some Hispanic leaders' participation in the GGL slating process, a large segment of the rank and file voted against the slated candidates—even those of their own ethnicity. Indeed, in this same time span only three of the nine Chicano GGL nominees received a majority of West Side support. In 1975, two of the four Chicano GGL candidates polled fewer West Side votes than their Chicano opponents, and another got fewer votes than an Anglo opponent running on an anti-GGL platform.[113] In contrast, both of the black GGL candidates between 1971 and 1975 received over 80 percent of the black vote.[114]

The disfavor in which the GGL was held by Hispanics was the result of GGL-controlled council policies during its heyday. The city's failure to appoint minority members to boards and commissions was well known. Between 1952 and 1974 only 10 percent of the 314 appointees to six important boards and commissions resided on the West Side.[115] Most of the appointees were businessmen, many of whom did not even reside in the city.[116]

The overriding policy goal of the GGL was commercial and residential development, which was largely achieved. However, some parts of the city benefited greatly, and others hardly at all. Freeway and access road construction to new suburban areas led to a huge expansion of the North Side, which was also promoted by decisions to build the South Texas Medical Center and the University of Texas at San Antonio there during the late 1960s and early 1970s.[117]

Concomitant with North Side development was a growing disparity in the delivery of city services to central city minorities.[118] Charles Cotrell found that in 1976 minority neighborhoods lagged well behind those of the North Side in services supported by federal revenue sharing funds, responsiveness of the zoning commission to neighborhood requests, street paving and repair, the drainage system, and public libraries.[119] Simmering dissatisfaction with council policies boiled into open political revolt in 1974 when the West Side community formed a grass roots organization called Communities Organized for Public Services (COPS), employing a model of confrontational tactics developed by Saul Alinsky's Industrial Areas Foundation. It succeeded in bringing the city's entrenched power structure to its knees by 1977.[120]

The beginning of the end of GGL's dominance of city hall occurred in 1973 when it lost three of the eight races in which it fielded candidates. Two years later it won only three of nine council positions, facing the "Independent Team" slate.[121] A major factor in its decline was a conflict between members of the business class favoring greater suburban development and those favoring the downtown area.[122] Faced with internal dissension and stunning defeat at the polls, the GGL chairman announced in 1976 that the organization had dissolved.[123]

A major change in San Antonio's electoral structure makes it extremely unlikely that the GGL will attempt a comeback. In 1976 the U.S. Department of Justice objected under the Voting Rights Act to the city's annexation of largely white suburbs, on the grounds that it diluted the votes of the city's minority population. As a remedy, the city adopted a council plan consisting of ten single-member district councilpersons and a mayor elected at large.[124] The West Side was now represented on council by Hispanics who did not have to meet the approval of an Anglo-dominated slating group. In 1981 Henry Cisneros, a candidate with strong West Side support who nonetheless attracted Anglo business backing, was elected mayor, becoming the first Chicano to occupy the post. (He had won a council seat in 1975 as a GGL candidate.) His council included four other Mexican Americans and one black. As in Dallas, the creation of single-member districts resulted in a diversity of interests represented on council that had not been witnessed in many decades.

CONCLUSION

We suggested at the beginning of this essay that the failure of racial minorities to achieve full and meaningful participation in local politics is often associated with nonpartisan slating groups. Having examined four such groups in major Texas cities, it is now time to elucidate this association.

Each of the four cities used an at-large election system at the time the slating groups were at their zenith of influence. The difficulty in winning office experienced by independent minority candidates—those not nominated by the slating groups—despite strong support from minority voters, points to vote dilution resulting from Anglo bloc voting. Dilution would have existed whether or not slating groups had operated in those cities. What, then, was their impact?

One important effect was *the dampening of issue-oriented campaigns.* All four slating groups strenuously discouraged their own nominees from waging campaigns built around issues. The "no-axe-to-grind" rule in both Abilene and Wichita Falls meant that issue-oriented candidates were not welcome. The same is implied by the unwillingness of the groups in these same two cities (and reportedly, those in Dallas and San Antonio as well) even to consider slating candidates who declared for office on their own initiative.

Over time the "no-axe-to-grind" policy put issue-oriented candidates on the defensive—not only the slating groups' candidates, but the independents as well. This was especially obvious in Abilene and Wichita Falls, where we carried out field work while the slating groups were dominant. Candidates told us they hesitated to raise issues for fear of being labeled demagogues or trouble makers. Leaders in the slating groups expressed their satisfaction that "politics" had been exorcised from elections.

In at-large cities where race is potentially divisive, however, a candidate representing racial minority interests must be able to air issues that overshadow purely racial ones—issues that appeal not solely to minority interests but to a substantial part of the majority electorate. An issue-oriented campaign is a major means by which a candidate representing minority interests can sometimes win cross-over votes from the majority bloc. Our study of the four Texas cities suggests that when the slating groups were at their strongest, this very important tool for building a winning coalition was effectively denied to independent minority leaders. The presence of the slating groups, then, added to the difficulties minority voters faced in overcoming a massive bloc vote among Anglos.

A second function of these particular slating groups was to coordinate the Anglo dominants' response to minority attempts to achieve greater political power. In its essence, this response was an exercise in the politics of tokenism.

By the late 1960s serious efforts in the minority communities were under way in all four cities to elect some of their preferred candidates. The gradual inclusion of selected minority persons in the internal nominating process and the slating of a few minority candidates were means of appearing to meet the political aspirations of minority groups.

That this was no more than appearance is indicated by the limited and very tentative role the minority community was accorded in the groups' internal slating process, and by the kind of minority candidates nominated. None of the slating groups allowed full and untrammelled minority involvement in the slating process. In some cases participation was by invitation. Not only were the rank-and-file minority voters excluded, but most of the minority leaders as well. In one case, participation at the "annual meeting" was open to all, but the makeup of the nominating committee was carefully controlled, and even then its recommendations could be overruled by the board of directors. In at least two cases, opinions of some minority leaders were sought by the nominating committee, although the minority leaders themselves were not allowed to take part in the inner deliberations of the slating group.

As a result, the candidates the slating groups finally nominated could not accurately be called the candidates of the minority groups' choice—not even when, occasionally, the slating group nominated candidates who themselves were black or Mexican American. The minorities' limited access to the slating process was reflected in the kind of minority persons typically slated. They were "safe" candidates who, like their Anglo counterparts, "didn't have an axe to grind," or in other words, did not wish to call attention to the particularized needs of their minority constituents or take an active part in seeing that those needs were met.

The result of the slating groups' coordinated response—the attempted cooptation of selected minority leaders by inviting them to take a limited role in the organization, and the substitution of the Anglo dominants' "minority candidates" for the minority community's choices—was to present to the public an image of moderate and reasonable compromise. "You cannot have your choice of candidate," the slating groups seemed to be saying to minority voters, "but at least you can have a council person of your own skin color." The groups may well have believed that this compromise would satisfy minority voters. And at a time when vote dilution litigation was beginning to attract public attention, they may have hoped to delude the courts as well into falsely identifying a minority officeholder with the minority groups' choice of candidate.

If so, they were probably mistaken on both counts. Most of the independent minority leaders to whom we talked in the various cities referred scornfully to the limits placed on their participation in the slating process. Judge Mahon, who wrote the opinion in *Lipscomb v. Wise,* the Dallas at-large dilution case, singled out for special criticism "the shadow of dilution" in "the high correlation between endorsement by the C.C.A. [the slating group] and victory citywide." Two blacks had been elected at large to the Dallas council prior to the trial, but only with the permission of the Citizens' Charter Association. Going directly to the heart of the slating group issue, he added, "Meaningful participation in the political process must not be a function of grace, but rather is a matter of right." [125] The implication is that minority persons elected under those circumstances, without minority voters having fair access to the slating group's nominating machinery, cannot properly be called candidates of the minority group's choice.

NOTES

1. Alfred B. Clubok, John M. De Grove and Charles D. Farris, "The Manipulated Negro Vote: Some Pre-Conditions and Consequences," *Journal of Politics* 26 (1964): 112–129.
2. See, for example, J. Leiper Freeman's observation that "many of the so-called nonpartisan local electoral systems might better be understood if viewed as complex

multiparty systems.'' Freeman, ''Local Party Systems, Theoretical Considerations and a Case Analysis,'' *American Journal of Sociology* 64 (November 1964): 283. While our own view is that many local nonpartisan systems can be seen as one-party systems, Freeman's argument that parties operate under the guise of nonpartisanship is identical to ours.

3. Leon D. Epstein, *Political Parties in Western Democracies* (New York: Praeger, 1967), 9.
4. City of Abilene EEO-4 Forms submitted to the Equal Employment Opportunity Commission State-Local Reporting Committee, 1981.
5. Rev. T. G. Oliphant, interviewed by Chandler Davidson, 8 February 1979, Ken Deckard, interviewed by Chandler Davidson, 7 February 1979.
6. Unpublished report by David Nix, ''The Founding of Citizens for Better Government,'' 1979.
7. Abilene *Reporter-News,* 6 March 1980.
8. Don Watts, interviewed by Chandler Davidson, 23 May 1979.
9. Defense Exhibit No. 75, *Maria Velasquez, et. al. v. Oliver Howard, et al.,* U.S. District Court, Northern District of Texas, No. CA 1-80-57.
10. Sample survey of voters in 1979 city elections (N = 156), conducted by Houston Interviewing, Houston, Texas, and supervised by the senior author.
11. Abilene *Reporter-News,* 16 December 1978.
12. *Velasquez v. Howard.*
13. This research was carried out under contract with West Texas Legal Services, plaintiffs' counsel, by the senior author of this paper.
14. *Robert's Rules of Order, Newly Revised,* a new and enlarged edition by Sarah Corbin Robert (Glenview, Ill.: 1970), 361–362. Except at mass meetings—as distinct from an organized society—the chair cannot make nominations unless provided for in the bylaws or by adoption of a motion (362).
15. Ken Deckard, interviewed by Chandler Davidson, 18 June 1980.
16. Lowell Maxey, interviewed by Eugene Jones, Spring 1979.
17. Ralph Hooks, interviewed by Chandler Davidson, 21 May 1979.
18. Abilene *Reporter-News,* 6 March 1979.
19. Joe Alcorta, interviewed by Luis Fraga, 8 August 1980.
20. Defendants' Exhibit No. 10, *Velasquez v. Howard.*
21. Calculations computed from data supplied by Abilene City Secretary.
22. Joe Alcorta, interviewed by Luis Fraga, 8 August 1980.
23. Ibid.
24. Ibid.
25. Letter to Abilene *Reporter-News,* 13 April 1980, from W. W. Dickenson.
26. Clarence W. Muehlberger, interviewed by Chandler Davidson, 12 December 1979.
27. The following example of ethnic hostility is taken *verbatim* from Mr. Muehlberger's interview: ''In the retail business I deal with a cross-section of Wichita Falls. The Blacks know me as 'Mr. Mule'. We've had to deal with their abusive language and their stealing. If they won't deal with us on our level, we'll deal with them on theirs.''
28. Guillermo ''Bill'' Garcia, interviewed by Chandler Davidson, 13 December 1979.
29. Ibid.
30. Mrs. Peggy McCullough, interviewed by Chandler Davidson, 12 December 1979.
31. Garcia interview.
32. Ibid.
33. Ibid.
34. Ibid.
35. Tommy Robinson, interviewed by Chandler Davidson, 10 September 1982.
36. Horace Boston, interviewed by Chandler Davidson, 10 September 1982.
37. Ibid.
38. Jody Cox, *Times* assistant managing editor, interviewed by Chandler Davidson, 10 September 1982.

39. Wichita Falls *Times,* 14 March 1976.
40. Ibid.
41. Ibid.
42. Muehlberger interview.
43. Wichita Falls *Times,* 14 March 1976.
44. Muehlberger interview.
45. Arthur Beyer, interviewed by Chandler Davidson, 10 December 1979; and Muehlberger interview.
46. Beyer interview.
47. Muehlberger interview.
48. Ibid.
49. Ibid.
50. Tom Fairclough, interviewed by Chandler Davidson, 13 December 1979.
51. McCullough interview.
52. Willis D. Hawley, *Nonpartisan Elections and the Case for Party Politics* (New York: John Wiley and Sons, 1973), 143.
53. *Charter, City of Dallas,* Tallahassee, Florida: Municipal Code Administration, 1973, xix.
54. Harold A. Stone, Don K. Price, and Katherine H. Stone, *City Manager Government in Nine Cities* (Chicago: Public Administration Service, 1940), 272.
55. Ibid., 272–273.
56. Ibid., 280.
57. Ibid.
58. Ibid., 271–272, 282, 287.
59. Ibid., 285.
60. Ibid., 286–287.
61. *Charter Amendments, City of Dallas,* Volume 2, 1930, 11–15.
62. Stone, Price and Stone, *City Manager Government,* 311.
63. *Dallas Morning News,* 4 April 1933.
64. Stone, Price and Stone, *City Manager Government,* 313–319.
65. Ibid., 328.
66. Ibid.
67. *Dallas Morning News,* 5 April 1939.
68. Kit Bauman, "A Collection of Dollars Represented by Men: Alex Bickley and the Dallas Citizens Council," *Dallas Times-Herald* (*Westward* magazine), 5 October 1980, 88.
69. *Dallas Morning News,* 15 July 1979.
70. Richard Austin Smith, "How Business Failed Dallas," *Fortune,* July 1964, 162.
71. Bauman, "Collection of Dollars," 94.
72. Molly Ivins, "Is Dallas Falling Apart?" *The Texas Observer,* 14 February 1975, 1; Bauman, "Collection of Dollars," 89; Smith, "How Business Failed Dallas," 214.
73. *Lipscomb v. Wise,* 399 F. Supp. 782–801 (Northern District of Texas, 1975), 736.
74. Ivins, "Is Dallas Falling Apart?", 1.
75. Ibid., 3.
76. *Lipscomb v. Wise,* 790, 794.
77. Arnold Fleischman, "The Adoption of the 8-3 Plan in Dallas" (manuscript, Department of Government, The University of Texas at Austin).
78. Ibid.
79. Stone, Price and Stone, *City Manager Government,* 330–331, 341.
80. *Lipscomb v. Wise,* 785–786.
81. Ibid., 784–791.
82. June Kronholz, "If Businessmen Find Dallas Friendly, That's Natural—They Run It," *Wall Street Journal,* 24 September 1979, 1.
83. John A. Booth and David R. Johnson, "Power and Progress in San Antonio Politics, 1836–1970," in *Community, Progress and Power: The Evolution of San Antonio,*

1836–1980, ed. John A. Booth, David R. Johnson, and Richard J. Harris (Lincoln, Nebraska: The University of Nebraska Press, forthcoming), chapter 2.

84. Ibid.
85. Ibid.
86. Luther Loe Sanders, "Nonpartisanism: Its Use as a Campaign Appeal in San Antonio, Texas, 1961–1971" (M.A. thesis, St. Mary's University, 1974), 52–53.
87. Booth and Johnson, "Power and Progress."
88. Ibid.; Sanders, "Nonpartisanism," 54.
89. Booth and Johnson, "Power and Progress."
90. Ibid.
91. Ibid.
92. Sanders, "Nonpartisanism," 59.
93. Ibid., 60.
94. Morgan Jones, interviewed by Chandler Davidson, 21 May 1979.
95. John Steen, past GGL president, interviewed by Luis Fraga, 30 June 1982; Sanders, "Nonpartisanism," 61.
96. Steen interview.
97. Sanders, "Nonpartisanism," 61.
98. Ibid., 63–64. In the 1970s the deliberations of the nominating committee became public, as a result of growing criticism of their secrecy.
99. Ibid., 64.
100. Ibid., 63–65.
101. Ibid., 74.
102. Ibid., 75.
103. Ibid., 69–72.
104. L. Tucker Gibson, Jr., and Robert R. Ashcroft, "Political Organizations in a Nonpartisan System" (Paper delivered at the Annual Meeting of the Southwestern Political Science Association, Dallas, Texas, 1977), 14.
105. Booth and Johnson, "Power and Progress."
106. Sanders, "Nonpartisanism," 74.
107. L. Tucker Gibson, "Mayoralty Politics in San Antonio," in Booth. Johnson, and Harris, *Community, Progress and Power,* chapter 9.
108. Ibid., 325; Robert Brischetto, Charles L. Cotrell and R. Michael Stevens, "Structural Change and Voter Participation in the Political Culture of San Antonio in the 1970s," in Booth, Johnson, and Harris, *Community, Progress and Power,* chapter 5.
109. Gibson, "Mayoralty Politics in San Antonio."
110. Ibid.
111. Ibid.
112. Brischetto, Cotrell, and Stevens, "Structural Change."
113. Ibid.
114. Ibid.
115. Ibid.
116. Thomas A. Baylis, "Leadership Change in Contemporary San Antonio," in Booth, Johnson and Harris, *Community, Progress and Power,* chapter 8.
117. Richard C. Jones, "San Antonio's Spatial Economic Structure from the Mid-1950s to the Late 1970s," in Booth, Johnson, and Harris, *Community Progress and Power,* chapter 6.
118. Booth and Johnson, "Power and Progress."
119. Charles L. Cotrell, *Municipal Services Equalization in San Antonio, Texas: Exploration in China Town* (San Antonio: St. Mary's University Department of Urban Studies, 1976) as summarized in Brischetto, Cotrell, and Stevens, "Structural Change," 160; and Peter A. Lapsha and William J. Sienbieda, "The Poverty of Public Services in the Land of Plenty: An Analysis and Interpretation," in *The Rise*

of the Sunbelt Cities, ed. David C. Perry and Alfred J. Watkins (Beverly Hills, California: Sage Publications, 1977), 180.

120. Paul Burka, "The Second Battle of the Alamo," *Texas Monthly,* December 1977, 218–230.

121. Gibson, "Mayoralty Politics in San Antonio," 318.

122. Gibson and Ashcroft, "Political Organizations," 25; Brischetto, Cotrell, and Stevens, "Structural Changes."

123. Gibson, "Mayoralty Politics," 318.

124. Charles L. Cotrell and Michael B. Stevens, "The 1975 Voting Rights Act and San Antonio, Texas: Toward a Federal Guarantee of a Republican Form of Local Government," *Publius* 8 (Winter 1978): 79–99.

125. 399 F. Supp. 790. The language was taken from *Graves v. Barnes* 343 F. Supp. 704 (W. D. Tex. 1972), aff'd sub nom. *White v. Regester* 412 U.S. 755 (1973).

7

Vote Dilution and the Voting Rights Act Amendments of 1982

Armand Derfner

The past two years have seen an extraordinary public debate over civil rights policy that has propelled the technical concept of ''vote dilution'' into national attention. The result is a new law, the Voting Rights Act amendments of 1982,[1] which is designed to recognize the tenacity of the vote dilution problem, to encourage the halting starts that have been made toward combating it, and to reject the efforts to shield vote dilution from effective challenge. The two-year-long debate also produced an ironic by-product—a Supreme Court decision, *Rogers v. Lodge,*[2] which goes far toward undoing the damage done by the earlier Supreme Court case of *Mobile v. Bolden.*[3]

Whether the new law will provide the intended relief, only time and court decisions will tell, but the first returns are encouraging. The lower courts have decided a number of cases under the amended Section 2, and have almost uniformly followed Congress' instructions faithfully. The Supreme Court has not finally decided any of the cases yet, but has given a preliminary approving signal in one significant case, and has made it clear that Section 2 is the first line of battle in voting discrimination cases.[4]

At this stage, then, it is appropriate to ask what we have, and what it means. To answer the second question we must also ask where the new provisions came from, and how they were passed.

In these four questions hangs the tale of one of the hardest fought civil rights battles of modern times.

WHAT DO WE HAVE?

On 29 June 1982, the President signed the Voting Rights Act amendments of 1982. The new law contains several major provisions, including an extension of Section 5 (under which certain ''covered'' jurisdictions are barred from instituting any new voting laws or procedures without first showing that the changes are nondiscriminatory), an extension of the bilingual assistance provisions (under which certain language minority voters are entitled to assistance in their own language when they vote), and a new provision entitling illiterate or handicapped people to assistance at the polls from a person of their choice rather than someone picked by the officials.[5]

Most centrally related to the concept of vote dilution, Section 2 of the Voting Rights Act was amended to incorporate a "results" test, allowing a voter to challenge a voting practice or procedure by showing that its "result" was discriminatory.[6] This amendment superseded the Supreme Court's holding in the 1980 *Mobile* case that such a challenge would be effective only if the proof showed that the practice or procedure had been intentionally designed or kept for the purpose of racial discrimination.

The ban on dilution, with the "results" test, is contained within Section 2(a) (The new language added by the amendment is italicized; the old language is bracketed.)

> 2(a). No voting qualification or prerequisite to voting or standard, practice or procedure shall be imposed or applied by any State or political subdivision [to deny or abridge] *in a manner which results in a denial or abridgement of* the right of any citizen of the United States to vote on account of race or color, or in contravention of the guarantees set forth in section 4(f)(2), as set forth in subsection (b).

In addition, during the course of the debate, the statute was expanded to include Section 2(b), a broad definition of what was being outlawed and what was not:

> 2(b). A violation of subsection (a) is established if, based on the totality of circumstances, it is shown that the political processes leading to nomination or election in the state or political subdivision are not equally open to participation by a class of citizens protected by subsection (a) in that its members have less opportunity than other members of the electorate to participate in the political process and to elect representatives of their choice. The extent to which members of the protected class have been elected to office in the State or political subdivision is one "circumstance" which may be considered, provided that nothing in this subsection establishes a right to have members of a protected class elected in numbers equal to their proportion of the population.

Although Section 2 is the only place where there is a definition of vote dilution, the same standard is adopted in several other provisions of the new law. One is in the "bailout" procedure, by which a jurisdiction covered under "preclearance" can gain release from that requirement. The 1982 amendments changed the old formula and made bailout depend upon an up-to-date showing of the jurisdiction's record on voting discrimination, including proof that the jurisdiction has

> eliminated voting procedures and methods of election which inhibit or dilute equal access to the electoral process.[7]

A second place where the Section 2 dilution standard is incorporated is in the Section 5 preclearance determination itself. Under the case of *Beer v. United States*,[8] a voting change submitted for preclearance is not objectionable unless it is "retrogressive," or unless it is so discriminatory as to violate the Constitution. The legislative history of the 1982 amendments indicates that in light of the results test written into Section 2, the *Beer* rule is expanded by authorizing a Section 5 objection if there is retrogression or a constitutional violation, *or* a violation of amended Section 2.[9]

WHERE DID IT COME FROM?

The language of Section 2(b) suggests the source of the new law. The critical language of the subsection is adapted from the Supreme Court's opinion in *White v. Regester*,[10] the 1973 decision which first struck down an election system (at-large elections) on the grounds that the system diluted the votes of black and Mexican American voters. The supporters of the new law believed that *White* had set up a workable, appropriate standard which was derailed by the later decision in *Mobile v. Bolden;* in *Mobile* the Supreme Court held that proof of the sort presented in *White* was insufficient without further proof that the system had been adopted or maintained for a discriminatory purpose. In amending Section 2, Congress was acting to restore the test of *White v. Regester* as it had been understood until *Mobile.*

The theme of racial vote dilution in districting dates back to 1965, when the Supreme Court first faced multimember districts in a districting plan. The Court held that multimember districts were not automatically unconstitutional, but warned that they might be invalid if they operated ("designedly or otherwise") to minimize or cancel out the voting strength of racial or political elements of the voting population.[11] This warning was repeated several times,[12] but it was not applied until a pair of cases were decided, in 1971 and 1973, testing at-large elections first in Indiana, then in Texas.

In the first case, *Whitcomb v. Chavis,* the Court rejected a challenge to the at-large elections in Marion County, Indiana, holding that the evidence did not establish vote dilution.[13] The Supreme Court made it clear there that dilution in an at-large system is not shown merely by blacks losing elections where the evidence suggested that the losses were the result of normal two-party politics and that blacks played effective roles in local politics. In the second case, however, the Supreme Court unanimously held that voters had successfully proved the unconstitutionality of at-large elections for the Texas State House of Representatives seats from Dallas County and Bexar County (San Antonio).

It was this latter case, *White v. Regester,* which became the center of the dispute over the 1982 Voting Rights amendments. In *White,* the Supreme Court took the formulation used since the first reapportionment cases and elaborated on it. First, the Court stressed that merely losing elections did not prove dilution:

> To sustain such claims, it is not enough that the racial group allegedly discriminated against has not had legislative seats in proportion to its voting potential.[14]

Then the Court went on to emphasize that the critical factor was the lack of equal opportunity for minority voters:

> The plaintiffs' burden is to produce evidence to support findings that the political processes leading to nomination and election were not equally open to participation by the group in question—that its members had less opportunity than did other residents in the district to participate in the political processes and to elect representatives of their choice.[15]

The Court went on to describe some of the factors that had led the lower court— in what the Supreme Court described as an "intensely local appraisal" of "the totality of the circumstances''—to conclude that the at-large elections in these two counties were unconstitutional.

The importance of *White* in 1982 lay as much in what it did not say as in what it did. First, although the language was less explicit than previous formulations, there was no indication that proof of discriminatory purpose was required. Second, although there was a discussion of formal barriers to registration and voting that had previously existed, those formal barriers were no longer in existence; therefore, it was apparent that the required "opportunity to participate" in the *White* opinion referred not simply to the absence of interference with registering and voting but to the realities of the political process. In effect, while the first sentence of the critical paragraph emphasized that there was no right to win elections, the rest of the paragraph made it clear that there was a right to have a fair opportunity.

Following *White v. Regester,* there were a number of cases applying the dilution test, most notably *Zimmer v. McKeithen,*[16] and these cases shared the basic theory of *White:* that minority voters were entitled to the opportunity to participate (and not simply in the sense of registering and voting), but that there was no guaranteed right to win elections; the other common thread of these cases was the absence of any suggestion that proof of discriminatory purpose was required.

In 1980, the Supreme Court put an end to these cases in its unexpected decision in *Mobile v. Bolden.* Although there was no single majority opinion in *Mobile,* the four-Justice opinion by Justice Stewart was generally thought of as the opinion of the Court. That opinion held that vote dilution under the Fourteenth Amendment could not be established without proof of a racially discriminatory purpose in the adoption or maintenance of the at-large election system. More decisive, though, was the way in which the four-Justice opinion treated the facts, which were quite similar to, and in some respects stronger than, the facts in *White v. Regester.* Where the Court in *White* had looked to the totality of the circumstances and had weighed each fact as part of a whole, the *Mobile* opinion isolated each fact which had led the lower courts to find dilution, and, looking at them separately, concluded that each factor was insufficient by itself to make out a showing of vote dilution.

By treating each item of evidence in isolation, and by sharply limiting the inferences which the lower courts were allowed to draw from the evidence, the *Mobile* court essentially overturned the *White* "totality of the circumstances" rule and rejected the very same proof that had been held sufficient in *White, Zimmer,* and numerous other lower court cases. As Congress was to see it, the *Mobile* decision eliminated the possibility of proving discriminatory purpose through circumstantial evidence and replaced it with a stringent rule demanding proof of discriminatory purpose and requiring that it be shown by direct evidence only.

The Supreme Court decision in *Mobile v. Bolden* brought judicial remedies for voting discrimination back to about what they had been before 1965—largely useless. That set the stage for discussions about ways of providing a statutory remedy that would be effective against voting discrimination and would allow a court to hold that a voting law or procedure is discriminatory without having to produce a purposeful "smoking gun."

As we shall see, *Whitcomb, White,* and *Bolden* formed the boundary points of

Congress's perception of the vote dilution issue, and thus shaped the legislation that became amended Section 2. *Mobile* was the case that Congress wanted to overturn; *White* was the rule Congress wanted to restore; and *Whitcomb* was the protection against the standard getting out of hand—because *Whitcomb* showed that the *White* rule would not extend to election systems in which minority voters appeared able to participate, just because they lost elections.

HOW DID WE GET HERE?

The result of the *Mobile* decision was devastating. Dilution cases came to a virtual standstill; existing cases were overturned and dismissed, while plans for new cases were abandoned. But apart from minority voters, a small group of lawyers, and critical comments in law reviews, there was no widespread outcry about the *Mobile* decision—at least not in 1980. The public outcry was to come a year later, after the legislative debate had gotten under way.[17]

Indeed, it is likely that *Mobile* would have become solidified, and vote dilution cases anachronisms, if not for the accident of timing that put the case just before the scheduled expiration date of the special provisions of the Voting Rights Act.

That expiration date was 6 August 1982, which made it a certainty that there would be a lively forum for consideration of voting discrimination, and that one of the topics in that debate would be the *Mobile* case. A look at the development of the Voting Rights Act shows why.

Voting Rights Act of 1965

The Voting Rights Act was passed on 6 August 1965, against a background of ninety years of failure to enforce the Fifteenth Amendment. The original heart of the Voting Rights Act was Section 4, which suspended literacy tests in certain "covered jurisdictions," mostly in the Deep South.

The suspension of the tests was for five years. During the five years, other remedies were in play, most important of which was Section 5, the preclearance provision. In 1965, Congress knew that in the past, whenever one type of discrimination had been blocked another had sprung up to take its place, sometimes within twenty-four hours. Section 5 was Congress's answer to this problem. Section 5 simply provided that in a covered jurisdiction no change in any voting law or procedure could be enforced until the change had been precleared by the jurisdiction through either a three-judge U.S. District Court in the District of Columbia or the Attorney General. In order to gain preclearance, the covered jurisdiction would have to show that its proposed change was not discriminatory in purpose and not discriminatory in effect. Section 5 was deliberately drawn as broadly as possible, to cover changes that could affect voting even in a minor way, because although Congress was confident that there would be widespread attempts to evade the Voting Rights Act, it could not predict exactly what forms those evasions would take.

There were several provisions of the new Voting Rights Act that were not limited to covered jurisdictions; the one that came to be most important was Section 2. The wording of this section, the simplest of all, was very similar to the language of the Fifteenth Amendment:

> No voting qualification or prerequisite to voting, or standard, practice or procedure, shall be imposed or applied by any State or political subdivision to deny or abridge the right of any citizen of the United States to vote on account of race or color. [Section 2 of the Voting Rights Act]

> The right of citizens of the United States to vote shall not be denied or abridged by any State on account of race, color or previous condition of servitude. [Section 2 of the Fifteenth Amendment]

The initial focus of efforts under the act was on registration and voting, through suspension of literacy tests. By 1970, as the initial five-year special coverage period was winding up, the literacy test suspension had resulted in registration of an estimated one million new black voters in the covered states.[18]

On the other hand, as black citizens overcame barriers to registering and casting ballots, new barriers were being erected to ensure that, while blacks might vote, they couldn't win. Congress's faith in the ingenuity of those who had been relying on discriminatory literacy tests was being quickly rewarded. A 1968 report of the Civil Rights Commission perceptively reported a sharp growth in vote dilution techniques as new methods of voting discrimination. The report specifically singled out redistricting measures, shifts to at-large elections, and changes in local government boundaries.[19]

Rejecting the argument that Section 5 should be limited to measures directly affecting the right to register and to cast a ballot, the Supreme Court in 1969 held that the broad reach of Section 5 covered these changes in "systems of representation" because, as the reapportionment cases recognized, "the right to vote can be affected by a dilution of voting power as well as by an absolute prohibition on casting a ballot."[20]

The trends perceived by the Civil Rights Commission in 1968 were the beginning of an epidemic of dilution methods in the covered jurisdictions. In fact, of the eight hundred changes to which the Attorney General has objected to date, the vast majority have involved changes in representational systems, or, to put it in plainer terms, gerrymanders and related tactics: redistricting; changes to at-large or multimember districts; annexations superimposed upon at-large election systems; majority-runoff requirements; and anti-single-shot methods such as full-slate laws and numbered places.[21]

Because of its effectiveness in checking the growth in vote dilution, Congress extended Section 5 for five years in 1970, and for seven more years in 1975. Both of the extensions in 1970 and 1975 were marked by vigorous debate in Congress and by extensive hearings and reports documenting the continuing abuses that justified the continued need for the preclearance remedy. Increasingly, these abuses fell in the area of vote dilution; and the 1975 hearings, reports, and floor debates are especially filled with account after account of gerrymandering, discriminatory at-large elections, improper municipal annexations, and similar methods that too often proved effective in keeping the newly registered black voters from exercising their votes effectively.[22] The administrative record under Section 5 demonstrated, though, that effective weapons against dilution could be developed.

The 1975 amendments also added a new dimension to the Voting Rights Act, in the form of provisions designed to protect certain language-minority voters (American Indian, Asian American, Alaskan Native, and Spanish-heritage) from discrimination. The key new provision, which is temporary, required bilingual assistance in some areas where language-minority voters are highly concentrated.[23] In addition, a clause was added to Section 2—the general ban on voting discrimination—prohibiting voting discrimination on account of language-minority as well as on account of race.

Prospects for Extension in 1982

The need to consider extending the Voting Rights Act by 1982 offered a perfect opportunity for trying to overturn the *Mobile* decision. In *Mobile,* the Supreme Court had considered the black voters' claims under three headings: the Fourteenth Amendment; the Fifteenth Amendment; and Section 2 of the Voting Rights Act. The Court had held that proof of purpose was required under both the Fourteenth and Fifteenth Amendments, and, since its cursory analysis of the legislative language and history of Section 2 persuaded the Court that the section was designed to do no more than to paraphrase the Fifteenth Amendment, it concluded that Section 2 must therefore have been intended to require proof of discriminatory purpose as well.[24]

This last holding gave Congress its opportunity. For, while the Supreme Court's decisions on the meaning of the Constitution are final, its interpretation of statutes is an interpretation of what the Court believes Congress intended. Congress is free to supersede the Supreme Court's interpretation of a statute by passing an amendment or a new statute spelling out in clearer language what it means (and what it believes the Supreme Court misconstrued). It was in this direction that civil rights organizations and lawyers looked for relief from *Mobile*.

Civil rights strategists meeting in late 1980 had three goals: (1) to extend Section 5; (2) to overturn *Mobile;* and (3) to extend the language-minority provisions of the Voting Rights Act. Each one of these tasks, taken separately, looked formidable. The conservative climate of the country had brought into office an administration that was perceived to be cool or even hostile to civil rights. In addition, each of the separate goals presented additional problems.

The extension of Section 5 could expect to face opposition because the replacement of violence and open fraud with more sophisticated techniques of dilution led many people to believe that voting discrimination had dropped so far that the severe remedy of requiring preclearance of every voting change—and only in some states—might no longer be justifiable.[25]

The amendment of Section 2 could expect opposition from those who were opposed to the results that had flowed from other holdings of discrimination based on proof of discriminatory effect. Many of these people feared that a standard that does not require proof of discriminatory purpose can be a code for racial quotas.

In this way, "effect" had picked up the same connotation that "affirmative action" has among many people today. For some people, these terms mean that people can be punished for innocent conduct because of proof based on "mere" statistics.[26]

The extension of the language-minority provisions could expect opposition based on the high cost of some of the bilingual assistance procedures, and from the growing anti-bilingual mood.

If each of the three goals seemed problematic, achievement of all three seemed out of the question. Yet, strategists made the decision early in 1981 to seek all three goals together, and to start with a draft bill that combined all three provisions. They did so with hope but pessimism, for there were few who thought Congress would pass any bill that included meaningful provisions extending preclearance *and* extending the language minority provisions *and* overturning *Mobile*. Nonetheless, the omnibus bill was launched.

On 7 April 1981, simultaneous bills were introduced in the House of Representatives, H.R. 3112, by Rep. Peter Rodino, and in the Senate, S. 895, by Sens. Charles Mathias, Edward Kennedy, and five other senators. These identical bills extended preclearance for ten years (until 1992), extended the language-minority provisions until 1992, and changed the language of Section 2 by replacing the words "to deny or abridge" with the words "in a manner which results in a denial or abridgement of." Accompanying statements underlined the fact that the reason for the Section 2 change was to eliminate the *Mobile* requirement of proving discriminatory purpose.[27]

In turning away from the *Mobile* rule, the supporters of the Section 2 amendment were seeking a return to the prior rule of *White v. Regester*. The term *result* was shorthand for that approach, and was chosen instead of the more familiar term *effect*, because *effect* had been the lightning rod for opposition to decisions in the highly controversial areas of employment and housing discrimination. The word *result* was chosen because it had not been so commonly used in this context and was thus a better candidate for an effort to define a term in precisely the way desired, without fear of confusion from other, seemingly analogous areas.

In moving to amend Section 2, the supporters of the change were under no illusions about the opposition. For one thing, it was clear that many civil rights opponents had seized upon the purpose-effect dichotomy as a way of opposing strong civil rights enforcement, and that the Voting Rights Act would be no exception. A graphic example occurred just as the planning was beginning at the end of 1980, when a set of amendments to the Fair Housing Act was successfully filibustered over the issue of purpose versus effect.[28]

House of Representatives

Because the 1980 elections had produced radical changes in the Senate, including likely opponents at the head of both the Judiciary Committee and the Constitution Subcommittee, the supporters of the bill decided to proceed first in the House of Representatives. There, the Subcommittee on Civil and Constitutional Rights, headed by Rep. Don Edwards, D-Cal., began hearings in May which continued for two months, through early July. During that period, the subcommittee heard more than one hundred witnesses, and its hearings eventually filled three volumes totaling over 2,800 pages.[29]

From the outset, the House subcommittee resolved to have exhaustive hearings, in order to lay to rest all doubts about whether voting discrimination was in fact still a major problem now that the outright denial of the right to vote was largely in the past. For this reason, the bulk of the House testimony focused on the continuing record of voting abuse, most of which consisted of different forms of dilution like gerrymandering, discriminatory annexations, use of at-large elections, and the like. The graphic testimony left no doubt that vote dilution could be just as corrosive and just as stifling as the outright vote denials that had been replaced.[30]

Moreover, although most of the testimony was presented to lay a basis for extending Section 5, no fewer than thirty witnesses also testified about the problems caused by the *Mobile* case, and the difficulty or near impossibility of proving discriminatory purpose in even the most egregious violations. Thus, the same testimony that supported extension of Section 5 also brought home the need for amending Section 2 to adopt a "results" test.

During the hearings, some concern was expressed about whether the Section 2 amendment was too open ended, and might allow the courts to find that a lack of proportional representation by itself was the kind of "result" that would establish a Section 2 violation. To remove this issue, the Judiciary Committee added a disclaimer sentence to the Section 2 amendment:

> The fact that members of a minority group have not been elected in numbers equal to the group's proportion of the population shall not, in and of itself, constitute a violation of this section.[31]

The committee report elaborated further on the meaning of amended Section 2. The committee bluntly disagreed with the Supreme Court's interpretation of Section 2 in *Mobile* and said the amendment would make clear "that proof of discriminatory purpose or intent is not required in cases brought under that provision."[32] The committee then discussed the types of evidence that would be appropriate, noting that its standards relied on *White v. Regester*. On the issue of proportional representation, the committee repeated the disclaimer that lack of proportional representation did not by itself constitute a violation, "although such proof, along with other objective factors, would be highly relevant."[33]

On 31 July 1981, the Judiciary Committee adopted the Voting Rights bill with the results test and the disclaimer, twenty-three to one.[34] Only Rep. Butler, R-Va., dissented from adoption of the results test and dissented equally from the *Mobile* "purpose" test, which he described as requiring a "smoking gun."[35] The bill also included a radically new bailout in place of the straight ten-year extension originally proposed. The new bailout included the requirement that a jurisdiction "have eliminated voting procedures and methods of election which inhibit or dilute equal access to the political process." In effect, this was a "reverse Section 2" case that must be established by any jurisdiction seeking to bail out from Section 5 coverage. The Judiciary Committee's explanation of this provision was similar to the explanation of Section 2, and referred to *White v. Regester* and *Zimmer v. McKeithen.*[36]

On 5 October 1981, the House of Representatives took the Voting Rights bill up, overwhelmingly rejected a series of amendments aimed primarily at relaxing the bailout, and finally passed the bill by the lopsided vote of 389 to 24.[37] The only quarrel with the results test came from Rep. Bliley, R-Va., who offered an amendment to eliminate the results test; the Bliley amendment was rejected by voice vote.[38]

Once the House overwhelmingly passed the Voting Rights Act extension on 5 October 1981, the focus of attention shifted to the Senate. Before activity began there, however, the president made his long-awaited statement on the act. After intense lobbying from all sides, a last-minute appeal by the attorney general led the president to back away from the generally supportive position and, instead, to come out for a "purpose" requirement and strongly oppose the "results" test.[39] From that point forward, the Justice Department, led by Attorney General Smith and Assistant Attorney General Reynolds, was an indefatigable foe of the Section 2 amendment and led the campaign against it.[40]

Senate

In the Senate, the hearings, which ran from late January through early March, focused almost exclusively on Section 2. Subcommittee Chairman Orrin Hatch, R-Utah, equated the results test with proportional representation, and the hearings were an intense battle between supporters of the amendment, who testified about the impossibility of dealing with serious voting discrimination under a "purpose" test, and opponents of the amendment, who insisted that without a requirement of discriminatory purpose, the section would inevitably require proportional representation and set up quota systems.[41]

The debate in the Senate subcommittee was extraordinarily subtle, at times almost metaphysical. Supporters of the results test argued, for example, that it focused correctly on whether evidence about the actual workings of an electoral system shows that minority voters are effectively shut out of the process in fact, rather than on the mindreading required by the purpose test. To this, opponents responded that the only coherent standard in a discrimination case is one based on purpose, while any standard that is not based on purpose will inevitably degenerate into a simple statistical exercise in which the number of minority officials elected will be the sole determinant of whether there is a violation. The supporters' rejoinder to this argument was that the results test was based on earlier cases like *White v. Regester* and *Zimmer v. McKeithen,* which had no purpose requirement and yet which adopted intelligible standards that did not involve any right to proportional representation. The opponents' response to this argument was that if *White* and *Zimmer* did not produce proportional representation, they must therefore have rested on proof of discriminatory purpose.[42]

While this battle was going on in the subcommittee hearings, senators were being lobbied intensively with discussions of legal philosophy and analysis of the subtleties of court opinions, as well as with traditional politics. On one side was an array of civil rights organizations, representing vocal constituents who were unusually well organized in almost every state, and who were urging protection of the most fundamental democratic right;[43] on the other side were staunch opponents led by a seemingly invincible president who was at the height of his popularity, but who had been badly hurt in the area of civil rights by gross blunders like the proposal to give tax exemptions to segregated private schools.[44] Supporters of the House bill had struck early by quietly lining up sixty-one cosponsors even before the House bill was introduced in the Senate in December 1981.[45] Many of the new cosponsors had not yet been subjected to pressure, and once the House bill was introduced in the Senate, they were pulled and tugged in every direction. The opponents included both the Judiciary Committee Chairman, Sen. Thurmond, R-S.C., and the Subcommittee Chairman, Sen. Hatch, R-Utah. Not only were these two men powerfully positioned and fiercely determined, but the structure and rules of the Senate give an enormous advantage to the side opposing passage of any bill. Moreover, because the Voting Rights Act had a deadline of 6 August 1982, the supporters were under pressure to pass the bill before the clock started running down; if they did not, time would be so short that supporters would have to compromise substantially in order to gain anything.

In the end, the maneuvering did not sway votes away from the Section 2 amendment, but by the time the Judiciary Committee met to consider the bill in late April, the Senate sponsors had decided that, in order to lay the proportional representation issue to rest, the Senate committee should follow the lead of the House committee and add language to Section 2 spelling out what it meant. The additional language, crafted chiefly by Senator Kennedy and Senator Dole, R-Kans., codified the approach of *White v. Regester* and responded to the frequently asked question, "Well, if you mean the *White* test, why don't you just say it in the statute itself?" The Kennedy-Dole language kept the original version of the Section 2 amendment as Section 2(a), and added a new Section 2(b) which adapted language from *White v. Regester* and reworded the House disclaimer on proportional representation.

With the new language, the Section 2 amendment was adopted in the Senate Judiciary Committee on 4 May 1982, by a vote of fourteen to four.[46] On the Senate floor, after a filibuster was broken on a massive cloture vote, the first amendment offered was by Sen. East, R-N.C., to delete the results test; the East proposal was overwhelmingly defeated by a vote of eighty-one to sixteen.[47]

A series of other amendments was offered, most of them dealing with Section 2, but some dealing with the bailout or the language assistance provisions. After a session that lasted until three o'clock in the morning of 18 June 1982, the Senate came back later that day and finally passed the bill by a vote of eighty-five to eight.[48]

In the end, all three provisions that the civil rights planners had aimed at from the beginning were adopted: extension of preclearance; extension of language assistance; and adoption of the results test. Even though each of the provisions had been amended, the amendments had not weakened the substance of what the proponents had sought. Ironically, the combination of the three goals had probably not weakened any of them, but rather strengthened them. The best example of that was the relative ease with which the complex bailout formula swept through the Senate.[49] This resulted in part from the opponents' preoccupation with Section 2 to the exclusion of anything else. When Senator Hatch began a floor speech attacking the bailout, his fellow subcommittee member, Sen. Grassley, R-Iowa, interrupted to ask why, if the issue was so important, no time had been devoted to it in the subcommittee hearings.[50]

On 29 June 1982, the President, who had announced his support of the Senate bill after it was approved by the Judiciary Committee—at which point he had no choice—signed the Voting Rights Act Amendments of 1982 into law.[51]

On Making Legislative History

Ordinarily, these clear-cut votes, accompanied by numerous statements that the "results" test was designed to overrule the *Mobile* purpose requirement, would have put the matter to rest. But a curious thing happened in the course of the Senate consideration of the bill. The opponents of the Section 2 amendment, while fighting every step of the way, began carefully positioning themselves for another battle after passage of the bill—a battle over the meaning of the Section 2 amendment.

This process began with claims by Senator Hatch and Assistant Attorney General Reynolds that *if* the cases to which supporters of the amendment looked, such as *White* and *Zimmer*, had not produced proportional representation, they must have been based on proof of discriminatory purpose.[52] For example, Senator Hatch voted against the Section 2 amendment and filed ninety pages of additional views with the committee report, largely attacking the results test and the amendment passed by the committee. In addition, though, he appended a two-page footnote to his additional views, in which he invited courts interpreting Section 2 to find that, notwithstanding his fears, and notwithstanding the statutory language and legislative history, amended Section 2 did in fact still have a purpose requirement.[53]

Still later, when the committee bill was called up for floor action, Senator Thurmond, as Judiciary Committee Chairman, designated Senator Hatch as floor manager. Such assignments are critical for later interpretations of legislation, because a standard rule of statutory construction is that the statements of floor managers carry great weight in interpreting a bill. It is highly unusual to designate as floor manager of a major bill someone who has been a strong opponent of the bill or its principal components. Ordinarily, the committee chairman is free to designate the floor manager of a bill, but in this case the bill's outraged sponsors cried foul to Majority Leader Baker, and suddenly it developed that Senator Hatch was floor manager only for the procedural motion to call up the bill, while Senator Mathias, the ranking Republican supporter of the bill, became floor manager of the bill itself.[54]

The positioning did not end there. Once the Judiciary Committee adopted the Kennedy-Dole amendment, the President announced that he would support the committee bill, and the Justice Department began claiming that it had achieved *its* goals in reaching a compromise—notwithstanding its unflinching opposition and the fact that the Justice Department's claims for the meaning of the amendment were rejected by its sponsors.[55]

Finally, when the bill was passed by the Senate and went back to the House to be conformed, Reps. Hyde and Lungren inserted statements in the *Congressional Record*, without making them on the floor, indicating that they were voting for the bill because they were satisfied that it did require proof of purpose.[56]

WHAT DOES IT MEAN?

After All This, What Does Section 2 Mean?

It has never been possible to define vote dilution in a single phrase, and even the *White* language inserted in Section 2(b) by the Senate committee is no more than a shorthand for a collection of facts (which vary from case to case) that would add up to the requisite lack of equal opportunity to participate successfully in the electoral process. Because some of the post-*White* and post-*Zimmer* cases treated possible factors in mechanical ways, both the House committee and, to an even greater extent, the Senate committee included discussions of what factors might be relevant, along with cautions about misuse of the factors. These two report passages are the most authoritative expressions of Section 2's meaning.

The House committee report said:[57]

> In determining the relevancy of the evidence the court should look to the context of the challenged standard, practice or procedure. The proposed amendment avoids highly subjective factors such [as] responsiveness of elected officials to the minority community. Use of this criterion creates inconsistencies among court decisions on the same or similar facts and confusion about the law among government officials and voters. An aggregate of objective factors should be considered such as history of discrimination affecting the right to vote, racially polarity [polarized] voting which impedes the election opportunities of minority group members, discriminatory elements of the electoral system such as at-large elections, a majority vote requirement, a prohibition on single-shot voting, and numbered posts which enhance the opportunity for discrimination, and discriminatory slating or the failure of minorities to win party nomination.[a] All of these factors need not be proved to establish a Section 2 violation.
>
> The amended section would continue to apply to different types of election problems. It would be illegal for an at-large election scheme for a particular state or local body to permit a bloc voting majority over a substantial period of time consistently to defeat minority candidates or candidates identified with the interests of a racial or language minority. A districting plan which suffers from these defects or in other ways denies equal access to the political process would also be illegal.

The Senate committee report said:[58]

> If as a result of the challenged practice or structure plaintiffs do not have an equal opportunity to participate in the political processes and to elect candidates of their

---

[a] These objective standards rely on *White v. Regester*, 412 U.S. 755 (1973) but [it] is not controlling since it established a constitutional violation.

choice, there is a violation of this section. To establish a violation, plaintiffs could show a variety of factors, depending upon the kind of rule, practice, or procedure called into question.

Typical factors include:[b]

1. The extent of any history of official discrimination in the state or political subdivision that touched the right of the members of the minority group to register, to vote, or otherwise to participate in the democratic process;
2. the extent to which voting in the elections of the state or political subdivision is racially polarized;
3. the extent to which the state or political subdivision has used unusually large election districts, majority vote requirements, anti-single shot provisions, or other voting practices or procedures that may enhance the opportunity for discrimination against the minority group;
4. if there is a candidate slating process, whether the members of the minority group have been denied access to that process;
5. the extent to which members of the minority group in the state or political subdivision bear the effects of discrimination in such areas as education, employment and health, which hinder their ability to participate effectively in the political process;[c]
6. whether political campaigns have been characterized by overt or subtle racial appeals;
7. the extent to which members of the minority group have been elected to public office in the jurisdiction.[d]

Additional factors that in some cases have had probative value as part of plaintiffs' evidence to establish a violation are:

whether there is a significant lack of responsiveness on the part of elected officials to the particularized needs of the members of the minority group.[e]

---

[b]These factors are derived from the analytical framework used by the Supreme Court in *White*, as articulated in *Zimmer*.

[c]The courts have recognized that disproportionate educational[,] employment, income level and living conditions arising from past discrimination tend to depress minority political participation, e.g., *White*, 412 U.S. 139 at 768; *Kirksey v. Board of Supervisors*, 554 F.2d 139, 145. Where these conditions are shown, and where the level of black participation in politics is depressed, plaintiffs need not prove any further causal nexus between their disparate socio-economic status and the depressed level of political participation.

[d]The fact that no members of a minority group have been elected to office over an extended period of time is probative. However, the election of a few minority candidates does not "necessarily foreclose the possibility of dilution of the black vote," in violation of this section. *Zimmer*, 485 F.2d at 1307. If it did, the possibility exists that the majority citizens might evade the section e.g., by manipulating the election of a "safe" minority candidate. "Were we to hold that a minority candidate's success at the polls is conclusive proof of a minority group's access to the political process, we would merely be inviting attempts to circumvent the Constitution. . . . Instead we shall continue to require an independent consideration of the record." *Ibid.*

[e]Unresponsiveness is not an essential part of plaintiff's case. *Zimmer; White* (as to Dallas.) Therefore, defendants' proof of some responsiveness would not negate plaintiff's showing by other, more objective factors enumerated here that minority voters nevertheless were shut out of equal access to the political process. The amendment rejects the ruling in *Lodge* v. *Buxton* and companion cases that unresponsiveness is a requisite element, 639 F.2d 1358, 1375 (5th Cir. 1981), (an approach apparently taken in order to comply with the intent requirement which the Supreme Court's plurality opinion in *Bolden* imposed on the former language of Section 2.) However, should plaintiff choose to offer evidence of unresponsiveness, then the defendant could offer rebuttal evidence of its responsiveness.

whether the policy underlying the state or political subdivision's use of such voting qualification, prerequisite to voting or standard, practice or procedure is tenuous.*f*

While these enumerated factors will often be the most relevant ones, in some cases other factors will be indicative of the alleged dilution.

The cases demonstrate, and the Committee intends that there is no requirement that any particular number of factors be proved, or that a majority of them point one way or the other.*g*

What Does Section 2 Not Mean?

There are several possible meanings of Section 2 which were urged or which may now be advanced but which have been explicitly and decisively rejected by the legislative history. One of these was the argument that the results test would require proportional representation, advanced by some in order to arouse opposition to the Section 2 amendment.[59] More pertinent now are several arguments to the effect that the Section 2 amendment really does almost nothing. This is known as the "never give up" approach, and there are at least two major issues in this category that the bill's supporters have anticipated and rejected.

Most critical is the argument that the Section 2 amendment still incorporates a purpose requirement. This argument was advanced in Congress, interestingly enough, by some of the same people who were claiming at the same time that Section 2 would bring proportional representation. No theory could have been more thoroughly, frequently, and vehemently rejected than this notion. It was repeatedly rejected in the Senate report, both in the majority views presented by Senator Mathias,[60] and equally emphatically by Senator Dole in his additional views;[61] both these sources refer explicitly to attempts by some to interpret the Section 2 amendment as including some form of purpose requirement, and make it clear that any such efforts are completely misplaced. The same thoughts were repeated on the Senate floor,[62] and finally in no uncertain terms by Senator Kennedy:

> Let there be no question then. We are writing into law our understanding of the *White* test. And our understanding is that this looks only to the results of a challenged law, in the totality of circumstances—with no requirement of proving purpose. But should the Highest Court in the land—or a majority of the Court—conclude there is a purpose element in *White*, then the Committee nonetheless has drafted a bill that does not incorporate this requirement, and that is the ultimate legislative intent of the bill we are adopting here tonight.[63]

---

*f*If the procedure markedly departs from past practices or from practices elsewhere in the jurisdiction, that bears on the fairness of its impact. But even a consistently applied practice premised on a racially neutral policy would not negate a plaintiff's showing through other factors that the challenged practice denies minorities fair access to the process.

*g*The courts ordinarily have not used these factors, nor does the Committee intend them to be used, as a mechanical "point counting" device. The failure of plaintiff to establish any particular factor, is not rebuttal evidence of non-dilution. Rather, the provision requires the court's overall judgment, based on the totality of circumstances and guided by those relevant factors in the particular case, of whether the voting strength of minority voters is, in the language of *Fortson* and *Burns*, "minimized or canceled out."

A related argument is that the references in the statutory language to the equal opportunity to participate refer only to the right to register and vote without interference, and that "equal access" is not a guarantee against dilution. This view, too, was explicitly rejected in a passage which noted and rejected the same notion as it appeared in the *Mobile* decision.[64]

Despite these clear statements, there have been and there will inevitably be more arguments pressing for a narrow interpretation of Section 2. This will be true not only in standard dilution cases, but also in cases by jurisdictions seeking to bail out of Section 5 coverage (who will have to provide a "reverse Section 2" case) that they "have eliminated voting procedures and methods of election which inhibit or dilute equal access to the electoral process." Thus far, all these arguments have been rejected.

THE EARLY SIGNS

The first cases decided under the amended Section 2 have given encouraging signs that Section 2 will be interpreted as Congress intended. In the first two years after the amendment of Section 2, approximately a dozen cases had been won by plaintiffs in lower courts, a similar number had been settled favorably, and a similar number of new cases had been filed.

One case, the Louisiana congressional districting plan (called the "Donald Duck" plan, after the appearance of one district), was struck down under Section 2.[65] In another case, a district court invalidated at-large elections in the city of Lubbock, Texas, as violating both the Constitution and Section 2. The Fifth Circuit disagreed with the constitutional holding because it found insufficient proof of purposeful discrimination, but agreed that the at-large elections violated Section 2.[66] In a third case, a court held that several state legislative districts in North Carolina produced discriminatory results in violation of Section 2. North Carolina requested a stay from the Supreme Court, arguing that the lower court had greatly exaggerated the scope of Section 2, but the stay was denied twice, first by Chief Justice Burger, and then on a request for reconsideration, by the unanimous Supreme Court as a whole.[67]

These decisions, and others, have included detailed and conscientious analyses of the background and meaning of Section 2, and have begun to create a body of law under Section 2 that can be used effectively to challenge vote dilution as Congress intended.

ANTI-CLIMAX: *ROGERS V. LODGE*

Two days after the Voting Rights Act Amendments of 1982 were signed into law, the Supreme Court handed down its decision in *Rogers v. Lodge,* holding that at-large elections in Burke County, Georgia, violated the Fourteenth Amendment.[68] The decision was not unexpected in the sense that most observers could not imagine how a majority of the Supreme Court, confronted with the outrageous facts in

Lodge and stung by nationwide criticism of the *Mobile* decision, could reverse two lower courts and find that the at-large elections in Burke County were not discriminatory. At the same time, there did not seem to be any way that a holding of discrimination in *Lodge* could be reconciled with *Mobile*, so observers waited to see how the Supreme Court would solve this puzzle.

As it developed, most of the justices thought the two cases required identical decisions; that is, the four justices who voted to strike down the at-large elections in *Mobile* also voted to strike them down in *Lodge*, while three of the justices who voted for the Mobile government also voted for Burke County. The difference was in Chief Justice Burger, who switched his vote from "constitutional" (Mobile) to "unconstitutional" (Burke County), and Justice O'Connor, who voted to hold the Burke County system unconstitutional whereas her predecessor, Justice Stewart, had voted to uphold Mobile's system.

The lower courts had found that the system was adopted in 1911 for reasons other than race, but that the continued maintenance of the at-large system was racially discriminatory. In affirming the lower courts, the Supreme Court examined the individual findings which contributed to the lower courts' ultimate finding of a discriminatory purpose in maintaining the at-large system, and approved their treatment together, rather than asking—as the *Mobile* Court had done—about the sufficiency of each factor in isolation. The net result was a holding that discriminatory purpose was required, but that it could be proved by an aggregate of factors that added up to a lack of equal opportunity to participate successfully.

Since that venture into deciding a dilution case under the Constitution, the Supreme Court has insisted that other vote dilution cases be decided under Section 2, and it has sent several cases back to lower courts for that purpose.[69] The meaning of dilution under the Constitution is therefore not certain, but that may become a moot question if the Section 2 cases continue to develop so that section 2 becomes a full and adequate remedy for vote dilution.

These and other questions are waiting for answers just beginning to develop, but there is no question that the debate that produced the new Section 2 has given a large push in favor of protecting minority voters from efforts to dilute their votes. If the courts read the law correctly, it will be an effective tool for combating vote discrimination.

NOTES

1. Public Law 97-205, 96 Stat. 131 (1982).
2. 458 L.Ed.2d 613 (1982).
3. 446 U.S. 55 (1980).
4. See *infra*, at notes 65–69.
5. The Voting Rights Act is codified at 42 U.S.C. § 1973. Section 5 was extended by amending the time periods in Section 4, 42 U.S.C. § 1973b; the extension of the bilingual provisions is in Section 203, 42 U.S.C. § 1973aa–1a; the aid to handicapped or illiterate voters is contained in a new Section 208, 42 U.S.C. § 1973aa–6.
6. 42 U.S.C. § 1973.
7. Section 4(a)(1)(F)(1), 42 U.S.C. § 1973b(a)(1)(F)(i).
8. 425 U.S. 130 (1976).

9. S. REP. NO. 97-417, p. 12n.31 (1982); 128 CONG. REC. S7095 (daily ed. 18 June 1982) (Sen. Kennedy); 128 CONG. REC. H3841 (daily ed. 23 June 1982) (Rep. Sensenbrenner).

10. 412 U.S. 755 (1965).

11. *Fortson v. Dorsey,* 379 U.S. 433 (1965).

12. *Burns v. Richardson,* 384 U.S. 73 (1966); *Abate v. Mundt,* 403 U.S. 182 (1971).

13. 403 U.S. 124 (1971).

14. 412 U.S. at 765–66.

15. *Ibid.*

16. 485 F.2d 1297 (5th Cir. 1973), aff'd on other grounds sub nom. *East Carroll Parish School Board v. Marshall,* 424 U.S. 636 (1976).

17. Compare the *Washington Post* editorials on 28 April 1980, and 11 February 1982, reprinted in the Senate Hearings. Hearings Before the Subcommittee on the Constitution of the Senate Committee on the Judiciary, on S.53, etc., Bills to Amend the Voting Rights Act of 1965, 97th Cong. 2d Sess., Vol. 1, 755, 770 (1982). Later, there were more than a hundred critical editorials in other newspapers from coast to coast, north and south. One of the most pungent was in the *Birmingham (Ala.) Post-Herald,* which said, "for one thing, many discriminatory voting and registration rules were adopted years ago by persons who are now dead. It would be a neat trick to subpoena them from their graves for testimony about their racial motivations." Nov. 13, 1981.

18. David Garrow, *Protest at Selma,* 19, 200 (1978).

19. United States Commission on Civil Rights, *Political Participation* (1968).

20. *Allen v. State Board of Elections,* 393 U.S. 544 (1969).

21. U.S. Justice Department figures printed in the House Hearings. Hearings Before the Subcommittee on Civil and Constitutional Rights of the House Committee on the Judiciary, on Extension of the Voting Rights Act, 97th Cong. 1st Sess., Part 3, 2243–44 (1981).

22. For example, H.R.REP. NO. 94-1968–11 (1975); S. REP. NO. 94-295, 15–19 (1975).

23. Section 4(f), 42 U.S.C. § 1973b(f); Section 203, 42 U.S.C. § 1973aa.

24. 446 U.S. at 61. The plurality view of the original meaning of Section 2 ignored most of the legislative history, which is described in S. REP. NO. 97-417, 17–19 (1982).

25. Rep. Henry Hyde typified this view, House Hearings 2. He later changed his mind. House Hearings 1816. See also Hyde, "Why I Changed My Mind on the Voting Rights Act," *Washington Post,* 26 July 1981.

26. This point of view is summarized in Sen. Hatch's additional views accompanying the Senate Report. S. REP. NO. 97-417, 139–51 (1982).

27. 127 CONG. REC. S3539 (daily ed. 7 April 1981) (Sen. Mathias); ibid. at S3540 (Sen. Kennedy); ibid. at H1311 (Rep. Rodino); ibid. at (Sen. Moynihan).

28. 38 *Congressional Quarterly* 3544 (1980).

29. Hearings Before the Subcommittee on Civil and Constitutional Rights of the House Committee on the Judiciary, on Extension of the Voting Rights Act, 6, 7, 13, 19, 20, 27, 28 May, 3, 5, 10, 12, 16, 17, 18, 23, 24, 25 June, and 13 July 1981, 97th Cong. 1st Sess. (1981).

30. At the conclusion of the Montgomery, Alabama, field hearing, Rep. Henry Hyde, R-Ill., the ranking minority member of the Subcommittee, announced that the testimony at the hearings had changed his mind, and that he would now support extension of Section 5. See Hyde, "Why I Changed My Mind," *Washington Post,* 26 July 1981.

31. H.R. REP. NO. 97-227, 48 (1981).

32. *Ibid.,* 29.

33. *Ibid.,* 30.

34. *Ibid.,* 3.

35. H.R. REP. NO. 97-227, at 70.

36. *Ibid.,* 42–43.

37. 127 CONG. REC. 7011 (Daily ed. 5 October 1981).

38. 127 CONG. REC. 6985 (Daily ed. 5 October 1981).
39. White House Press Release, 6 November 1981, reprinted at Senate Hearings 763. See *Los Angeles Times,* 6 November 1981; *Washington Post,* 7 November 1981.
40. 40 *Congressional Quarterly,* 170–71, 520–21 (1982); 14 *National Journal* 592 (1982).
41. *Compare* Senate Hearings at 1417 (Archibald Cox) with ibid. 74 (William French Smith).
42. *Compare* Senate Hearings 797 (Armand Derfner) with ibid. 1679 (William Bradford Reynolds).
43. See Barton Gellman, "The New Old Movement," *New Republic,* 6 September 1982, p. 10.
44. 40 *Congressional Quarterly* 86 (1982). The Administration's efforts were rejected by the Supreme Court in *Bob Jones Univ. v. United States,* 461 U.S. __ (1983).
45. The House bill was introduced as S. 1992, on 16 December 1981.
46. S. REP. NO. 97-417, at 75. After a number of other amendments were defeated, the bill was reported out by the Committee by a vote of 17 to 1, with Sen. East, R-N.C., the sole dissenter.
47. 128 CONG. REC. S6965 (Daily ed. 17 June 1982).
48. 128 CONG. REC. S7139 (Daily ed. 18 June 1982).
49. Amendments dealing with the bailout provisions were rejected by votes of 65-31, 78-19, 58-32, 74-16, 73-19, 64-28, 66-28, 81-12, and 81-12 again. 128 CONG REC. D781, D789–90 (daily eds. 17 and 18 June 1982).
50. 128 CONG. REC. S6650–51 (Daily ed. 10 June 1982) (remarks of Sen. Grassley).
51. See 18 Weekly Comp. Pres. Docs. 846 (29 June 1982).
52. SENATE HEARINGS 1696, 1701 (William Bradford Reynolds).
53. S. REP. NO. 97-417, at 104–05 n.24.
54. 128 CONG. REC. S6941 (daily ed. 17 June 1982). See also ibid. at S7095 (Daily ed. 18 June 1982) (remarks of Sen. Kennedy, referring to the change). Some of the reasons for not giving as much weight to opponents' explanations of a bill are discussed in *Ernst & Ernst v. Hochfelder,* 425 U.S. 185, 204 n.24 (1976).
55. See William Bradford Reynolds, Letter to the Editor, *Washington Post,* 31 May 1982, A16.
56. 128 CONG. REC. H3842–45 (daily ed. 23 June 1982).
57. H.R. REP. NO. 97-227, at 30–31.
58. S. REP. NO. 97-417, at 28–29.
59. See, *e.g.,* SENATE HEARINGS*** 773.
60. S. REP. NO. 97-417, at 27–28.
61. *Ibid.,* 193–95.
62. 128 CONG. REC. S7095 (daily ed. 18 June 1982).
63. *Ibid.* The same view was expressed again by one of the co-authors of the original House bill. 128 CONG. REC. H3841 (daily ed. 23 June 1982) (remarks of Rep. Sensenbrenner).
64. S. REP. NO. 97-417, at 30 & n.120.
65. *Major v. Treen,* 547 F.Supp. 325 (E.D.La. 1983).
66. *Jones v. City of Lubbock,* 727 F.2d 364 (5th Cir. 1984).
67. *Gingles v. Edmisten,* __ F. Supp. __ (E.D.N.C. 1984), *stay denied,* No. A-653 (27 February 1984) (Burger, C.J.), *reapplication for stay denied,* No. A-653 (5 March 1984) (By the Court).
68. 458 U.S. 613 (1982).
69. *E.g., Escambia County v. McMillan,* __ U.S. __ (1984).

REMEDIES

8

Enforcement of Section 5 of the Voting Rights Act

Drew S. Days, III and Lani Guinier

The Voting Rights Act of 1965 has been hailed as by far the most effective federal civil rights statute. While diligent efforts have been made to achieve compliance with laws prohibiting discrimination in housing, education, employment and the like, meaningful remedies for proven violations in these areas have come only after years of litigation.[1] Administration of the preclearance provisions of the Voting Rights Act, in contrast, has prevented in a matter of days electoral changes likely to undercut or retard meaningful minority participation at the ballot box.[2]

The most important temporary provision of the act, discussed in this chapter, is Section 5, which requires certain state and local governments, "covered jurisdictions," to preclear changes in voting procedures with either the Department of Justice or the United States District Court for the District of Columbia. The preclearance triggering formula for Section 5 coverage is in Section 4. It applies to states or other political jurisdictions which employed a literacy test for voter registration on 1 November 1964, 1 November 1968, or 1 November 1972, and whose voter registration or turnout in the 1964, 1968, or 1972 presidential elections was less than 50 percent of the voting age population. The preclearance triggering formula now covers nine states in their entirety and parts of thirteen others. Most of the covered jurisdictions are in the South.

The Voting Rights Act was originally passed in response to compelling evidence of continuing interference with attempts by black citizens to exercise the franchise despite prior congressional efforts to end such practices. In upholding the constitutionality of the act in response to challenges by several southern states, the Supreme Court observed in *South Carolina v. Katzenbach:*

> Congress had found that case-by-case litigation was inadequate to combat widespread and persistent discrimination in voting, because of the inordinate amount of time and energy required to overcome the obstructionist tactics invariably encountered in these lawsuits. After enduring nearly a century of systematic resistance to the Fifteenth Amendment, Congress might well decide to shift the advantage of time and inertia from the perpetrators of the evil to its victims.[3]

As assistant attorney general for civil rights from March 1977 to December 1980, Days, pursuant to 28 C.F.R. 51.3, reviewed, with the assistance of his staff, thousands of voting changes subject to the preclearance provisions of the Voting Rights Act, lodged objections to 120 of those changes determined to have a discriminatory purpose or effect, and sought the assistance of the courts in enforcing the act. Guinier was his special assistant at the Department of Justice.

Congress' decision to "shift the advantage of time and inertia" to the victims of voting discrimination has clearly paid dividends in significant increases in voting turnouts by minorities, in the numbers of minority candidates running for office, and in the number of minority-elected officials directly attributable to the operation of the Voting Rights Act.

It would be unfortunate, however, to conclude from the *relative* effectiveness of the act that over a century of injustice against minority voters has been remedied and that we need no longer fear that new strategies will be devised to reverse or retard what few gains have been achieved since the act came into existence.

Though the act has been on the books since 1965, any fair assessment of its enforcement history would reflect that it has been a meaningful weapon for less than a decade except against the most direct forms of discrimination. It was not until 1969 that the Supreme Court made clear that private parties could sue to obtain compliance by covered jurisdictions with provisions of Section 5,[4] and not until 1971 that the Justice Department received explicit Supreme Court approval to require that changes in polling place locations and in boundary lines by means of annexations receive approval pursuant to Section 5 procedures.[5]

Moreover, procedures for enforcing Section 5 of the Voting Rights Act have been the subject of lengthy court challenges, several of which had to be resolved by the Supreme Court, almost every year since it was enacted.[6] *United States v. Board of Commissioners of Sheffield, Alabama*[7] provides some measure of the degree to which such litigation threatened the continued validity of Section 5 enforcement. There, the Supreme Court was faced with the question of whether voting changes enacted by a city which is within a state designated for coverage under Section 5 of the Voting Rights Act of 1965 must be precleared under Section 5 before they become effective. The Court held that they did. One can gain some sense of the consequences for enforcement of the Voting Rights Act had *Sheffield*'s challenge succeeded by looking at the department's experience between 1965 and May 1977. During that period, it received more than 3,600 submissions of more than 8,100 proposed changes by political units like Sheffield. Fifty-six percent of all Section 5 submissions and 58 percent of the changes in all submissions during that period were from such entities.[8] Even though this challenge to Section 5 enforcement was unsuccessful, meaningful enforcement of Section 5 was effectively stalled between the December 1976 three-judge court decision in *Sheffield* and the Supreme Court ruling in March 1978.

One must also acknowledge, in assessing the act's effectiveness, that covered jurisdictions have made literally hundreds of changes that have never met the preclearance requirement of Section 5,[9] despite congressional expectations that there would be substantial voluntary compliance.[10] Even during periods of vigorous enforcement of the act the department has not been able to ensure that every electoral change by covered jurisdictions, or indeed most of them, was subjected to the Section 5 process. It never received adequate resources from Congress systematically to canvass changes since 1965 that had not been precleared, to obtain compliance with preclearance procedures, or even, in a few cases, to ascertain whether submitting jurisdictions had complied with objections to proposed changes. It is not uncommon for the department to find out about changes made several years earlier from a submission made by a covered jurisdiction seeking preclearance of a more recent enactment. For example, there is the case of the City of Greenville, Pitt County, North Carolina. In February 1980, the Department of Justice received a submission from Greenville, a city with a 25 percent black population, seeking preclearance of voting changes that became law in 1970, 1972, 1973, 1975 and 1977 without satisfying Section 5 requirements.[11] In this instance, it should be noted, the submission was prompted by inquiries the department made based upon an FBI survey of voting changes in North Carolina conducted at the Civil Rights Division's request. Though the department found most of the changes were nondiscriminatory, an objection was lodged to the city's switch from a plurality to majority vote system for election of city council because of its discriminatory consequences for black voters. Viewed in the most positive light, the Greenville experience does point up the fact that many precleared changes come ultimately to the department's attention.

For minorities in Greenville and elsewhere, however, electoral gains since 1965 have not taken on such a permanence as to render them immune to attempts by opponents of equality to diminish their political influence. Annexations; shifts from ward to at-large elections or, as in Greenville, from plurality win to majority vote;[12] and changes from pure at-large to numbered posts or in the size of electoral bodies can in any given community deprive minority voters of fair and effective procedures for electing candidates of their choice. It is still too early to conclude that the effects of decades of discrimination against blacks and other minorities have been eradicated and that minorities are now in a position to compete in the political arena against nonminorities on an equal basis without the assistance of the Voting Rights Act.

Furthermore, it bears noting that Section 5 enforcement still must be concerned with many minor changes that have a direct effect upon the process of casting ballots, even though most of the serious challenges to minority electoral gains have come recently from redistrictings and annexations. In April 1978, for example, New Orleans, Louisiana, submitted five proposed polling place changes two days *after* the changes went into effect for April first elections in that jurisdiction. The department concluded that one of the changes had had a discriminatory effect upon the participation of black voters in the election. In that instance, the polling place was changed only fourteen days before the election from a private home located in a 92 percent black district to an elementary school in another, noncontiguous district. Advertisements placed in the daily newspaper up to 30 March contained the address of the old polling place. On the day prior to the election and on election day itself, the correct polling location was given out but the public school was incorrectly identified. The new polling place, located approximately sixteen blocks from the old one, required voters, many of whom were elderly and without automobiles or convenient access to public transportation, to cross an interstate highway about 170 feet wide in order to cast their ballots. Not surprisingly, in view of these obstacles to casting their ballots, many black voters stayed home on election day.[13]

Between early 1977 and the end of 1980, the attorney general, on the recommendation of the assistant attorney general, authorized the assignment of over three thousand federal observers to monitor elections in covered jurisdictions.[14] In almost every case, the assignment of observers was based upon a judgment that physical interference, intimidation, or pressure was likely to be directed at minority voters if the federal observers were not there. Minority advances in the electoral process have been especially vulnerable during the last few years when thousands of jurisdictions were reapportioning themselves and making other alterations in their political structures on the basis of results of the 1980 census.[15]

The discussion thus far has attempted to describe certain strengths and weaknesses of the enforcement scheme created by Congress in 1965. One cannot assess adequately the act's effectiveness, however, without understanding the administrative standards by which the department has traditionally evaluated submissions.[16]

Under Section 5, the attorney general must determine whether an electoral change submitted for preclearance has the purpose or will have the effect of denying or abridging the right to vote on account of race or color. Once the department receives a submission, the first step should be to discern whether the covered jurisdiction has provided enough data on the change to allow a meaningful evaluation of its nature and impact. If the information is insufficient, then the department normally requests further data. Among the types of information needed by the department are population and voting figures (by race or national origin); election results showing the existence of racial bloc voting or polarization and the extent to which minorities have been able to elect candidates of their choice; census maps; and some explanation of which, if any, alternatives were considered before the submitted change was adopted. The department also should seek to identify knowledgeable minority persons and organizations in the submitting jurisdiction in order to elicit their concerns on the proposed change.

This information should be subjected to a two-pronged analysis. First, the department must determine whether there is evidence of intentional discrimination. Second, it should assess the prechange level of minority political power and decide whether that power is augmented, diminished, or not affected by the change. If there is evidence of intentional discrimination, no further inquiry is necessary and the department should object. In the absence of such evidence, where the change augments the ability of minority groups to participate in the political process, fully recognizes legitimate minority political strength, and gives evidence of no discriminatory result, then the core objective Congress sought to achieve under Section 5 has been satisfied. Thus, the submitting jurisdiction has met its burden and the change is normally precleared. Where the change promises to diminish or leave unaffected minority political power, further inquiries must be made as to whether the proposed change has a discriminatory result or whether the submitting jurisdiction adopted the proposed change despite the availability of equally acceptable alternatives that would have given minorities a fairer opportunity to elect candidates of their choice.

For example, assume that in a community with a 25 percent minority population, local officials can create a compact and contiguous set of four city council districts where minorities are likely to have a sizable population advantage in one district. When the jurisdiction submits instead, however, a plan that is not compact or contiguous, reflects substantial population deviations from district to district, or is otherwise drawn in a fashion that frustrates any prospect that minorities will gain control of one district in the plan,[17] the department is likely to object. Assume, on the other hand, another set of facts in which it can be shown that no fairly drawn redistricting plan will result in minority control of one district because of dispersed minority residential patterns, for example. The department's response would not be to demand that the jurisdiction adopt a crazy-quilt, gerrymandered districting plan to ensure proportional minority representation. Nor would the department object to a plan that does not ensure minority control of a district where a community can show that racial bloc voting is not a significant consideration and that minority candidates or ones favored by minority voters regularly run and win even from districts where nonminority voters are in control.

In each of these instances, the department objective has not been to dictate any particular result, and the scope of its review is limited to election law changes. Moreover, the statutory scheme has been interpreted by the Supreme Court to preempt judicial review of the department's enforcement decisions.[18] Such a loophole raises the specter of political abuse.[19] Nevertheless, the record of enforcement of Section 5 has generally been impressive in protecting against the creation of unfair new obstacles to meaningful minority advancement. This is precisely what Congress determined would be necessary when it originally passed the Voting Rights Act to ensure that the gains so far achieved in minority political participation would not be destroyed through new discriminatory procedures and techniques.

FIGHT FOR EXTENSION

In June 1982, Congress extended Section 5 coverage for twenty-five years. This was the longest extension ever enacted. In May 1981, as the previous seven-year period of coverage was nearing the end, the Subcommittee on Civil and Constitutional Rights of the Judiciary Committee of the House of Representatives undertook a thorough examination, including two months of hearings, of the record of compliance and enforcement under the act since 1975. In connection with that consideration, several bills were introduced to extend the special provisions for ten years.[20] With the assistance of a coalition of 155 civil rights groups ("the civil rights industry," as it was sometimes called),[21] an extensive hearing record was compiled documenting some of the enforcement problems described earlier and the continued need for Section 5.[22]

Witness after witness testified about the current conditions in each of the major covered states. There was testimony that registration and voting sites were purposely made inaccessible, and registration hours limited, in order to discourage free exercise of the franchise by minority voters.[23] There was testimony about physical violence and intimidation.[24] There was testimony that more jurisdictions had made discriminatory voting changes rejected by the Justice Department since 1975 than in the ten years after the act's passage in 1965.[25] Witnesses testified to the absence of a secret ballot, the refusal of jurisdictions to appoint minorities as deputy registrars and poll watchers, efforts by whites in majority-black counties to maintain political power through purging statutes, and annexations and changes in electoral systems designed to dilute minority voting strength.[26] Other witnesses testified to the deterrent effect of the act and the real fear that the gains made by minority voters as a result of the act would be extremely vulnerable without its protections.

By 29 June 1982, when President Reagan signed into law the twenty-five-year extension, there were very few congressional holdouts actively opposed to the 1965 law.[27] A broad consensus had developed heralding the virtues of the "most effective civil rights law ever passed."[28] Nevertheless, support for the continued protection of the preclearance provisions of the Voting Rights Act did not come easily.

At the beginning of the debate on extension, many subsequent congressional supporters were very skeptical about the need for a federal voting law.[29] In questioning the first witness at the first House hearing, Representative Henry Hyde (R., Ill.) sounded a refrain that was to become the heart of the House debate. "I would suggest," Mr. Hyde argued, "the issue is, how long is enough? After seventeen years of history, the South, the white power structure, has made progress, the blacks have made progress in terms of registering, in terms of being elected to office. At some point, you have to recognize an effort has been made and provide some incentive for that effort to continue."[30]

Several proposals to amend Section 5 were made with Reagan administration support. These changes would have altered fundamentally the enforcement scheme. Three of them—nationwide preclearance, restrictions on preclearance, and mandatory notice—would have paralyzed any meaningful enforcement of the act and were all rejected.[31] The fourth proposal was a substantially weaker version of the compromise "bailout" provision that eventually became a part of the act.

In sum, none of the Reagan administration proposals was ultimately accepted as initially formulated. Somewhat ironically, however, they provided the ninety-seventh Congress with an opportunity to reconsider the reasons for the act's original passage and to reaffirm the basic goals and objectives. The result of this debate over first principles produced the longest extension, by the greatest margin, in the act's history.

Nationwide Preclearance

The most popular argument of opponents of the 1982 extension of the 1965 preclearance mechanism was that if the requirements of Section 5 were continued, then they should apply nationwide.[32] Congress rejected this proposal for four basic reasons. First, the Supreme Court had found shortly after the act's passage and again only a year prior to the extension vote that the coverage formula was "rational in both practice and theory" and not punitive.[33]

Second, the Supreme Court's support for the coverage formula was based in significant part on the extensive Congressional findings of discrimination in the affected jurisdictions. Without similarly detailed and persuasive evidence of the need for preclearance in jurisdictions other than those presently covered, members of Congress were aware that serious constitutional questions were presented by the prospect of applying this "uncommon exercise of congressional power" to the nation as a whole.[34]

Third, those who argued for nationwide coverage did not recognize that the act already contained a section allowing a court to order preclearance in a state or political subdivision not presently covered by the triggering formula. Nor did they really understand the nature of the preclearance process.

Finally, evidence of the serious administrative problems with nationwide preclearance was presented. Although parts of twenty-two states were already covered, nationwide coverage would have required Justice Department review of the laws of forty-one states not covered and of tens of thousands more political subdivisions. At the time of the House Hearings, slightly more than a dozen Civil Rights Division employees reviewed all submissions from covered jurisdictions; the staff would have been inundated by the avalanche of voting change submissions to be reviewed within sixty days from every state, county, and city in the country.[35]

The Congress ultimately realized that the tremendous volume of new submissions would divert, for no good reason, the attorney general's resources from those areas currently covered by the act where continued voting discrimination against racial and language minorities had been shown to exist.

Restricting Preclearance

The Reagan administration floated a proposal in June 1981 to restrict the types of voting changes subject to preclearance review by limiting the preclearance requirement to those types of changes that had elicited the most objections from the Justice Department. Congress never followed up on this proposal for the same reasons that had prompted it to devise the original preclearance mechanisms in 1965: jurisdictions simply do not limit their efforts to discriminate to one type of voting practice. Congress determined that a procedure for monitoring all prospective voting changes was necessary to reach and correct those discriminatory practices that replaced schemes that had been successfully challenged.

Prior administrations had found in enforcing the act that the discriminatory potential in seemingly innocent or insignificant changes could be determined only after the specific facts of the change were analyzed in context. The original coverage formula, which Congress retained, allowed for such a factual analysis. Moreover, by 1981 it was clear that all changes had to be submitted, and election officials could not argue persuasively that they did not understand their responsibilities under the act. If a complicated formula to limit preclearance had been adopted, much energy would have been spent resolving new disputes over whether a change fell inside or outside the new coverage provisions. The present law, as extended, defines changes broadly and places the emphasis properly on whether the jurisdiction, and not the change, is covered.

Mandatory Notice Provision

The administration also considered a proposal to replace the automatic preclearance requirement of Section 5 with a "mandatory notice" provision. Covered jurisdictions would have had to inform the Justice Department of proposed voting changes, but the attorney general would then have had to seek a court injunction in order to prevent a change from taking effect. No longer would the attorney general have been able simply to object to a change and thereby preclude its implementation.

Congress rejected the mandatory notice provision for several reasons. First, the present administrative preclearance process is more efficient than court review. This was evident from the overwhelming number of jurisdictions choosing Justice Department preclearance. Covered jurisdictions may seek preclearance administratively, or seek a declaratory judgment in court. As of July 1981, of the thirty-five thousand voting changes proposed by covered jurisdictions since Section 5 was enacted, less than two dozen had been reviewed by the District Court for the District of Columbia at the option of covered jurisdictions.[36]

Second, the proposal would have switched the burden of proof from the local authorities, where it had been since 1965, to the attorney general. Shifting the burden of proof to the attorney general would have been time-consuming in the initial stages, and the resulting litigation would have clogged the dockets of already overburdened courts. It would also have negated the fundamental premise underlying the original act: that the advantage of time and inertia should be on the side of the victims of discrimination and not with the perpetrators.[37]

BAIL-OUT

The one change in the original enforcement scheme that was adopted was a new bail-out provision. A condition of the 1982 extension was a more liberal release mechanism that would provide jurisdictions the opportunity to terminate coverage in advance of the year 2009, the date for termination of the twenty-five-year extension. This change reflected a compromise between civil rights groups who supported a straight extension of the act and those members of Congress whose sympathies were with the elected officials who had to comply with the act. The nature of the compromise demonstrated the surprising strength of the civil rights lobby on this issue.[38]

On 17 June 1981, Representative Hyde introduced H.R. 3948, the main focus of which was an amendment to the bail-out provisions in Section 4(a). Under H.R. 3948, administrative preclearance provisions would have remained indefinitely; however, a covered jurisdiction would have been allowed to bail out immediately if it could satisfy four limited requirements to the satisfaction of a local federal court.

The avowed purpose of Mr. Hyde's bail-out proposal was threefold. First, he hoped to provide incentives for covered jurisdictions to do more than remove overt barriers to minority participation such as literacy tests and poll taxes. He argued that his bail-out proposal was designed to encourage jurisdictions to make their electoral systems more accessible to all eligible voters. Second, he wanted to reward those jurisdictions which had complied with the letter and spirit of the law. Finally, he predicted that some modification of existing law was necessary to gain a consensus in support of the act's extension.

In introducing his bail-out proposal, Mr. Hyde admitted that his second reason, regarding "saintly jurisdictions," may have been based more on theory than hard evidence.[39]

In fact, nothing in the hearing record identified covered jurisdictions where minorities no longer would have benefited from the protections of Section 5 or where voluntary efforts had been made to increase the opportunity for minority participation.

Mr. Hyde was able, nevertheless, to garner bipartisan support for his bail-out concept, and the amendment as enacted was considerably tougher than his original proposal. Many of Mr. Hyde's conservative colleagues embraced the idea of an easier bail-out once it became clear that the record for continued preclearance was established by the House hearings. They seized upon the notion of a compromise bail-out as an opportunity to accomplish through the back door what was becoming increasingly unpopular to do directly. Some House members hoped that a loose bail-out would be a sieve through which covered jurisdictions could easily slip.

On the other hand, proponents of the act's extension were also receptive to Mr. Hyde's arguments. Supporters of the preclearance provisions were interested in a compromise that would generate broad bipartisan endorsement without weakening the act's effectiveness. They also were sympathetic to the concept of an incentive bail-out. Whereas the preclearance requirement had been destined to expire in 1982 by providing "automatic bail-out" for covered jurisdictions, the Hyde proposal suggested a new premise for release. Hyde's proposal introduced a behavior-oriented standard for determining the expiration of preclearance. To the act's supporters, this seemed a fair way to give currently covered jurisdictions notice of what was required of them, as well as the incentive to do more than simply maintain a status quo that grandfathered in discriminatory pre-1965 election laws and practices. Moreover, as initially introduced and as it passed the House, the amendment had no expiration date. Civil rights supporters were intrigued by the opportunity to obtain permanent Section 5 coverage.

Representative Hyde's proposal, therefore, became the core of a compromise amendment that incorporated the key features of H.R. 3948. The compromise enlarged the number of jurisdictions eligible to bail-out, used a behavior-oriented test of compliance with the law, and delineated standards for affirmative steps that a jurisdiction would have to take in order to show that it had complied with the spirit as well as the letter of the law. The major features of the substitute amendment were that (1) jurisdiction of the bail-out suit was retained in the District of Columbia, (2) states and counties within wholly covered states could now bail-out if they met the objective standards of compliance themselves and could also show compliance by governmental units within their territory, and (3) jurisdictions, in order to obtain release, were obligated to eliminate discriminatory methods of election and other structural barriers to full minority participation.

The compromise bail-out provision was reported out by the House Judiciary Committee as a substitute amendment to H.R. 3112 by a vote of twenty three to one. The guiding principle behind the compromise was that it should not be manipulable by jurisdictions whose past practices of serious, sustained electoral discrimination had been the basis for Section 5 coverage in the first place. The cosponsors' rationale for amending the existing bail-out provision was not to make it easy for a jurisdiction to do the minimum amount in order to terminate the Section 5 protections of its citizens but rather to encourage jurisdictions to act consistently in a nondiscriminatory fashion.

Nonetheless some House members, as well as the administration and several conservative Senators were dissatisfied with the final compromise.[40] They argued that the standards would be impossible to meet. Amendments were introduced in the House and Senate to remove jurisdiction for bail-out suits to local courts, to allow states to bail-out even though cities and counties within the state were not in compliance, to allow jurisdictions to bail-out although they had been sued for substantial voting rights violations and opted to settle the litigation, and to allow bail-out by jurisdictions to which federal examiners had been assigned as a result of certified complaints of voter harassment and intimidation to the attorney general. Each of these proposed amendments was considered and resoundingly defeated.[41]

The House Judiciary Committee bail-out compromise in H.R. 3112 was subsequently endorsed by an overwhelming margin in Congress and became part of the new act. Members of the House of Representatives had been persuaded by civil rights lobbyists that it was fair and achievable.[42]

The bail-out provision in the new statute links behavioral modification to termination of Section 5 coverage, although a twenty-five-year limit was added in the Senate, terminating Section 5 coverage for any jurisdiction that fails to bail-out by the year 2009. It is now the responsibility of the Department of Justice to investigate thoroughly the facts of each bail-out application to preclude premature release of jurisdictions that have not complied fully and in a timely manner with their responsibilities under Section 5 or that have not eliminated discriminatory election methods such as at-large elections, majority vote requirements, and staggered terms. The Justice Department's burden is vigorously to defend against the declaratory judgment action brought by a covered jurisdiction if minorities in that jurisdiction would still benefit from the protections of Section 5. Although Congress attempted to legislate an interlocking set of provisions to set the standards for release, the effectiveness of these additions to the Section 5 enforcement scheme will depend largely on judicial interpretation, Justice Department resources and commitment, and, of course, the ability of civil rights organizations and other advocacy groups to monitor the initial bail-out attempts and to exercise freely their right to intervene.[43]

CONCLUSION

It took Congress over one hundred years after the Emancipation Proclamation meaningfully to address major obstacles to black participation in the electoral process. Since 1965, however, in areas of the country where racial discrimination had historically excluded blacks from any real role in political life, the Voting Rights Act has made it possible for thousands of blacks to register, cast ballots, and elect candidates of their choice. The number of blacks holding elective office has increased significantly. But "one swallow does not make a spring." That Congress found it necessary in 1970, 1975 and again in 1982 to extend the Voting Rights Act reflects the depressing fact that simple-minded as well as sophisticated efforts persist to deprive blacks and other minorities of an opportunity to participate fully in the political process.

On the other hand Congress has demonstrated a greater commitment over the past twenty-five years to eradicating the vestiges of racial discrimination in voting than in any other area of our national life. Of course, federal laws were enacted during the same period to ensure nondiscrimination against blacks in education, housing, employment, public accommodations and federally funded programs. As in the voting rights area, however, initial legislative action has not ended racially exclusionary practices; further steps are clearly warranted. Yet, the political atmosphere, both in and out of Congress, appears hostile to any additional governmental efforts to eradicate lingering barriers in these areas. Indeed, the prevailing attitude among nonminorities in America is that blacks, other minorities, and women have received more than enough assistance to deal with current discriminatory practices or to overcome any present effects of past discrimination, despite so much solid evidence to the contrary. The 1982 extension of the Voting Rights Act, when placed in this context, must be regarded as an exceptional act of congressional candor and courage even when tempered, as it was, by political expediency.

Under the 1982 extension, the Section 5 preclearance mechanism will remain in force for another twenty-five years. Whether Congress will be confronted anew in 2009 with requests for further extensions depends upon several major factors. First, the current administration and all subsequent governments in Washington must enforce its provisions vigorously. The "advantages of time and inertia" should remain with the victims of voting discrimination and not be shifted back to the perpetrators. Secondly, both the executive and judicial branches of the federal government must ensure that the new bail-out provisions of the act are implemented in a manner consistent with the intent of Congress. They should not become a "sieve" through which offending jurisdictions can escape from Section 5 preclearance, but they should provide an incentive to "reformed" political entities to regain control over their electoral processes. Finally, the act's ultimate success will turn on the extent to which blacks and other minorities make meaningful use of the tools it provides for opening up opportunities in the political process.

Given the current climate in Washington it is extremely unlikely that we as a nation will realize before 2009 the hope expressed in 1966 by the Supreme Court in upholding the act's constitutionality: that we arrive at "the day when truly 'the right of citizens of the United States to vote shall not be denied or abridged by the United States or by any State on account of race, color or previous condition of servitude.' "[44] If we do, it will only be as a result of the extraordinary vigilance of civil rights lawyers, lobbyists, and community organizers.

NOTES

1. See, for example, *Hills v. Gautreaux,* 425 U.S. 284 (1976) (expanding scope of remedies under the 1968 Fair Housing Act); *Swann v. Charlotte-Mecklenburg Board of*

Education, 402 U.S. 1 (1971) (school desegregation remedies expanded seventeen years after *Brown* decision); and *Griggs v. Duke Power,* 401 U.S. 424 (1971) (construing 1964 Civil Rights Act provisions outlawing discrimination in private employment).

2. See Extension of the Voting Rights Act of 1965: Hearings on S. 1992 before the Subcommittee on the Constitution of the Senate Judiciary, 97th Cong., 2nd Sess. (1 March 1982) (statement of William Bradford Reynolds, Assistant Attorney General, Civil Rights Division, Attachments A-2, E-1 and E-2) (hereinafter cited as Hearings on S. 1992).

3. *South Carolina v. Katzenbach,* 383 U.S. 301, 327–28 (1965).

4. *Allen v. State Board of Elections,* 393 U.S. 544 (1969).

5. *Perkins v. Matthews,* 400 U.S. 379 (1971).

6. *South Carolina v. Katzenbach,* (1966) (challenge to Act's constitutionality); *Allen v. State Board of Elections,* (1969) (private enforcement of §5; broad scope of coverage); *Perkins v. Matthews,* (1971) (Section 5 coverage for polling place changes, annexations, and redistricting); *Georgia v. United States,* 411 U.S. 526 (1973) (upholding Attorney General's Section 5 preclearance procedures); *Connor v. Waller,* 421 U.S. 656 (1975) (exclusive jurisdiction of D.C. district court to adjudicate racial purpose or effect of voting changes denied preclearance); *City of Richmond v. United States,* 422 U.S. 358 (1975) (reconciling Section 5 requirements and racially dilutive annexations); *Beer v. United States,* 425 U.S. 130 (1976) (establishing ''non-retrogression'' principle); *United Jewish Organizations v. Carey,* 430 U.S. 144 (1977) (use of racial criteria in reapportionment); *Briscoe v. Bell,* 432 U.S. 404 (1977) (challenge to 1975 extension of Act); *Morris v. Gressette,* 432 U.S. 491 (1977) (nature of Attorney General's review); *United States v. Board of Comm'rs of Sheffield,* (1978); *Wise v. Lipscomb,* 437 U.S. 535 (1978) (Section 5 coverage); *Berry v. Doles,* 438 U.S. 190 (1978) (Section 5 coverage); *Dougherty County Board of Education v. White,* 439 U.S. 32 (1978) (Section 5 coverage); and *City of Rome v. United States,* 446 U.S. 156 (1980).

7. 435 U.S. 110 (1978).

8. *United States v. Board of Commissioners of Sheffield,* Jurisdictional Statement of United States, 13–14.

9. Senate Committee on the Judiciary, Report on S. 1992, S. Rep. No. 417, 97th Cong., 2nd Sess. 12–13 (1982) (hereinafter ''S. Rep.''); House Committee on the Judiciary, Report on H.R. 3112, H. Rep. No. 227, 97th Cong., 1st Sess. 13 (1981) (hereinafter ''H. Rep.'').

10. See, e.g., *Perkins v. Matthews, supra* at 396; S. Rep. at 47–48.

11. Objection letter from John Huerta, Acting Assistant Attorney General, to A. Louis Singleton, Esq. (7 April 1980).

12. See H. Rep. at 18, 42–43; S. Rep. at 10 and 54 n.184.

13. Objection letter from Drew S. Days, III, Assistant Attorney General to Ernest Salatich, Assistant City Attorney, New Orleans (12 May 1978).

14. Report of the United States Commission on Civil Rights, *The Voting Rights Act: Unfulfilled Goals,* 268–269 (1981). Also see, Hearing on S. 1992 (1 March 1982) (statement of Wm. Bradford Reynolds).

15. S. Rep. at 12 n. 31.

16. This section describes the department's practices based on record evidence of the period from 1965 to 1977 and from the authors' personal knowledge for the period 1977 to 1980. See also *Procedures for the Administration of Section 5 of the Voting Rights Act of 1965,* 28 C.F.R. §51 ff. (1980). Justice Department practices under the Reagan Administration have been the subject of recent charges that Section 5 objections have often been interposed where Republican candidates, as well as minorities, stood to gain from opposition to proposed reapportionment plans, i.e., designed to serve partisan political ends. *See* Pear, ''Justice Department and Courts Expand Redistricting Role,'' *New York Times,* 6 June 1982. See also Pear, ''Backdated Memo on Rights is Conceded,'' *New York Times,* 21 January 1983; Taylor, ''Louisiana Plan for Re-

districting is Struck Down," *Wall Street Journal,* 27 September 1983; and Editorial, "Gerryduck in Louisiana," *New York Times,* 1 October, 1983 (failure to object politically motivated).

17. The determination of what percentage of black or other minority population will produce a realistic chance that a candidate acceptable to that community will be elected has to take into consideration that in many jurisdictions rates of minority registration and voting are substantially below those for non-minorities. Consequently, in most instances, a 51 percent minority population district will not create a meaningful opportunity. The Department of Justice has, consequently, rejected reapportionment plans that do not take such factors into consideration, often seeking districts in excess of 65 percent minority population. Since lower minority registration and voting are often the products of past discriminatory practices, such an approach is consistent with constitutional and statutory requirements. The Supreme Court has so held. *United Jewish Organizations v. Carey,* 430 U.S. 144, at 164 (1977).

18. *Morris v. Gressette,* 432 U.S. 491 (1977).

19. See note 16, *supra.*

20. H.R. 3112 was introduced by Representative Rodino; S. 1992 was introduced by Senators Kennedy and Mathias. These bills, as introduced, would also have amended Section 2.

21. S. Rep. at 210 (Minority Views of Senator East).

22. S. Rep. at 9–14.

23. Hearings on Extension of the Voting Rights Act before the Subcomm. on Civil and Constitutional Rights of the House Comm. on the Judiciary, 97th Cong. Sess., at 173, 377–79, 820–836 (hereinafter House Hearings).

24. Ibid., 289, 821.

25. H. Rep. at 11.

26. House Hearing at 1566, 1587, 377–78, 581, 584.

27. The motion to concur in Senate amendments of H.R. 3112, to amend the Voting Rights Act of 1965 and to extend the effect of certain provisions passed the House of Representatives unanimously on 23 June 1982, 128 Cong. Rec., *supra* at H. 3840; S. 1992, the identical bill, passed the Senate by a vote of 85-8, 128 Cong. Rec. at S. 7139 (daily ed. 18 June 1982).

28. 128 Cong. Rec. S. 7123-36 (daily ed. 18 June 1982); also see remarks of Senator Hatch, an early opponent of S. 1992, recognizing, as Chairman of the Senate Subcommittee on the Constitution that "nearly every witness acknowledged some need for the continuance of Section 5 coverage." S. Rep. at 159–60.

29. Representative Henry Hyde, a key minority member of the House Subcommittee on Civil and Constitutional Rights, characterized the provisions of Section 5 as "controversial" and a "drastic remedy" when the Subcommittee first convened on 6 May 1981 to take testimony on extension of those provisions. In his opening statement Congressman Hyde said, "One of the most important and controversial issues before this Congress will be whether or not to extend certain expiring sections of the Voting Rights Act, as amended in 1975. . . . I believe it is fair to say that there are some individuals in the other body who would like to see the preclearance provisions expire altogether in 1982. . . . In short, my view is that the handful of Southern States have been in the penalty box for nearly 17 years; they have improved their voting rights records, and hence ought to be treated like every other jurisdiction in the land. The infringement of their sovereignty imposed by the selective application of preclearance for 17 years ought to be ended." House Hearing 2-3.

30. Ibid., 12.

31. See, e.g., Cong. Rec. H.6975-79, Harnett Amendment to make preclearance nationwide rejected by voice vote (daily ed., 5 Oct. 1981); compare 128 Cong. Rec. S. 7083-86 (daily ed., 18 June 1982).

32. President Ronald Reagan in his speech to the NAACP National Convention on 29 June 1981, argued against regional coverage. *New York Times* 30 June 1981, 1.

33. *South Carolina v. Katzenbach,* at 330.
34. S. Rep. at 15; H. Rep. at 34.
35. See 28 CFR §51.8; *Georgia v. United States,* 411 U.S. 526, 539–540, 541 n. 13 (1973); *United States v. Uvalde Consolidated Independent School District,* 625 F.2d 547 (5th Cir. 1980).
36. Senate Hearings, Statement of Wm. Bradford Reynolds, *supra,* Attachment A-2 at 10 n. 12.
37. *Georgia v. United States; South Carolina v. Katzenbach.*
38. B. Gellman, "The New Old Movement," *The New Republic,* 6 September 1982, 12.
39. House Hearings at 1822.
40. H. Rep. at 54 (Supplemental Views of Hon. Henry Hyde and Hon. Dan Lungren); S. Rep. at 160-165 (Additional Views of Senator Hatch); Ibid. at 59.
41. 127 Cong. Rec. H. 6945-48, 6966-74, 6979-82 (5 Oct. 1981). 128 Cong. Rec. S. 6967-7000 (June 17, 1982) and S. 7075-7139 (18 June 1982).
42. H. Rep. at 32; S. Rep. at 44, 59. 127 Cong. Rec. H.6844 (daily ed., 2 Oct. 1981) (statement of Edwards); 128 Cong. Rec. S.6650 (daily ed. 10 June 1982) (statement of Mathias); 128 Cong. Rec. S.6988 (daily ed. 17 June 1982) statement of Dole.
43. "Any aggrieved party may as of right intervene at any stage in such action." 42 U.S.C. 1973c, Pub. L. 97-205, Section 2(b) (4) (9).
44. *South Carolina v. Katzenbach,* at 337.

9

The View from Georgia and Mississippi
Local Attorneys' Appraisal of the 1965 Voting Rights Act

Howard Ball,
Dale Krane and Thomas P. Lauth

INTRODUCTION

This essay examines the views of city and county attorneys from Georgia and Mississippi regarding the controversial preclearance provision of the 1965 Voting Rights Act. Compared with the problem in some areas of civil rights enforcement, such as housing and education, it is relatively easy with regard to voting rights to identify the target population whose behavior needs changing if policy is to be effectively implemented.[1] Yet, until recently, most appraisals of voting rights enforcement have been made from the perspective of federal officials charged with implementing the law rather than from the vantage point of local officials who must comply with it. The views from city hall and the county courthouse examined here represent an important perspective which has generally been missing from past assessments.

Voting as a State Responsibility

The sine qua non of a democratic society is the right of each member to participate in the process of public leadership selection and to have his or her vote freely cast, fairly counted, and equally weighted. The voting rights struggle in the United States during the middle decades of this century has been an effort to guarantee this aspect of popular governance.

In America the responsibility for conducting elections has resided with state and local governments. In fact, there is no constitutional provision for a national right to vote.[2] State governments have the prerogative to set voting qualifications, subject, of course, to certain national limitations (for example, the Fifteenth, Nineteenth, Twenty-fourth and Twenty-sixth Amendments and such statutory provisions as the Voting Rights Act). This locus of responsibility for conducting elections has often enabled local majorities (political, if not always numerical)[3] to deny the franchise to racial minorities located in the same jurisdiction. The discriminatory effects of the white primary, the literacy test and poll tax, and such nonstatutory techniques as economic sanctions and personal intimidation are too well known to be recounted. After severe setbacks to minority rights resulting from the Supreme Court's decisions in the *Civil Rights Cases* (1883)[4] and *Plessy v. Ferguson* (1896)[5], the protection of civil rights returned to the agenda of the national government in the 1940s and 1950s with the Court's decisions in *Smith v. Allwright* (1944), *Brown v. Board of Education* (1954),[6] and the passage of the 1957 Civil Rights Act.

For the first time since the Civil Rights Act of 1875, black citizens began to expand the scope of their conflict[7] with tyrannical local majorities to the national level, where they were then able to form a legislative coalition with other minorities and become part of a national majority on voting rights and other civil rights issues. Thus it can be seen that American federalism has sometimes facilitated the denial of voting rights to black citizens and at other times made it possible for them to use the national government in their struggle to overcome discrimination.

To date, the Voting Rights Act of 1965[8] stands as the most important piece of national legislation prohibiting electoral discrimination in state and local government. In the last ten years, Section 5 of the act has been particularly important in this regard. Section 5 calls for administrative (or judicial) preclearance of all proposed voting changes, before they are put into practice, to determine whether their purpose or effect is to deny or dilute the voting rights of black or minority-language citizens. As passed, the act was an affirmation of the principles contained in the Civil Rights Acts of 1957, 1960 and 1964, as well as a statement of objectives regarding the elimination and prohibition of discriminatory voting practices. However, like any other statute, the Voting Rights Act is not self-enforcing, and an examination of its effectiveness must go beyond the language of the act itself to the corpus of rules, decisions, and informal practices which unfold during the act's implementation. The purpose of this essay is to examine the act in this larger context, paying special attention to the ways in which officials from covered jurisdictions view the enforcement process.

Voting Rights Implementation and Federalism

Several problems plague voting rights implementation. Although the officials from covered jurisdictions represent an easily identifiable segment of the population within their locales (unlike the more diversified "target populations" in housing and education rights enforcement), the change required of them has been substantial.[9] It amounts to the acknowledgment in deed if not in attitude of the legitimacy of black participation in local political processes.

Federalism confounds the task of voting rights enforcement because compliance must be achieved within the context of intergovernmental relations. Those being called upon to comply are often policy makers in their own right at another level of government. There is no official hierarchy or chain of command. Because of this, the Voting Section of the Civil Rights Division at the Department of Justice assumed from the outset that they alone could not effectively enforce voting rights policy but had to rely upon some cooperation from local officials. Yet those whose cooperation is most needed also have the potential to veto statutory enforcement.[10]

Although the Voting Rights Act contains criminal sanctions for noncompliance, the Department of Justice has been very reluctant to use them, for fear of losing a case and thereby undermining the credibility of the department's ultimate threat.[11] Further, unlike many kinds of federal policy where a financial carrot can induce compliance from even the most unwilling subnational government, voting rights policy is "fiscally dry," in that department officials have no funds to offer or deny.

Also, in striking contrast to other bureaucratic agencies, the Voting Section's Submission Unit cannot ordinarily delay its decisions; otherwise, it violates the act's sixty-day time limit. And finally, the department's Civil Rights Division lacks sufficient staff to maintain field offices throughout covered jurisdictions. Given this situation, coercion has not been an effective means of achieving compliance. To the extent that compliance has been achieved, it has tended to come about more through a quasi-voluntary consensus among the contending parties.[12]

If officials from covered jurisdictions are going to comply with the Voting Rights Act, they must be both willing and able to do so, for they share the responsibility with federal officials of implementing this crucial civil rights legislation. Ability to comply entails not only the requisite decision-making authority possessed by nearly all local officials, but also knowledge of what is expected. The issuance of procedures for administration of the act in 1971 (28 CFR 51) informed covered jurisdictions about the requirement to submit voting changes for preclearance and told them not only about the kinds of changes that must be submitted, but about the types of supporting evidence required. Nevertheless, some jurisdictions continue to claim ignorance regarding their obligation to comply with the act and, more important, others disregard the act entirely when initiating voting changes.

SUBNATIONAL OFFICIALS
THE MISSING LINK IN VOTING RIGHTS POLICY

"Shared Responsibility" as an Enforcement Philosophy

From the passage of the Voting Rights Act in 1965 to the present, the political leadership in the Civil Rights Division has believed that "the Justice Department has neither the personnel nor the resources to become the primary enforcer of the Voting Rights Act."[13] Trapped in the crossfire from segregationists and civil rights marchers, the Assistant Attorney General for Civil Rights, Burke Marshall, and Deputy Attorney General Nicholas Katzenbach adopted an enforcement strategy in 1965–66 that relied on "the smallest possible federal intrusion into the conduct of state affairs"[14] and tried "to avoid *at all costs* an occupation of the South by federal troops, lawyers, registrars, and marshalls."[15] Instead, it was hoped that successful implementation would depend on measured actions by the national government in combination with responsible subnational officials acting out of respect for the national law, and on the political pressure exerted by local black citizens. In his 1978 testimony before the House Judiciary Subcommittee on Civil and Constitutional Rights, Drew Days III, Assistant Attorney General for Civil Rights under President Carter, reiterated this same enforcement posture.

> It might be appropriate that we explain, generally, how we view the role of the Civil Rights Division in enforcing the Voting Rights Act. We are an enforcement agency—that is, we are charged with the responsibility for enforcing the Voting Rights Act through preclearance procedures, litigation, and examiner-observer activities—*but we do not have sole responsibility for vindicating voting rights* [our emphasis]. Under the Voting Rights Act we share that responsibility with private litigants, as well as with the very jurisdictions subject to the Act. . . . It was never contemplated that an official of the federal government would be on hand in each jurisdiction to prevent violations of this act. While we do have a substantial role in monitoring compliance, it is impossible for a unit [the Voting Section] which consists of 17 attorneys and 15 paralegals to be looking over the shoulder of officials in some 1,115 jurisdictions.[16]

"Shared responsibility," Days argued, was in accord with original congressional intent.

Voting section personnel and their political managers, responsible for implementing a unique piece of federal legislation with a very small staff, utilized the "bottleneck" principle implicit in the Section 5 preclearance requirement. Since the act froze voting patterns as of 1 November 1964, any covered jurisdiction seeking to alter its electoral rules and procedures had to gain a federal imprimatur either from the U.S. District Court in Washington, D.C. or the U.S. Attorney General. Because the legal route was so time consuming and costly, most jurisdictions chose the administrative one. Therefore, in terms of implementation theory it made eminent sense for a small, resource-poor enforcement unit to have "the target population pass through a central point rather than having to be sought out by the controllers."[17]

Such a bottleneck strategy operates best as a constraint on noncompliance when the target population (that is, the officials in the covered jurisdictions) is an unwilling partner in the implementation of government policy. However, reliance on this type of reactive enforcement posture—waiting for the target population to come to the central clearance point—poses two dangers to the accomplishment of the act's objectives: covered jurisdictions could (1) be content to leave election procedures unchanged (Section 2 of the amended 1982 Voting Rights Act enables plaintiffs to challenge existing voting procedures enacted prior to 1965), or (2) make changes and fail to submit as required by law. In the first case, discriminatory election practices would remain legally frozen in place, except when constitutional challenges in federal court resulted in changes. In the second case, discriminatory changes would escape detection in the absence of an effective mechanism for monitoring the actions of the geographically dispersed covered jurisdictions.

To avoid these two dangers, the Justice Department's philosophy since 1965 has been to keep a low profile and rely instead on "sharing the enforcement responsibility" with local minority groups and election officials. Simply put, it has been up to black and white political leaders to work out their differences to the satisfaction of both parties before the local community files for a Section 5 preclearance. The voting change(s) submission, embodying the locally hammered-out compromise is then *routinely* approved by the U.S. Attorney General or by the Washington, D.C. District Court. The key assumption, and the "Catch-22" in the department's enforcement strategy, is that there will be a viable minority political community in each of the more than 7,000 (not 1,115) covered jurisdictions—a countervailing power that will be able to dissuade local white leaders from taking actions to dilute the newly won minority franchise. Without this critical political force, the Department's bottleneck strategy rests only on the dubious assumption that election officials have the capacity and more important the will to uphold the Voting Rights Act despite the South's long history of massive resistance to civil rights law.

The spirit of the department's approach is expressed in Drew Days's 1981 congressional testimony:

> For while I regarded it as my central responsibility under the Act to ensure against changes having a discriminatory purpose or effect with respect to minority participation in the electoral process, I was also determined to carry out that mission in a manner that was fair to the submitting jurisdictions and properly respectful of the integrity of their electoral processes.[18]

This concern for the integrity of local elections has been translated into an informal advice-giving and consultative relationship between the personnel in the voting section and local attorneys who are filing preclearance requests. The following comment from the attorney in charge of the submission unit illustrates the nature of preclearance counseling.

> [Local jurisdictions] want guidelines; they want to know what we are going to look for. They're going to revise their city charter and the city attorney will call me up to ask [my advice]. . . . And this is a widespread type of request. . . . They have a job to do and they want to get our clearance. . . . We'll do what we can for them . . .; we try to make things go smoothly for them so they can hold elections.[19]

The purpose behind an enforcement strategy based on the discussion and negotiation of a voting change prior to its submission is two-fold: (1) the reduction of resistance to the Section 5 requirement; and (2) the reduction of alienation between local and federal officials. By adopting an almost fraternal relationship between professionals, the Voting Section believes it maximizes the level of compliance with the act. As one local attorney in a Mississippi town that has benefited from this type of advice told us: "It's easier to work with them [the Voting Section staff] than with the electric power company."

The Voting Section staff claims, furthermore, that over 90 percent of all voting changes are reported to the attorney general and that the unreported 10 percent are the most insignificant and the least dangerous with respect to vote dilution.[20] Given the historic hostility of whites in these locales to voting rights policy, this estimate is indeed remarkable.

Agency personnel believe that their alleged success is directly attributable to their role as peacemakers between the population groups and to their enforcement strategy of informal advice, discussion, and negotiation to iron out the differences between the two sides. Yet ever since the first days of the act's implementation, controversy over the extent of its success has been sharp. Spokesmen for pressure groups like the NAACP and the Voter Education Project have been joined by governmental bodies such as the U.S. Commission on Civil Rights and the General Accounting Office in their criticism of the strategy.[21] While these organizations applaud the department's Section 4 activity (ending vote denial), they uniformly decry its failure to effectively enforce Section 5 (preventing vote dilution). These negative assessments are based on the persistent underrepresentation of blacks in elected as well as appointed offices throughout the covered jurisdictions. For example, the Southern Regional Council in its 1982 report on Georgia, based on 1980 census data, observed that in twenty-seven counties in the southwestern part of the black belt, only four of the 127 county commissioners elected to office were black.[22] The three counties with minority officials have relatively large black populations or have single-member districts. Supporting evidence for the weakness of Section 5 enforcement throughout other parts of the South includes continuing use of ingenious racial gerrymanders and the grossly unfair distribution of public goods and services to black neighborhoods.[23]

A Courthouse View of Section 5 Enforcement

Given the Justice Department's long-standing "shared responsibility" philosophy of enforcement, it is curious that little attention has been paid to the opinions of officials in the covered jurisdictions whose responsibility it is to abide by the Voting Rights Act. Section 5 requires that a preclearance submission must be made "by an appropriate official" of the "submitting authority" (28 CFR Part 51.2). Typically, the submitting authority—whether a municipality, school, or utility district, or a county—employs a local attorney, often hired on a case-by-case basis, to act as the appropriate official. (The "appropriate official" for one of the covered states is, of course, the state's attorney general. These legal officers are not the focus of this article.) Except in the 1978 General Accounting Office Report,[24] the crucially relevant views of these attorneys generally have been ignored. As part of a larger study of Section 5 implementation,[25] we conducted in 1980 a mail survey of Georgia and Mississippi city/county attorneys to fill this information gap.[26] The responses to the inquiries provide interesting glimpses into the attitudes and behavior of local officials who must initiate the preclearance process. While the images drawn from this limited survey capture only certain aspects of the enforcement process, the answers of the local attorneys nevertheless reveal much about their own compliance behavior and thus permit some basis for appraising the degree of protection for minority voters that is possible through "shared responsibility."

For purposes of analysis, the responses of the attorneys have been grouped into categories that reflect the percentage of black citizens in a given jurisdiction. This arrangement was adopted because the significance of Section 5 protection varies with the proportional size of the minority population. Where fewer black citizens live in a community, the temptation to discriminate is less. At the other end of the population spectrum, where blacks constitute a sizeable majority and are politically organized, the need for Justice Department assistance is not great. But in communities where black citizens are not dominant but constitute a viable political force, electoral politics may become an intense struggle fought many times along racial lines.

The first requirement for full compliance with Section 5 is, quite simply, that the local attorneys must know the law and what must be done when their jurisdiction decides to alter its electoral procedures. Effective enforcement in a federal system depends on the capacity of national officers to transmit the necessary information (e.g., the federal regulations) in a clear, consistent, and understandable manner. Failure to ensure that the responsible local officials receive and comprehend appropriate procedural rules can easily confound enforcement by creating an alibi for noncompliance. (It should be noted that the typical city in the Southeast has a population in the 2,500–5,000 range. Culpable ignorance of Section 5 procedures may be inexcusable in Atlanta, Georgia or Charleston, S.C., but in towns like Smut Eye, Alabama or Chunky, Mississippi, the *Federal Register* may not be available in the local library, if a library, in fact, exists.)

Because Section 5 enforcement hinges on the local attorney's knowledge of federal policy and procedures, the availability of information about the act directly conditions compliance. Table 9-1 provides an overview of the intergovernmental communication process between the covered jurisdictions and Washington, D.C., as perceived by those local attorneys who personally have filed preclearance requests (59.2 percent). While almost two-thirds of the attorneys who filed submissions stated that the department had sent them information about the act, only 50.0 percent said that the department was their primary source of information about procedures. The free-answer comments about sources of information indicate that approximately 45 percent of the attorneys who have made Section 5 requests did not receive any information from the department prior to the submission and instead relied on their state's attorney general for advice.[27] Of those attorneys who had made Section 5 submissions, 60.8 percent rated the assistance they received from the department as "adequate" or "more than adequate." The principal complaints about assistance were lack of timely reply, ambiguous answers to questions, and difficulty in identifying the appropriate Justice Department official.[28]

It is important to recall that the Civil Rights Division did not announce Section 5 regulations until 1971, and it was not until 1973 that the Voting Section prepared information packets which were mailed to local legal officers. Current policy is to send out information on request rather than systematically to mail information and/or updates, as is done by other federal agencies.[29] The responses show that slightly over one-third of the city/county attorneys who made submissions claimed not to have received information from the Justice Department about Section 5 preclearance. Viewed in light of the Civil Rights Division's passive policy of information dissemination, this suggests that the division may be missing an opportunity to increase compliance by not actively contacting or educating as many attorneys as possible.

Since the burden of proof under Section 5 procedures is on the submitting authority, officials in the covered jurisdictions ought to know what counts as evidence of nondiscriminatory changes. Kenneth Culp Davis has argued that administrative actions should be subject to predetermined or prospective rules which are

Table 9-1.   Sources of information about Section 5 procedures

City/county attorneys in agreement with statement	Percent minority population in jurisdiction					
	100–60	59–50	49–40	39–25	24–0	Totals
Personally submitted a preclearance request to Department of Justice (DOJ)	58.8	91.7	63.6	61.0	42.4	59.2
	(17)	(12)	(22)	(41)	(33)	(125)
City/county attorneys who have submitted a preclearance request:						
DOJ has sent information about submission procedures	50.0	45.5	71.4	60.2	85.7	63.5
	(10)	(11)	(14)	(25)	(14)	(74)
DOJ was jurisdiction's primary source of information about VRA	30.0	36.4	35.7	64.0	64.2	50.0
	(10)	(11)	(14)	(25)	(14)	(74)
DOJ assistance was:						
a) adequate	60.0	45.5	50.0	72.0	64.3	60.8
b) inadequate	40.0	54.5	50.0	28.0	35.7	39.2
	(10)	(11)	(14)	(25)	(14)	(74)
Attorneys' self-described knowledge of DOJ standards for evaluating Section 5 submissions:						
a) familiar with standards	11.1	18.2	35.7	24.0	7.7	20.8
b) unsure or unaware of standards	88.9	81.8	64.3	76.0	92.3	79.2
	(9)	(11)	(14)	(25)	(13)	(72)

One-hundred twenty-five Georgia and Mississippi attorney respondents. Figures in parentheses indicate percentage base.

known in advance by the affected parties.[30] With 79 percent of the attorneys who have filed submissions stating that they were either "unsure" or "unaware" of the Civil Rights Division's standards for Section 5 determinations, it is likely that many local attorneys remain misinformed and perplexed about the act's Section 5 requirements. Ignorance on the part of local officials can even lead to the rejection of a submission, as explained by the voting section's submission unit attorney:

> As election administrators, they might suspect that if they don't submit, they're going to get into some kind of trouble, even if it [the change] is not discriminatory. There could be a challenge of the election or something will happen, or they'll look bad, like this county attorney in _____ County, where he just wasn't aware of the requirement. He was new and making the submission a week before the election. And having the election called off, he probably looks pretty bad and so do the others there, and he doesn't like that, I'm sure.[31]

While the department may not be able to prevent every newly appointed attorney from making a costly error, it could follow the General Accounting Office's advice and institute a regular training program throughout the covered states.[32]

Turning to the actual steps taken to obtain a preclearance, we see from Table

9-2 that a majority of the attorneys (60.8 percent) with preclearance experience contacted the department prior to filing a submission. As corroborated by the comments of the Voting Section staff (see previous section), most local attorneys who made prior contact telephoned and/or wrote Washington to seek guidelines and discuss points of difference. Materials accompanying a submission usually included a copy of the local ordinance and other pertinent records, such as census data, voter registration figures, and maps. (It is quite common for a covered jurisdiction to include multiple changes—for example, moving a dozen polling places or the annexation of eighteen separate parcels of land—in a single submission. To comply with the law, covered jurisdictions typically mail a cover letter for the whole package of changes and append a collection of supporting materials. What is crucial for the Submission Unit in the Voting Section is that the covered jurisdiction has submitted a "clear statement" of the proposed electoral change and evidence of its nondiscriminatory character. Based on the responses to the ques-

Table 9-2. Actions taken to comply with Section 5 preclearance requirement

	Percent minority population in jurisdiction					
City/county attorneys in agreement with statement:	100–60	59–50	49–40	39–25	24–0	Totals
Communicated with DOJ prior to a Section 5 submission	60.0	45.5	78.6	60.0	57.1	60.8
	(10)	(11)	(14)	(25)	(14)	(74)
Communication prior to a Section 5 submission via:						
a) letter	12.5	28.6	42.1	25.0	41.2	32.8
b) telephone	75.0	71.4	52.6	62.5	41.2	56.7
c) personal visit	12.5	0.0	5.3	6.3	5.9	6.0
d) State Attorney General	0.0	0.0	0.0	0.0	5.9	1.5
e) U.S. Congressman	0.0	0.0	0.0	6.3	5.9	3.0
	(8)	(7)	(19)	(16)	(17)	(67)
Materials included in Section 5 submission: *						
a) local ordinance	60.0	81.8	92.8	72.0	71.4	75.7
b) census data	10.0	27.3	57.1	48.0	57.1	45.2
c) voter registration data	50.0	36.4	78.6	72.0	71.4	64.8
d) maps	40.0	54.5	78.6	68.0	92.8	68.9
e) report by consultant	20.0	9.1	57.1	8.0	14.3	20.3
f) statement by local citizen group(s)	30.0	18.2	21.4	28.0	28.6	25.7
g) other	30.0	36.4	42.9	20.0	35.7	31.1
	(10)	(11)	(14)	(25)	(14)	(74)
Contacted DOJ while Section 5 submission was still pending	50.0	45.5	64.3	71.4	53.8	58.0
	(10)	(11)	(14)	(21)	(13)	(69)
Election proceeded while Section 5 submission was still pending	44.4	30.0	50.0	36.8	35.7	36.4
	(9)	(10)	(14)	(19)	(14)	(66)

*Multiple responses permitted.

Georgia and Mississippi attorneys who have personally submitted preclearance requests. Numbers in parentheses indicate percentage base.

tionnaire, city/county attorneys include approximately three different types of sup-plemental materials with their cover letter.) Beyond these items, some Section 5 submissions also contained reports from consultants, court proceedings, resolu-tions of the city council or county board, and occasionally even statements of sup-port from local minority group leaders. It is not surprising to learn that once sub-missions were sent to the U.S. Attorney General, a majority (58.0 percent) of the local attorneys continued to track their progress by contacting the voting section while the submissions were under review.

Another crucial component of compliance concerns the conduct of elections prior to approval of a preclearance request. Despite the claims of the voting sec-tion that such elections are not a serious problem,[33] over one-third (36.4 percent) of the sampled attorneys who personally made submissions asserted that elections proceeded in their jurisdictions while Section 5 submissions were still under re-view. This disregard for federal procedures calls into question the effectiveness of the department's ability to monitor election officials. In fact, improvement of its ability to discover elections that proceeded while a submission was pending is one of the principal recommendations for strengthening Voting Rights Act enforce-ment made in the 1978 General Accounting Office report.[34] Despite the office's sharp criticism on this point, the department has continued to deny that it is guilty of faulty monitoring.[35]

A collateral problem with monitoring elections that proceed while a submis-sion is pending arises out of a covered jurisdiction's deliberate decision not to make electoral changes. When asked about the manner of elections in the city or county and the length of time that this form had been used, 40 percent of the local attor-neys who had never filed a preclearance request typically answered with responses like "50 years" or "forever."[36] This suggests that many jurisdictions have evaded the reach of Section 5 of the Voting Rights Act by not modifying their election laws or procedures. Put bluntly, in this type of governmental unit, local white po-litical power holders may have decided to defend the status quo ante in the hope of outlasting the lifespan of the act.

For all of the voting section's work to make the submission process conve-nient, the feeling that there is federal intrusion into local affairs persists. Just un-der 70 percent of the local attorneys who participated in the submission process claimed that the Justice Department asked them for additional information above and beyond that incorporated in the jurisdiction's original submission documents. The sense of intrusion is heightened by the Civil Rights Division's necessary mo-dus operandi of validating submission materials through its institutionalized net-work of local minority contacts. To counterbalance its lack of field staff, the vot-ing section maintains a permanent registry of minority officials, minority group leaders, and other informed citizens to help evaluate the impact of a proposed vot-ing change. Describing his reliance on local "whistleblowers," the submission unit's line attorney explained:

> It doesn't seem likely that there are a whole lot of very discriminatory changes out there that haven't been submitted. There might be some. . . . If there were real big problems, I think we would have heard about them. . . . If they're really controver-sial like that, they'll get caught quickly by civil rights groups.[37]

White officials, as indicated in Table 9-3, are quite aware of this monitoring by the Voting Section through local black community groups. Curiously, the Voting Section does not often request the FBI to visit local officials as a means of encouraging the flow of accurate information about proposed voting changes.

From the viewpoint of the local attorneys, the Voting Section's adherence or nonadherence to the legislatively mandated sixty-day time limit for notification also exacerbates the sense of federal intrusion. While just half of the attorneys who have submitted preclearance requests said they received word of the U.S. Attorney General's decision by the sixtieth day, the other half claimed notification arrived after the legal deadline, with some letters (4.1 percent) arriving more than four months after the proposed voting change was submitted. Much of this irritation stems from confusion on the part of local attorneys over the tolling of the sixty-day period.[38] *Georgia v. United States*[39] permits the clock to be restarted whenever the U.S. Attorney General requests additional information and that information is returned to Washington, D.C.

Though confusion exists about the timing of the sixty-day clock, the usual Section 5 decision, even if it arrives late by local perceptions, is either one of approval or of approval contingent upon one or two minor revisions. The depart-

Table 9-3.   Perceptions of Justice Department preclearance policy

City/county attorneys in agreement with statement:	Percent minority population in jurisdiction					
	100–60	59–50	49–40	39–25	24–0	Totals
DOJ has requested more information after initial submission of preclearance documents	50.0 (10)	70.0 (10)	85.7 (14)	68.0 (25)	64.3 (14)	68.5 (73)
DOJ has sought information from sources outside your office	77.8 (9)	50.0 (10)	85.7 (14)	100.0 (15)	64.3 (14)	77.4 (62)
DOJ has sent an officer to your jurisdiction to seek more information	0.0 (10)	9.1 (11)	21.4 (14)	16.7 (24)	7.1 (14)	12.3 (73)
DOJ has suggested: a) significant revision(s)	10.0	20.0	16.7	23.5	16.7	18.1
b) minor revisions, if any	90.0 (10)	80.0 (10)	83.3 (12)	76.5 (17)	83.3 (12)	81.9 (61)
DOJ has informed your jurisdiction of its decision in: a) 60 days or less	60.0	72.7	35.7	52.4	53.8	50.7
b) 61–90 days	30.0	9.1	28.6	28.6	23.1	23.3
c) 91–120 days	10.0	18.2	28.6	14.3	15.4	21.9
d) 121 days or more	0.0 (10)	0.0 (11)	7.1 (14)	4.8 (21)	7.7 (13)	4.1 (73)

Georgia and Mississippi attorneys who have personally submitted a preclearance request. Figures in parentheses indicate percentage base.

ment's concern for the integrity of local election processes is substantiated by the high proportion (81.9 percent) of proposed voting changes approved without significant revision. Both the responses to open-ended questions and in-depth interviews with Civil Rights Division personnel indicate that the Voting Section's presubmission counseling and guidance of local attorneys is actually a form of intergovernmental negotiation that usually resolves problems prior to the submission of the formal request for preclearance.[40] Wholesale revisions occur rather infrequently (18.1 percent) and tend to be concentrated among the submissions from racially divided "battleground" jurisdictions (i.e., those communities with a minority population in the 25 to 60 percent range). The lesson for covered jurisdictions is straightforward: when the presubmission communication process breaks down (or is not attempted), the likelihood of significant revisions in a submission increases.

Although the U.S. Attorney General, through February 1981, interposed only 815 objections to some 35,000 voting changes submitted since 1965 (2.3 percent), objections to submissions from Georgia (17.4 percent) and Mississippi (11.9 percent) were considerably higher.[41] Election changes that most commonly have engendered objections are method of election (41.3 percent) and annexations (29.9 percent).[42] Besides the substantive disagreement over the discriminatory effect of a proposed voting change, city/county attorneys expressed strong dislike for the department's handling of the objection process. Attorneys representing covered jurisdictions that had experienced an objection uniformly were upset by the department's failure to explain or justify satisfactorily the basis for the interposition of an objection. While the number of cases in Table 9-4 is quite small, nevertheless the basis for local exasperation is evident. Explanatory comments by attorneys (e.g., "I do not recall any reasons being cited," or "the Department said it would adversely affect members of the minority race") make it clear that the local attor-

Table 9-4.   Interposition of an objection to a voting change

City/county attorneys in agreement with statement	Percent minority population in jurisdiction					
	100–60	59–50	49–40	39–25	24–0	Totals
Has the U.S. Attorney General ever imposed an objection?	6.3 (16)	25.0 (12)	30.4 (23)	11.8 (34)	5.9 (34)	14.3 (119)
Of jurisdictions under an imposed objection:						
DOJ provided detailed information in support of their objection	0.0 (1)	0.0 (3)	0.0 (7)	50.0 (4)	0.0 (2)	11.7 (17)
The objection has been resolved	0.0 (1)	67.0 (3)	57.0 (7)	75.0 (4)	50.0 (2)	58.8 (17)
Elections proceeded while an objection was still pending	0.0 (1)	33.0 (3)	71.4 (7)	25.0 (4)	50.0 (2)	47.0 (17)

Georgia and Mississippi attorneys. Figures in parentheses indicate percentage base.

neys felt that they were not being adequately informed of the reasons for an objection. Eventually, most objections are resolved, yet about half of the jurisdictions under an objection (47 percent), according to their attorneys, proceeded with elections prior to the removal of the objection. It is possible to consider these few cases as part of the imperfections associated with any enforcement responsibility; on the other hand, what appear to be outright violations of the act call to mind the General Accounting Office's allegations that the Civil Rights Division fails to follow up objections.[43]

The Consequences of "Shared Responsibility"

In light of the responses to the survey questions, what can be said in summary about the compliance of covered jurisdictions and their "appropriate officials" with respect to the Voting Rights Act? As mentioned earlier in this essay, the Voting Section staff believes that their enforcement strategy results in the submission of over 90 percent of all voting changes. Unfortunately our data do not allow a direct test of this contention. Nonetheless, the figures in Table 9-5 are suggestive, viewed within the context of southern whites' hostility to minority political power and their tenacious efforts to frustrate the purpose of the Voting Rights Act (illustrated in the two case studies that follow).

Of the attorneys who responded to the questionnaire, approximately 60 percent stated that they had personally filed one or more proposed electoral changes with the U.S. Attorney General. Jurisdictions represented by these attorneys are probably by and large in compliance with the act. Another group of attorneys (11.2 percent) had not personally filed a preclearance request, but stated that their jurisdiction had made submissions since 1965. This set of jurisdictions may also be in compliance with Section 5. The remaining attorneys (29.6 percent) did not file preclearance requests nor were they aware of any submissions made by their jurisdictions. Election law changes—especially inasmuch as they are construed so broadly by the Justice Department to include changes in polling places, annexations, as well as balloting procedures—typically occur fairly frequently in cities and counties. It seems quite probable that many of the jurisdictions in this latter category—comprising almost one-third of the total—have in fact made such changes

Table 9-5.   Section 5 compliance behavior by city/county attorneys

Attorney has personally made a submission	59.2
Attorney has not made a submission, but knows jurisdiction has made a submission since August 1965	11.2
Attorney has not made a submission nor does he know if jurisdiction has made a submission since August 1965	29.6
	100.0
	(125)

Georgia and Mississippi attorneys. Figure in parentheses indicates percentage base.

and have not reported them to the Justice Department. If this is the case in even half of these jurisdictions, then there is a larger noncompliance rate in these two states than the 10 percent overall figure estimated by the department.

In addition to outright noncompliance by failing to tender required submissions, there is a likelihood that some of these jurisdictions have remained in compliance precisely to frustrate the spirit of the act. In other words, discriminatory voting procedures may have been in place at the time the Voting Rights Act was passed in 1965, and local officials have refused to make badly needed electoral changes for fear that the Justice Department under Section 5 will require them to modify their discriminatory rules as a prerequisite to approving their submissions.[44]

A second conclusion suggested by the data is that some local attorneys have learned to play the Section 5 preclearance game to the full advantage of their jurisdiction. Table 9-2 indicates that 36.4 percent of the local attorneys said that their communities went ahead with elections even though a preclearance request was still pending. While this may partly indicate ignorance of correct procedures, it seems also to reflect a rational strategy according to which attorneys presented the Voting Section with a fait accompli and gambled (with very good odds) that the Justice Department's solicitude for smoothly working local election processes would override any decision to abort the election. Other attorneys, we discovered, withheld contemplated voting changes until a week or two before the upcoming election in a ''brinkmanship'' effort to take advantage of the Voting Section's posture of accommodation. In still other cases, local attorneys followed a strategy of protracted negotiations over every minute detail of a preclearance request or interposed objection. Their purposes were to delay as long as possible any change and to obtain through attrition the smallest amount of change acceptable as ''nondiscriminatory.'' While this short list of compliance ''games'' played by local attorneys is not exhaustive, each strategy falls under the aegis of Section 5, and thus the Voting Section staff in the Civil Rights Division must constantly develop counterstrategies.

These avoidance activities exemplify the basic shortcoming inherent in an enforcement philosophy of ''shared responsibility.'' To compensate for the minimal resources provided for by Congress to enforce the 1965 Voting Rights Act, the Department of Justice had to devise an enforcement procedure that relied heavily on the ''good faith'' of state and local officials to uphold national policy, even one that many of these local officials themselves strongly disliked. Prevented from constructing a far-reaching and powerful enforcement organization, the Civil Rights Division translated the 1965 Voting Rights Act into a series of regularized procedures—the preclearance process—that eased the costs of compliance for the local officials throughout the area of the covered jurisdictions and also reduced the costs of enforcement for the Justice Department. Unfortunately, ''shared responsibility,'' while lowering the cost of Section 5 enforcement, has not purchased adequate compliance with the 1965 Voting Rights Act. This tradeoff between vigorous enforcement of Section 5 and the maintenance of amicable relationships with local officials traps Voting Section personnel in an administrative quandary that allows local election officials to exploit the Section 5 process to the detriment of the minority franchise.

INACTION AND CONFRONTATION
TWO LOCAL RESPONSES TO SECTION 5

As a group, local attorneys interviewed in Mississippi and Georgia regarding county and municipal implementation of Section 5 voiced similar attitudes about the civil rights legislation. Their responses suggested, however, some diversity of voting rights compliance in their jurisdictions. To demonstrate what this diversity may entail in concrete terms, we present a brief examination of two small cities and their different responses to the requirements of the Voting Rights Act and Justice Department regulations.

The View from Attala County, Mississippi

Kosciusko is the largest city in Attala County, which is located in the center of the state.[45] Of Kosciusko's 9,383 residents, 64 percent are white and 36 percent are black. Although the county has some small industry, it is basically a farming region. The blacks, many of whom own property and farm, have been involved only marginally in local politics. In the 1960s, during the early days of integration in Mississippi, there were monthly meetings between the elected white and black leaders. A local Baptist minister, the head of Attala County NAACP, was the primary black leader consulted by whites during this period.

Through 1962, the city's voters elected one representative from each of four wards plus one at-large representative. With the passage of the Voting Rights Act, Kosciusko (and some other cities in Mississippi) went to the at-large system of electing five aldermen with the proviso that the candidates had to maintain residency in the various wards. From the 1960s to 1977, at-large elections were held in Kosciusko. In 1966, county land was annexed by the city. It was not precleared with the Justice Department. The mayor later said: "I don't know how the 1966 voting changes never got up to D.C. It didn't enter my mind."

After Section 5 guidelines were formulated and distributed by the department in 1971, there was little understanding of their scope and meaning by the public officials in Kosciusko and by its city attorney. "They didn't give us hardly any guidelines at all," the mayor said. "I didn't believe that we were required to file the preclearance."

The city attorney was more emphatic in his criticism of the department. The 1971 guidelines were poorly written, he said. But until the threat of litigation loomed, local officials did not attempt to get clarification.

There were no communications between them and the department until litigation began in 1976. Unlike traditional voting rights litigation, said the local attorney, where lawyers had case law to work with such as in the one person, one vote cases, they had little to aid them when forced to comply with the Voting Rights Act and the 1971 regulations.

Kosciusko officials claimed that they had found out about the 1966 noncompliance (failure to seek preclearance for the annexation) in 1976 when the city came under court order by the U.S. Court of Appeals, Fifth Circuit, to do away with at-large elections. These elections were declared unconstitutional, and U.S. District Court Judge William Keady ordered Kosciusko to come up with a new election plan. The city responded with an at-large election system with no residency requirements.

At this point, the black Baptist minister and NAACP leader in Attala County called the department and indicated to attorneys in the Voting Section that there was no 1966 preclearance of the annexation. In May 1977, Kay Butler, an attorney in the litigation unit of the department's voting section, filed a motion in U.S. District Court in Mississippi, seeking to enjoin Kosciusko from holding elections under the new plan on the grounds that blacks would not have an opportunity to elect any black representatives. At the same time, the department asked Kosciusko attorneys to submit a copy of the 1966 annexation ordinance for preclearance review.

Toward the end of the month, Judge Keady ordered Kosciusko to redraw ward lines within ninety days and then hold a special election, or the Court would redraw the lines. At this moment, Kosciusko officials had their first informal contacts with Butler.

Prior to her talks with white officials, she had spoken with the black minister about the situation in Kosciusko. The white leaders were not pleased with this type of communication. While "happy" with their black population with whom they said they had good relations, they were angry with those blacks who spoke to Justice Department attorneys. "The Department of Justice have representatives in Kosciusko—the NAACP. They've got that Bowen [David Bowen-D: 2d C.D. Mississippi] in congress," said the mayor. Furthermore, he believed that the blacks had "a toll-free line to the Justice Department. . . . Some blacks make a career out of informing for the Justice Department."

In Butler's conversations with the mayor ("she was a very nice woman," he said), and with the city attorney and members of the city council, she indicated that the department expected to see a five-ward city, apportioned in accordance with the one person, one vote principle. If that were done, then the 1966 annexation would be precleared. The Kosciusko white officials wanted to keep their at-large system.

After Butler returned to Washington, Kosciusko leaders, black and white, sat down to work out a plan which was then submitted to Judge Keady and the department in August 1977. The plan included the annexed area, and established four wards plus one at-large seat. Two of the newly created wards had black population majorities.

The department approved the submission in September. In October, Judge Keady signed an order that validated the redistricting, and the following month, Kosciusko had municipal elections. For the first time in its history, two black aldermen were elected to city council.

The Floyd County, Georgia $230,000 Preclearance

Between 1965 and 1980, jurisdictions in Georgia failed to submit at least 362 voting changes.[46] A 1982 study of local officials' compliance with the Voting Rights Act concluded that Georgia "state and local officials have violated Section 5 provisions with impunity.[47] Regarding Justice Department rejections of proposed voting changes between 1975–1980, Georgia ranked second, with 17 percent, only to Texas, with 36 percent. (Mississippi ranked third, with 12 percent.)[48]

"Annexations [are] the most commonly enacted voting changes that are implemented [in Georgia] without seeking Justice Department or D.C. U.S. District Court approval," according to the study.[49] The Rome, Georgia, case involved sixty annexations between 1964 and 1975, as well as a 1966 change in the city charter that in effect created a new governmental structure. Rome is a city of 31,000 located in Floyd County in the northeastern portion of the state, with a population that is 77 percent white and 23 percent black.

Prior to 1966, Rome's city charter, enacted in 1918 by the Georgia General Assembly, provided for a nine-person city commission and a five-person board of education. Candidates for both bodies were elected concurrently on an at-large basis by plurality vote. Those for city commissioner were required to run from one of nine residential districts. There were no residency requirements for board of education candidates.[50]

The basis for the bitter dispute between the city and the department was the Georgia General Assembly's passage of several laws of local application in 1966— a year after passage of the Voting Rights Act. The laws, passed on the recommendation of Rome city officials, amended Section 4 of the 1918 law that had established Rome's governmental machinery. For commissioners, these modifications included: 1) three residential districts instead of nine; 2) three numbered posts in each residential district; 3) a majority vote requirement; and 4) staggered terms. For the board of education, the enlarged six-person board was to be elected at large, with residency requirements and staggered terms.

In 1974, Rome officials submitted a proposal for a minor annexation to the Justice Department for preclearance. Once it examined the history of the city, the department discovered fifty-nine other unreported annexations as well as the 1966 election changes. The Voting Section immediately requested Rome to submit these changes for formal preclearance. The city initially refused to do so, and the department convinced a local federal court to enjoin the city from holding elections—an injunction which remained in force until 1980.

Rome then submitted the requested material in 1975, arguing that the 1966 omnibus voting changes had not originally been submitted because of "oversight." (These changes were later justified as enabling the city to comply with the one person, one vote doctrine.)

After reviewing the previously unreported changes, the department interposed an objection to thirteen of the sixty annexations which involved areas that had heavy white populations; and it objected to a number of the 1966 municipal changes on grounds that they diluted the black vote. In order to comply with the Voting Rights Act, the department said, the city must change dilutionary features of the 1966 voting law. Rome officials refused to do so, however, arguing that they could not be sued under the Voting Rights Act as a "political subdivision" as defined in the act's Section 4.

With elections still not allowed by 1979, the city sued the department in the U.S. District Court for the District of Columbia, still claiming that the department did not have the power to review the city's voting changes because Rome was not a political subdivision covered by the act. The suit also requested that the city be allowed to bail out from coverage of the act because it had not been involved in racially discriminatory actions, as proven by absence of civil rights litigation during the previous seventeen years. The court issued a summary judgement in support of the department's jurisdiction to review the city's voting changes.

Rome then appealed to the Supreme Court in April 1979, requesting that the justices issue a declaratory judgement that the Rome procedures had neither the purpose nor effect of denying or abridging the right to vote on account of race, color, or membership in a language minority. It continued to claim that it was not a political subdivision covered by the act, and to request that it be allowed to bail out from coverage.

While the appeal was pending, the city petitioned the department for permission to conduct an interim election using the 1966 election rules which had been partially objected to. No resolution was worked out, however, until after the Supreme Court announced its decision in April 1980, in *City of Rome v. United States*.[51] The six to three decision written by Thurgood Marshall upheld the Justice Department's authority to preclear voting changes in cities such as Rome. Justice Marshall's opinion stated that the city came within the act

> . . . because it is part of a covered state. Under the plain language of the statute, then, it appears that any bail out action to exempt the city must be filed by, and seek to exempt all of, the state of Georgia. . . . When an entire state is covered, it is irrelevant whether political units of it might otherwise come under Section 5 as 'political subdivisions.' . . . Our conclusion is that, under the express statutory language, the city is not a political subdivision for purposes of Section 4 (a) 'bail out.'[52]

After the decision was announced, the city negotiated a settlement with the department. Residency requirements were abandoned along with numbered posts, staggered terms, and the majority requirement.

An election was set for 2 December. A black campaigned for city commissioner and two more ran for the board of education. (Prior to 1980, only four blacks had ever sought office in Rome. None had won, although one had received a plurality vote but was defeated by a white in the runoff.) In the 1980 election, a black won a seat on the commission and another won a seat on the board.

The costs of Rome's six years of resistance to the department's enforcement efforts were extremely high. City elections were not held during this period, and over $230,000 in tax revenues were spent in legal fees.

Comparison of the Two Events

There were several similarities between the Kosciusko and Rome interactions with the federal government.

1. Both cities initially responded to the 1965 act by instituting voting changes that diluted the votes of their black minorities.
2. Neither city precleared their voting changes before implementation; Kosciusko's noncompliance lasted eleven years, while Rome's lasted over fourteen.
3. Both cities claimed to have "accidentally" learned of their earlier noncompliance.

4. City attorneys in Kosciusko and Rome complained about the lack of information provided by the Justice Department (yet neither attorney evidently requested this needed information).
5. Officials' hostility to the Voting Rights Act was so great in both cities that they attempted to stonewall the federal government once their noncompliance was discovered.
6. In both cities, an immediate result of the department's review and modification of the voting changes was the election of blacks to local government for the first time.
7. The federal judicial orders from the Fifth Circuit in the Mississippi case, and from the U.S. Supreme Court in the Georgia case, had major impact in both cities.

There were also some interesting differences between the Kosciusko and Rome strategies.

1. At some point, Kosciusko local officials saw the value of resolving the dispute through intensive informal discussions with black local leaders and the department rather than choosing the appeal route.
2. There was a grudging willingness by Kosciusko officials to sit down with the black representatives to decide on new ward lines for the city.
3. The 36 percent black population in Kosciusko was larger than Rome's 23 percent.
4. Kosciusko's local leaders, while opposed to federal intervention, showed greater flexibility in their dealings with the department than did Rome's.

However, local white officials in both cities shared a common disdain for the federal voting rights statute, one which took the form of noncompliance with Section 5 regulations for over a decade in both cities, as well as a basic rejection of the objective of the act—eradication of barriers to effective minority participation in the democratic processes of local government.

To its credit, the Justice Department staff, when it finally learned of the noncompliance, took effective action. And, in both cases, the courts played a major role in accommodating the conflicting interests, thus exemplifying the federal judiciary's "conditioning impact" on voting rights enforcement.[53]

CONCLUSION

Elsewhere we have described Voting Rights Act implementation as an intergovernmental bargaining process between the Justice Department and officials from covered jurisdictions.[54] This process often produces minimal compliance. Where voting changes are approved, the affected black population may not be harmed, but its relative voting strength also may not be substantially improved. Although critics of the Justice Department contend that its approach to administering Section 5 preclearance requirements results in missed opportunities to bolster the voting rights of blacks, department officials answer that a more vigorous enforcement strategy (if it were possible with their limited resources) would likely lead to even greater resistance to the act than presently exists.

The department holds that the level of compliance with the act is high despite the hostile attitudes of local officials and their own administrative limitations. Negotiations to work out potentially troublesome changes result in a relatively high rate of preclearance and the remaining undetected changes are probably minor and benign in any case. By encouraging covered jurisdictions to continue to participate in the preclearance process, the Justice Department believes it has made improvements possible in the voting status of black Americans. By not insisting on a more radical departure from the status quo in voting practices, the strategy of negotiated settlements has minimized resistance and reduced the need for coercion.

However, the data from local officials and the two case studies contained in this essay suggest that the level of noncompliance may be much higher than department officials suspect or at least are willing to acknowledge. From the beginning, the Justice Department has known that it could not achieve compliance with the Voting Rights Act by itself from Washington. Without personnel in place in the field to monitor local government voting activities, it has had to rely on local officials to assume a major share of the responsibility for voting rights enforcement.

This cooperative effort based on the concept of "shared responsibility" to achieve political equality for black Americans has been successful in only some jurisdictions; instances of local ignorance and deliberate avoidance are numerous. Eighteen years after the passage of the Voting Rights Act the task of changing long-standing behavior patterns among officials from covered jurisdictions continues to be a difficult one.

NOTES

1. For a discussion of the importance of this factor in achieving implementation of statutory objectives see Paul Sabatier and Daniel Mazmanian, "The Implementation of Public Policy: A Framework for Analysis," *Policy Studies Journal,* 8 (Special issue #2, 1980): 538–560; and for a discussion of implementation differences among civil rights policy areas see Harrell R. Rodgers, Jr. and Charles S. Bullock, III, *Law and Social Change: Civil Rights Laws and Their Consequences* (New York: McGraw-Hill, 1972).

2. Daniel Grant and H. C. Nixon, *State and Local Government,* 2nd Ed. (Boston: Allyn and Bacon, 1968), 155.

3. For a discussion of the relationship between the proportion of a political jurisdiction's population which is black and the stringency of voting registration requirements in the early 1960s, see Donald R. Matthews and James W. Prothro, *Negroes and the New Southern Politics* (New York: Harcourt, Brace and World, 1966).

4. 109 U.S. 3 (1883).

5. 163 U.S. 537 (1896).

6. 347 U.S. 483 (1954).

7. For a discussion of the "scope of conflict" notion see E. E. Schattschneider, *The Semi-Sovereign People* (New York: Holt, Rinehart and Winston, 1960), 1–18.

8. 42 U.S.C. 1977.

9. Sabatier and Mazmanian, "Implementation of Public Policy," 543–544.

10. Ibid., 546.

11. Drew Days, III, Testimony on the Extension of the Voting Rights Act, Subcommittee on Civil and Constitutional Rights, House Committee on the Judiciary, Washington, D.C., July 1981.

12. Aaron Wildavsky, *Speaking Truth to Power* (Boston: Little, Brown and Co., 1979), 142–152.

13. *Jackson Clarion Ledger* (Jackson, Mississippi), 16 June 1978, 11.

14. David J. Garrow, *Protest at Selma: Martin Luther King, Jr. and the Voting Rights Act of 1965* (New Haven: Yale University Press, 1978), 21–22.

15. Howell Raines, *My Soul is Rested* (New York: Bantam Books, 1978), 372.

16. *Jackson Clarion Ledger*, 16 June 1978, 11.

17. Andrew Dunsire, "Implementation Theory," in *Implementation, Evaluation and Change* (U.K.: The Open University, 1980), 5–54.

18. Drew Days, III, Testimony, 1981.

19. Interview with David Hunter, Staff Attorney, Voting Section, Civil Rights Division, U.S. Department of Justice, 1 September 1977, Washington, D.C.

20. Interview with Gerald Jones, Chief, Voting Section, Civil Rights Division, U.S. Department of Justice, 2 September 1977, Washington, D.C.

21. See, for example, the following reports by the U.S. Commission on Civil Rights. *Political Participation: A Study of the Participation by Negroes in the Electoral and Political Processes in 10 Southern States Since Passage of the Voting Rights Act of 1965*, May 1968; *The Voting Rights Act: Ten Years After*, January 1975, chaps 3–6 328–335, 344ff passim; *The Voting Rights Act: Unfulfilled Goals*, September 1981, 64–76, 89–91. Also see U.S. Comptroller General, U.S. General Accounting Office, *Voting Rights Act—Enforcement Needs Strengthening*, 6 February 1978, 10–19; 26–32 passim.

22. Raymond Brown and Duane McMahon, *The State of Voting Rights in Georgia in 1982* (Atlanta: The Southern Regional Council, 1982), 35–43.

23. See for example, Armand Derfner, "Racial Discrimination and the Right to Vote," *Vanderbilt Law Review*, 26 (April 1973): 523–584; Frank Parker, "County Redistricting in Mississippi: Case Studies in Racial Gerrymandering," *Mississippi Law Journal*, 44 (June 1973): 391–424; Richard Engstrom, "Racial Discrimination in the Electoral Process: The Voting Rights Act and the Vote Dilution Issue," in *Party Politics in the South*, ed. Robert P. Steed, Lawrence W. Moreland, and Tod A. Baker (New York: Praeger Publishers, 1980), 197–213; Mack H. Jones, "The Voting Rights Act and Political Symbolism," Paper presented at the annual meeting of the Southern Political Science Association, Gatlinburg, Tennessee, November 1979.

24. As part of the data collection for the eventual 1978 report, the General Accounting Office conducted a survey of state and local officials, minority organizations, and "private citizens with expressed interest in minority voting rights." The sample included states covered by the 1975 amendments to the Voting Rights Act (see chapter 7 of the 1978 General Accounting Office report, *Voting Rights Act—Enforcement Needs Strengthening*, for more details).

25. Howard Ball, Dale Krane, and Thomas P. Lauth, *Compromised Compliance: Implementation of the 1965 Voting Rights Act* (Westport, Conn.: Greenwood Press, 1982).

26. To obtain the views of local attorneys on Section 5 requirements, the authors mailed questionnaires to 159 county attorneys in Georgia and 82 in Mississippi, and to 236 city attorneys in Mississippi. While the responses do not constitute a random sample (125 jurisdictions replied out of a total of 477, for a 26 percent response rate), the responses come from a wide range of jurisdictions by population size, racial mix, and degree of urbanization. It is, of course, possible that attorneys who were most hostile to the preclearance requirement were least likely to respond; the opposite is also a possibility. There is no good prima facie reason to choose between these potential sources of bias. Despite its limitations, this survey is the only available in-depth ex-

amination (of which we are aware) of those individuals who must actually comply with the act. A copy of the questionnaire may be obtained from the authors.

27. Several of the questions asked for further explanation of a particular answer. For example, the question about "primary source of information" read as follows:

> Was the Department of Justice your jurisdiction's primary source of information about the 1965 Voting Rights Act?
> Yes ( )   No ( )
> If no, please explain

Some of the interpretations of the attorneys' attitudes and behavior offered in this article are derived from these open-ended follow-up questions.

28. These complaints were garnered from both open- and closed-ended questions.
29. See Ball, Krane, and Lauth, *Compromised Compliance*, 116–125.
30. Kenneth Culp Davis, *Discretionary Justice: A Preliminary Inquiry* (Baton Rouge: Louisiana State University Press, 1969).
31. Hunter interview.
32. 1978 GAO report, *Voting Rights Act—Enforcement Needs Strengthening*, 20.
33. Letter from Kevin D. Rooney, Assistant Attorney General for Administration, Department of Justice, submitted to the Honorable Abraham Ribicoff, Chairman, Committee on Governmental Affairs, U.S. Senate, Washington, D.C., 7 June 1978.
34. 1978 GAO report, *Voting Rights Act—Enforcement Needs Strengthening*, 20.
35. Rooney, letter to Ribicoff.
36. Based on examination of open-ended comments written on questionnaire.
37. Hunter interview.
38. This confusion is apparent in the free comments to the authors' questionnaire.
39. 411 U.S. 526 (1973).
40. For more detail on the character of this intergovernmental negotiation, see Ball, Krane, and Lauth, *Compromised Compliance*, chapter 5.
41. U.S. Commission on Civil Rights, *The Voting Rights Act: Unfulfilled Goals* (Washington, D.C.: September 1981), 184, table 6.2.
42. Ibid.
43. 1978 GAO report, *Voting Rights Act—Enforcement Needs Strengthening*, 15.
44. Howard Ball, Testimony on the Extension of the Voting Rights Act, Subcommittee on Civil and Constitutional Rights, House Committee on the Judiciary, 25 June 1981, Washington, D.C.
45. Kosciusko information is based on interviews with local officials, 6 March 1978 and news reports of the events in the *Kosciusko Star-Herald*, 5 and 26 May, 2 June, 29 September, and 6 October 1977.
46. Raymond Brown and Duane McMahon, *The State of Voting Rights*, 29.
47. Ibid., 24.
48. U.S. Commission on Civil Rights, *The Voting Rights Act: Unfulfilled Goals*, 67.
49. Brown and McMahon, *State of Voting Rights*, 29.
50. Data about Rome events are based on material from Douglas J. Mathis and L. Doyle Mathis, *The Voting Rights Act and Rome (Georgia) City Elections* (Athens, Georgia: Institute of Government, 1981), and *City of Rome v. United States*, 446 U.S. 156 (1980).
51. 446 U.S. 156 (1980).
52. Ibid. 131.
53. Ball, Krane, and Lauth, *Compromised Compliance*, 110–112.
54. Ibid., Part Three.

10

At-Large Elections and One Person, One Vote
The Search for the Meaning of Racial Vote Dilution

James Blacksher and Larry Menefee

In 1964, citizens of Birmingham, Mobile, and Gadsden convinced the Supreme Court of the United States that the Constitution guarantees equal voting rights for white people in Alabama *(Reynolds v. Sims).*[1] The problem was that the legislature of Alabama had since 1901 refused to reapportion itself and was tightly controlled by the thinly populated, rural "black belt" counties.[2] Many of these smaller counties had majority black populations, but blacks at that time were not allowed to vote.[3] Only after passage of the Voting Rights Act of 1965 would the door to voter registration—held shut since 1901 by the institution of white supremacy—be opened to black Alabamians.[4] The conflict that underlay the issues in *Reynolds v. Sims,* therefore, was between the fast growing white suburbs and a dwindling white "oligarchy" in the rural black belt counties.[5]

The plight of the suburbanites was that the state and federal courts had for decades steadfastly refused to enter the reapportionment fray, the "political thicket" *(Colegrove v. Green).*[6] But two years earlier, the Supreme Court had provided a breakthrough, ruling that the malapportionment claims of Tennessee's big cities were justiciable *(Baker v. Carr).*[7] The task facing the Alabama plaintiffs was to identify what constitutional rights and remedies were available to them. The Court responded in *Reynolds v. Sims* by announcing that the Fourteenth Amendment requires state legislatures to apportion themselves by population. The new constitutional maxim of one person, one vote was born, over strong objections from Justices Harlan, Stewart, and Clark that no such substantive principle was expressed or implied in the Constitution. The *Reynolds* majority, however, relied on the growing list of decisions under the Fifteenth Amendment, which prohibits racial discrimination in voting, to find in the Fourteenth Amendment an analogous (if unspoken) principle that proscribed undervaluation of citizens' votes based on their place of residence. This transposition of Fifteenth Amendment principles into the Fourteenth provided (white) Mobilians what they had sought: representational strength in the Alabama legislature in proportion to their numbers.

The cases following *Reynolds v. Sims* immediately recognized that the new one person, one vote constitutional norm could most perfectly be realized by creation of multimember districts or at-large voting plans, which likely would disadvantage racial minorities, the groups protected by the Fifteenth Amendment. Eventually, in *Whitcomb v. Chavis*[8] and *White v. Regester,*[9] the Court confronted this problem, ruling that the submergence of blacks' and Mexican Americans' voting strength through multimember legislative districts was unconstitutional in Texas but not in Indiana.

After *White v. Regester,* the lower federal courts, led by the Fifth Circuit, attempted to extract from the Supreme Court's opinions legal guidelines for cases where racial groups claimed that at-large elections were "diluting" or "cancelling out" their voting strength, underweighting their votes just as effectively as malapportioned districts would have done. But there was clear discontent on the part of some justices with the way this case law was developing.

Once again, the white suburbs of Mobile, Alabama, were on hand to present the Supreme Court with the opportunity to finish what it had begun with *Reynolds v. Sims.* In *City of Mobile v. Bolden,*[10] the Court reversed the Fifth Circuit's affirmance of a federal district court's ruling that at-large voting in Mobile city elections unconstitutionally diluted the votes of the black minority in the manner condemned by *White v. Regester.* The Court was deeply divided, and there was no majority rationale for reversal. A plurality led by Justice Stewart held that black voters would have to prove a racially invidious purpose behind the at-large plan in order to prevail. They distinguished minority vote dilution from population malapportionment, which violates the Fourteenth Amendment regardless of its intent. And, in the plurality's view, an at-large apportionment perfectly satisfied the one person, one vote rule.

A review of the evolution of the *Reynolds* doctrine as it affected racial minorities suggests that constitutional priorities have been misplaced by the Court's inability to discover judicially manageable standards for multimember-district vote dilution. The competing theories in the several *Bolden* opinions further underline the need for a standard of proof that reconciles the new constitutional right of majority rule with the explicit constitutional demand for the protection of racial groups.

For Mobile, as a microcosm, the historical results of *Reynolds* were dramatically felt and not without irony. In *Reynolds,* voters who resided in the predominantly white suburbs of Mobile convinced the Supreme Court that the Civil War amendments to the Constitution, which hitherto had been thought to prohibit only diminution of voting rights on the basis of race, also embodied the affirmative right of population majorities to representational control of their elected governments. In *City of Mobile v. Bolden,* officials elected by these same white suburbs convinced the Court that the unwritten one person, one vote doctrine, engrafted in large part from the Fifteenth Amendment, is a more fundamental right than the right to be free from racial discrimination, in the respect that violation of the majoritarian right requires only proof of adverse effects, while violation of the racial minority's comparable right requires proof of invidious intent as well.[11] Subsequently, in *Rogers v. Lodge,*[12] a clear majority of the Court accepted the *Bolden* plurality's intent requirement. It appears that, in terms of constitutional priorities, the white majority in Mobile may have commandeered the Fifteenth Amendment.

JUDICIAL DEVELOPMENT OF THE
CONSTITUTIONAL RIGHT OF MAJORITARIAN RULE

In 1971 Justice Harlan would write about the reapportionment decisions of the 1960s that they "can be best understood . . . as reflections of deep *personal* commitments by some members of the Court to the principles of pure majoritarian democracy." [13] Any analysis of the constitutional implications of at-large elections must begin with a review of how a fundamental constitutional right of majority control came to be recognized.

Baker v. Carr: The Question Is Manageability

Voters in the metropolitan areas of Memphis, Nashville, Chattanooga, and Knoxville, Tennessee, were the plaintiffs in *Baker v. Carr.*[14] Their complaint was that mass migration to the cities since the Tennessee legislature was last reapportioned in 1901 had caused the 1901 statute to become "unconstitutional and obsolete." [15] The less populated rural counties, it was argued, enjoyed disproportionate political strength in relation to the cities. Breaking with what was thought to be well-established precedent, the Court ruled seven to two that the complaint made out a justiciable claim under the Fourteenth Amendment and sent the case back to the lower court without delineating the elements of proof that would entitle the underrepresented counties to relief or the shape of judicial remedies that would be permissible. The majority accepted the argument of Solicitor General Archibald Cox, as *amicus curiae,* that, notwithstanding the political nature of the controversy, a constitutional violation could be detected by reference to "well developed and familiar" equal protection standards.[16] The basis of the Court's ruling thus postponed resolution of the substantive issue dividing the justices: what judicially manageable standards were available to decide apportionment disputes?

The majority opinion, written by Justice Brennan, repudiated the widely held interpretation of earlier cases to the effect that malapportionment controversies presented inherently nonjusticiable political questions. According to Brennan, a dominant characteristic of political questions was "the lack of satisfactory criteria for a judicial determination. . . ." [17] And, unlike admittedly nonjusticiable guaranty clause claims, attacks on malapportioned state legislatures could be addressed—on a case-by-case basis—to determine if the alleged "discrimination reflects *no* policy, but simply arbitrary and capricious action." [18] But by sidestepping the task of articulating a manageable equal protection standard, even for the case at hand, the majority reined up short of proposing any substantive constitutional right to apportionment by equal population.

A significant feature of the majority opinion in *Baker v. Carr* was its reliance on Fifteenth Amendment cases to support its two major premises: (1) that merely because legislative apportionments dealt with the allocation of political strength among groups of voters they did not necessarily present nonjusticiable political questions,[19] and (2) that apportionments may infringe voting rights which are subject to protection under the Fourteenth Amendment.[20] Rights guaranteed racial minorities by the Fifteenth Amendment were clearly appropriate subjects for judicial intervention in state electoral affairs, lifting alleged violations of these explicit constitutional rights "out of the so-called 'political' arena and into the conventional sphere of constitutional litigation." [21] These Fifteenth Amendment precedents, thought the *Baker* majority, provided reliable assurance that at least some forays into the political thicket could be managed by the judiciary.

In his famous dissent, joined by Justice Harlan, Justice Frankfurter moved immediately to rebut the majority's reliance on Fifteenth Amendment case law as justification for discovering population-based voting rights in the Fourteenth Amendment. "[T]he relationship between population and legislative representation" he began, "[is] a wholly different matter from denial of the franchise to individuals because of race, color, religion or sex." [22] The difference lay in the express language and underlying purpose of the Constitution itself. There has been "an explicit and clear constitutional imperative" guiding judicial intervention in state government when the issue was disfranchisement of blacks. [23] But there was no reference to a right to "representation proportioned to the geographic spread of population" in the Fourteenth Amendment, and none had been intended. [24]

Aside from his view that the Fourteenth Amendment was never intended to provide a general basis for regulating the apportionment process, Justice Frankfurter saw three jurisprudential concerns that made judicial consideration of population malapportionment claims inappropriate: (1) the need to avoid federal judicial involvement in legislative policy-making, (2) the difficulty of devising manageable standards for judgment, and (3) the problem of providing proper remedies. [25] Of these three, the "dominant consideration" was the lack of manageable standards. [26] The "principle of numbers," [27] mere mathematical equality of population, was compelled by neither the Constitution, Anglo-Saxon tradition, nor common logic, [28] and the limitless practical and political factors that must inform a fair apportionment scheme were simply too complex for courts to standardize. Justice Frankfurter feared that in future reapportionment decisions the Court would be able to surmount what he saw as intractable problems of manageability and the absence of any clear constitutional mandate only by making "[the Justices'] private views of political wisdom the measure of the Constitution. . . ." [29]

Justice Harlan's separate dissent seconded Justice Frankfurter's focus on the problem of unmanageability and went a step further, concluding that

> lack [of] standards by which to decide such cases as this, is relevant not only to the question of "justiciability," but also, and perhaps more fundamentally, to the determination whether any cognizable constitutional claim has been asserted in this case. [30]

Because apportionment issues were "basically matters appropriate only for legislative judgment," there could be no Fourteenth Amendment violation "so long as . . . a possible rational legislative policy" was available to support the plan. He rejected the suggestion that the equal protection clause required equally weighting each person's vote and thought it was "surely beyond argument" that apportionment decisions had to take into account "factors other than bare numbers." [31]

Justices Clark and Stewart wrote separate concurring opinions. They agreed with the dissenters that the equal protection clause did not require population equality among districts or more than a rational basis to uphold legislative apportionments, and they insisted that the judgment of the Court was not based on theories to the contrary. Justice Clark simply concluded that Tennessee's apportionment had strayed so far from its original design that it was totally irrational—a "crazy quilt."[32] Justice Stewart, on the other hand, declined to reach the merits at all, basing his vote for reversal on the yet untested allegation of the complaint "that Tennessee's system of apportionment is utterly arbitrary—without any justification in rationality."[33]

The divided Court in *Baker v. Carr* thus opened the door heretofore shut to consideration by federal courts of claims by voters in overpopulated legislative districts that the Constitution afforded them some still undefined protection against malapportionment. The key would be judicial manageability. Obviously, this was a Court in search of a clear constitutional norm—as clear as the Fifteenth Amendment's explicit condemnation of state policies that denied or abridged the right to vote on account of race.

Reynolds v. Sims: A New Fundamental Constitutional Right Is Born

Two years after *Baker v. Carr,* the Court attempted to resolve the knotty problem of articulating a manageable equal protection apportionment standard by rejecting altogether the traditional equal protection rationality yardstick and by establishing a new affirmative, fundamental constitutional right based on population. In *Reynolds v. Sims,*[34] over the strong objections of Justices Stewart, Clark and Harlan, the majority concluded that the "easily demonstrable" rule of one person, one vote was the "fundamental goal" and "plain objective" of the Constitution.[35] Since the new equal population principle was determined to be an affirmative constitutional right of the individual voter, it would not be necessary for federal courts to thrash about in the political thicket sorting out the rational legislative apportionment goals from the irrational ones. Historical, economic, and other group interests, no matter how legitimate, could not justify more than a minor deviation from the equal population norm. Both houses of the state's bicameral legislature must be apportioned by population.

Justice Frankfurter was no longer on the Court, but Justices Clark, Stewart, and Harlan continued vigorously to disagree with the notion of a constitutional right of population equality. Because of the pivotal role he would play in the development of minority rights in apportionment law, Justice Stewart's concurring opinion in *Reynolds* and his dissent in the companion case, *Lucas v. Forty-Fourth General Assembly of Colorado*[36] provide an appropriate focus on the fundamental differences between the majority and the dissenters.

Justice Stewart argued that the superficially neat criterion of one person, one vote did not in fact answer the problem left by *Baker v. Carr* of finding a judicially manageable equal protection standard: (1) because the Fourteenth Amendment neither imposed nor permitted such a rule,[37] and (2) because it did not address the realities of apportionment politics and thus did not as a practical matter provide judicial manageability.[38] Chief Justice Warren's majority opinion had found a right to equal voting strength in the Fourteenth Amendment by referring to prior

Fifteenth Amendment race discrimination precedents. Warren considered it "undeniabl[e]" and "repeatedly recognized that all qualified voters have a constitutionally protected right to vote and to have their votes counted." [39] This critical assertion, the constitutional predicate for explication of a one person, one vote rule, was supported solely by a long list of Fourteenth and Fifteenth Amendment decisions dealing with racial discrimination against black voters. [40] These Fifteenth Amendment cases, thought the majority, held the key to discovery of manageable standards under the equal protection clause as well. Since "the Fifteenth and Nineteenth Amendments prohibit a State from *overweighting* or *diluting* votes on the basis of race or sex," [41] it may be inferred that the Fourteenth Amendment, without explicitly naming voting rights, prohibits diluting any citizen's vote on the basis of population or geographic residence.

Justice Stewart's dissent in *Lucas* opened with a sharp rejoinder to this constitutional analysis. He contended that the reapportionment cases had

> nothing to do with the denial or impairment of any person's right to vote. Nobody's right to vote has been denied. Nobody has been deprived of the right to have his vote counted. The [Fifteenth Amendment] voting rights cases which the Court cites are, therefore, completely wide of the mark. [42]

Justice Stewart flatly disputed the assertion that the equal protection clause required the states to apportion their legislatures on a population basis. He agreed with Justice Frankfurter and with Justice Harlan's detailed presentation of historical evidence that its framers never intended the Fourteenth Amendment to confer any voting rights and, most particularly, never intended that it inhibit to any extent the states' exercise of apportionment policymaking. [43] In other words, Justice Stewart believed that the majority's discovery in the Constitution of a "fundamental principle . . . of equal representation for equal numbers of people . . . is not correct, simply as a matter of fact." [44]

The *Reynolds* majority based its holding on a much broader principle than population equality, defining the denial of equal voting rights as including any form of underweighting or diluting the *strength* of a citizen's vote. [45] This conclusion, said the Court, flowed from the bedrock principle of representative government that

> each and every citizen has an inalienable right to full and effective participation in the political processes of his State's legislative bodies. . . . Full and effective participation by all citizens in state government requires, therefore, that each citizen have an equally effective voice in the election of members of his state legislature. Modern and viable state government needs, and the constitution demands, no less. [46]

The majority acknowledged that the apportionment process is "complex and many-faceted," involving "factors other than population." [47] It did not, therefore, limit its constitutional view of effective representation to geographic malapportionments. Rather, the Chief Justice's opinion condemned undervaluations of citizens' voting power "by any method or means" [48] and "no matter what their form." [49] Specifically included among the dilutive factors which would be prohibited was racial discrimination; indeed, race cases decided under both the Fourteenth and Fifteenth Amendments were cited as the primary support for the broader requirement of effective representation.[50] Nevertheless, at least in terms of judicial standards, the *Reynolds* majority clearly inferred that the newly found equal population rule should enjoy primacy among other considerations, including race. "Population is, of necessity, the *starting point* for consideration and the controlling criterion for judgment in legislative apportionment controversies."[51] This was because population malapportionment would always be "easily demonstrable,"[52] and its dilutive *effect* would be obvious, regardless of the legislators' otherwise benign motives.[53] As for minority groups, the Court was convinced that there was ample constitutional protection for them even as it made the right of majoritarian rule the paramount constitutional concern.[54]

Again, Justice Stewart strenuously disagreed. To him, the apparent simplicity and manageability of one person, one vote were illusory, both ideologically and practically. As a matter of practical, political fact, Stewart thought, legislative apportionment had to be concerned with too many other important factors to be reduced to a mere numbers game. It was "a process of accommodating *group* interests,"[55] it had to be guided by the ideal of ensuring "effective representation . . . of the various groups and interests making up the electorate,"[56] and as a practical matter it had to approximate the ideal "by a realistic accommodation of the diverse and often conflicting political forces operating within the State."[57] Consequently, thought Justice Stewart, the measure of the fairness of an apportionment scheme could not be reduced to the equation of one person, one vote, which he called "the uncritical, simplistic, and heavy-handed application of sixth-grade arithmetic."[58] He viewed with alarm the danger that the new equal population rule

> forever freezes one theory of political thought into our Constitution, and forever denies to every State any opportunity for enlightened and progressive innovation in the design of its democratic institutions, so as to accommodate within a system of representative government the interests and aspirations of diverse groups of people, *without subjecting any group or class to absolute domination by a geographically concentrated or highly organized majority.*[59]

Thus, Justice Stewart saw a "strongly felt American tradition of preventing the submergence of the society's many diverse interests . . . by the majority's monolithic command."[60] Racial discrimination was not directly at issue in *Reynolds*. But Justice Stewart's warning about the potential damage to political minorities of an unyielding one person, one vote rule seemed to foreshadow the plight of racial groups in particular.

Both Stewart and Harlan argued that, putting aside the shaky constitutional underpinnings of one person, one vote, its adoption still would not solve the Court's problem of finding manageable criteria for judgment, would not, in other words, lead them out of the poiltical thicket. For example, questions about the number of districts required or permitted and whether their boundaries had been gerrymandered would remain.[61] And what rule would govern the use of single-member versus multimember districts or some combination of the two?[62] Prophetically—and ominously, from the standpoint of racial minorities, Justice Stewart warned: "I do not understand why the Court's constitutional rule does not require the abolition of districts and the holding of all elections at large."[63]

The dissenters in the 1964 reapportionment cases believed that the Court had gone too far by erecting the new, fundamental constitutional right of population equality in legislative apportionments. They would have retained the equal protection rationality standard as the proper constitutional measure of these political decisions, disturbing at most only those plans they could agree were mere "crazy quilts." But the one person, one vote rule of *Reynolds v. Sims* was unequivocal and generally would be greeted with approval by the nation. All that remained were questions about the ultimate shape of the new rule: what state and local governmental bodies would be subject to it, what deviations from absolute mathematical equality would be tolerated by the Court, what remedies would be required and, in particular, how the vulnerable interests of geographically insular, racial minorities would be safeguarded now that majority rule was the paramount law of the land.

Refining *Reynolds:* The Continuing Importance of Manageability

In the first six or seven years after *Reynolds,* the Court was occupied primarily with fleshing out the equal population requirements. The rule was extended to local governments, *Avery v. Midland County,*[64] and the justices struggled to find guidelines for how close to perfect mathematical equality legislatures must come. A more relaxed degree of population variance was permitted for legislative reapportionment than for congressional redistricting. Throughout these years, Justices Harlan and Stewart continued to express their opposition to the one person, one vote rule of *Reynolds.* Justice Harlan felt bound to follow *Reynolds,* but not to extend it.[65] Justice Stewart, however, still refused to accept the constitutional rule of *Reynolds* in any context.[66] He persisted in the view that legislative apportionment at both the state and local levels was "too subtle and complicated a business to be resolved as a matter of constitutional law in terms of sixth-grade arithmetic."[67] But it seemed clear that the simplicity of the population equality rule was precisely what attracted the Court's majority. Strict and comprehensive application of one person, one vote to local bodies, for example, avoided the necessity of devising standards to detect when municipal apportionment schemes actually diluted the fundamental voting rights *Reynolds* had been concerned with. Otherwise, as Justice White pointed out, in each case the Court would have to determine if the state legislature had delegated sufficient power to the local government to trigger *Reynolds* rights,[68] and it would become bogged down in arguments that local government functions were "administrative" or "executive" as opposed to "legislative."[69] So it is fair to say that population equality gained stature and was further extended as an established rule of equal protection in large part because its simplicity of statement was thought to give it judicial manageability.

Yet, even in its most straightforward applications, one person, one vote did not relieve the Court of the burdens of seeking out more flexible standards for handling the variegated, intensely political problems of reapportionment. In the early going, the Court placed the burden on the states to justify more than *de minimis* or "minor" deviations from "pure" population equality.[70] Dissenting, Justices Harlan and Stewart pointed out that such a rule stood on its head the traditional judicial presumption of constitutional validity accorded state laws; they would have left plaintiffs with the burden of proving that the population variances had an "invidious purpose . . . or effect." [71] This difficult standard of state justification for failure to achieve "pure" population equality enjoyed its finest hour in *Kirkpatrick v. Preisler* [72] and *Wells v. Rockefeller*, [73] companion congressional reapportionment cases. Majority opinions written by Justice Brennan declared that any relaxation of the Court's demand for districts drawn as close to mathematical equality as practicable would encourage legislatures not to aim for pure equality. [74] Justices Harlan, Stewart, and White dissented, charging that the majority had repudiated the teaching of *Reynolds* that exact mathematical equality was not constitutionally required. [75]

The constitutional pronouncements of *Kirkpatrick* and *Wells* were indeed "Draconian." [76] Justice Brennan acknowledged the validity of the dissenters' warnings that such an unyielding mathematical standard would actually facilitate gerrymandering directed against unpopular social and political minorities. [77] But the majority interpreted *Reynolds* to establish strict population equality as the "basic" constitutional command, one that overrode even concerns about diluting the effective representation of "distinct social and economic interests." [78] The common contention of the three dissenters and Justice Fortas' concurring opinion was that, in its quest for judicial manageability, the *Kirkpatrick-Wells* majority had allowed the siren song of simplicity to distract it from the constitutional predicates of *Reynolds v. Sims*. Justice White called it "a confusion of priorities": [79]

> Today's decisions on the one hand require precise adherence to admittedly inexact census figures, and on the other downgrade a restraint on a far greater potential threat to equality of representation, the gerrymander. Legislatures intent on minimizing the representation of selected political or racial groups are invited to ignore political boundaries and compact districts so long as they adhere to population equality among districts using standards which we know and they know are sometimes quite incorrect. [80]

It did not take long for the Court to recognize and to retreat from the illusory manageability of *Kirkpatrick*'s strict equality standard. The real world of state and local government interests simply could not wear such a mathematical straitjacket, no matter how clear and simple it appeared. *Abate v. Mundt* [81] approved a county government apportionment that varied even further from population equality than had the *Kirkpatrick* districts, naming as its reason for not insisting on strict equality the need for "flexibility in municipal arrangements." [82] Then in *Mahan v. Howell* [83] the Court limited the *Kirkpatrick* rule to congressional districting and announced a more flexible standard of "substantial equality" [84] for state legislative apportionments. As further refined in the same term by *Gaffney v. Cummings*, [85] the rule for state apportionments placed the threshold burden on plaintiffs to show a variance from substantial population equality [86] and permitted the states to rebut a prima facie case with a "rational" explanation rather than demonstration of "governmental necessity." [87]

Both *Mahan* and *Gaffney*, in relaxing the *Kirkpatrick* rule, proclaimed renewed commitment to the proposition that pure population equality, notwithstanding its superficial neatness, could not be used as an excuse to avoid considering countless other factors that affected equal representation. And, once again, Justice White's majority opinion in *Gaffney* warned of the affirmative constitutional danger that lay in relegating to the newfound right of population equality too great a role in assuring equal protection in apportionment schemes.

> An unrealistic overemphasis on raw population figures, a mere nose count in the districts, may submerge these other considerations and itself furnish a ready tool for ignoring factors that in day-to-day operation are important to an acceptable representation and apportionment arrangement.[88]

The passage from *Gaffney* was quoted most recently in *Brown v. Thompson*,[89] one of the first of the post-1980 census reapportionment cases considered by the Supreme Court. The Court held that Wyoming's policy of providing at least one representative to each county outweighed a population deviation of 60 percent below the mean in Niobrara County.[90] Justice Brennan's dissenting opinion sought to minimize the precedential value of the Wyoming case,[91] but the majority opinion, written by Justice Powell, clearly heralds a renewed willingness on the part of the Court to give priority to nonpopulation considerations in assessing representational fairness. It accepted the legislature's finding that "the opportunity for oppression of the people of this state or any of them is greater if any county is deprived a representative in the legislature than if each is guaranteed at least one (1) representative."[92] The majority recalled the teaching of *Reynolds* that "the character as well as the degree of deviations from a strict population basis" must be considered.[93] So, in spite of the disclaimer that "[t]his does not mean that population deviations of any magnitude necessarily are acceptable,"[94] the holding of *Brown v. Thompson* takes a quantum leap beyond the already growing uncertainty over what size population deviations will satisfy constitutional demands on state legislative reapportionments.

A companion case to *Brown v. Thompson*, dealing with a congressional redistricting plan in New Jersey, has escalated the trend toward vagueness on the other end of the one person, one vote spectrum. In *Karcher v. Daggett*,[95] the Court struck down, as unjustifiably excessive, a maximum population deviation between the largest and smallest districts of only 0.6984 percent. Simply because other plans with somewhat smaller population deviations had been available, the state's burden, under *Kirkpatrick v. Preisler*, to make a good faith effort to achieve perfect population equality was not satisfied.[96] Writing for the five-member majority, Justice Brennan candidly confessed the "unusual rigor" of the standard for congressional districts,[97] and reasserted its vitality: "We thus reaffirm that there are no *de minimis* population variations, which could practicably be avoided, but which nonetheless meet the standard of Art. I, sec. 2 without justification."[98]

So, as of today, with the possible exception of its approach to congressional redistricting, the Supreme Court remains committed to a case-by-case evaluation of apportionment plans under the imprecise standards of substantial equality and rational state interests. There is no strict guidance for legislators and lower courts,[99] and there is concededly a continuous spectrum of possible mathematical variances and political concerns that must somehow be weighed to discern violations of the equal protection clause, even where the state plan is challenged solely on the basis of population inequality.

AT-LARGE VOTE DILUTION:
THE DEVELOPMENT OF STANDARDS AVOIDED

Before *City of Mobile v. Bolden*

The question of whether multimember districts, which by their nature provide perfect mathematical equality, nonetheless violate the equal protection clause when they submerge the voting strength of racial minorities was one of the first post-*Reynolds* issues the Court had to take up. But in *Fortson v. Dorsey*,[100] the Court decided to postpone what promised to be its most difficult task in forming manageable standards for the fledgling constitutional right of one person, one vote. The majority reaffirmed that feature of the *Reynolds* holding which declined to make multimember districts unconstitutional per se.[101] But it left open the possibility that in particular cases multimember districting would offend the equal protection clause if there was proof that "designedly or otherwise [it] would operate to minimize or cancel out the voting strength of racial or political elements of the voting population."[102]

The following year in *Burns v. Richardson*,[103] a case in which the Court was primarily concerned with reassuring state legislatures that their serious reapportionment efforts would be treated with great deference by federal courts, it repudiated the district court's attempt to confront the political realities of multimember districting in a multiracial society. The lower court had disapproved Hawaii's proposal of multimember senatorial districts for Oahu because it "enabl[ed] the same constituency to elect four representatives and three senators" and did not take into account "community of interests, community of problems, socio-economic status, political and racial factors."[104] In vacating the decision, the Supreme Court remained convinced that mathematical equality alone would ordinarily guard against racial discrimination, and it repeated *Fortson*'s call for particular proof that minority vote dilution would occur "designedly or otherwise."[105] Exactly what evidence of dilution would suffice was not spelled out, but dictum in Justice Brennan's majority opinion indicated that the Court had in mind not proof of a purposeful gerrymander so much as "the demonstration that a particular multi-member scheme effects an invidious result. . . ."[106]

The issue continued to be avoided until 1971, when finally it was addressed on the merits for the first time in *Whitcomb v. Chavis*.[107] Delivering the opinion of a deeply divided Court, Justice White rummaged through several theories but stopped short of articulating manageable criteria for constitutional assessment of at-large voting. The three-judge district court had held unconstitutional Indiana's legislative reapportionment plan insofar as it established one multimember district for all of Marion County (Indianapolis), but had approved a 28 percent maximum population variance among the districts in the state. The Supreme Court reversed on both counts, upholding the Marion County multimember district but rejecting the population variance as too large.

At the outset, Justice White reaffirmed the teaching of earlier opinions that the underlying principles of *Reynolds v. Sims* protected minority groups from having their votes devalued by multimember districts, just as they protected voters in mathematically malapportioned districts.[108] He recalled that both the Fourteenth and Fifteenth Amendments had been designed in particular "to protect the civil rights of Negroes."[109] Significantly, the majority opinion concluded that multimember districting could violate the Fourteenth Amendment by effectively denying blacks an equal opportunity "to participate in the political processes and to elect legislators of their choice,"[110] even if the apportionment plan had not been designed purposefully to dilute blacks' votes—that is, even if there had been no racial gerrymandering.[111] The Court thus seemed to acknowledge its responsibility to guard against the use of the new one person, one vote rule in a way that would affirmatively disadvantage the racial groups who were supposed to be the primary beneficiaries of the Fourteenth Amendment.

Nevertheless, the majority could not agree that the record in *Whitcomb v. Chavis* sufficiently proved constitutionally objectionable undervaluation of the black vote in Indianapolis. Clearly, what prevented them from affirming the ruling against the multimember district was their inability to distinguish the lower court's rationale from a theory of proportional representation. The district court had based its conclusion of unconstitutionality solely on the fact that disproportionately few blacks had actually been elected.[112] Blacks were regularly (if not proportionately) slated as candidates by the Democrats,[113] and election returns exhibited bloc voting more along party lines than along racial lines.[114] When the Democrats won, the black candidates won, and when the Republicans won, the black candidates lost.

> If this is the proper view of this case, the failure of the ghetto to have legislative seats in proportion to its population emerges more as a function of losing elections than of built-in bias against poor Negroes. The voting power of ghetto residents may have been "cancelled out" as the District Court held, but this seems a mere euphemism for political defeat at the polls.[115]

Thus, thought Justice White, the district court's holding "is not easily contained."[116] In other words, it provided no judicially manageable basis for distinguishing prohibited debasement of an insular minority's voting strength from "the more general proposition that any group with distinctive interests must be represented in legislative halls."[117] Affirmance of the district court's reasoning, it seemed, would mean that any geographically concentrated group—Democrats, Republicans, union members, university communities, religious or ethnic groups—could demand its own "safe" single-member districts.[118]

But if Justice White's majority opinion exposed the hazards in the district court's logic, it did not chart what an acceptable course would be either. There was no clear inference, for example, that the Court would have found a denial of equal protection in the Marion County multimember district had the record demonstrated consistent racial bloc voting and the failure of either major party to slate black candidates. Justice White named a number of additional evidentiary factors, absent in *Whitcomb*, which might or might not be considered necessary to establish a Fourteenth Amendment violation: blacks' inability to register and vote, to join and participate in the political party of their choice, to command legislative responsiveness to their particularized needs.[119] The standards for proving minority vote dilution were left undefined, and the strength of the Court's commitment to assuring that the rule of *Reynolds* would not become one *white* person, one vote remained uncertain.

In his separate opinion in *Whitcomb*, Justice Harlan mocked the majority's "inability to measure what it purports to be equalizing"[120] and said it vindicated Justice Frankfurter's view that voting power was too elusive and complex a notion for courts to handle.[121] But Justice Harlan's point, once again, was that *Reynolds* itself had been wrong; that population equality was no fairer or more accurate a measure of voting strength than the still standardless proscription of racial vote dilution. The necessary corollary of this argument seemed to be that continued adherence to the one person, one vote formula demanded development of workable criteria for detecting racially discriminatory debasement of voting power in at-large apportionment schemes as well.

The Court appeared unequivocally to affirm its commitment to the minority vote dilution implications of the *Reynolds v. Sims* rule by its unanimous decision in *White v. Regester*.[122] This was the first case in which the Court had actually held that a multimember district scheme was unconstitutional. But while they affirmed the district court's judgment rejecting proposed at-large voting in Dallas and Bexar (San Antonio) counties as part of the Texas House of Representatives reapportionment plan, the justices once again sidestepped any systematic analysis of the minority vote dilution phenomenon and, thus, did not articulate uniform, manageable standards for determining when it violates the equal protection clause. The basis of the decision was restricted more or less to a recapitulation of the district court's factual findings and to cryptic announcements that the Court was not inclined to overturn them. The litany of earlier Supreme Court bouts with multimember districts was recited. But no attempt was made to explain exactly why the record in this case demonstrated an equal protection violation when that in *Whitcomb v. Chavis* did not. And there was no new attempt to distill from the many precedents cited the evidentiary standards for proving "that multi-member districts are being used invidiously to cancel out or minimize the voting strength of racial groups."[123]

The trial court findings of fact selected for inclusion in the Supreme Court's opinion in *White v. Regester* are difficult to catalogue. There was a history of *de jure* discrimination against black voters in Texas,[124] and Mexican Americans "had long suffered from . . . invidious discrimination and treatment in the fields of education, employment, economics, health, politics and others."[125] In Dallas County, only two blacks had been elected to the house since Reconstruction,[126] and in Bexar County only five Mexican Americans had been elected.[127] The Court did not, however, say whether others had been defeated by racially polarized voting. There was a powerful, white-dominated Democratic Party organization in Dallas that ignored blacks' concerns and used racial campaign tactics to defeat candidates supported by the black community,[128] but no mention was made of any similar slating group in San Antonio. Cultural and language barriers had resulted in depressed Mexican American voter registration in Bexar County,[129] but no mention was made of the black registration rate in Dallas. The district court had found "that the Bexar County legislative delegation in the House was insufficiently responsive to Mexican-American interests."[130] Requirements that candidates run for numbered places and win by a majority of the total vote, "neither in themselves improper nor invidious, enhanced the opportunity for racial discrimination. . . ."[131] The Court gave no hint of the priority it attached to any of these facts; instead, it approved the district court's conclusion of unconstitutionality based on the "totality of the circumstances."[132] The Court credited the trial judges with a "special vantage point" from which they could make "a blend of history and an intensely local appraisal of the design and impact of the . . . multimember district in light of past and present reality, political and otherwise."[133]

Following *White v. Regester,* the lower federal courts, particularly in the Fifth Circuit, found themselves presented with a growing number of challenges by blacks to multimember district plans. This proliferation of cases, concerning mostly county and municipal election schemes, was probably attributable more to the pervasiveness of the problem than to any perceived clarity of the Supreme Court's mandate. The leading case was *Zimmer v. McKeithen,*[134] which addressed the at-large election of the police jury (county commission) and school board in a small, rural Louisiana parish. In *Zimmer,* the en banc Court of Appeals for the Fifth Circuit, in a majority opinion by Judge Walter Gewin, attempted "to establish some standards as to what is required to 'minimize or cancel out' black voting strength . . . ."[135] That is, the Fifth Circuit set for itself the task that the Supreme Court had heretofore avoided: providing trial courts with evidentiary norms for deciding racial vote dilution cases. The teaching of *Zimmer v. McKeithen* would, in fact, guide federal courts throughout the nation until *City of Mobile v. Bolden* was handed down.

The *Zimmer* majority rejected the district court's reasoning that because an at-large apportionment plan by definition provided a zero population deviation it could not dilute the voting strength of blacks.

> Inherent in the concept of fair representation are two propositions: first, that in apportionment schemes, one man's vote should equal another man's vote as nearly as practicable; and second, that assuming substantial equality, the scheme must not operate to minimize or cancel out the voting strength of racial elements of the voting population.[136]

A districting plan that met population equality requirements could still be constitutionally challenged as racially discriminatory if there was proof of *either* a racially motivated gerrymander *or* that the plan would *operate* to dilute black voting strength.[137] The court declined to consider evidence of a racial purpose behind the at-large scheme, because it found that the apportionment was constitutionally infirm in the way it operated. As the Fifth Circuit read the cases, it was a districting plan's operation, after all, that the Supreme Court had been concerned with in *Whitcomb v. Chavis* and *White v. Regester.* From these two cases, therefore, the *Zimmer* court gleaned "a panoply of factors, any number of which may contribute to the existence of dilution."[138] These were concisely catalogued as the famous four "primary" factors and four "enhancing" factors:

[W]here a minority can demonstrate a lack of access to the process of slating candidates, the unresponsiveness of legislators to their particularized interests, a tenuous state policy underlying their preference for multi-member or at-large districting, or that the existence of past discrimination in general precludes the effective participation in the election system, a strong case is made. Such proof is enhanced by a showing of the existence of large districts, majority vote requirements, anti-single shot voting provisions and the lack of provision for at-large candidates running from particular geographical subdistricts. The fact of dilution is established upon proof of the existence of an aggregate of these factors.[139]

In setting out these standards for proving unconstitutional dilution, the court emphatically disavowed any intention that they be used to require mere proportional representation: "clearly, it is not enough to prove a mere disparity between the number of minority residents and the number of minority representatives."[140]

Over the next seven years, the so-called *Zimmer* factors preempted the field and were used—practically to the exclusion of all other evidentiary criteria—to govern the outcomes of scores of reported and unreported at-large dilution cases.[141] Meanwhile, the Supreme Court was sending out signals of dissatisfaction with the *Zimmer* approach—and with the unanimous *White v. Regester* decision that underlay *Zimmer*. On direct appeal, *Zimmer* itself was affirmed on the narrow ground that a judicially ordered reapportionment plan must adopt single-member districts, unless there were extraordinary justifications for another type plan;[142] the Court expressly reserved approval of the Fifth Circuit's constitutional theory of dilution. In *Wise v. Lipscomb*,[143] three other justices joined a concurring statement by Justice Rehnquist labeling the *Zimmer* analysis an "amorphous theory." *Washington v. Davis*[144] and *Arlington Heights v. Metropolitan Housing Development Corp.*[145] established an apparently comprehensive intent requirement for proof of equal protection claims, without discussing the impact of such a rule on apportionment cases. And dialogue among the Justices on related issues in *Beer v. United States*[146] and *United Jewish Organizations v. Carey*,[147] strongly hinted at a movement toward an intent requirement in dilution cases. Finally, the question was presented squarely to the Court in *City of Mobile v. Bolden*.

City of Mobile v. Bolden: Still Searching for Manageable Standards

In *City of Mobile v. Bolden*, the justices fully engaged the lingering problem of at-large vote dilution cases caused by the lack of clearly enunciated judicial standards, but no majority could agree on a solution. However, it is fair to say that *Bolden* contained a five to four vote disapproving the *Zimmer v. McKeithen* analysis—at least, by itself—as a satisfactory formula for detecting unconstitutional vote dilution. But the Court did not fill the vacuum left by *Zimmer's* demise; Justice White correctly noted that the *Bolden* decision "leaves the courts below adrift on uncharted seas. . . ."[148]

Invidious purpose is the constitutional standard for at-large vote dilution endorsed by Justice Stewart in *Bolden:* using the evidentiary guides set out in *Washington v. Davis, Arlington Heights* and *Personnel Adm'r of Mass. v. Feeney*,[149] "[a] plaintiff must prove that the disputed plan was 'conceived or operated as [a] purposeful device to further racial discrimination'. . . ."[150] To reach this conclusion, Justice Stewart was required to distinguish multimember district dilution problems from the genre of vote dilution condemned by *Reynolds v. Sims;* no one has suggested that proof of invidious purpose is necessary to establish a one person, one vote claim. He did so by limiting the scope of *Reynolds* to prohibition of mathematically demonstrable population malapportionments. Consequently, he said in *Bolden,* every at-large system perfectly satisfies the one person, one vote principle, and no citizen within it can complain that his vote is "diluted" in the *Reynolds* sense.[151] This disposition of the *Reynolds* precedents, and his narrow reading of the Fifteenth Amendment as completely satisfied where the right to register and vote is not formally restricted, cleared the way for Justice Stewart to include racial vote dilution claims in the category of attacks on facially neutral laws, which, under *Washington v. Davis* and *Arlington Heights,* must be proved to have an invidious purpose in order to make out an equal protection violation.

Justice Stevens disagreed with the Stewart plurality's selection of an *Arlington Heights* intent standard for at-large dilution cases, because, in his view, reference to the subjective intent of some lawmakers would merely lead the courts into a different kind of political thicket and would open the floodgates to endless litigation.[152] Instead, Justice Stevens drew on his dissenting opinion in *Cousins v. City Council of Chicago,*[153] written while he was on the court of appeals, and proposed a constitutional standard that would demand proof, based on the objective effects of the apportionment plan, that it was entirely motivated by the desire to curtail the strength of a political minority and had no other rational justification.[154] Justice Stevens sought to distinguish *Reynolds v. Sims* and its progeny by naming two different categories of vote dilution, one which requires strict constitutional scrutiny of voting practices and one which does not.[155] The first category, he argued, involves practices, like poll taxes or literacy tests, which restrict individuals' access to the ballot, while the second category concerns practices which, in his view, affect the political strength of discrete groups without inhibiting any individual's right to vote. According to Justice Stevens, population malapportionments interfere with individual voting rights and thus fall into the strict scrutiny category, but at-large dilution cases concern only group rights and thus fall into the second category. Put differently, Justice Stevens viewed the at-large problem as simply another gerrymander case, indistinguishable from claims that equally populous district boundaries had been drawn purposefully to fragment the voting strength of a political group. He harked back to Justice Frankfurter's warning about the difficulty of devising judicially manageable standards to govern intensely political apportionment decisions.[156] He urged a rule of deference to legislative bodies that would acknowledge the constitutional acceptability of their use of racial and other group-based considerations in the apportionment process—so long as invidious discrimination was not obviously their *sole* concern. Under this standard, racial groups would have no greater claim for judicial protection than would any religious, ethnic, economic or political groups.[157]

In his separate opinion, Justice White stood by the "totality of circumstances" dilution standard he had authored in *Whitcomb v. Chavis* and *White v. Regester* and which he found faithfully codified in *Zimmer v. McKeithen.*[158] Justice White thought that the *White v. Regester–Zimmer* criteria were entirely consistent with the equal protection intent requirement of *Washington v. Davis* (which he had also authored), implying—though not saying so explicitly—that proof of intent might be required in at-large dilution cases.[159] And he defended the manageability of the *White–Zimmer* analysis, accusing the Stewart plurality of "viewing each of the factors . . . in isolation, and ignoring . . . the totality of circumstances approach we endorsed in *White v. Regester, Washington v. Davis,* and *Village of Arlington Heights v. Metropolitan Housing Development Corp. . . .*"[160]

Justice Marshall insisted that at-large dilution and population malapportionment were only different manifestations of the same *Reynolds* violation, so that the effect-only standard of proof was equally applicable to both.[161] But Justice Marshall endorsed the "intensely local appraisal" of *White v. Regester* as "the proper test" for proving effective vote dilution.[162] Thus Marshall agreed in substance with Justice White, although White appeared more willing to view *White v. Regester* as an intent standard. Justice Marshall did, however, embellish the *White v. Regester* principles with a concise definition of his own:

> Unconstitutional vote dilution occurs only when a discrete political minority whose voting strength is diminished by a districting scheme proves that historical and social factors render it largely incapable of effectively utilizing alternative avenues of influencing public policy.[163]

It was this definitional "combination of an electoral structure and historical and social factors"[164] that Justice Stewart attacked as "gauzy sociological considerations [that] have no constitutional basis."[165]

Actually, the hands-off standard proposed by Justice Stevens was substantially the same as the rationality standard which Justice Stewart had once persistently advocated in population malapportionment cases; now in *Bolden,* Stewart accepted mathematical equality as a fundamental right. So far as the *Bolden* opinions of Justices Stewart and Stevens were concerned, the equal population guarantee of majority control was a constitutional right more fundamental and more deserving of strict judicial enforcement than the right to be free from racial vote diminution, notwithstanding the explicit racial focus of the Fifteenth Amendment, from which the unexplicit one person, one vote rule had been extrapolated. Yet it seems clear that they arrived at this result, to borrow a phrase from Justice Stewart's *Feeney* opinion,[166] "in spite of" rather than "because of" its historical and constitutional inversion of values. Both justices seemed heavily—perhaps entirely—influenced by their inability to discern judicial manageability in the dilution theories of Justices White and Marshall, theories which undeniably suffer from tendencies toward amorphousness. Thus the single most intelligible message of *City of Mobile v. Bolden* was that a fragmented Supreme Court was still searching for a judicially manageable constitutional theory of at-large vote dilution.

Post-*Bolden* Developments: The *White-Zimmer* Standard Rehabilitated

The decline of *Zimmer v. McKeithen* proved to be shortlived. In *Rogers v. Lodge,*[167] the Court affirmed the Fifth Circuit's reliance on the *Zimmer* factors to find racially discriminatory intent in the maintenance of an at-large election scheme in Burke County, Georgia. The six-member majority led by Justice White did not answer the contention of the dissenters that the facts in *Rogers* could not be distinguished from those found insufficient to prove intent in *Bolden*.[168] Instead, Justice White's opinion distinguished the two cases, "[f]irst, and fundamentally," on the trial court's acknowledgement in *Rogers* that purposeful discrimination is the "ultimate issue" and, secondly, on the district judge's awareness that the *Zimmer* factors were not the exclusive indicia of such a purpose.[169] Consequently, the Court held, even though the district court used the *Zimmer* analysis "[f]or the most part," its conclusion of invidious intent was not clearly erroneous and thus survived appellate review, in light of the Court's newfound deference to the trial judge's finding of fact, when racial motivation is the issue.[170] It appears, therefore, that *Rogers v. Lodge* has restored the *White v. Regester–Zimmer v. McKeithen* standard for constitutional challenges of election systems that dilute the voting strength of racial minorities. Only now the trial judge must conduct his or her "intensely local appraisal" of the "totality of circumstances" and then pronounce a conclusion of purposeful discrimination in order to avoid reversible error.

Justice Powell wrote a dissenting opinion,[171] joined by Justice Rehnquist, based on his conclusion that the evidence in *Rogers* was no different in kind from that found insufficient by the *Bolden* plurality to prove invidious intent.

Justice Stevens also dissented,[172] but on grounds that extended the reasoning of his *Bolden* dissent. He reiterated and elaborated the argument that a subjective intent approach was not "an acceptable, judicially-manageable standard for adjudicating cases of this kind."[173] Stevens still subscribed to a rationality test, explaining that he would consider any electoral structure to be irrational and invalid if its only demonstrable justification was "to assist a dominant party to maintain its political power."[174] And he persisted in the view that racial minorities should not be afforded "special protection" not available to any other political groups.[175] However, Justice Stevens seemed to soften this stance to the extent of making racial discrimination "presumptively irrational," requiring states to come forward "to identify legitimate local policies that might justify" election system features that have "an adverse impact on the minority's opportunity to participate in the political process."[176] His vote for reversal in *Rogers* apparently was based on his belief that the racial discrimination clearly demonstrated in Burke County's election scheme could be cured by eliminating the majority runoff and numbered post requirements, obviating the need to assess the at-large apportionment itself.[177]

Rogers was handed down only two days after the President signed into law the Voting Rights Amendments of 1982,[178] in which Section 2 of the Voting Rights Act[179] was amended to codify the *White–Zimmer* standard for racial vote dilution cases.[180] The amended Section 2 "is designed to restore the legal standard that governed voting discrimination cases prior to the Supreme Court's decision in *Bolden*."[181] Congress, however, has labeled the *White–Zimmer* analysis a "results" test.[182] According to the Senate Judiciary Committee, "[t]he intent test focuses on the wrong question and places an unacceptable burden upon plaintiffs in voting discrimination cases."[183]

In apparent disagreement, a clear majority of the Supreme Court has now approved that aspect of the *Bolden* plurality's opinion that subjected attacks on multimember district election schemes to the invidious intent requirement "generally applicable to Equal Protection Clause cases." [184] However, thanks to Congress, litigants challenging dilutive at-large schemes in the future, as a practical matter, may not be burdened with the need to prove invidious intent. In recent decisions, the Supreme Court has made it clear that such claims must be addressed under the new statutory standard, not under the constitutional standard. [185] Thus the amendment to Section 2 of the Voting Rights Act could postpone indefinitely further inquiry by the Court into the constitutional dilemma. But even a shift to Section 2's results standard will leave open, at least to some extent, the question of what electoral, political, social, and geographical circumstances surrounding at-large systems amount to abridgement of minority voting rights. Ultimately, the Court cannot avoid a thorough examination of the principles of electoral fairness set in motion by *Reynolds,* as they apply to political minorities. Indeed, the extensive dictum in the several opinions by the justices in *Karcher v. Daggett*[186] indicate a growing interest in exploring the corresponding rights of political groups who are not protected by the Voting Rights Act, such as political parties. If so, the inquiry may be reopened on a constitutional footing sooner rather than later.

TOWARD A CONSTITUTIONALLY ADEQUATE AND JUDICIALLY MANAGEABLE STANDARD OF AT-LARGE VOTE DILUTION

The constitutional rules for protecting racial minorities in the apportionment process cannot be written on a clean slate. The history of race relations in the United States, the adoption of the Civil War amendments to the Constitution, and the Supreme Court's full acceptance of *Reynolds v. Sims* ought to constrain judicial inclinations to erect from scratch theories of minority representation that might appeal to some personal notions of doctrinal purity. In particular, the Court ought not countenance use of the Fourteenth and Fifteenth Amendments to assure electoral majorities not merely parity but a constitutional advantage over voters who are in the racial minority. There are many creditable theoretical approaches to an analysis of minority representation.[187] The final test of these theories should not only be whether they are judicially manageable, politically fair, and consistent with democratic ideals, but whether they can be reconciled with the existing constitutional record.

The Necessity of Recognizing a Fundamental Constitutional Right of Racial Minorities to Be Free from At-Large Vote Dilution

A constitutionally unacceptable flaw in the standards for proving at-large vote dilution advanced by the Stewart and Stevens opinions in *City of Mobile v. Bolden* and by Justice White in *Rogers v. Lodge* is that they subordinate the racial minority's right of judicial protection to the majority's right of electoral rule. Not only are blacks and other racial minorities required to carry a heavier burden of proof than are majority groups in order to safeguard for themselves an "equally effective voice" in legislative apportionments, but the invidious intent standard actually *presumes* that when majority voting strength is safeguarded the minority has no further right to complain. In this respect, the theories advanced in *Bolden* and *Rogers* are wrong as a matter of fact and as a matter of constitutional priorities—according to the basic rationale of *Reynolds v. Sims* and its progeny, including in particular the arguments of Justice Stewart and the other dissenters in the reapportionment cases.

The one person, one vote rule is a child of the "living Constitution."[188] The dissenters in the reapportionment cases showed that the framers of the Fourteenth Amendment did not intend for it to interfere with the states' plenary power to regulate the franchise, and no member of the Court has found explicit proof to the contrary. Nor has any member of the Court disagreed with oft-repeated reminders that the "end of discrimination against the Negro was the compelling motive of the Civil War Amendments."[189] The *Reynolds v. Sims* majority discovered the fundamental right to an equally effective vote in the Fourteenth Amendment by interpolation of the Fifteenth Amendment's explicit condemnation of abridging voting rights on the basis of race or color. But the *Reynolds* dissenters argued that assurance of representational control by population majorities could not find its source of legitimacy in either the Constitution or Anglo-Saxon tradition. One needn't rehash and choose sides in these arguments or challenge the validity of the *Reynolds* principles to accept the proposition that, *in terms of constitutional priorities*, if vote dilution of any kind is unconstitutional, racially based abridgment of voting strength is *no less* objectionable than population-based vote dilution. Whether it is the voting strength of Negroes that has been devalued or that of some other "racial, ethnic or cultural" minority, it is offensive to the primary purpose of the Fourteenth Amendment in both its original and modern contexts.[190] State-supported racial discrimination is the first concern of this constitutional value system because it is "illegal, immoral, unconstitutional, inherently wrong, and destructive of democratic society."[191] Since this is so, judicial rules of enforcement which subordinate and even handicap the ability of racial minorities to avoid submergence of their electoral strength by the racial majority undermine the plan of the Constitution.

The expulsion of racial voting rights from the constitutional penumbra of *Reynolds v. Sims* also works a special historical injustice on blacks in the United States. From the time the first African was brought by a Dutch slaver to the North American shore in the seventeenth century, majority rule in this country has meant, first and foremost, white rule.[192] As the Civil War opened, even free Negroes were denied the right of suffrage in an overwhelming majority of the northern states;[193] only five New England states and New York had permitted blacks to vote.[194] Both before and after adoption of the Fifteenth Amendment, at-large election plans were employed throughout the country to cancel out the voting strength of blacks and other racial and ethnic minorities.[195] The so-called Progressive Reform Movement at the turn of the twentieth century prominently featured at-large voting as a device for politically neutralizing readily mobilized racial, ethnic, and economic minority groups and for putting in office the "best" citizens from all-white business and professional classes.[196] Of course, in the South the first order of business for the reformers was the near total disfranchisement of blacks, whose manipulable votes had proved to be an embarrassing but irresistible source of corruption to white politicians.[197] Many of the state laws which today prescribe at-large elections for municipalities, county commissions, and school boards in the South were enacted during the Progressive Period,[198] when blacks could not vote and thus could not participate in the apportionment decisions. Until the mid-twentieth century, in southern states like Florida and Alabama, white voters frequently enjoyed the special representational benefits of single-member districts in the white-only Democratic primary elections for local government, while the general elections—the only ones in which the few black voters could participate—were conducted at large.[199]

Moreover, during the sixty to seventy years of black disfranchisement in the South, minority control was the general rule for the all-white state legislatures.[200] The strangleholds of the less populous rural counties over the urban areas in Tennessee and Alabama were the malapportionment conditions which offended the Supreme Court in *Baker v. Carr* and *Reynolds v. Sims*. The Alabama legislature was in 1964 effectively controlled by the black belt counties,[201] in which blacks who held population majorities were not allowed to vote—until the Voting Rights Act passed in 1965, a year after *Reynolds* was decided. It would be farfetched to suppose that newly enfranchised black voters actually could have gained control of the legislature if the federal courts had not ordered reapportionment, and no one would suggest that the three-judge district court, the liberal urban lawyers and the Warren Court were co-conspirators in a conscious litigation program designed to head off a black takeover in Alabama. But there is no doubt that powerful white politicians in Alabama were alert to the implications of impending black reenfranchisement with respect to the reapportionment issue.

Indeed, Walter Perry of Jefferson County urged the legislators from the heavily-Negro populated counties to surrender power to the urban areas of the state because the cities were "the last depositories of conservatism" in Alabama and their own counties would soon see Negroes voting in large numbers.[202]

The coincidence of events is loaded with poignant irony. History seems to have its own imponderable way of making sure that the politically powerful land on their feet, and, in a 1964 Alabama, *Reynolds* surely was an idea whose time had come. It can at least be said that the entire historical backdrop of *Reynolds v. Sims* substantially increases the constitutional imperative of ensuring judicial protection against dilution of blacks' voting strength that is fully commensurate with the protection of majority rule.

Assessing the *Bolden* and *Rogers* Opinions

If a proper standard for determining at-large racial vote dilution must at once be faithful to constitutional priorities and offer reasonably consistent judicial manageability, then none of those described in the several *City of Mobile v. Bolden* opinions succeeds, even with the embellishments of *Rogers v. Lodge*.

Justice Stewart cast the representational interests of blacks into the *Washington v. Davis* dust bin of rights which have no fundamental, independent claim to strict judicial protection and which, therefore, must be purposefully impaired before a constitutional violation occurs. In arriving at this conclusion, he had to make a similar categorical decision about the right of geographic population majorities not to have their voting strength diluted. If population malapportionment offended no fundamental constitutional concern—was itself only another suspect statutory classification—then even overpopulated districts would not be constitutionally objectionable unless they were totally irrational or unless an invidious legislative purpose to discriminate against voters in those districts could be shown. On the other hand, if one person, one vote was a fundamental constitutional right, then at-large racial vote dilution had to be distinguished from dilution resulting from population imbalances if proof of more than effective debasement of blacks' voting power was to be required. By choosing the latter alternative, Justice Stewart abandoned the positions he had maintained since his dissent in *Reynolds* concerning both the constitutional necessity of population equality and the realities of dilution.

Where previously Justice Stewart had insisted that the Fourteenth Amendment conferred no voting rights and was not intended to restrict state apportionment decisions, in *Bolden* he accepted the rule of *Reynolds* that the equal protection clause guarantees to each voter "an equally effective voice."[203] Where before he had protested the transposition of Fifteenth Amendment principles into reapportionment cases, contending that no one's right to vote is denied or impaired by apportionment decisions, he now agreed that dilution of representational strength abridges the right to vote under the Fourteenth Amendment (though not within the meaning of the more explicit Fifteenth).[204] Where in the earlier cases Justice Stewart argued that equal voting strength could not be measured solely by the "sixth-grade arithmetic" of population equality, but had to take account of the complex political realities involved in accommodating group interests, in *Bolden* he concluded that the *Reynolds* requirement of an equally weighted, fully effective vote is *completely* satisfied by population equality, so that blacks fenced out of a "unitary" at-large district cannot claim that their "vote has been 'diluted' in the sense in which that word was used in the *Reynolds* case."[205]

At bottom, Justice Stewart seemed unwilling to include at-large vote dilution within the proscription of *Reynolds v. Sims* because it was "difficult to perceive how [its] implications . . . could rationally be cabined."[206] But the invidious intent standard he adopted does not promise to solve the manageability problem. In fact, as Justice Stevens has argued forcefully,[207] it is likely to make the judicial task even more uncertain. Because most apportionment decisions have fully realized political intentions, to argue that racial groups are disadvantaged in the process by accident is to ignore reality.[208] An evidentiary standard for detecting discriminatory intent that allows courts honestly to identify and to condemn every legislative decision that purposefully advantages one racial group at the expense of another in the apportionment process would sweep broadly indeed. Justice Stevens even argued that "the facts of political life would deny legislatures the right to perform the districting function."[209] On the other hand, as Justice Marshall points out, if the intent standard requires federal courts to accept legislators' apportionment choices "so long as they sufficiently mask their motives through the use of subtlety and illusion,''[210] or so long as they can point to some nonracial justification for the districting scheme, it will be impossible for disadvantaged blacks to prevail. In between these two extremes are countless other problems presented by an intent standard that threatens either legislative independence, judicial manageability, or the constitutional guarantee of an equally effective voice for racial minorities.[211] Some of these questions have already been raised.

For example, what if invidious racial motives are mixed with legitimate nonracial apportionment considerations? The Stewart plurality in *Bolden* would condemn legislation that was racially motivated ''at least in part.''[212] Justice Stevens disagrees; he ''do[es] not believe otherwise legitimate political choices can be invalidated simply because an irrational or invidious purpose played some part in the decision-making process.''[213] If racial discrimination need not be the exclusive purpose, how much relative weight must it carry? How many lawmakers must share the invidious motive? What if the legislators innocently rubber-stamp racially intended proposals of local officials?[214] Must the most influential decisionmakers be identified and their motives scrutinized?[215] How much deference must be accorded in-court denials of invidious motives by decisionmakers?[216] Must discriminatory intent be detected in a discrete legislative decision, or may the court consider the cumulative purpose of a series of laws enacted over the years?[217] What if an apportionment plan was originally adopted for the purpose of diluting black voting strength but has acquired legitimate, nonracial justifications in intervening years?[218] These questions only begin the tangled inquiry into the meaning of an intent standard of unconstitutional vote dilution. However long *Arlington Heights* survives in other equal protection contexts, it seems unlikely to succeed as a guide for judicial investigation of at-large election schemes. Not only does such a standard leave unresolved the problem of judicial manageability, it arguably aggravates it. No other member of the Court has rebutted Justice Stevens' convincing argument that the ''unseemly''[219] case-by-case examination of lawmakers' motives places the federal judiciary not just in a ''political thicket'' but in ''a vast wonderland of judicial review of political activity,''[220] and that it ''cannot possibly satisfy the requirement of impartial administration of the law. . . .''[221]

The *Rogers* majority held that the White–Zimmer analysis is simply a particular application of the equal protection intent standard, a conclusion that is at least debatable in view of vigorous disagreement by both Congress and the *Rogers* dissenters. Justice White did not identify which state actors are guilty of improper motivation,[222] unless his reference to the discretion Burke County's state legislators have over purely local affairs[223] means that they necessarily are the culprits. Nor did he attempt to respond to the contentions of Justices Stevens and Marshall that a motivation analysis should be irrelevant when violation of the constitutionally protected right to an equally effective vote is at issue, not just the denial of a ''constitutionally gratuitous benefit.''[224] As the Senate Judiciary Committee said, the intent test focuses on the wrong question. An intent requirement is particularly objectionable when population majorities are not burdened with this added element of proof in order to obtain judicial relief.

Whether it is denominated as ''intent'' or ''results,'' the *White–Zimmer* standard cannot claim judicial manageability adequate to serve the fundamental voting rights it seeks to analyze. The "access to the political process" standard espoused by Justices White and Marshall cannot promise much greater hope of manageability. At the very least, it probably deserves the "amorphous" label some members of the Court bestowed on it.[225] Most of the cases which concluded under the *Zimmer v. McKeithen* guidelines that at-large schemes were constitutional could not honestly be distinguished analytically from those which reached a contrary result—on any basis other than the varying personal views of the trial and appellate judges who decide them.[226] Capriciousness is an inherent risk of the "intensely local appraisal" of each "totality of circumstances."

To the extent that Justice Marshall embellishes the *White v. Regester–Zimmer v. McKeithen* standard by calling for proof of "historical and social factors" which make it difficult for the "political minority" to influence public policy by means outside the at-large election process, he might introduce more uncertainty and hence even less judicial manageability. The quality and quantity of proof sufficient to demonstrate that blacks are unable to influence elected officials through "a variety of other political, social and economic groups"[227] or are unable to form effective out-of-office factions to "serve as watchdogs on the performance of the government"[228] are sure to vary widely from case to case and from court to court.

Of all the members of the Court, Justice Stevens alone explored the policy concerns underlying the search for a manageable standard of dilution. But he simply readopted, sometimes verbatim, his lengthier analysis of gerrymandering in *Cousins v. City of Chicago*,[229] when he sat on the court of appeals. And by applying to *Bolden* his *Cousins* rationale for approving allegedly gerrymandered city council districts in Chicago, Justice Stevens would make it literally impossible to challenge any at-large election system on constitutional grounds.

Cousins was the classic gerrymander case, involving single-member districts which had been reapportioned by incumbent council members to preserve their old wards at the expense of racial and political groups who were out of power. A majority of the Seventh Circuit panel ruled that there was sufficient evidence of inculpatory remarks by the aldermen drawing boundary lines to remand the case for a new trial on the issue of racial gerrymandering.[230] But it rejected the claims of politically unaligned "independent voters," citing a line of cases holding that allegations of nonracial, purely political gerrymandering were nonjusticiable.[231] Dissenting, Judge Stevens thought that the rights of nonracial political groups should be identical to those of racial minorities in the apportionment process.[232] He rejected the "easy distinction" between racial and political gerrymandering afforded by the language of the Fifteenth Amendment, concluding that the Fourteenth Amendment gave the same protection to all politically cohesive groups.[233] But he recognized that a standard of proof available to every group had to be drawn narrowly if legislative bodies were to be left free to carry out the legitimately political reapportionment function. So Stevens distinguished gerrymander cases from those which he perceived as challenging practices that diminished an individual's voting strength and which required a compelling state justification. In his view, claims that equally populated districts nevertheless diluted someone's voting strength did not concern individual rights but group rights, and the voting rights of a group were not entitled to the same strict protection as those of the individual.[234]

In his *Cousins v. City of Chicago* dissenting opinion, Justice Stevens considered seven possible judicial standards for addressing what he had denominated as group-based gerrymander claims. Six of them he found unacceptable: (1) no judicially manageable standard is available, so gerrymander issues are entirely nonjusticiable; (2) if mathematical equality is achieved, then courts may inquire no further into vote dilution; (3) to prevail, the complaining group must demonstrate that invidious discrimination is the sole purpose of the districting plan; (4) conversely, any taint of invidious intent would invalidate the plan; (5) discriminatory subjective motives on the part of the plan's sponsors would invalidate it; and (6) any plan which denied a group its proportionate share of population majority districts would violate their constitutional rights.[235] What Justice Stevens finally settled on as "a workable guideline for judicial management of gerrymandering litigation" was the old equal protection rationality standard: plantiffs must show that the districting plan "rests on grounds wholly irrelevant to the achievement of a valid state objective."[236]

In *City of Mobile v. Bolden*, Justice Stevens took his *Cousins* analysis of the gerrymander problem with its rational basis answer and transposed it without modification to litigation attacking at-large districting. But, by its own terms, Stevens' *Cousins* theory doesn't work in the at-large context. Because there is no at-large apportionment scheme that can fail the rationality test, none is wholly irrelevant to the achievement of a valid state objective. Every at-large plan can display as legitimate objectives the defenses advanced by the City of Mobile: perfect mathematical equality, encouragement of citywide perspectives on the part of elected officials, discouragement of ward-heeling, and so forth. Justice Stevens' description in *Cousins* of a single-member district plan that would survive a gerrymander challenge illustrates the futility of attacking at-large schemes under his theory:

> If the basic plan is designed to follow historic political boundaries, natural barriers, or reflects a consistent endeavor to achieve compactness to the extent allowed by the requirements of contiguity, and, of course, if the equal population requirement is met, rarely if ever could a plan be attacked as wholly irrational.[237]

Every districting plan that relies completely on citywide or countywide voting follows precisely the political and natural boundaries of the jurisdiction and is perfectly compact, contiguous, and equally populated. There can be no "inexplicable, grotesque shapes, reminiscent of *Gomillion*, or the Massachusetts shoestring or the Illinois saddlebag . . . [a] pattern . . . explicable only by reference to a purpose to segregate or to disadvantage a definable group. . . ."[238]

Perhaps because he realized that every at-large apportionment should satisfy the test of rationality, Justice Stevens seemed to modify his position in *Rogers*. There he suggested that Burke County's election system might be irrational, not because it required all candidates to run at large, but because the numbered places, majority-vote requirement, and lack of residency subdistricts seemed to him to have no other purpose than "to assist a dominant party to maintain its political power," a policy which Justice Stevens summarily concluded is "arbitrary and capricious."[239] He would leave it open for state defendants "to identify legitimate local policies that might justify the use of such rules,"[240] but his skepticism that such "local" justifications could exist seems clear. With these features eliminated, Stevens is convinced, "a well-organized minority [could] elect one or two candidates to the county board."[241] But even if Justice Stevens' prediction of minority successes in a plurality-win at-large system is plausible, it is not, as he insists, "apparent."[242] This was illustrated in the latest at-large dilution case before the Supreme Court, *Escambia County v. McMillan*.[243] Majority vote and numbered place requirements provided unnecessary additional protection for the bloc-voting white majority in Escambia County, Florida. Blacks were only 20 percent of the population, and although two black candidates had made the runoffs in the countywide primary elections, neither had led the field in the first primary.[244] By vacating and remanding the case to the court of appeals for reconsideration under the amended Voting Rights Act, the Court did not reach the merits of the dilution claim, and Justice Stevens was not required to confront the adequacy of a theory that limited relief to elimination of barriers to a plurality victory.

More to the point, it is not at all clear why the traditional rationale for numbered places, majority-vote requirements and no residency requirements is less legitimate or less rational than that supporting at-large voting itself: increasing the likelihood that all seats will be filled by candidates who have "county-wide perspectives" and who are unbeholden to any "ward-heelers" (i.e., assuring that all the winners are those who are most acceptable to the entire county electorate). The features Justice Stevens would strike down as arbitrary and capricious merely "enhance" the objectives of at-large plans generally, and the Court has expressly held that they are "neither in themselves improper nor irrational."[245] Assisting a dominant party to maintain its political power is a natural tendency of all at-large schemes and a necessary corollary of their confessed objectives. Nor does it seem to be any more odious a policy than that of preserving incumbencies, a reapportionment policy that the Court has found not to be unconstitutional per se.[246]

If one accepts the thesis that there is a constitutional obligation to develop a judicially manageable standard for detecting racial vote dilution in at-large election schemes—a predicate Justice Stevens subscribes to—then the reasons for the failure of his *Cousins* standard should be explored. It may be that Stevens wrongly insisted that his gerrymander constitutional rule be universally available to every social, economic, or political group, not just to racial or ethnic groups as the panel majority in *Cousins* concluded. If limited to racial or ethnic discrimination, a less deferential standard of purposeful discrimination—such as the focus on lawmakers' subjective motives called for by the *Cousins* majority and the *Bolden* plurality—might intrude less on the political functions of apportionment. That is, legislators would be constitutionally free to wheel and deal over the relative strengths of Republicans and Democrats, the blue collar vote and the silk stocking vote, the liberals and the conservatives—so long as such conscious manipulation of voting power was not applied to blacks, Puerto Ricans, ethnic Jews, and so forth. But putting aside Stevens' ethical objection to providing one group equal protection rights that are denied another group, even this limitation of the subjective intent rule leaves all the problems of judicial unmanageability previously shown to be associated with Justice Stewart's application of *Arlington Heights* to the apportionment process. Justice Stevens' objections to the approach of the *Bolden* plurality and the *Rogers* majority still have validity.

Serious questions can also be raised about Stevens' distinction between individual and group voting rights as a justification for applying strict scrutiny to mathematical deviations from equality and a more deferential standard to gerrymandered districts. Political scientists and theorists have criticized the Court's failure to analyze carefully the meaning of such grand generalities as political equality, equally weighted votes, equally effective votes, equal representation, and voting strength.[247] However, the Supreme Court's repeated insistence on the provision of an "equally weighted" and "equally effective" vote necessarily implies that each voter must have an equal opportunity to affect the election *result*.[248] This requires more than the provision of equally weighted voting "shares," that is, the same mathematical number of voters per representative. Even in the strictly technical or theoretical sense, equipopulous single-member districts do not provide the individual voter an equal probability of deciding the outcome of the election, except in the special case where none of the voters has factional predispositions.[249] This special case, of course, does not exist in the real world. Equally populated districts, therefore, simply create *groups* on the basis of geography. To determine whether individual voters have equally effective voices, reference must be made to the voting propensities of other voters both within and without a particular person's district as well as to the relative size of the district.[250] So, from both theoretical and practical standpoints, an individual's voting strength cannot be divorced from the voting strength of the group in which he or she is placed by the election structure. Justice Stewart, who also would reserve strict judicial scrutiny for dilution of individual voting rights and require stricter proof of the debasement of a group's voting strength, at least alluded to the logical weakness of this distinction:

> It is, of course, true that the right of a person to vote on an equal basis with other voters draws much of its significance from the political association that its exercise reflects, but it is an altogether different matter to conclude that political groups themselves have an independent constitutional claim to representation.[251]

But the phenomenon of racial vote dilution is offensive not because of any independent constitutional claim of the racial group, *qua* group, but because, in the same respect that an overpopulated district undervalues the individual voting rights of its residents, so are the individual voting rights of each member of the disadvantaged racial group diminished. To say that one circumstance injures personal or individual rights while the other injures only group rights is analytically inaccurate. If members of a geographically concentrated, cohesive racial group find themselves split into voting minorities among several election districts, each will suffer inequality of his or her voting strength, and the Stevens-Stewart distinction between individual and group rights cannot explain why he or she ought to be required to advance, additionally, proof that the apportionment-makers intended to accomplish this dilution. As one theoretician says: "The inequality here would be particularly invidious if the districts had been deliberately designed to bring about this result; but even if it came about by accident, the inequality is real (and substantial) nonetheless.''[252] This group-individual distinction is made all the more anomalous by more recent statements by Justice Stevens and other members of the Court recognizing that fairness of group participation in the political process may be more important constitutionally than mere numerical equality.[253]

The most logical explanation for the miscarriage of Stevens' *Cousins* rationale in the *Bolden* context is that he failed to observe that at-large districting is not just another potential gerrymander. Rather, it is a decision not to district at all. It is a legislative decision not to engage at all in the political process of apportioning seats to geographic areas, but instead to allow the same citywide or countywide majority to control all of the seats. Since no political apportionment choices are made, there is no chance for them to be made invidiously or irrationally. Meanwhile, under the rational basis standard, the at-large scheme enjoys its guaranteed, boilerplate acceptability. The rational basis standard may or may not be a workable, constitutionally acceptable approach to claims that equally populated districts have been drawn to carve up the voting strength of a protected group. But it will always flop as a measure of at-large dilution.

So we return to the unique dilemma presented by at-large elections because of the firm grip *Reynolds v. Sims* has established in constitutional jurisprudence. Before *Reynolds,* all of the ''political thicket'' problems Justice Stevens has sought to avoid in his gerrymander analysis were considered to be a sufficient justification for barring federal court intervention in all types of malapportionment cases. As the reapportionment dissenters strained to show, one person, one vote is one of several possible antidilution formulas and is distinguishable from others primarily by the ''sixth grade'' simplicity of its statement. Its elevation to the status of fundamental constitutional right may facilitate gerrymandering of other sorts, as the Court has always acknowledged.[254] But the constitutional requirement of population equality presents a special problem with regard to at-large voting. Because an at-large plan offers majority group legislators an opportunity to avoid altogether the political and judicial risks of having to share power with racial minorities in the apportionment process, and because it is absolutely unassailable from the standpoint of population equality, there arises a constitutional imperative that the explicitly intended beneficiaries of the Fourteenth and Fifteenth Amendments be provided fundamental and certain protection from discrimination by at-large plans. The several proposals in *City of Mobile v. Bolden* and *Rogers v. Lodge* fall short of this mark.

One Proposal for a
Constitutional Standard of At-Large Vote Dilution

If the history of *Reynolds v. Sims* and its progeny teaches anything, it is that attempts to formulate a single constitutional standard of vote dilution that will succeed in every situation will probably fail. As the dilemma created by Justice Stevens' proposal to apply to at-large schemes the same standard of proof he used in a gerrymander situation shows, one is not likely to discover a universal equation for equally effective voting strength.[255] Proposed here—without demanding that it should be the exclusive standard for all at-large situations—is one promising measure of unconstitutional vote dilution caused by at-large election plans.

> An at-large election scheme for a state or local multirepresentative body is unconstitutional where jurisdictionwide elections permit a bloc voting majority, over a substantial period of time, consistently to defeat candidates publicly identified with the interests of and supported by a politically cohesive, geographically insular racial or ethnic minority group.

The balance of this chapter defends the appropriateness of this standard.

Any successful standard for analyzing an at-large system should detect the same kind of devalued voting strength that one person, one vote measures. It must also promise judicial manageability: a reasonable degree of reviewability and consistency of result in a variety of circumstances and in a variety of courts. At the same time, it must avoid either outlawing multimember districting per se or becoming merely a guarantee of proportional representation.

Although *Reynolds v. Sims* used broad, majestic language to define the constitutional entitlement, speaking in terms of "fair and effective representation for all citizens,"[256] the actual holdings of the reapportionment cases and their progeny have limited strict judicial scrutiny to problems of geographic or territorial districting. All other forms of underrepresentation have been left in the thicket of political choices legislative bodies are still free to make, subject only to more deferential judicial prohibitions of capriciousness and invidious intent.

To be consistent with this policy of judicial restraint, a standard of at-large vote dilution must be based not on a measure of group proportionality but on a determination that the underrepresentation complained of is specifically attributable to—is proximately caused by—the choice of at-large over single-member districting. The operative question must be whether the inability of members of an identifiable minority group to have their choices registered in an at-large election would be possible or permissible in a districted system.

For example, consider a hypothetical city where residents on one side of the railroad tracks make up a clearly identifiable working-class district. Analysis of at-large elections will show (a) whether any candidate was the clear choice of the workers and (b) whether, nonetheless, opposition from political forces outside the working-class district were powerful enough to defeat the workers' favorite. If it can be demonstrated that single-member districts could not be drawn without the likelihood of at least one district having a workers' majority, it can also be shown that the at-large election result would clearly be contrary to the constitutionally required result had there been a districted election plan. If not, then the use of voting at large rather than by districts would be of no consequence, in the *Reynolds* sense that an identifiable geographic population is entitled solely by the weight of its ballots to select its own representative. Of course, this is precisely the difference an at-large scheme is designed to make; perhaps next time the working-class district will join with other political interests to form a new majority coalition. Or perhaps the district will be divided into new political factions and will no longer express a clear workers' choice. The occasional at-large disadvantage suffered by the working-class area, gauged by a districted election standard, is counterbalanced by occasional winner-take-all victory or by shifting political characteristics.

The problem with the at-large scheme arises when, through a number of elections, the pattern persists of a politically cohesive district having its choices defeated by a citywide majority that always rallies behind the district's opponents. Here, then, is an unrelieved series of electoral results that, if they had occurred in districted elections, would have violated the one person, one vote rule. The problem has been observed solely on the basis of voting patterns; there is no need to inquire into the (probably very interesting) political stories behind the election returns in order to discern a real debasement of the district's voting power—the same kind of vote devaluation *Reynolds* was concerned with.

But when is such dysfunctioning of an at-large plan a constitutional problem? Is an economic group like our hypothetical working-class district entitled to protection? Or what if the district had been politically cohesive on the basis of party affiliation—a Democratic district, for example? These are the social, economic and political conflicts that have traditionally been left for resolution by the political process without intervention by courts.[257] However, dictum in the several opinions of the justices in *Karcher v. Daggett*[258] shows that a majority of the Court may now be sympathetic to claims by nonracial, partisan political groups that gerrymandering directed against them violates the equal protection clause. This sentiment was made even more explicit in the recent action of the Supreme Court refusing to stay the New Jersey district court's order on remand approving 1984 congressional elections under a plan proposed by the Republicans, instead of the plan adopted by the Democratic controlled state senate.[259] In a concurring opinion, Justice Stevens explained that his vote to uphold the district court's decision was based on the lower court's finding that the senate plan was "an intentional gerrymander in favor of certain Democratic representatives."[260] Justice Brennan wrote a much longer dissenting opinion, joined by Justices White and Marshall, in which he insisted that the Court's first decision in *Karcher* was based solely on the unacceptably large population deviations in New Jersey's original districting plan and not on disapproval of its partisan gerrymandering.[261] It is significant that only two other members of the Court joined this protest by Justice Brennan:

> We have never concluded, nor in my view should we conclude, that the existence of noncompact or gerrymandered districts is by itself a constitutional violation. Therefore, absent unconstitutional population variances, or other findings of unconstitutionality such as discrimination on racial or ethnic lines, the District Court should implement the alternative plan that is most faithful to the districts included in the most recent plan enacted by the State.[262]

Regardless of what constitutional voting rights the Court ultimately assigns to political parties, having derived a fundamental right of majority rule from the Fourteenth and Fifteenth Amendments, the federal judiciary is obliged to afford commensurate protection against minority vote dilution by at-large schemes on the basis of race or ethnicity. Claims of racial vote dilution resulting from at-large elections, unlike claims of racially gerrymandered single-member districts, necessarily force federal courts to resolve a direct conflict between two constitutional criteria of fair representation, majority rule and nondiscrimination against racial minorities.

Justice Stevens has consistently opposed the adoption of a constitutional rule of vote dilution, such as the one proposed here, that extends only to racial or ethnic groups and not to other social, economic or political factions.[263] His dissenting opinion in *Rogers* eloquently defends this position.[264] His policy concerns, even though they purport to express nothing more than a personal view, have obvious merit. Perhaps he is right that the voting guarantees of the Fourteenth Amendment should be expansive enough to protect all types of political factions. Indeed, the *White–Zimmer* analysis, criticized by Justice Stevens and this chapter as unmanageable, appears not to be limited to racial groups.[265] The standard of at-large dilution proposed here could easily be extended to all political groups as well. This chapter does not contend that its own or any workable judicial rule must be confined to the benefit of racial or ethnic groups. Rather, it argues that, if the Court's prudential reluctance to overextend federal judicial involvement in state and local political affairs so warranted it, restriction of an at-large dilution rule to racial or ethnic minorities could be justified constitutionally. What Justice Stevens fails to acknowledge is that the special protection of racial groups, which he would consider valid as ''a legislative choice rather than [as] a constitutional principle,''[266] has already been made as an explicit constitutional choice by the Civil War amendments. The obligation to construct a constitutional jurisprudence that fully assures racial equity cannot, therefore, be avoided in the name of federal–state comity.

In the context of single-member district reapportionment, it may be possible, as Justice Stevens would have it, for the judiciary to abstain from interfering with the political competition and from affording racial minorities protection not available to other political or social groups without totally abandoning the policy of the Fifteenth Amendment. If single-member district boundaries must be drawn according to population, any bloc-voting racial majority must at least bear the risk of being forced to share political power with the racial minority, either because of the political constraints of reapportionment or because total emasculation of the minority's strength would offend even a narrow, rational basis standard of judicial review. But at-large elections guarantee a no-risk exclusion of minority choices by a sufficiently cohesive majority bloc, free from the vicissitudes of reapportionment and from the threat of disapproval by federal courts under a rationality standard. If the purpose of the Fifteenth Amendment is not to be sacrificed entirely to the newfound Fourteenth Amendment guarantee of majority rule, at least in the special case of at-large elections, the Court must adopt a less deferential constitutional standard of racial vote dilution. It would seem that the Court must acknowledge that a constitutionally intolerable problem exists when an at-large scheme consistently, systematically dilutes the voting strength of a geographically isolated racial or ethnic minority.

So the proposed formula satisfies the criterion that it detect in the at-large scheme the same kind of vote devaluation for racial or ethnic groups that the population equality rule discovers for any other geographic group in a districted plan. Black voters are injured by at-large elections only if the election returns show that districted elections satisfying the one person, one vote rule would likely have required a more favorable result. To demonstrate this, the black voters must be residentially concentrated enough and politically cohesive enough that a putative districting plan would contain majority-black districts[267] whose clear electoral choices were in fact defeated by at-large voting. If blacks' residences are substantially integrated throughout the jurisdiction, even if they vote as a bloc for unsuccessful candidates, the at-large district can't be blamed for their defeat. The constitutional standard thus would only protect black votes from diminution proximately caused by the districting plan (or, rather, by the lack of one); it would not assure blacks proportional representation.

The proposed at-large dilution standard also avoids conditions so strict as to make at-large voting unconstitutional per se, a rule the Court has steadfastly disavowed.[268] The plan would not be unconstitutional if the defeat of minority-favored candidates were only episodic. There must be a consistent, systematic pattern of blacks' choices being submerged by a bloc-voting racial majority. If at-large schemes are to be permitted at all, judicial review must tolerate occasional defeat of even a racial minority's choices, so long as the electoral track record does not demonstrate that such defeat is generally predictable. Where election results over a period of time reflect a genuine ability of the black minority to have some of its choices prevail, regardless of the political explanation for it, the at-large scheme would be constitutionally unobjectionable.[269] Predictability is the distinguishing feature between vote dilution and merely losing elections in the at-large context. A constitutional rule that provides a presumption of validity to at-large elections on the basis of population equality at least owes vulnerable racial minorities protection from *systematic* cancellation of their voting strength by the racial majority.

In terms of certainty and consistency, this standard promises to be nearly as manageable as the population equality rule. It avoids the vagaries of legislative and/or political dynamics which are the subjects of both the Stewart *Arlington Heights* standard and the *White–Zimmer* criteria favored by White and Marshall. Instead, it focuses on voting patterns discernible almost entirely in census or registered voter data and in the election returns. In this way, it responds to Justice Stevens' demand for objective evidence. Ignoring such factors as the history of official racial discrimination and its lingering effects, the circumstances and legislative representations surrounding adoption or retention of the at-large plan, and the responsiveness of elected officials to minority interests is justified for the same reason that these factors are irrelevant to the one person, one vote inquiry: they simply are not necessary for detecting the constitutional offense. These factors and others like them may well indicate that impermissible vote dilution exists, but they are either causes or symptoms of such dilution, not the most direct and reliable means of measuring it.

By insisting on proof of some of these causes or symptoms, with unspecified quality or quantity, the *White–Zimmer* standard both demands too much of vote dilution victims and promotes capricious results. On the other hand, racial bloc voting and the failure of black candidates, the "important evidence of purposeful exclusion" named in Justice White's *Rogers* opinion,[270] may, indeed, require too little to stand alone as proof of unconstitutional dilution. In addition, the complainants should have to demonstrate that the clear choices of minority voters were defeated systematically by the racial majority voting as a bloc and that the minority is residentially concentrated enough to benefit from a geographical districting scheme.

No doubt, the proposed standard demands some exercise of judicial discretion. Confronting the facts characterizing elections in a particular locality, the court must decide whether the minority group is geographically insular and politically cohesive, whether candidates are publicly identified with and supported by minority interests, whether their defeat is attributable to majority bloc voting, and whether the frequency and duration of minority vote submergence are substantial. But these observations are not qualitatively more difficult to make with a reasonable degree of certainty than are those associated with population malapportionment claims: what percentage variance is substantial enough to make out a prima facie case, and what state governmental interests are substantial enough to justify mathematical imbalances. Consideration of some of the more obvious questions about application of the proposed at-large dilution standard will illustrate its judicial manageability.

The ultimate criterion of geographic insularity is whether single-member districting would produce any majority black districts. *Whitcomb v. Chavis, White v. Regester, City of Mobile v. Bolden* and *Rogers v. Lodge* all presented situations where racial residential segregation was obvious; indeed, the potential availability of some districts with black or Hispanic majorities has been clear in virtually every reported case challenging at-large elections. Otherwise, a single-member district remedy would not have been sought in the first place. There are counties and cities, however, where the racial minority is small enough and dispersed enough to prevent it from being a majority in any one district. Such was the case for Mexican Americans in *Wise v. Lipscomb*.[271] The court-ordered change to district elections in Dallas, in order to afford some council seats for the larger black minority, purportedly reduced the political effectiveness of Mexican Americans, because, it was alleged, they were in a better position to influence at-large elections. The Supreme Court reversed the Fifth Circuit's imposition of single-member districts exclusively and approved the city council's mixed plan of eight single-member districts and three at-large seats, although on grounds ostensibly unrelated to the complaint of Mexican Americans.

Under the at-large dilution standard proposed here, Dallas's Mexican American community would be entitled neither to demand nor to oppose districted elections. Without the possibility of at least one district with a Mexican American population majority, they could not prove devaluation of their voting strength by the at-large plan. But neither could the Mexican American claim of advantage in an at-large system, because of their particular ability to play coalition politics, undermine the entitlement of blacks to a district election remedy for the demonstrable dilution of their vote. Because the residentially dispersed Hispanic voters could not be assured of having their choices succeed, solely on the weight of their ballots, under either an at-large or districted system, their contention that the at-large plan offered them a greater degree of influence would fall short of a constitutional standard that refuses to recognize a right to proportional representation and (solely due to considerations of judicial restraint) restricts justiciable claims to those based on geographic grouping. Their situation illustrates the truism that only one of the proportional representation electoral forms can provide fair representation and equally effective voting strength to literally every voter. But the nonjusticiable Mexican American claim ought not bar judicial relief for the larger and more residentially concentrated black community.

Whether a racial group is politically cohesive depends on its demonstrated propensity to vote as a bloc for candidates or issues popularly recognized as being affiliated with the group's particularized interests. The concept of particularized interests was one feature of the district court's opinion with which the Supreme Court had no difficulty in *Whitcomb v. Chavis*,[272] and again in *White v. Regester*[273] and *City of Mobile v. Bolden*.[274] However, the Court has perhaps too casually taken for granted the supposition that disproportionately small numbers of minority elected representatives were caused by racial bloc voting.[275] Obviously, one candidate will always win a majority of blacks' votes in a head-to-head contest. Consequently, in every jurisdiction there are likely to be elections without racially charged issues where blacks may be said to have picked a winner, in the sense that a majority of blacks voted for the successful candidate. But the only elections of consequence to the constitutional inquiry would be those where an overwhelming majority of blacks supported one or more candidates. The distinction between a mere majority and an overwhelming bloc vote is no more uncertain than is the population variance needed to establish a one person, one vote claim; but neither is susceptible of precise formulation.

Ordinarily, receiving the racial minority's bloc support would be the best and necessary indication that a candidate is identified with the minority's particularized interests. The candidate may or may not be a member of the racial minority. In *Bolden,* for example, white candidates who received black political endorsement and who did not win a majority in the first election were assured of a devastating white majority backlash in the runoff.[276] But, whether they are white or black, Mexican American or Anglo, to trigger the at-large dilution phenomenon the candidates must be known *publicly* to have the political backing of the racial minority; otherwise there will be no signal to mobilize the majority's bloc vote and no opportunity to test their inclination to defeat candidates because they are favored by the minority.

The mere existence of bloc voting on the part of a racial majority and/or minority group does not establish at-large dilution. There must also be proof that the minority's clear choices are defeated consistently by a majority bloc vote. The question was raised, in *McMillan v. Escambia County*,[277] how much white crossover voting for black candidates would foreclose finding that there was a white bloc vote. The district court concluded that a white vote of any size sufficient to defeat the combined strength of clear black support plus white crossovers constituted a majority bloc vote for the purpose of proving effective at-large dilution.[278] This view is consistent with the standard of at-large vote debasement proposed here: it is the ability of an antagonistic majority, regardless of defections from its ranks, consistently to defeat minority choices that defines the amount of bloc voting required to invoke judicial relief. An extreme example would be a city with a 10 percent black population and with a ten-member council all elected at large. If black candidates could count on nine-tenths of the black vote but only four ninths of the white vote, they would face consistent defeat notwithstanding a substantial white crossover, and blacks would be entitled to single-member districting so long as they were geographically concentrated enough to benefit from it. But, taking this example a step further, if the city council had only five seats, the 10 percent black minority could not successfully challenge an at-large election plan under the proposed constitutional standard. In these circumstances, blacks would have to prove that the council size was itself a device for racial discrimination, that it was intended to prevent black representation or that it perpetuated prior de jure discrimination, in order to make out a constitutional claim.[279]

Similarly, what constitutes the "consistent" defeat of minority-favored candidates would require some exercise of judicial discretion. A 50 percent success rate certainly would discredit an at-large dilution claim, and even a substantially smaller success rate could do so if the occasional black candidate victories reflected a genuine ability of black voters to play coalition politics—as was the case, for example, in *Whitcomb v. Chavis,* where blacks regularly appeared on the Marion County Democratic ticket and won when the Democrats won.[280] But where token numbers of blacks were "cued" into office by the white political establishment and did not reflect the exercise of real black political choice, their victories would not outweigh the defeat by white bloc voting of candidates chosen by the black community.[281] On the other hand, the proposed standard would recognize the possibility that a city or county with a long history of racial vote dilution could be transformed to the point where the results of two or three recent elections demonstrated the genuine ability of blacks' choices to be elected. Such results would defuse constitutional attacks on the at-large scheme, at least in the *Reynolds* sense.

What constitutes a "substantial period of time" for the manifestation of at-large racial vote dilution also calls for considered judicial development. Probably more than a single minority-choice candidacy is needed to satisfy the underlying meaning of the proposed standard. In *Bolden,* the expert political scientist testified that fifteen to twenty years' experience would be desirable, but it would be dangerous, obviously, to suggest a hard and fast rule for how long the minority candidate track record must be. At least some clear minority choices must have run; otherwise, there would be no evidence of either minority political cohesiveness or how the at-large system would operate on minority choices. However, even if no blacks, for example, had offered for city council, it is likely that black candidates or whites identified with black interests would have sought election in overlapping county commission, school board, state, or federal contests, and these election results may in appropriate circumstances provide credible proof of how the at-large city elections would dilute black voting strength.[282]

The factors of "consistent" minority defeat over a "substantial period of time" may be the most likely judicial gray areas and could require a limited inquiry into local political dynamics. But such an inquiry can be guided, under the proposed standard, by a much more articulable, more fully realized notion of the nature of impermissible at-large dilution than is possible under either the subjective intent standard of the *Bolden* plurality or the "access to the political process" standard of *White v. Regester*. It certainly promises little more difficulty in terms of judicial manageability than does the still fluctuating one-person, one-vote rule, and it answers the *Bolden* plurality's questions about how a "theory of group representation could rationally be cabined."

CONCLUSION

As a constitutional rule, one person, one vote, the equal protection guarantee of majority control, is actually derived from cases decided under the Fifteenth Amendment, whose explicit purpose is the protection of racial minorities from abridgement of their voting rights. Nevertheless, when the Supreme Court created the right of population equality in *Reynolds v. Sims,* it simultaneously elevated it to a position of constitutional primacy in the judicial scrutiny of apportionment schemes. Though it was founded on the broader, more complicated notion that each citizen is entitled to equally weighted and equally effective voting strength, one person, one vote was made the starting point for analyzing districting plans because it could be simply stated and, it was at first thought, could be managed with consistency by the courts. But from the beginning the Court was unsure about how to handle the obvious problem created for racial minorities by multimember districts and at-large voting. Unlike the "sixth-grade arithmetic" of one person, one vote, racial vote dilution could not easily be measured without resorting to formulas that appeared either to make multimember districts unconstitutional per se or to require racial proportional representation, propositions that were thought to offend traditional American political values.

However, the Court continued to insist that its failure to strike down multimember plans that allegedly submerged blacks' voting strength was not to be understood as any denigration of the constitutional priority of the rights asserted, but was simply because there were no readily available judicially manageable standards for detecting this form of vote diminution. In only one case, *White v. Regester,* did it find unconstitutional racial vote dilution caused by multimember districting, and even there the Court declined fully to explore and explicate any uniform constitutional standard for judgment. In *City of Mobile v. Bolden,* a deeply divided Court brought out at least four separate theories for managing at-large dilution, none of which captured a majority of the justices. In *Rogers v. Lodge,* a clear majority accepted the insistence of the *Bolden* plurality on proof of an invidious legislative purpose to invalidate an at-large election scheme on constitutional grounds. However, *Rogers* reinstated the formulae of *White v. Regester* and *Zimmer v. McKeithen* as sufficient proof of such intent.

Any evidentiary standard of racial vote dilution due to at-large elections that demands a greater quantum of proof than that required to challenge population malapportionment works an intolerable inversion of constitutional and historical priorities. Even the reapportionment dissenters, while denouncing the constitutional legitimacy of the population equality rule, conceded that the first purpose of the Fourteenth and Fifteenth Amendments was safeguarding the rights of racial minorities. But the standard of proof adopted by the four-member Stewart plurality in *Bolden* and adopted by a majority of justices in *Rogers* would demand stricter proof of vote dilution on the part of blacks than it does of population majorities: it is enough to show that voting strength is effectively diminished by numerical inequality, but black voters in multimember districts must prove that an at-large plan has the purpose as well as the effect of diluting their votes. Moreover, the intent formula is unlikely to afford the sought-after judicial manageability, because it requires federal judges to look into the subjective motives of lawmakers, an inquiry that courts have always recognized to be fraught with uncertainty and perilously involved in the legislative process. Similarly, the at-large dilution standards of Justices White and Marshall are vulnerable to criticisms of unmanageability, because they depend on the inherent vagaries of "access to the political process" and "a blend of history with an intensely local appraisal." The strict burden of proof adopted by Justice Stevens from his earlier analysis of single-member district gerrymandering would absolutely immunize all at-large schemes from challenges of racial discrimination. Thus none of the theories advanced in *Bolden* adequately conforms to the dual constitutional policies of (1) assuring commensurate protection for the voting strength of the majority and racial minorities and (2) providing a judicially manageable standard of proof that neither outlaws multimember districts per se nor requires proportional representation.

This article proposes a standard for detecting at-large vote dilution that promises to meet both of the foregoing criteria:

> An at-large election scheme for a state or local multirepresentative body is unconstitutional where jurisdictionwide elections permit a bloc voting majority, over a substantial period of time, consistently to defeat candidates publicly identified with the interests of and supported by a politically cohesive, geographically insular racial or ethnic miniority group.

The claim of appropriateness made by this formula rests on the following features:

1. It measures the same kind of apportionment-related vote debasement as does one person, one vote and does not demand additional inquiries about the purpose of the plan.
2. It does not presume that every combination of multimember districting and racial bloc voting will be objectionable, but instead requires proof that systematic racial discrimination actually results from the plan's operation.
3. It does not rely on comparisons between the number of minority representatives and the size of the minority population, nor does it presume that racial minorities will always vote as a bloc or always support candidates of their own race; consequently it does not demand proportional representation.
4. By focusing almost solely on racial patterns readily discerned in the election returns and in census data, it avoids excessive investigation of the community's underlying historical, political, and social dynamics and thus promises to be judicially manageable.

Like every other constitutional or legal standard of proof, the one proposed here, once it is applied to actual circumstances, may require refinement and modification, demand recognition of some exceptions, and confess some shortcomings. But it does represent a serious analysis of the fundamental and unique dilemma presented by multimember districting in the development of one person, one vote as a constitutional requirement. Other racially discriminatory voting practices, though no less injurious and objectionable than at-large elections, may well be subject to different, perhaps more or less stringent standards of proof. But in the now established jurisprudence of *Reynolds v. Sims* and its progeny, multimember districts are a special case. They confront federal courts with a compelling obligation to reconcile the new rule of population equality with its constitutional and historical roots. Because an at-large plan at the same time perfectly satisfies the one-person, one-vote requirement and perfectly affords the optimum conditions for diluting the voting strength of racial minorities, the Supreme Court cannot avoid the duty of working out an evidentiary standard for evaluating at-large schemes that truly does not subordinate the rights of racial minorities to the right of majority rule.

 Rogers v. Lodge is now the controlling constitutional precedent, and the statutory codification of the *White–Zimmer* standard in the Voting Rights Amendments of 1982 is likely to encourage the Supreme Court's steadfast reluctance to examine at-large vote dilution as a constitutional issue in greater depth. But it ought to. The Court should begin focusing on the critical, still unresolved question of under what circumstances at-large schemes actually have the adverse racial impact that has only been presumed to exist in the cases to date; and it should give up its constitutionally irrelevant preoccupation with what legislative reasons might justify such discriminatory effect. Until then, litigants can look forward to some capricious results in the courts, and local governments will continue to be without either the guidance or the incentive to correct the constitutionally unfair features of their election systems.

NOTES

1. 377 U.S. 533 (1964).
2. *E.g.,* Richard Cortner, *The Apportionment Cases* (Knoxville 1970), 160–63; Comment, "Alabama's Unrepresentative Legislature," *Alabama Law Review* 14 (1962): 403, 406.
3. See *United States v. Alabama,* 252 F.Supp. 95 (M.D.Ala. 1966). See generally: Steven F. Lawson, *Black Ballots: Voting Rights in the South, 1944–1969* (New York 1976); J. Morgan Kousser, *The Shaping of Southern Politics* (New Haven 1970); William W. Rogers, *The One-Gallused Rebellion: Agrarianism in Alabama, 1865–1896* (Baton Rouge 1970); Sheldon Hackney, *Populism to Progressivism in Alabama* (Princeton 1969); Malcolm C. McMillan, *Constitutional Development in Alabama, 1798–1901: A Study in Politics, the Negro and Sectionalism* (Chapel Hill, North Carolina 1955); V. O. Key, Jr., *Southern Politics* (New York 1949).
4. Lawson, *Black Ballots; House Comm. on the Judiciary, Report on Voting Rights Act Extension,* H.R. Rep. No. 97-227, 97th Cong., 1st Sess. 13–21; Jane Reed Cox and Abigail Turner, *The Voting Rights Act in Alabama: A Current Legal Assessment.*
5. Cortner, *The Apportionment Cases,* 161 (quoting McMillan), 307.
6. 328 U.S. 549, 556 (1946).
7. 369 U.S. 186 (1962).

8. 403 U.S. 124 (1971).
9. 412 U.S. 755 (1973).
10. 446 U.S. 55, 64 L. Ed. 2d 47, 100 S Ct. 1490 (1980).
11. See Armand Derfner, "Pro Affirmative Action in Districting," *Policy Studies Journal* 9 (1981): 851.
12. 50 U.S.L.W. 5041 (1 July 1982).
13. *Whitcomb v. Chavis*, 403 U.S. 124, 166 (1971) (separate opinion of J. Harlan) (emphasis in the original).
14. 369 U.S. 186, 204 and n. 23 (1962). See Cortner, *The Apportionment Cases*, 51 *et seq.*
15. 369 U.S. at 193.
16. 369 U.S. at 226.
17. 369 U.S. at 210, *quoting Coleman v. Miller*, 307 U.S. 433, 454–55 (1939).
18. 369 U.S. at 226.
19. 369 U.S. at 209, *citing Nixon v. Herndon*, 273 U.S. 536, 540 (1927), 369 U.S. at 229–30, *citing Gomillion v. Lightfoot*, 364 U.S. 339 (1960).
20. 369 U.S. at 208, *citing United States v. Classic*, 313 U.S. 299 (1941); *Ex parte Siebold*, 100 U.S. 371 (1880).
21. 369 U.S. at 230.
22. 369 U.S. at 266, 267.
23. 369 U.S. at 285, 300.
24. 369 U.S. at 301.
25. 369 U.S. at 277–78.
26. 369 U.S. at 282–83.
27. 369 U.S. at 308.
28. "To assume that political power is a function exclusively of numbers is to disregard the practicalities of government . . . ." 369 U.S. at 279, *quoting MacDougall v. Green*, 335 U.S 281, 283 (1948).
29. 369 U.S. at 301.
30. 369 U.S. at 337.
31. 369 U.S. at 332–33.
32. 369 U.S. at 254.
33. 369 U.S. at 265.
34. 377 U.S. 533 (1964).
35. 377 U.S. at 559–60, 563.
36. 377 U.S. 713, 744 (1964).
37. 377 U.S. at 745.
38. 377 U.S. at 750–51.
39. 377 U.S. at 554.
40. 377 U.S. at 554–55, *citing Ex parte Yarbrough*, 110 U.S. 651 (1884); *United States v. Mosley*, 238 U.S. 383 (1915); *Guinn v. United States*, 238 U.S. 347 (1915); *Lane v. Wilson*, 307 U.S. 268 (1939); *United States v. Classic*, 313 U.S. 299 (1941); *Ex parte Siebold*, 100 U.S. 371 (1880); *United States v. Saylor*, 322 U.S. 385 (1944); *Gomillion v. Lightfoot*, 364 U.S. 339 (1960); *Nixon v. Condon*, 286 U.S. 73 (1932); *Smith v. Allwright*, 321 U.S. 649 (1944); *Terry v. Adams*, 345 U.S. 461 (1953).
41. 377 U.S. at 557 (emphasis added).
42. 377 U.S. at 744 (footnote omitted).
43. 377 U.S. at 745–46 n.6, *citing Baker v. Carr*, 369 U.S. 186, 266, 301 (1962) (J. Frankfurter dissenting); *Reynolds v. Sims*, 377 U.S. 533, 589 (1964) (J. Harlan dissenting).
44. 377 U.S. at 745.
45. 377 U.S. at 555, 562, 563.
46. 377 U.S. at 565.
47. 377 U.S. at 566.
48. 377 U.S. at 563.

49. 377 U.S. at 563 n. 40, *quoting Colegrove v. Green*, 328 U.S. 549, 569–71 (1946) (J. Black dissenting).
50. 377 U.S. at 563, *citing Lane v. Wilson, supra*, 307 U.S. at 275, and *Gomillion v. Lightfoot, supra*, 364 U.S. at 342 (condemning "sophisticated as well as simple-minded modes of discrimination"); 377 U.S. at 566.
51. 377 U.S. at 567 (emphasis added), at 560–61.
52. 377 U.S. at 563.
53. 377 U.S. at 562–63, 565, 579–80.
54. 377 U.S. at 565.
55. 377 U.S. at 749 (emphasis added).
56. *Ibid.*
57. *Ibid.*
58. 377 U.S. at 750.
59. 377 U.S. at 748–49 (emphasis added).
60. 377 U.S. at 751.
61. 377 U.S. at 621, 750 n.12.
62. 377 U.S. at 621, 750.
63. 377 U.S. at 750 (footnote omitted).
64. 390 U.S. 474 (1968).
65. *Avery v. Midland County*, 390 U.S. at 487–88.
66. *Ibid.*, 390 U.S. at 510.
67. 390 U.S. at 510.
68. 390 U.S. at 481.
69. 390 U.S. at 482.
70. *Swann v. Adams*, 385 U.S. 440, 443–44 (1967); *Kilgarlin v. Hill*, 386 U.S. 120, 122 (1967).
71. *Swann v. Adams, supra*, 385 U.S. at 447–48.
72. 394 U.S. 526 (1969).
73. 394 U.S. 542 (1969).
74. *Kirkpatrick v. Preisler* 394 U.S. at 531.
75. 394 U.S. at 550 (J. Harlan dissenting).
76. *Ibid.* at 549.
77. Compare 394 U.S. at 133–34 with 394 U.S. at 551–52 (J. Harlan) and 554–55 (J. White).
78. 394 U.S. at 533.
79. 394 U.S. at 555.
80. *Ibid.*
81. 403 U.S. 162 (1971).
82. 403 U.S. at 185.
83. 410 U.S. 315 (1973).
84. 410 U.S. at 326.
85. 412 U.S. 735 (1973).
86. 412 U.S. at 740–41.
87. *Mahan v. Howell*, 410 U.S. 315, 326 (1973).
88. 412 U.S. at 749.
89. 103 S.Ct. 2690 (1983).
90. *Ibid.* at 2696.
91. *Ibid.* at 2700.
92. *Ibid.* at 2694 (footnote omitted).
93. *Ibid.* at 2697, *quoting Reynolds, supra*, 377 U.S. at 581.
94. 103 S.Ct. 2697.
95. 103 S.Ct. 2653 (1983).
96. *Ibid.* at 2657.
97. *Ibid.* at 2659.
98. *Ibid.* at 2660 (footnote omitted).

99.   Andrea J. Wollock, ed., *Reapportionment: Law and Technology* (National Conference of State Legislatures, Denver 1980), 12–19.
100.   379 U.S. 433 (1965).
101.   379 U.S. at 436.
102.   379 U.S. at 439.
103.   384 U.S. 73 (1966).
104.   384 U.S. at 87.
105.   384 U.S. at 88.
106.   *Ibid.*
107.   403 U.S. 124 (1971).
108.   403 U.S. at 141–44.
109.   403 U.S. at 149.
110.   *Ibid.*
111.   403 U.S. at 149–55.
112.   403 U.S. at 148–49, 164.
113.   403 U.S. at 150 n. 30.
114.   403 U.S. at 134 n. 11, 150–53.
115.   403 U.S. at 152–53.
116.   403 U.S. at 156.
117.   *Ibid.*
118.   *Ibid.*
119.   403 U.S. at 149–50, 155.
120.   403 U.S. at 169.
121.   403 U.S. at 170.
122.   412 U.S. 755 (1973).
123.   412 U.S. at 765.
124.   412 U.S. at 766.
125.   412 U.S. at 768.
126.   412 U.S. at 766.
127.   412 U.S. at 768.
128.   412 U.S. at 767.
129.   412 U.S. at 768.
130.   412 U.S. at 769.
131.   412 U.S. at 766.
132.   412 U.S. at 769.
133.   412 U.S. at 769–70.
134.   485 F.2d 1297 (5th Cir. 1973) (en banc), *aff'd sub nom.*, *East Carroll Parish School Board v. Marshall*, 424 U.S. 636 (1976) ("without approval of the constitutional views expressed by the Court of Appeals").
135.   *Zimmer v. McKeithen*, 485 F.2d at 1309 (J. Coleman, dissenting in part).
136.   485 F.2d at 1303 (footnote omitted).
137.   *Ibid.* at 1304 (footnote omitted).
138.   *Ibid.* at 1305.
139.   *Ibid.* (footnotes omitted).
140.   *Ibid.* (footnote omitted).
141.   For comprehensive summaries of the reported racial vote dilution cases, see Steve Bickerstaff, "Reapportionment By State Legislatures: A Guide For the 1980's," *Southwestern Law Journal* 34 (1980): 607, 647–48, notes 326–33; Paul Bonapfel, "Minority Challenges to At-Large Elections: The Dilution Problem," *Georgia Law Review* 10 (1976): 353.
142.   *East Carroll Parish School Bd. v. Marshall*, 424 U.S. 636 (1976).
143.   437 U.S. 535, 549 (1978).
144.   426 U.S. 229 (1976).
145.   429 U.S. 252 (1977).
146.   425 U.S. 130 (1976).

147. 430 U.S. 144 (1977).
148. 100 S.Ct at 1519.
149. 439 U.S. 891 (1979).
150. 100 S.Ct. at 1499–1500, *quoting Whitcomb v. Chavis,* 403 U.S. at 149.
151. 100 S.Ct. at 1499, 1506.
152. 100 S.Ct. at 1513–14.
153. 466 F.2d 830, 848–52 (7th Cir. 1972) (Stevens, dissenting).
154. 100 S.Ct. at 1512.
155. 100 S.Ct. at 1508–09.
156. 100 S.Ct. at 1514 n. 15.
157. 100 S.Ct. at 1510.
158. 100 S.Ct. at 1514, 1518.
159. 100 S.Ct. at 1517–19.
160. 100 S.Ct. at 1519 (citations omitted).
161. 100 S.Ct. at 1527.
162. 100 S.Ct. at 1524, 1537 n.33.
163. 100 S.Ct. at 1524 n.7.
164. *Ibid.*
165. 100 S.Ct. at 1504 n.22.
166. 99 S.Ct. at 2296.
167. 102 S.Ct. 3272 (1982).
168. 102 S.Ct. at 3281–82 (J. Powell dissenting).
169. 102 S.Ct. at 3280–81.
170. 102 S.Ct. at 3278–79, *citing Pullman-Standard v. Swint,* 102 S.Ct. 1781 (1982).
171. 102 S.Ct. at 3282.
172. 102 S.Ct. at 3284.
173. *Ibid.*
174. 102 S.Ct. at 3288.
175. 102 S.Ct. at 3293.
176. 102 S.Ct. at 3288.
177. *Ibid.* and n. 22.
178. Pub.L. No. 97–205 (June 29, 1982).
179. 42 U.S.C. § 1973.
180. Senate Comm. on the Judiciary, Rpt. on S.1992, S.Rep. No. 97–417, 97th Cong., 2d Sess. 2, 27, 28n., 113 (1982).
181. *Ibid.,* 15.
182. Pub.L. No. 97-205, § 3; S. Rep. No. 97–417, at 2.
183. S.Rep. No. 97–417, at 16.
184. *Rogers v. Lodge,* 102 S.Ct. at 3275.
185. *Escambia County v. McMillan,* S.Ct. (Mar. 27, 1984); *Cross v. Baxter,* 103 S.Ct. 1515 (1983).
186. 103 S.Ct. at 2669–70, 2676 n.28 (J. Stevens, concurring); *ibid.* at 2687 (J. White, dissenting); *ibid.* at 2689 (J. Powell, dissenting).
187. *E.g. see* "Symposium on the Theory and Practice of Representation," *Ethics* 91 (1981): 353 *et seq.*
188. *See Oregon v. Mitchell,* 400 U.S. 112, 148–49, 278 (1970) (J. Douglas and J. Brennan separate opinions); Carl A. Auerbach, "The Reapportionment Cases: One Person, One Vote—One Vote, One Value," *Supreme Court Review* (1964): 75. Charles Reich, "Mr. Justice Black and the Living Constitution," *Harvard Law Review* 6 (1963): 673, 715, 751–52.
189. *Baker v. Carr,* 369 U.S. at 385 (J. Frankfurter, dissenting); *accord, e.g., Regents of the University of Calif. v. Bakke,* 438 U.S. 265, 291 (1978) (J. Powell); *Slaughter House Cases,* 16 Wall. 36, 21 L.Ed. 394 (1873); *Loving v. Virginia,* 388 U.S. 1, 10 (1967); *Whitcomb v. Chavis,* 403 U.S. 124, 149 (1971).

190. *Regents of the University of California v. Bakke,* 438 U.S. 265, 292–96 (1978) (J. Powell).

191. *Ibid.* at 296 n. 35, *quoting.* Alexander Bickel, *The Morality of Consent* (New Haven 1975), 133.

192. See Winthrop Jordan, *White Over Black: American Attitudes Toward the Negro, 1550–1812* (Chapel Hill 1968).

193. Chilton Williamson, *American Suffrage from Property to Democracy, 1760–1860* (Princeton 1960), 277–78.

194. *Oregon v. Mitchell,* 400 U.S. 112, 255–56 (1970) (Opinion of Justices Brennan, White and Marshall), *citing* William W. Van Alstyne, "The Fourteenth Amendment, the 'Right' to Vote, and the Understanding of the Thirty-Ninth Congress," *Supreme Court Review* (1965): 33, 70.

195. *E.g.,* Melvin G. Holli, "Social and Structural Reform," in *The City Boss in America,* ed. Alexander Callow (New York 1976), 215–224. T. Harry Williams, Richard Current and Frank Freidel, *A History of the United States Since 1865* (New York 1959), 164.

196. Bradley Robert Rice, *Progressive Cities: The Commission Government Movement in America, 1901–1920* (Austin 1977), xvi, 4–18, 26–29, 34–51, 60–61. See also Samuel P. Hays, "The Politics of Reform in Municipal Government in the Progressive Era," *Pacific Northwest Quarterly* 55 (1964): 157–69; Charles A. Beard, *American City Government* (New York 1912); James Weinstein, "Organized Business and the City Commissioner and Manager Movements," *Journal of Southern History* 28 (May 1962): 166–82.

197. Kousser, *The Shaping of Southern Politics,* 45–47, 130–38; Hackney, *Populism to Progressivism in Alabama,* chap. 8; McMillan, *Constitutional Development in Alabama,* chap. 14.

198. *E.g., City of Mobile v. Bolden, Kirksey v. City of Jackson,* 663 F.2d 659 (5th Cir., 1981); *McMillan v. Escambia County,* 638 F.2d 1239, 1244 (5th Cir. 1982) *on rehearing,* 688 F.2d 960 (5th Cir. 1982) *voc. and rem.,* ____ S.Ct. ____ (Mar. 27, 1984); *McGill v. Gadsden County Commission,* 535 F.2d 277 (5th Cir. 1975); *Kendrick v. Walder,* 527 F.2d at 51 (J. Pell dissenting).

199. *E.g., McMillan v. Escambia County,* 638 F.2d at 1244 n. 10 (Florida).

200. *See* Cortner, *The Apportionment Cases,* chap. 1, 160–62.

201. Comment, "Alabama's Unrepresentative Legislature," 406, citing Farmer, *The Legislative Process In Alabama* (1949) 24; McMillan, *Constitutional Development in Alabama,* 283–309, 360–70.

202. Cortner, *The Apportionment Cases,* 177, quoting the *Birmingham Post-Herald,* 4 July 1962, 9.

203. *Compare Lucas v. Forty-Fourth General Assembly of Colorado,* 377 U.S. 713, 745–46 (J. Stewart, dissenting), *with City of Mobile v. Bolden,* 100 S.Ct. at 1506.

204. *Compare Lucas,* 377 U.S. at 744, *with Bolden,* 100 S.Ct. at 1498–99, 1505–06, and *Connor v. Finch,* 434 U.S. 407, 416 (1977).

205. *Compare Lucas,* 377 U.S. at 749; *Avery v. Midland County,* 390 U.S. 474, 509 (1968) (J. Stewart, dissenting); *Whitcomb v. Chavis,* 403 U.S. 124, 163,(1971) (J. Stewart, concurring and dissenting); *Sixty-Seventh Minnesota State Senate v. Beer,* 406 U.S. 187, 203 (1972) (J. Stewart, dissenting), *with Bolden,* 100 S.Ct. at 1506.

206. *Bolden,* 100 S.Ct. at 1505–06 n. 25.

207. *Bolden,* 100 S.Ct. at 1513–14; *Rogers v. Lodge* 102 S.Ct. at 3286–92.

208. *Bolden,* 100 S.Ct. at 1513; *accord, Gaffney v. Cummings,* 412 U.S. at 753 ("[I]t is most unlikely that the political impact of [a reapportionment] plan would remain undiscovered by the time it was proposed or adopted, in which event the results would be both known and, if not changed, intended.").

209. *Bolden,* 100 S.Ct. at 1513.

210. *Bolden,* 100 S.Ct. at 1536–37.

211. *E.g. see Beer v. United States*, 425 U.S. 130, 148 n. 4 (J. Marshall dissenting), *citing, inter alia*, Ely, "Legislative and Administrative Motivation in Constitutional Law," *Yale Law Journal* 79 (1970): 1205.
212. 100 S.Ct. at 1502 n. 17.
213. *Bolden*, 100 S.Ct. at 1513.
214. See *McMillan v. Escambia County*, 638 F.2d 1239, 1247 (5th Cir. 1981), *appeal and cert. pet. dismissed*, 102 S.Ct. 17 (1980).
215. See Jurisdictional Statement, 14–16, *City of Pensacola v. Jenkins*, No. 80–1946, *appeal dismissed*, 102 S.Ct. 17 (1980).
216. See *McMillan v. Escambia County*, 638 F.2d at 1244–45.
217. See *Rogers v. Lodge*.
218. Compare *McMillan v. Escambia County*, 638 F.2d at 1247 n. 16, *with City of Richmond v. United States*, 422 U.S. 358, 375–78 (1975).
219. *Rogers*, 102 S.Ct. at 3290 n. 28 (J. Stevens dissenting), *quoting* Karst, "The Costs of Motive-Centered Inquiry, *San Diego Law Review* 15 (1978): 1163, 1164–65.
220. *Ibid.* at 3292.
221. *Ibid.* at 3289.
222. *Ibid.* at 3281 (J. Powell dissenting); *ibid.* at 3290 (J. Stevens dissenting).
223. *Ibid.* at 3280.
224. *Ibid.* at 3288 (J. Stevens dissenting), *citing Bolden*, 446 U.S. at 121 (J. Marshall dissenting).
225. *Bolden*, 100 S.Ct. at 1512 (J. Stevens concurring); *Wise v. Lipscomb*, 437 U.S. 535, 549 (1978) (J. Rehnquist).
226. *E.g., compare cases cited in* Bickerstaff, "Reapportionment by State Legislatures," 647 n. 167.
227. 100 S.Ct. at 1524 n. 7.
228. *Ibid.*
229. 466 F.2d 830, 847 (7th Cir. 1972) (J. Stevens dissenting).
230. 466 F.2d at 843–44.
231. 466 F.2d at 845.
232. 466 F.2d at 848.
233. 466 F.2d at 848–50.
234. 466 F.2d at 851–53, 855.
235. 466 F.2d at 853–58.
236. *Ibid.* at 859, *quoting Turner v. Fouche*, 396 U.S. 346, 362 (1970).
237. 446 F.2d at 859.
238. *Ibid.*
239. *Rogers*, 102 S.Ct. at 3288 (J. Stevens dissenting).
240. *Ibid.*
241. *Ibid.*
242. *Ibid.*
243. __ S.Ct. __ (Mar. 27, 1984).
244. *Escambia County v. McMillan*, No. 82-1295, Jurisdictional Statement, 107a-09a.
245. *White v. Regester*, 412 U.S. at 766.
246. *E.g., Gaffney v. Cummings*, 412 U.S. at 753; *Ely v. Klahr*, 403 U.S. 108, 113 n. 5 (1971); *Burns v. Richardson*, 384 U.S. 73, 89 n. 16 (1966).
247. *E.g.*, Robert Dixon, "The Warren Court Crusade for the Holy Grail of 'One Man–One Vote,'" *Supreme Court Review* (1969): 219, 277, cited in Bernard Grofman, "Fair and Equal Representation," *Ethics* 91 (1981): 477, 480 n. 8; Jonathan W. Still, "Political Equality and Election Systems," *Ethics* 91 (1981): 367, 375, 388, 394; Ronald Rogowski, "Representation in Political Theory," *Ethics* 91 (1981): 395, 417; Jane J. Mansbridge, "Living with Conflict: Representation in the Theory of Adversary Democracy," *Ethics* 91 (1981): 466, 470.
248. Rogowski, "Representation in Political Theory," 419–20. See also Still, "Political Equality," 388.

249. Still, "Political Equality," 379–80; Grofman, "Fair and Equal Representation," 478.
250. Still, "Political Equality," 380–83.
251. *Bolden*, 100 S.Ct. at 1506 (footnote omitted).
252. Still, "Political Equality," 382.
253. *Karcher v. Daggett*, 103 S.Ct. at 2671 (J. Stevens, concurring); *accord, ibid.* at 2683 (J. White, dissenting); *ibid.* 2689 (J. Powell, dissenting).
254. *See* note 77 above. *Reynolds v. Sims*, 377 U.S. at 578–79.
255. Rogowski, "Representation in Political Theory," 396; As Robert Dixon put it:

> "one man, one vote" should be perceived as a symbol of an aspiration for fairness, for avoidance of complexity, for intelligibility in our representational process—indeed, for a sense of meaningful membership in the *polis*. These are legitimate aspirations, but there is no single, simple formula for their accomplishment.

Robert G. Dixon, Jr., *Democratic Representation* (1968), 268, quoted in Gordon E. Baker, "An Historical Tour Through the Political Thicket: Tracing the Steps of the Late Robert G. Dixon, Jr.," *Policy Studies Journal* 9 (1981): 825, 831. See Auerbach, "The Reapportionment Cases," 22 ("The principle of 'One Person, One Vote,' by itself, is confusing").
256. *Reynolds v. Sims*, 377 U.S. at 566.
257. *Gaffney v. Cummings*, 418 U.S. 733 (1973).
258. 103 S.Ct. 2676 n. 28. (J. Stevens, concurring); *Ibid.* at 2687 (J. White, joined by JJ. Burger, Powell, and Rehnquist, dissenting); *Ibid.* at 2689 (J. Powell, dissenting).
259. *Karcher v. Daggett*, 52 U.S.L.W. 3717 (30 Mar., 1984).
260. *Ibid.*
261. *Ibid.*
262. *Ibid.* (footnote omitted), *citing Gaffney v. Cummings*, 412 U.S. 735, 752–54 and n. 18 (1973).
263. *See* 466 F.2d at 848–50.
264. *Rogers*, 102 S.Ct. at 3293–94.
265. *Rogers*, 102 S.Ct. at 3286; *ibid.* at 3292 (J. Stevens dissenting).
266. *Ibid.* at 3294 (J. Stevens dissenting).
267. Carpeneti, "Legislative Apportionment: Multimember Districts and Fair Representation," *University of Pennsylvania Law Review* 126 (1972): 696–96.
268. *Compare Fortson v. Dorsey*, 379 U.S. at 437–39, *with City of Mobile v. Bolden*, 100 S.Ct. at 1499.
269. *E.g., see Leadership Roundtable v. City of Little Rock*, 499 F.Supp. 579, 590 (E.D. Ark. 1980), *aff'd*, 661 F.2d 701 (8th Cir. 1981).
270. *Rogers*, 102 S.Ct. at 3279.
271. 437 U.S. 535 (1978).
272. 405 U.S. at 134–35 and n. 12.
273. 412 U.S. at 767.
274. 100 S.Ct. at 1506–07.
275. *Compare Whitcomb v. Chavis*, 403 U.S. at 133–34 and n. 11 *with White v. Regester*, 412 U.S. at 766–67; *City of Mobile v. Bolden*, 100 S.Ct. at 1502 (blacks never elected to city government "apparently because of the prevasiveness of racially polarized voting").
276. *Bolden v. City of Mobile*, 423 F. Supp. at 388–89.
277. 638 F.2d 1239 (5th Cir. 1981), *on rehearing*, 688 F.2d 960 (5th Cir. 1982), *vac. and rem.,* __ S.Ct. __ (27 Mar., 1984).
278. *McMillan v. Escambia County*, 638 F.2d at 1241 n. 6.
279. Cf. *Sixty-seventh Minnesota State Senate v. Beer*, 406 U.S. 187 (1972). This example well illustrates the distinction made here by the proposed standard of at-large racial vote dilution and the standard for proving that other facially neutral devices, practices or procedures related to voting unconstitutionally disadvantage racial groups. The proposed at-large standard essentially sets up an effect-only test of the choice

between multimember and single-member districting—on the basis that such a test is necessary to reconcile Fourteenth and Fifteenth Amendment policy with the *Reynolds v. Sims* precedents. But it leaves other voting practices subject to the general rules for proving Fourteenth and Fifteenth amendment violations, which post-*Bolden* appellate decisions have uniformly understood to require proof of invidious purpose or intent. *E.g., Rogers v. Lodge, Kirksey v. City of Jackson, Washington v. Finlay* 664 F.2d 913 (4th Cir. 1981); *McMillan v. Escambia County.*

280.   403 U.S. at 150 and n. 29. See also *Leadership Roundtable v. City of Little Rock,* 449 F.Supp. 579 (E.D. Ark. 1980), *aff'd* 661 F.2d 701 (8th Cir. 1981).

281.   *E.g., McMillan v. Escambia County,* 638 F.2d at 1241 n. 6.

282.   *E.g., Brown v. Moore,* F.Supp 1123, 1126 (S.D. Ala. 1976), *aff'd per curiam,* 575 F.2d 298 (5th Cir. 1978), *vacated and remanded sub nom. Williams v. Brown,* 446 U.S. 236 (1980), *reaff'd on remand* 542 F.Supp. 1078 (S.D. Ala., 1982), *aff'd* 706 F.2d 1103 (11th Cir. 1983), *aff'd* 104 S.Ct. 520 (1983).

11

Alternatives to Single-Member Districts

Edward Still

Most elections in the United States are held using single-member districts or at-large elections or some combination of the two. Variations include plurality or runoff elections; nonpartisan or partisan elections; at-large elections with or without subdistrict residency requirements and numbered places; and staggered or concurrent terms. There are a multitude of other voting systems, a few of which will produce more minority representation than the typical ones now in use in this country. This chapter will discuss four systems designed to produce more minority representatives—the single transferable vote, the limited vote, the cumulative vote, and "add-on" representatives. After the mechanism of each system is examined in turn, the possibility of its adoption or approval by a court will be discussed.

An examination of single-member district elections reveals several problems. In an area with two well-organized parties or factions, at-large elections may produce a winner-take-all situation in which the majority party or faction could capture all seats despite a razor-thin popular plurality over the minority party. If the two groups are normally distributed over a large number of single or multimember constituencies (that is, partisan strength varies along the bell shaped curve) and have 90 percent of the vote between them, the ratio of the number of seats won by each will be

$$\left\{ \frac{1-S}{S} \right\} = \left\{ \frac{1-V}{V} \right\}^{K}, \tag{1}$$

where S is the percentage of seats won by the party, and V is the percentage of votes received by the party, and K is 3. This is called the "cube law." If Party A receives 55 percent of the vote, the cube law predicts that A will get nearly 65 percent of the seats.[1] Empirical research has shown that K is actually less than 3 in most situations. It has been found as low as 0.71 in 1966–1970 congressional elections and as high as 4.4 in the Electoral College, 1828–1968.[2]

An example of the cube law in operation is the 1972 Democratic presidential preference primary in Alabama. Each candidate for delegate was required to run in a single-member district and was requested to indicate his or her preference for president on the qualification form. These preferences were given wide publicity. George Wallace's organization "slated" an official candidate whenever more than one Wallace candidate was running, while the opposition to Wallace usually hid behind the label "uncommitted" and was uncoordinated with an identifiable faction. No delegate committed to Wallace ran in four of the twenty-nine districts, and the Wallace delegate was unopposed in one district. Uncommitted delegates won in only two of the twenty-four contested races. The total vote in those contests was 377,606 for Wallace delegates and 179,768 for delegates committed to no one or to other candidates. Thus with only 68 percent of the votes, the Wallace organization won 91 percent of the contested delegate positions.[3] Wallace's victory reflects both the use of highly disciplined voting by his supporters and the nearly clean sweep that can result from small majorities.

When district lines are eliminated altogether—that is, when the elections are at-large—it is even easier for the majority to win all the seats. Fairfield, Alabama, is divided into six residential districts, with two council members elected from each, but all are voted on at large. In the 1972 municipal election nine races could be characterized as black-white contests. In those nine races, 42 percent of the vote was cast for black candidates, yet no black candidates were elected.[4] Thus 58 percent of the vote yielded 100 percent of the seats.

This trend toward majority control or overrepresentation can be increased by allowing a mere plurality rather than a majority to win an election. Thus, as the number of candidates increases, the plurality required to win decreases. The 28 February 1974 British general election demonstrates the problems inherent in plurality victories in single-member districts. Figure 11-1 shows the results of that election (excluding Northern Ireland).[5]

These results demonstrate both the diversity of representation that results from single-member districts in comparison to a winner-take-all at-large system and the lack of relationship between votes and seats. The Conservatives won five fewer seats than Labour even though they received two hundred thousand votes more.

In the general election in 1979, the largest party received the largest share of the votes, but the overrepresentation of the large parties was as gross as before. Figure 11-2 shows the votes cast and seats won for the entire United Kingdom, including the twelve Northern Ireland seats (listed among the "others"). Similar results occurred in the June 1983 election. The Conservatives received over two-thirds of the seats with only 44 percent of the vote, while the Labour Party won nine times as many seats as the Liberal-Social Democratic Alliance with only 2 percent more votes.[6] These elections "manufactured" majorities for the Conservatives, as many electoral systems do.[7]

Party	Votes		Seats	
	Number (in thousands)	Percent	Number	Percent
Conservative	11,869	38.8	297	47.7
Labour	11,649	38.0	301	48.3
Liberal	6,058	19.8	14	2.2
SNP	633	2.1	7	1.1
PC	168	0.5	2	0.3
Others	248	0.8	2	0.3

Figure 11-1.   SNP = Scottish Nationalist Party; PC = Plaid Cymru, the Welsh Nationalist Party. Source: *Representation: Journal of the Electoral Reform Society* 14 (1974): 15.

	Votes		Seats	
Party	Number (in thousands)	Percent	Number	Percent
Conservative	13,698	43.9	339	53.4
Labour	11,510	36.9	268	42.2
Liberal	4,314	13.8	11	1.7
SNP	504	1.6	2	0.3
PC	133	0.4	2	0.3
Others	1,063	3.4	13	2.0

Figure 11-2.   Source: Data compiled by the author from articles listed in footnote 6.

Thus while it is true that "[t]he very essence of districting is to produce a different—more 'politically fair'—result than would be reached with elections at large, in which the winning party would take 100 percent of the legislative seats,"[8] the results leave much room for improvement in terms of accurate reflection of the voters' wishes. At a minimum, a majority of representatives should not represent the second largest bloc of voters.

These unrepresentative results could be caused by manipulation of district boundaries by one or more parties—usually called gerrymandering.

> Where a system offers in theory such fruitful opportunities, it is too much to expect party managers to refrain from using them. Consequently, the district system, combined with party politics, has resulted in the universal spread of the gerrymander. . . . The gerrymander is simply such a thoughtful construction of districts as will economize the votes of the party in power by giving it small majorities in a large number of districts, and coop up the opposing party with overwhelming majorities in a small number of districts.[9]

The U.S. Supreme Court has taken note "that the location and shape of districts may well determine the political complexion of the area. District lines are rarely neutral phenomena."[10]

Gerrymanders can be rather sophisticated. They need not be the obviously distorted shapes that first gave rise to the term "gerrymander." The maps in Figure 11-3 show the political consequences of two districting plans for a city, neither of which looks suspicious. The first plan follows the major roads to the center of the city and results in a clean sweep for the majority party. A plan using the city center and its northern and southern suburbs as three districts results in a two to one majority for the smaller party. Likewise, 31 percent could win control of a five-member board by carefully drawing themselves into majorities in three districts.

This kind of gerrymander is not unusual. In 1970 New Orleans redrew its five city council districts. (There were also two at-large seats.) As had been true for some years, the districts were five elongated areas running north-south. Since the black neighborhoods were arranged along an east-west axis, the 45 percent black minority was completely submerged in the white majorities of each district. The city redrew the plan to meet Department of Justice objections, but drew only one black-majority district.[11]

Even a fairly drawn plan that results in a roughly proportional distribution of

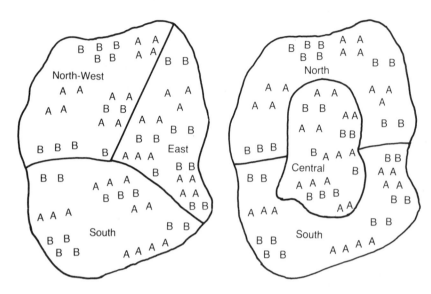

	Party A	Party B		Party A	Party B
N.W.	12,000	11,000	C.	14,000	9,000
E.	12,000	11,000	N.	11,000	12,000
S.	12,000	11,000	S.	11,000	12,000
Votes	36,000	33,000		36,000	33,000
Seats	3	0		1	2

Figure 11-3. Two examples of "sophisticated" gerrymanders. Source: Enid Lakeman, *How Democracies Vote: A Study of Electoral Systems* (London: Faber and Faber, 1974), 79.

seats between the two parties or races may be unfair to some citizens. Those who cannot affect the outcome in their own districts, such as black residents in a white-majority district or Republicans in a Democratic district, may take faint consolation from the overall parity their race or party has. Unfortunately for them, the U.S. Supreme Court has held that as long as the entire apportionment plan does not result in a disproportionate number of the seats going to blacks, whites have not had their right to vote abridged on grounds of race.[12] The Supreme Court thus views apportionment as a group right rather than an individual right.

Is there a method of election that recognizes the associational rights of whites and blacks to form groups to win elections as well as the individual right to cast an effective ballot? Surely any majoritarian system that can leave 49 percent of the people in a district or in the whole political unit with nothing to show for having gone to the polls except a patriotic feeling is not the answer. Instead, we should search for a voting system which meets as many of the following criteria as possible:

1. Proportionality between representation and group strength.[13]
2. Generality of operation in a variety of sociopolitical conditions. The plan should

not be so specific that it can only operate successfully in very limited situations. This condition also allows for temporal changes in the relative size or voting patterns of voting groups.

3. Resistance to gerrymandering or other manipulation.
4. Minimization of "wasted" votes. Wasted votes occur in two situations: when votes are cast for losing candidates; or when a group casts more votes than necessary for a winner to the detriment of another candidate supported by the same group.

As we have seen, single-member district plans can meet the first of these criteria, but are not resistant to gerrymandering. In a few cities mixed plans of single-member and at-large seats have resulted in some black representation, but there is no guarantee that the unique factors which make such a plan work in one city can be duplicated in another.[14]

The limited vote, cumulative vote, and single transferable vote systems meet more of these criteria than do single-member districts. All three use multimember districts and could be employed to elect all members of a governing body at large or members from two or more multimember districts if the number of seats is large. The systems differ in the manner in which the voters indicate a preference for candidates.

LIMITED VOTING

In a limited vote system the voter may cast fewer votes than the number of at-large seats to be filled. In theory such a system prevents the majority from making a clean sweep of all seats by voting a straight ticket. Theory has usually been borne out in practice. Between 1867 and 1885, Great Britain used the limited vote in thirteen three-member constituencies with two votes for each elector. Except in Glasgow and Birmingham, no party won all three seats.

Japan has used the limited vote with each voter having one vote in three-, four-, or five-member constituencies during this century. In 1980 the results of the election for the Japanese House of Representatives were as shown in Figure 11-4. Even though this election, as have many others, manufactured a majority, the results during this century have been much more representative than single-member districts used in Britain.[15]

The limited vote is subject to some manipulation. A well-disciplined majority

Parties	Votes (percent)	Seats (percent)
Liberal Democratic Party	47.9	55.6
Socialists	19.3	20.9
Komeito	9.0	6.4
Democratic Socialist Party	6.6	6.3

Figure 11-4. Source: Data compiled by the author from papers and book cited in footnote 15.

	Candidates				
Votes	A	B	C	D	Z
20.25%	X				
20.25%		X			
20.25%			X		
20.25%				X	
19.0%					X

Figure 11-5.

can win all seats by evenly dividing its votes among its full slate if the minority is smaller than

$$\frac{\text{(total votes cast)}}{\text{(number of seats)} + \text{(number of votes to be cast by each voter)}} . \tag{2}$$

Thus, a minority voting group of less than 20 percent would lose an election in which the majority strategically split its votes in a "one vote for four seats" election. If A, B, C, and D were the candidates of a majority party whose voters had been instructed very carefully so that one-fourth of the party voted for each candidate, the results would be as shown in Figure 11-5. On the other hand, if the minority party had only 21 percent of the total vote, it would have been guaranteed one seat by casting all its ballots for one candidate.

The majority could have been smaller or less well organized and still have won all seats if each voter had had a larger number of votes (in relation to the number of seats to be filled). The following Figure 11-6 shows a "three votes for four seats" election:

	Candidates				
Votes	A	B	C	D	Z
42%					X
14.5%	X	X	X		
14.5%	X	X		X	
14.5%	X		X	X	
14.5%	X	X	X	X	
	43.5%	43.5%	43.5%	43.5%	42%

Figure 11-6.

Note that it would not make much difference to the results if a "full ballot" or "anti-single-shot" provision required each voter to vote for three. The minority group would have to vote for two other candidates of their group or would have to help the majority candidates. The limited vote is thus subject to some manipulation, both in setting the ratio of votes to seats and in strategic voting.

The ratio of votes to seats is quite important in this type of election. Generally the smaller the ratio between the number of votes (to be cast by each voter) and the number of seats to be filled, the smaller the minority party can be and still be assured of one seat. The deficiencies of limited voting are magnified if there

Slate	Example 1 Votes (percent)	Seats	Example 2 Votes (percent)	Seats
A	40	6	85	6
B	35	3	10	3
C	25	0	5	0

Figure 11-7.

are three or more cohesive slates of candidates in the election, and each voter casts votes equal to more than half of the seats to be filled. In such a situation, the plurality will be able to elect its whole slate, while the leftover seats will be won by the second largest group. Figure 11-7 shows two examples of this phenomenon. Assume that each voter casts six votes and nine seats are to be filled. In example 1, Slate A has been overrepresented at the expense of slate C, with Slate B in a roughly proportional position. In example 2, Slate B is now the beneficiary of the leftover seats, while the plurality has been underrepresented. If the majority group is unimaginative or not well enough organized to vote strategically, the majority leaders can promote straight ticket voting for a number of candidates equal to the number of votes each voter has. This will limit the minority to the leftover seats.

On the other hand, a disciplined minority could conceivably win as many seats as each voter has votes if the "majority" spread its votes among a large number of candidates. Assume a 25 percent minority group is voting as shown in Figure 11-8 in a three votes for four seats election. The winners would be A, B, C, and M. The example works just as well whether candidates M-W are of the same political group or they are supported by several minorities smaller than the A-B-C group. In either case, the rule of proportionality has been violated. This example also shows the potential for manipulation by encouraging false or "straw man" candidacies in the opposing group.

CUMULATIVE VOTING

Some of the deficiencies in limited voting can be cured by cumulative voting. In the classical form of cumulative voting each voter has as many votes as there are

Votes	A	B	C	M	N	O	P	Q	R	S	T	U	V	W
25%	X	X	X											
20%				X	X	X								
20%							X	X	X					
20%				X					X	X				
15%												X	X	X

Figure 11-8

seats to be filled and may cumulate them among a smaller number of candidates. Illinois used a cumulative vote procedure for its general assembly between 1870 and 1980. Each legislative district elected three representatives. Each voter had three votes which could be cast as follows:

>1 for each of 3 candidates
>1½ for each of 2 candidates
>3 for one candidate

Very few districts elected three representatives from the same party. The provision of some minority representation in nearly every district meets one of our criteria, but cumulative voting requires even more strategic voting than limited voting systems. In a two-party situation, the strategy is usually made by the party headquarters when it decides to nominate one, two, or three candidates.[16]

In a cumulative vote system, the most cautious policy for a minority group is to cumulate its votes for one candidate. The minority will achieve some representation if its strength is more than

$$\frac{1}{1 + (\text{number of seats})},\qquad (3)$$

which is the same share of the total vote necessary to achieve representation in a single limited vote system.

All of this assumes that there can be tight control over the number of candidates and discipline on the part of voters to vote as instructed. In some cases in Illinois, the parties tacitly or by agreement nominated only three candidates between them so that the voters had no choice in the general election. In 1970 the Illinois Constitution was amended to require a party to nominate two or three candidates, not one, thus eliminating the no-choice situation.[17]

Deciding how many candidates to nominate (or to have campaign actively) can be the most important decision the local party committee makes, especially when each party's expected vote is within the 40 to 60 percent range. Figure 11-9 shows the election results of various nomination strategies where Party B receives 50 percent to 60 percent of the total vote. "Nomination" in this context includes only candidates the party is actively supporting, not "straw men" nominated to comply with a minimum nominations requirement (like that of Illinois). The letters in each cell of the table indicate the party identification of winners of

	Number of candidates	If party B nominates:		
		1	2	3
and party A nominates:	1	ABB	ABB	ABB
	2	AAB	ABB	AAB
	3	AAB	ABB	BBB

Figure 11-9.

	Candidates					
Voters	A	B	C	D	E	F
25	3					
38		1.5	1.5			
36				1	1	1
1				1.5	1.5	
100	75	57	57	37.5	37.5	36

Figure 11-10.

the election if the respective party's supporters' do not split their tickets between parties and give equal support to all the party's candidates. If the party nominates two candidates, the voters cast one and a half votes for each; if the party nominates three, the voters cast one vote for each.

Anomalous results occur where both parties overestimate their strength: the minority party A wins two seats when it nominates two and B nominates three. This results as follows: A would split its 40 to 50 percent share of the votes among two candidates, thus giving each 20 to 25 percent. B's 50 to 60 percent of the voters would be splitting their votes among three candidates with the result that each would get 17 to 20 percent of the vote. If A has more than 40 percent, it is assured of two seats. If A overreaches even more by nominating three when the majority party nominates three, A will lose entirely.[18]

The foregoing examples have been based on two well-organized parties. Cumulative voting is likely to produce even more skewed results in plurality-win "nonpartisan" elections in which the number of candidates for each group is not so easily controllable. Just as in limited voting, a bloc voting minority could obtain an unfairly large representation.

Even the requirement of runoffs, if candidates do not obtain a majority or some other quota—might not solve the problem. An at-large election—whether carried out with majoritarian, limited, or cumulative voting, and which requires a runoff for some or all eventual winners—divides voters in the first election into three groups: those who wasted their votes on losers, those who cast effective votes for winners, and those who cast partially effective votes for candidates who will be in the runoff. Figures 11-10 and 11-11 show how some voters may be allowed to cast more votes for winners than others. In an election with one hundred voters with three votes each, seventy-five votes would be the "quota" for election, since

	Candidates				
Voters	M	N	P	Q	R
50	1.5	1.5			
20			1.5	1.5	
21				1.5	1.5
19			1.5		1.5
100	75	75	58.5	61.5	60

Figure 11-11.

four candidates could win one-fourth of the three hundred votes to be cast. (The results of this example would be no different if the quota for election without runoff were set at sixty-one, which is the Droop quota, discussed on page 259.)

The minority of twenty-five has "plumped" for A and elected her. In the runoff between B, C, D, and E, the twenty-five supporters of A will be the deciding factor if the other two groups continue dividing their votes equally between their respective candidates.

In other elections, it may be the majority casting more effective votes which decides the winners (see Figure 11-11). Here the majority elected its two candidates and will help decide the third winner in the runoff.

PROPORTIONAL REPRESENTATION

Limited voting and cumulative voting systems are sometimes referred to as "semi-proportional" because they achieve more proportionality than single-member or multimember plurality or majority elections, but less than complete proportionality. Nearly complete proportionality can be achieved using some form of a proportional representation system.

These systems come in various sizes and shapes. Two basic types are the party-list system and the single transferable vote (STV).[19] In the party-list form, the voter casts his votes for the party, seats are allocated to the parties on the basis of the percentage of votes received, and the winning candidates are taken from the top of the party lists.

The list system of proportional representation requires that parties be sufficiently organized to prepare lists ranking their candidates. In places where white voters discriminate against black candidates, it would probably be necessary for blacks to organize their own party. This would have the effect of segregating blacks and probably hindering further amelioration of racial tensions.

On the other hand, STV allows the voter complete freedom to pick candidates, in any order. The voter marks his ballot preferentially, that is, first choice with "1," second choice with "2," and so on.

The operation of STV can be shown in the following simple election. Let us imagine that A, B, and C belong to one party (or bloc voting racial group), and X, Y, and Z belong to the other, and all six contended for three seats on the council. After the polls had closed, the counters would first sort the ballots into piles corresponding to the first preference marked on each. (The description that follows assumes a hand count of paper ballots. With optical character recognition readers and computers, the count could be carried out faster, but in essentially the same way.) Let us assume the results of this are as follows:

A	1,801
B	350
C	300
X	820
Y	500
Z	229
Total	4,000

If this were an election using a single limited vote for three seats, it is clear that the 60 percent who voted for the ABC party would have elected only one representative. Thus, proportionality would not have been achieved. However, because of the second and successive preferences on most of the ballots in an STV election, this imbalance can be rectified. The first thing we realize is that A has too many votes: if they were more evenly distributed, B or C could have been elected. But how many is "too many"? When Thomas Hare first suggested the single transferable vote, he used the number of votes divided by the number of seats to be filled. In this election that would be

$$\frac{4,000}{3} = 1,333. \tag{4}$$

However, this is not the minimum number of votes that each winner could get and exclude the possibility of more "winners" than seats to be filled. The least votes each winner could get is one more than

$$\frac{\text{number of votes}}{(\text{seats to be filled}) + 1}. \tag{5}$$

This is called the Droop quota, named after H. R. Droop, its inventor. Since there are three seats, the quota is one more than a fourth of the total of the votes polled: the quota would therefore be 1,001.

Party A attained eight hundred votes more than the quota and would be declared elected. The next step is to transfer A's eight hundred surplus votes in accordance with the wishes of his supporters. The ballots of A would be divided into subparcels according to the second preference marked on each. Assume the result is as follows:

B is the second choice on	1,296
C is the second choice on	264
Z is the second choice on	40
Total with second preferences	1,600
Ballots with no further preferences	201
Total	1,801

In this case there are eight hundred surplus votes, while there are sixteen hundred ballots on which a next preference has been marked. Each candidate (B, C, Z) should receive half of his subparcel of A's surplus. Figure 11-12 indicates the results of the transfer.

Since no candidate (except A) now has a quota, the candidate with the fewest votes is eliminated and his votes transferred to the next available preference (A, who is already elected and unavailable, would receive no more votes). Figure 11-13 shows the results of that transfer.

As a result of this distribution of Z's votes, B and X each obtain a quota of votes and are declared elected.

In the example, the majority party has ended the election with a majority of the representatives, but the minority party is not excluded. Long-term experience in the Republic of Ireland, Australia, Malta, and several American cities indicates

	Votes		
Candidate	Previous	Transferred from A	New Total
B	350	648	998
C	300	132	432
X	820		820
Y	500		500
Z	229	20	249

Figure 11-12.

that STV actually achieves proportionality and the effective use of more votes.[20] The Droop quota formula guarantees that a party casting at least

$$\frac{1}{(\text{seats to be filled}) + 1} \tag{6}$$

votes will have a representative, just as in cumulative voting and single limited vote systems. However, in cumulative and limited voting it may be difficult for a larger minority party to achieve more than one seat; STV usually results in a party with strength equal to several quotas electing several representatives. STV is not nearly so open to manipulation as the other two by either strategic voting or encouragement of ''straw men'' to waste the opponents' votes.

STV is a flexible system that will work in nonpartisan, two-party, or multiparty situations. In multiparty situations, formal and informal agreements encourage voters to give their preferences to closely allied parties after their first few preferences.[21] About the only institutional modification that can be made in STV that will affect proportionality is the number of seats. As Figure 11-14 shows, the Droop quota as a percentage of total votes falls rapidly until the number of seats reaches ten; above ten, the difference another seat or two makes is small.[22] In STV elections, as in most types of elections, the larger the number of seats in a district, the more likely the election is to have proportional results.[23]

STV is not without its inconsistencies. It sometimes violates the reduction principle (that the elimination of a losing candidate ought not to affect the identity of the winners), but this can also occur in plurality elections, limited voting, cumulative voting, and the first stage of two-stage elections.[24]

	Votes		
Candidate	Previous	Transferred from Z	New Total
B	998	20	1,018
C	432		432
X	820	200	1,020
Y	500	29	529

Figure 11-13.

# of seats	Droop quota as %
2	33.3
3	25
4	20
5	16.7
6	14.3
7	12.5
8	11.1
9	10
10	9.1
11	8.3
15	6.3

Figure 11-14.

It has also been claimed that STV is perverse in that a candidate may lose because he or she gets too many first place votes. Doron and Kronick have used the election as shown in Figure 11-15, as an example. If two are to be elected, the

	Choices			
Voters	1st	2nd	3rd	4th
9	W	Z	X	Y
6	X	Y	Z	W
2	Y	X	Z	W
4	Y	Z	X	W
5	Z	X	Y	W

Figure 11-15.

quota would be ten, but in this example the authors assumed it was nine. In this election, W would be the first winner; Z's five votes would be transferred to X, who would be the second winner.

If the first two preferences of the voters on the third line are reversed, X would have eight first place votes, but Y would be the candidate eliminated this time. Y's four votes would be transferred to Z, making him a winner.[25]

This "perverse" result is a function of the "Condorcet effect" among the voters on the second, fourth, and fifth lines. Condorcet theorized that the winner of a multi-candidate election ought to be the one who wins all head-to-head contests with the other candidates. There are times, as in this case, when the winner varies in each pairwise election. If the fifteen voters on the second, fourth, and fifth lines were presented with pairwise elections of X, Y, and Z, they would vote as follows:

$$X \ vs \ Y \quad\quad Y \ vs \ Z \quad\quad X \ vs \ Z$$

$$11 \quad 4 \quad\quad 10 \quad 5 \quad\quad 6 \quad 9 \quad\quad\quad (6)$$

A majority of these fifteen voters (but not the same majority each time) prefer X to Y, Y to Z, and Z to X in pairwise elections. This circularity would cause problems in almost any type of election.[26]

ADD-ON VOTING

A fourth method might be called "topping up" or "add on," that is, achieving proportionality by the addition of representatives to those already elected by single- or multi-member constituencies. Variations of this system are used in West Germany, Sweden, Iceland, Denmark, and Puerto Rico. In Denmark and Sweden, thirty-nine or forty seats are allocated on the basis of the total vote for each party's district representatives (elected by a list system of proportional representation). In West Germany and Iceland, the voter actually votes twice—once for a constituency representative in a single-member district and once for a party. Half of the members of the West German Bundestag are chosen from party lists in numbers sufficient to give each party its correct proportion of the total membership.[27]

In Puerto Rico, the relative proportion of seats for parties is decided by reference to the votes for governor. If the majority party wins more than two-thirds of the seats in either house, that house can be increased in size by up to one-third in order to correct for underrepresentation of minority parties. If the largest party also obtains less than the two-thirds of the votes for governor, the minority parties are entitled to the full one-third additional members at large, allocated among the minority parties according to their relative strength. If the largest party's gubernatorial candidate obtains more than two-thirds of the total vote, the minority parties are entitled to additional representation only to the extent necessary to give all parties proportional strength in the legislature.[28]

These systems differ slightly in the manner of choosing the individuals who fill the add-on positions. In all the countries except Puerto Rico, the party organization decides on the priority of its national or regional list candidates, who are usually also its constituency candidates. In Puerto Rico, the losing candidates of each minority party are ranked according to the vote each received in his or her constituency.

All of these topping up systems achieve nearly perfect proportionality, but each has its drawbacks, especially in nonpartisan elections in which the minority group is a racial or ethnic minority rather than a political party. Topping up systems can only work for ethnic or racial groups if they form their own parties or if the law treats each group like a party. If racial parties were formed and add-on seats were distributed on the basis of votes cast for minority candidates (as in Sweden), a minority group would have to run candidates even in districts it was sure to lose, thus giving up its ability to influence the election of some constituency members. On the other hand, there might be a philosophical objection (among all races) to making an explicit guarantee of racial or ethnic representation that would accompany proportionality based on each group's percentage of the total population, without regard to how they voted.

PROSPECTS FOR CHANGE

There is little chance that the courts will order any of these nonmajoritarian plans into effect as a remedy in a case brought by a racial or ethnic minority. There are several reasons for this.

First, in the absence of survey data showing how different ethnic groups vote in city elections, litigants must continue to rely on aggregate data analysis based on precinct returns. These data can only be useful if there are appreciable racial differences from precinct to precinct. If the races are residentially segregated—and they typically are—a single-member district plan will probably be an improvement over at-large voting.

Second, the U.S. Supreme Court has made a political science judgment that single-member districts are adequate to protect the rights that are at stake in ordinary malapportionment cases. It has repeatedly instructed lower courts to adopt single-member district plans when the courts have to apportion a state or locality.[29] Since courts are supposed to remedy only that which is unconstitutional or unlawful, they are not likely to adopt a proportional or semiproportional system without a showing that no other system is adequate.

Third, the courts have shown a bias against claims of a right to proportional representation,[30] probably because "proportional representation" has been misunderstood by the courts to be something like a quota system that requires racial or ethnic balance in elective bodies. Three of these methods of election discussed in this chapter are not quota systems of that sort but allow for the creation of "voluntary constituencies" based on whatever issues the voters feel are important. Limited voting, cumulative voting, and STV could all work without regard to race, if the voters stopped thinking race was important. In contrast, racially safe single-member districts tend to encourage further residential segregation and harden the separation between the races.[31] However, in a recent case, the U.S. Supreme Court held that a court may require the use of plurality elections rather than runoffs for two at-large seats on a nine-member council because "[r]emoval of the [runoff] requirement . . . might enhance the chances of blacks to be elected to the two at-large seats . . . but would surely not guarantee that result."[32] This case may indicate some hope for convincing courts that proportionality is a reasonable measure of fairness.

Fourth, the U.S. Supreme Court has shown little concern that those who support the losers in an election are effectively unrepresented. In a case involving the underrepresentation of blacks in Indianapolis, the Court said:

> As our system has it, one candidate wins, the others lose. Arguably the losing candidates' supporters are without representation since the men they voted for have been defeated; arguably they have been denied equal protection of the laws since they have no legislative voice of their own. This is true of both single-member *and* multimember

districts. But we have not yet deemed it a denial of equal protection to deny legislative seats to losing candidates, even in those so-called "safe" districts where the same party wins year after year.[33]

This approval of a win-lose system is part of the cultural mind-set of the Supreme Court. Majoritarian systems have been part of the American scene for two hundred years, therefore they must be legitimate, the justices believe. The problem is that majoritarian systems create winners who take all rather than winners who share in power, thus making politics into a battle for total victory rather than a method of governing open to all significant groups.[34]

Even if the courts will not impose one of these nonmajoritarian systems, state or local governments could voluntarily adopt such a plan with little chance of its being voided on federal constitutional grounds. One commentator has recently argued that cumulative, limited, or single transferable vote systems would be discriminatory, but could probably be justified on the basis that the state has an interest in remedying past discrimination or in increasing minority representation.

> Any [plan] to improve minority representation, however, would also be discriminatory. Cumulative or proportional voting systems, for example, can improve the ability of minorities to elect representatives. Where these schemes replace majority win systems, it is unlikely that the majority will elect as many representatives as it could under the prior electoral system. This loss in ability to elect representatives is sufficient to support a prima facie violation of equal protection.[35]

This argument is based on cases in which the Supreme Court has reviewed affirmative action plans which favored blacks to the disadvantage of whites and on cases in which blacks have been excluded from the electorate or been subject to schemes which diluted their votes.[36] These cases are inapposite, however, when a majoritarian system is replaced by a proportional system in which representation is shared by several groups. This makes the new system more like voluntary desegregation of schools in which no whites are excluded to make room for blacks (as in *Bakke*), but all share the integrated school system. Since the election schemes discussed in this chapter do not purposely overrepresent the minority and do not dilute the effectiveness of white voters who live in black majority districts, there is no invidious discrimination at all.

In the few times that STV has been challenged in federal court, it has withstood attacks on the grounds that it denies equal protection and a republican form of government.[37] Charges that STV or cumulative voting violated state constitutional provisions allowing each citizen to vote for all elective officers have been successful in some cases.[38]

Each of the systems discussed provides more proportionality of representation than single-member districts. Cumulative voting would be most subject to strategic voting and would be the least attractive of the four for that reason. Limited voting would probably be a half-way solution, but would have the problem of wasted votes. Add-on systems would tend to perpetuate racial separation. Clearly STV is the most attractive of the four in terms of proportionality and its resistance to manipulation.

NOTES

1. Enid Lakeman, *How Democracies Vote: A Study of Electoral Systems* (London: Faber and Faber, 1974), 56; W. J. M. Mackenzie, *Free Elections: An Elementary Textbook* (London: George Allen and Unwin Ltd., 1958), 52.
2. Edward R. Tufte, "The Relationship Between Seats and Votes in Two-Party Systems," *American Political Science Review* 67 (1973): 540–547; Rein Taagepera, "Seats and Votes: A Generalization of the Cube Law of Elections," *Social Science Research* 2 (1973): 257–275; Bernard Grofman, "For Single-Member Districts Random is not Equal," in Bernard Grofman, et al., eds., *Representation and Redistricting Issues* (Lexington, Mass.: Lexington Books, 1982), 55–58.
3. Records of Alabama Democratic Party, Birmingham, Alabama.
4. *Nevett v Sides,* U.S. District Court for the Northern District of Alabama, C.A. 73-529, case file.
5. *Representation: Journal of the Electoral Reform Society* 14 (1974): 15.
6. "Margaret Thatcher Assumes Her Office as Prime Minister," *New York Times,* Late City Edition, 5 May 1979, p.1, col.6; *London Sunday Times,* 12 June 1983, p. 2, col. 4.
7. Douglas W. Rae, *The Political Consequences of Electoral Law,* (New Haven: Yale University Press, 1971), 74–77. Professor Hermens argues that such manufactured majorities are a good feature because the role of an election system is to create a consensus, not take a census. F.A. Hermens, *Democracy and Proportional Representation,* Public Policy Pamphlet 7 (Chicago: University of Chicago Press, 1940), 4–6.
8. *Gaffney v Cummings,* 412 US 735, 753 (1973).
9. John R. Commons, *Proportional Representation* (New York: Thomas Y. Crowell & Company, 1896), 49–51.
10. *Gaffney v Cummings,* 412 US 735, 753 (1973).
11. *Beer v United States,* 425 US 130 (1976).
12. *United Jewish Organizations v Carey,* 430 US 133, 166 (1977).
13. For various measures of bias and proportionality see Louis Maisel and Gerald J. Lieberman, "The Impact of Electoral Rules on Primary Elections: The Democratic Primaries in 1976," in *The Impact of the Electoral Process,* ed. Louis Maisel and Joseph Cooper, Sage Electoral Studies Yearbook III (Beverly Hills: Sage Publications, 1977), 48; Bernard Grofman, "Measures of Bias and Proportionality in Seats-Votes Relationships" (Unpublished research paper, April 1982).
14. Francine F. Rabinowitz and Edward K. Hamilton, "Alternative Electoral Structures and Responsiveness to Minorities," *National Civic Review* 69 (1980): 371–385, studied four mixed-plan cities and found "a movement toward [proportional] black representation." However, Richard L. Engstrom and Michael D. McDonald, "The Election of Blacks to City Councils: Clarifying the Impact of Electoral Arrangements on the Seats/Population Relationship," *American Political Science Review* 75 (1981): 344–54, found that blacks are not elected to mixed-plan city councils in proportion to their population percentages.
15. Theodore McNelly, "Limited Voting in Japanese Parliamentary Elections" (Paper read at Annual Meeting of American Political Science Association, Denver, Colo., 2–5 September 1982), 7. Limited voting is now used in New York city council, Philadelphia city council (at-large members only), most Pennsylvania county commissions, and some Connecticut municipal elections. Sandra Featherman, "Limited Voting and Local Governance: A View from the Politician's Seat," Paper read at Annual Meeting of the American Political Science Association, Washington, D.C., August 1980); Lakeman, *How Democracies Vote,* 82–87.
16. Lakeman, *How Democracies Vote,* 89; Commons, *Proportional Representation,* 93;

Robert G. Dixon, Jr., *Democratic Representation: Reapportionment in Law and Politics* (New York: Oxford University Press, 1968), 523–25; Jack Sawyer and Duncan MacRae, Jr., "Game Theory and Cumulative Voting in Illinois: 1902–1954," *American Political Science Review* 56 (1962): 937.

17. Ill. Const., Art. IV, 2, para. b (repealed 1980). Illinois now uses single-member districts for the election of all legislators. For an insightful discussion of the campaign to repeal cumulative voting, see David H. Everson and Joan A. Parker, "The Illinois Cutback Initiative and its Aftermath," (Paper read at Annual Meeting of the American Political Science Association, Denver, Colo., 2 Sept. 1982).

18. Sawyer and McRae, "Games Theory and Cumulative Voting," 938.

19. Various forms of proportional representation are described in detail in Lakeman, *How Democracies Vote*, 92 *et seq.*, and Douglas W. Rae, *The Political Consequences of Electoral Laws* (New Haven: Yale University Press, 1971).

20. Lakeman, *How Democracies Vote*, 231–69, 284–86; George H. Hallett, Jr., *Proportional Representation: The Key to Democracy* (New York: National Municipal League, 1940), 105–47; Rae, *Political Consequences*, 110–11.

21. Peter Mair and Maria Maguire, "The Single Transferable Vote and the Irish General Election of 1977," *Economic and Social Review* 9 (1978): 319–27.

22. Lakeman, *How Democracies Vote*, 128.

23. Rae, *Political Consequences*, 114–19.

24. Gideon Doron, "Is the Hare Voting System Representative?" *Journal of Politics* 41 (1979), 918–22.

25. Gideon Doron and Richard Kronick, "Single Transferable Vote: An Example of a Perverse Social Choice Function," *American Journal of Political Science* 21 (1977): 303–11.

26. Richard G. Niemi and William H. Riker, "The Choice of Voting Systems," *Scientific American* 234, no. 6 (1976): 21–27.

27. P.J. Taylor and R.J. Johnston, *Geography of Elections* (Harmondsworth, England: Penguin Books, 1979), 70–74.

28. Puerto Rico Const., Art. III, §7; Puerto Rico Laws, Tit. 16, §3272. Parties with less than 5 percent of the vote are not included in the calculations.

29. *Chapman v Meier*, 420 US 1 (1975); *Mahan v Howell*, 410 US 315 (1973); *Connor v Johnson*, 402 US 690 (1971).

30. *City of Mobile v Bolden*, 446 US 55, 75–6 (1980). On the other hand, Puerto Rico's "add-on" representation system has been upheld against a claim of unconstitutionality. *Fuster v Buso*, 102 DPR 327 (1974), app. dis. sub nom. *Cerezo v Buso*, 419 US 1098 (1975).

31. Russell Hayman, "Affirmative Action and Electoral Reform," *Yale Law Journal* 90 (1981): 1829.

32. *City of Port Arthur, Texas, v United States*, 51 USLW 4035 (13 Dec. 1982). The case was decided under §5 of the Voting Rights Act.

33. *Whitcomb v Chavis*, 403 US 124, 153 (1971).

34. Marc V. Levine, "Institution Design and the Separatist Impulse: Quebec and the Antebellum American South," *Annals of the American Academy of Political and Social Science* 433 (September 1977): 62.

35. Hayman, "Affirmative Action and Electoral Reform," 1823 (footnotes omitted).

36. *Fullilove v Klutznik*, 448 US 448 (1980); *Regents of the University of California v Bakke*, 438 US 265 (1978); *Gomillion v Lightfoot*, 364 US 339 (1960); *Kirksey v Board of Supervisors*, 554 F2d 139 (5th Cir) (en banc), cert. denied 434 US 968 (1977).

37. *Campbell v Board of Education*, 310 FSupp 94 (SD NY 1970); *Moore v Election Commissioners of Cambridge*, 309 Mass 303, 35 NE2d 222 (1941); *Reutener v City of Cleveland*, 107 Ohio St. 117 (1923).

38. For cases holding in favor of STV on this ground, see *Moore* and *Reutener, supra* note 37, and *Johnson v City of New York*, 274 NY 411, 9 NE2d 30 (1937). Cases

holding STV violated such a constitutional provision include *People ex rel. Devine v Elkus*, 59 Cal App 396, 211 P 34 (1922); *Wattles ex rel. Johnson v Upjohn*, 211 Mich 514, 179 NW 335 (1920). Cumulative voting was ruled void under the state constitution in *Maynard v Board of District Canvassers*, 84 Mich 228, 47 NW 756 (1890).

PROSPECTS

12

Black Electoral Participation and the Distribution of Public Benefits

Milton D. Morris

Black Americans have pursued very few goals as vigorously or persistently as they have pursued the right to participate fully in the political life of the country. They have devoted so much to this goal for at least three reasons: their commitment to the basic democratic values of representative politics; the symbolic importance of full involvement, especially since their exclusion had been so clearly linked to their subordination and exploitation; and their conviction that through politics they could influence government to act to improve their social and economic status.

The emphasis on securing tangible benefits from political participation is supported by traditional beliefs about how democracy works as well as by the experience of many ethnic groups. In this society, political participation has always been perceived as a means of influencing the actions of government. The history of urban politics in this country is dominated by the successful efforts of ethnic minorities to influence the distribution of the benefits at the disposal of local governments.[1]

On the other hand, the black experience amply demonstrates that those groups lacking the capacity to influence government have received very little. Their streets were the last paved or went unpaved; they were farthest from the parks and recreational facilities; their neighborhoods were less frequently or properly patrolled by the police; they received the least attractive government jobs; and in virtually all areas of benefit distribution, they were generally served last and least. Dr. Martin Luther King, Jr., expressed the conviction of many blacks in asserting, "Voting is the foundation stone for political action. With it the Negro can vote out of office public officials who bar the doorway to decent housing, public safety, jobs, and decent integrated education."

Of course, the relationship between political participation and the distribution of benefits by government is not simple and direct and is therefore extremely difficult to measure. One reason for this difficulty is that the most common form of political participation, voting, allows the individual to express support for or op-

This paper is reprinted, with editorial changes, from *The Right to Vote*, a conference report published by the Rockefeller Foundation in October 1981.

position to broad policy positions or individual candidates but usually not for specific interests. Another is that policy decisions by government are usually products of competing demands or pressures, making it difficult to observe the impact of a specific demand on a final decision. Social scientists nevertheless believe that citizens' confidence in the relationship between political participation and governmental action is of intrinsic importance to the political system. That belief encourages political participation, which, in turn, legitimizes government. Although historically, blacks have expressed strong belief in the ability of groups like theirs to influence the political system, they also have had persistent doubts, especially about the effectiveness of their participation in electoral politics.

Dr. King reflected these doubts in a 1968 comment: "In the past two decades Negroes have expended more effort in quest of the franchise than they have in all other campaigns combined. Demonstrations, sit-ins, and marches, though more spectacular, are dwarfed by the enormous number of man-hours expended to register millions, particularly in the South." Noting, however, the failure of electoral politics to bring about the far-reaching changes blacks sought, he declared that "the time is short for social science to illuminate this critical area. If the main thrust of Negro effort has been and remains substantially irrelevant, we may be facing an agonizing crisis of tactical theory."[2]

Recent experiences have also given cause for doubts by blacks about the effectiveness of their electoral participation. After playing an apparently critical role in the election of a president in 1976, many blacks expressed disillusionment with what they perceived as meager benefits that accrued from that support. Moreover, in the 1980 presidential election, the black vote had virtually no impact on the outcome. A president was elected with a smaller proportion of the black vote (less than 7 percent)—and on the basis of positions that diverge more sharply from those maintained by most blacks—than any other president in this century.

The doubts of blacks about their political effectiveness extend even to those localities where blacks have gained political power by capturing the mayor's office or gaining control of the city council. Many blacks expected that with these achievements they would be able to influence the distribution of public benefits to improve their economic opportunities. For several reasons, these expectations have been largely unrealized.[3] Today, there is widespread skepticism about whether such electoral successes will make a difference in the efforts of blacks to improve their economic status or to obtain a more equitable allocation of public benefits.

This paper attempts to review the state of our knowledge about the effectiveness of black electoral participation in influencing the distribution of public benefits—the goods, services, and opportunities at the disposal of government. The increasing emphasis by blacks on converting their political strength into economic advancement requires careful scrutiny of the opportunities for and obstacles to such a conversion. In this regard, it is important to determine how their political power might be harnessed to increase responsiveness by government; what we might learn from recent experience about the conditions under which they can influence the distribution of benefits; whether political styles and decision-making procedures have changed over time to such an extent that traditional techniques or resources are now substantially less effective means of exerting influence; and whether governments, national or local, are still able to distribute substantial and valuable resources desired by blacks. Answers to these questions can help shape political strategies and suggest realistic expectations from political participation. Moreover, they can help us assess the real cost of the failure by blacks to utilize fully their political power or of efforts by others to dilute that power.

FEATURES OF BLACK ELECTORAL PARTICIPATION

Although the political system is expected to be responsive to citizen demands, in reality it tends to be most responsive to those individuals or groups who wield special influence. This influence might derive from strategic location within decision-making institutions, specialized knowledge, or especially effective levels or modes of political participation. This study focuses on two modes of political participation, voting and holding public office, because they are easily observed and measured and are prominent types of routine political participation.

The Black Vote

Undoubtedly, the most powerful political resource available to blacks is their voting strength. As approximately 11 percent of the national electorate, and by far the most cohesive of the racial or ethnic groups in that electorate, blacks indeed have the potential for formidable political power. Moreover, their strategic location in several large states and in large metropolitan areas seems to further enhance this power in national elections as well as elections in localities where they are concentrated.

Although the size, cohesiveness, and strategic location of the black vote confer the potential for considerable influence, the level and character of that vote and the conditions under which it occurs determine the actual influence. The available evidence suggests that the black vote is seriously and persistently underutilized. Moreover, some characteristics of black political behavior, as well as structural and procedural features of the political system, tend to undermine the effectiveness of that vote.

The extent of the underutilization of the black vote is reflected in data for presidential and congressional elections between 1964 and 1982 (Table 12-1). Those data confirm what is already well known: blacks vote at much lower rates than whites. Roughly half of all blacks who were eligible to vote failed to do so in 1980, and more than half failed to do so in 1976. Data gathered by the Joint Center for Political Studies on the 1980 election and recent studies of overreporting in post-election surveys indicate that these data may substantially overstate actual participation.

The most striking fact about the level of black voting reported in 1980 is that it was almost 7 percentage points below the level for 1964. This decline has occurred even though the Voting Rights Act of 1965 paved the way for millions of southern blacks to enter the electorate, even though the level of education for blacks has been increasing, and even though there are signs of an increase in the size of the black middle class—all developments which should have produced a substantial *increase* in the level of black voting.

The decline in black voting is disappointing to those who see the vote as one of the principal means of influencing government. However, it must be viewed in relationship to other major developments affecting the electorate as a whole. One is the adoption in 1968, of the Twenty-sixth Amendment, which extended the franchise to eighteen-year-olds. All of the available evidence indicates that eighteen-to-twenty year olds are the least likely age group in the electorate to vote.[4] The addition of this age group to the electorate has, therefore, resulted in a substantial reduction in overall voting levels. Since there is a larger proportion of eighteen-to-twenty year olds in the black population than in the total population, their effect on black voting rates has been especially strong, reducing the effect of the southern voters enfranchised by the Voting Rights Act.

Another noteworthy development is that there has been an even steeper decline for the electorate as a whole than for the black electorate. The data in Table 12-1 indicate that the gap between the white electorate and the black electorate, which had been about 11 to 13 percentage points for most of the 16-year period, was down to about 10 percentage points in 1980. (This assumes that overreporting rates remain constant over time. Here, too, indications are that the Census Bureau's data somewhat overstate the turnout rate, since the official vote tabulations reveal that only 52.9 percent of the total voting-age population actually voted, compared to 59.8 percent who reported having voted).

More disturbing than the overall decline in voting is that voting rates for the

Table 12-1. Reported voter participation of persons of voting age by race, 1980, 1976, 1972, 1968, and 1964 (in thousands)

Subject	Presidential election				
	1980	1976	1972	1968	1964
Black					
Number who reported that they voted	8,287	7,273	7,032	6,300	6,467[a]
Percent of voting age population who reported that they voted	50.5	49	52	58	57[a]
Percent of registered population who reported that they voted	84.1	83	80	87	NA
White					
Number who reported that they voted	83,855	78,808	78,166	72,213	70,204
Percent of voting age population who reported that they voted	60.9	61	64	69	71
Percent of registered population who reported that they voted	89.1	89	88	92	NA

NA = Not available
[a] Includes persons of "other" races.
Source: U.S. Bureau of the Census, Current Population Survey, 1977; data for 1980 is from the unpublished results of the 1980 post-election survey.

higher socioeconomic groups have remained relatively high while those for lower socioeconomic groups have plunged.[5] Even though specialists stress that socioeconomic characteristics are among the most powerful determinants of voting behavior, with low-status individuals much less likely to vote than those of high status, the current trend is surprising and ominous. The socioeconomic factors alone do not seem to account satisfactorily for the falloff. Cavanagh suggests that it might reflect declining attention to policies and programs of direct interest to low-income people.

The literature on black voting behavior identifies four broad sets of factors that contribute to low voter turnout. These are 1) the social and psychological scars of a history of subordination and deliberate exclusion from politics; 2) current socioeconomic and psychological characteristics of the black population; 3) structural or procedural arrangements that discourage voting; and 4) institutional and leadership styles within black communities.

Unlike any other racial or ethnic group in the society, the overwhelming majority of the black population was, for decades, denied by law the most basic political rights. Even after this officially sanctioned exclusion from politics ended, an array of equally effective indirect and unofficial devices accomplished the same result. This history of exclusion left scars whose full depth and effects are still not fully known. Clearly, however, it denied blacks the opportunity to develop, through use, the skills and attitudes vital to political participation; it denied them the development of strong convictions about their right to participate; and it undermined the transmission of participatory attitudes to succeeding generations.[6]

Most of the recent research on black voting behavior focuses on socioeconomic and psychological characteristics as impediments to increased voting. As we noted earlier, a large body of research has shown that in general, the propensity to participate in politics increases as one moves up the socioeconomic scale. According to Verba and Nie, "Political participation is predominantly the activity of wealthier, better educated citizens with high status jobs."[7] A distressingly large segment of the black population remains at the bottom of the socioeconomic scale. In 1976, 27 percent of blacks between ages twenty and twenty-three did not have a high school education, while only 15 percent of whites were in this situation. Similarly, only one in ten blacks aged twenty-five to thirty-four had a college education, compared to one in four whites.[8] The gap remains equally wide with respect to occupation and income levels. These socioeconomic conditions are formidable barriers to the full use of black voting strength.

Certain psychological characteristics have also been shown to affect voting levels. Most important in this regard are feelings of effectiveness in influencing government (political efficacy) and level of trust in government. Social scientists agree that the higher the levels of political efficacy and political trust, the higher the level of voting is likely to be. They also agree that blacks exhibit relatively lower levels of these attitudes than whites do. These attitudes among blacks are believed to be the products of distinctive socialization experiences, experiences and perceptions of government, and historically subordinate status in the society.[9]

Procedural or structural factors also are believed to impede or discourage black voting. Among the procedural factors are registration and residency requirements for voting. Some studies emphasize that because they increase the effort required to vote and eliminate the highly mobile, they discourage especially those of low socioeconomic status.[10]

And of course, as this book amply demonstrates, vote dilution itself has a strong and pervasive negative effect on black voting. Racially gerrymandered legislative districts and at-large or multimember districts do not directly interfere with the right to vote, but they remove one of the major incentives for blacks *to* vote—that is, to select a representative who will represent their interests.

Particular political styles and institutional roles within black communities also seem to affect voting levels. An important feature of black politics has been the heavy reliance on mediating institutions or individuals. Institutions such as the church and national civil rights organizations, as well as individual community leaders, historically have been advocates for blacks, acting as intermediaries between blacks and public officials. Their effectiveness in articulating black interests probably has reduced the perceived need for individual political action.

Insight into the effects of such mediators is provided by Charles Hamilton's study of client-patron relations in some black neighborhoods of New York City. Although the study is limited to a single program in one city, its findings might very well be more broadly applicable. Hamilton suggests that the introduction of several major social programs aimed at neighborhood improvement, with the participation of residents and an accompanying cadre of program leaders and community activists, resulted in the development of a patron-recipient relationship which is

> hardly likely to lead to the kind of politicization that maximizes political influence. Indeed, such a relationship creates a model of process-product-participation that does not stress the efficacy of a major process (electoral politics) in the political system. Recipients receive benefits (products), but these are not a function of their voting (active participation). Rather, recipients receive these benefits through nonactivity and passivity or through episode protest politics.[11]

Hamilton suggests that this depoliticizing effect might be partly responsible for the extremely low voting level for the incumbent black representative in the neighborhoods studied.

White urban ethnic groups, on the other hand, tended to develop political relationships in which they provided support to a party or candidate in return for specific benefits. Such a relationship was built on the necessity to vote and thus encouraged voting. Hamilton observes, however, that in his study, the patron isolated the individual from the political arena in which decisions are actually made. To the extent that this picture holds generally, it suggests that programs intended to be beneficial to blacks might have had the unintended effect of reducing voting by blacks.

Although all the specific reasons for relatively low turnout by blacks are not clear, it seems clear that the electoral power of the black population is substantially underutilized. A number of events since 1980 point to a substantial increase in black registration and voting, a development that augurs well for greater influence on government. However, the relationship between the vote and decisions about distribution of benefits is neither clear nor direct. In the traditional model of representative government, the vote elects representatives whose decisions embrace both the particular good of constituents and the general good of the society. In our highly competitive political arena, distributive policy decisions are rarely clear-cut responses to a specific group.

In general, one might distinguish between three broad means of exerting influence through voting. First, and farthest removed from specific interests, is the traditional representational path in which the vote legitimizes decision-makers and reflects the broad values of the electorate. Blacks as voters can influence policy direction through a choice of candidates, and that influence can be decisive when the black community is cohesive while the rest of the electorate is evenly divided. Here, however, the vote does not shape specific policy decisions. Second, the vote is a commodity that the voter trades to a candidate or party in return for specific benefits on the assumption that the candidate or party receiving that vote has the capacity to deliver the desired benefits. This is epitomized in the big-city machine politics of the past in which various white ethnic groups were prominent elements. Third, the voter may gain influence by selecting a racial or ethnic compatriot who is presumed to have a special attachment to and understanding of his/her group, and whose election, in addition, has symbolic value for that group. Although the black vote is influential to some extent in all three ways, its use in electing black representatives has been particularly important and deserves special attention.

Black Office Holding

In any hierarchy of participatory activities, holding elective office ranks at the very top. For blacks, winning elective office has been a deep and long-standing aspiration. It has had considerable symbolic value, and, even more important, it offers especially valuable opportunities to influence public policy, particularly the distribution of benefits.

To a great extent, the black elected official (BEO) provides the principal link between the black vote and the distribution of benefits. BEOs are the products of black votes, and they are in many respects the focus of black expectations for a more responsive government. The increase of recent years in the number and variety of elective offices held by blacks is directly linked to the growth and geographical distribution of the black electorate. The emergence of the big-city black mayor since the mid-1960s, for example, is primarily the result of changes in the racial composition of the cities involved. Whether as members of Congress, mayors, city councilmembers, or law enforcement officials, BEOs come mainly from majority-black constituencies, or must depend on a large black vote augmented by a small share of the nonwhite vote to win.

In elections in which black candidates compete with whites for elective office, not only is the black vote for the black candidate generally overwhelming, but even in a losing cause, the level of voting rises above the usual level for that electorate.[12] This was the case in recent mayoral elections in Chicago, Boston, and Philadelphia, where blacks were candidates and black turnout was unusually high, equalling or surpassing that of whites. (This consistently strong level of support by blacks is accompanied by a high level of expectations. Several case studies

Table 12-2. Change in number of black elected officials by category of office, 1970–1983

Year	Total BEOs N	Total BEOs % Change	Federal N	Federal % Change	State N	State % Change	Substate regional N	Substate regional % Change	County N	County % Change	Municipal N	Municipal % Change	Judicial/law enforcement N	Judicial/law enforcement % Change	Education N	Education % Change
1970	1,469	—	10	—	169	—	—	—	92	—	623	—	213	—	362	—
1971	1,860	26.6	14	40.0	202	19.5	—	—	120	30.4	785	26.0	274	28.6	465	28.5
1972	2,264	21.7	14	0.0	210	4.0	—	—	176	46.7	932	18.7	263	-4.0	669	43.9
1973	2,621	15.8	16	14.3	240	14.3	—	—	211	19.9	1,053	13.0	334	27.0	767	14.6
1974	2,991	14.1	17	6.3	239	-0.4	—	—	242	14.7	1,360	29.2	340	1.8	793	3.4
1975	3,503	17.1	18	5.9	281	17.6	—	—	305	26.0	1,573	15.7	387	13.8	939	18.4
1976	3,979	13.6	18	0.0	281	0.0	30	—	355	16.4	1,889	20.1	412	6.5	994	5.9
1977	4,311	8.3	17	-5.6	299	6.4	33	10.0	381	7.3	2,083	10.3	447	8.5	1,051	5.7
1978	4,503	4.5	17	0.0	299	0.0	26	-21.2	410	7.6	2,159	3.6	454	1.6	1,138	8.3
1979	4,607	2.3	17	0.0	313	4.7	25	-3.8	398	-2.9	2,224	3.0	486	7.0	1,144	0.5
1980	4,912	6.6	17	0.0	323	3.2	25	0.0	451	13.3	2,356	5.9	526	8.2	1,214	6.1
1981	5,038	2.6	18	5.9	341	5.6	30	20.0	449	-0.4	2,384	1.2	549	4.4	1,267	4.4
1982	5,160	2.4	18	0.0	336	-1.5	35	16.6	465	3.6	2,477	3.9	563	2.6	1,266	-0.08
1983	5,606	8.6	21	16.7	379	12.8	29	-17.1	496	6.7	2,697	8.9	607	7.8	1,377	8.8

Source: Joint Center for Political Studies, *Focus* 12 (1984): no. 1, 8.

of big-city black mayors suggest that the unrealistically high level of public expectations create unique pressures on the mayor and set the stage for swift and deep disillusionment of the black electorate.)

Table 12-2 shows that, since 1970 (when the annual survey of black elected officials began), the number of BEOs has grown by approximately 300 percent. Moreover, there has been growth during every year. In fact, while overall black voting levels do not reflect the profound impact of the Voting Rights Act of 1965, gains in the number of blacks holding elective office clearly do.

While blacks outside the South had made some progress in electing blacks to public office, the obstacles to black voting and officeholding in the South before the enactment of the Voting Rights Act limited severely the opportunities for blacks to win public office even when they were a distinct majority. However, since passage of the act, the South has experienced the most rapid growth in the number of BEOs, going from 703 in 1970 to 3,140 in 1982, an increase of 346.7 percent (Table 12-3).

Although there has been encouraging progress in winning elective office, that progress masks the fact that blacks are still severely underrepresented among elected public officials: Blacks are now 11.6 percent of the total population of the country, but they hold just over 1 percent of the elective offices. Such severe underrepresentation is partly a product of the distinctly racial character of voting in the society and partly the result of vote dilution, which continues to limit severely their opportunities to win elective offices.

While there have been candidates such as Mervyn Dymally, Wilson Riles, Edward Brooke, and others who have won office in a statewide electorate that is overwhelmingly white, they are the exceptions to the rule. Most blacks must depend for their election on black votes. This reality makes especially devastating the use of dilutionary measures. To assess the full costs of vote dilution, we must consider the available evidence about the relationship between electoral participation by blacks and the distribution of benefits to them.

ASSESSING THE EFFECTS OF ELECTORAL PARTICIPATION ON THE DISTRIBUTION OF PUBLIC BENEFITS

What difference does electoral participation by blacks make in the level and kinds of benefits they receive from government? Do blacks obtain benefits they would not have received otherwise? As we indicated earlier, to establish causal relationships between political participation and policy outcomes is quite difficult. Nevertheless, several analysts have explored the impact on benefit distribution of black political participation generally, and for the specific effects of voting, holding elective office, or the holding of a specific office such as mayor.[13]

Public benefits at the disposal of government include the broad array of services, facilities, employment and other opportunities affected by governmental action. Although some of these benefits have always been distributed in direct response to political considerations, others are distributed on the basis of other criteria. Furthermore, the basis for benefits distribution changes over time in response to

Table 12-3.   Change in number of black elected officials by region and
state, 1970–1982

State	1970	1982	Growth (percentage)
Northeast	238	577	142.4
Connecticut	31	54	74.2
Maine	0	4	*
Massachusetts	8	28	250.0
New Hampshire	0	0	0.0
New Jersey	73	170	132.9
New York	75	192	156.0
Pennsylvania	49	123	151.0
Rhode Island	2	6	200.0
Vermont	0	0	0.0
North Central	396	1,090	175.3
Illinois	74	325	339.2
Indiana	30	67	123.3
Iowa	5	6	20.0
Kansas	6	26	333.3
Michigan	110	293	166.4
Minnesota	8	10	25.0
Missouri	65	147	126.2
Nebraska	2	6	200.0
North Dakota	0	0	0.0
Ohio	89	184	106.7
South Dakota	0	0	0.0
Wisconsin	7	16	128.6
South	703	3,140	346.7
Alabama	86	269	212.8
Arkansas	55	219	298.2
Delaware	9	22	144.4
District of Columbia	8	254	3,075.0
Florida	36	118	227.8
Georgia	40	271	577.5
Kentucky	41	79	92.7
Louisiana	64	372	481.3
Maryland	43	82	90.7
Mississippi	81	424	423.5
North Carolina	62	266	329.0
Oklahoma	36	82	127.8
South Carolina	38	235	518.4
Tennessee	38	127	234.2
Texas	29	207	613.8
Virginia	36	93	158.3
West Virginia	1	20	1,900.0

State	1970	1982	Growth (percentage)
West	130	308	136.9
Alaska	1	2	100.0
Arizona	7	15	114.3
California	105	239	127.6
Colorado	7	14	100.0
Hawaii	1	2	100.0
Idaho	0	0	0.0
Montana	0	0	0.0
Nevada	3	8	166.7
New Mexico	3	6	100.0
Oregon	0	6	*
Utah	0	1	*
Washington	4	15	275.0
Wyoming	1	0	− 100.0

*Not meaningful.

Source: T. E. Cavanagh and D. Stockton, *Black Elected Officials and Their Constituencies* (Washington, D.C.: Joint Center for Political Studies, 1983).

governmental reform and the professionalization of certain activities. Not surprisingly, then, virtually all studies of the effects of black electoral participation are tentative, largely impressionistic, and limited in scope.

Although influence at the national level is important to blacks and indeed has been the primary focus for most blacks, studies of the effects of electoral participation focus primarily on the local level. Localities are much more manageable units of analysis than the nation as a whole, and the character of local politics better facilitates the attempt to relate electoral activity to benefit distribution.

The growing body of literature on the implications of black electoral participation can, for convenience, be reviewed in terms of three broad approaches to influence. The first explores the extent to which black electoral participation affects local decision-making generally; the second focuses on a single type of benefit, employment; and the third type looks for change in policy priorities reflected in expenditure patterns.

General Impact on Political Decision-Making

All of the major studies of the relationship between black electoral participation and the distribution of public benefits suggest that electoral participation does indeed make a difference, albeit a limited difference. The most extensive examination of this relationship is still that done more than a decade ago by William Keech (1968), which was based on case studies of Tuskegee, Alabama, and Durham, North Carolina. Keech found that electoral participation made an important difference in both localities. Participation brought about changes in the outcome of elections; "in the distribution of public services, including garbage collection, street paving, recreational facilities, and fire stations; in the employment of blacks by the city governments''; and in eliminating some forms of discrimination. Keech reported of Tuskegee that ''Negro votes brought a radical change in the distribution of public services, including garbage collection, street paving, and recreational facilities. Negroes were hired for the first time to municipal service positions and appointed to boards and commissions.''[14]

Keech found, however, that the vote was much less effective in eliminating the effects of past discrimination, in bringing about drastic change, or in preventing discriminatory practices in the private sector. Of course, his study occurred at a time when southern blacks were still just beginning to overcome the formidable array of obstacles to the ballot, and resistance to blacks in politics was still very strong even in the two jurisdictions he studied. We do not know whether his findings would have been very different a decade later.

A recent study of the distribution of benefits in Chicago examined four broad areas of service delivery to determine what kinds of forces influenced distributional decisions. Although the focus was not on the impact of black electoral participation, the effects of blacks on some of these distributional decisions were examined. The study stated that ''the data strongly suggest that local officials respond to black demands and protests by providing black neighborhoods with a greater share of available resources. Black wards primarily gained swimming pools, athletic fields, and playgrounds.''[15] In general, however, the study concluded that distribution of benefits was not generally the result of rational political calculation but was ''largely a function of past decisions, population shifts, technological changes and reliance upon technical-rational criteria, and professional values.''[16]

This study of Chicago raises a number of questions about the sources of influence on decision-making in large, complex cities. Have cities moved from politically determined decisions to technical-rational decisions, thereby gradually reducing the room for influence from black political activities? One extensive critique of this Chicago study concludes that it probably understated the degree to which efforts to provide political benefits to racial and ethnic groups influenced administrative decisions.[17]

Public Employment

Several studies examine the impact of electoral participation on benefits to blacks in the area of public employment. Not only has there been a tradition of distributing some municipal jobs as political rewards, but these jobs have been an opportunity ladder for many disadvantaged ethnic groups. Blacks, like these earlier groups, have relied on a steadily expanding public sector for jobs and particularly for the upward mobility these jobs provide. Blacks have held a disproportionately large number of local government jobs.

In his classic study of the Negro in Chicago politics, Harold Gosnell's discussion of the effects of Negro politics centered mainly on the employment benefits that resulted from black support of the city's political machine. He concluded that, ''Participation in politics has brought a certain number of more or less desirable jobs to the group.'' He suggested that jobs such as those in the postal service were "less the result of specific political pressures than [they have been] the product of the general participation of Negroes in local politics."[18]

Of course, relating black public employment increases to electoral participation is more complex than it might seem initially. The size and composition of the local labor force and the introduction of equal employment opportunity requirements at the initiative of the federal government are important factors that might affect level of employment opportunities for blacks independently. Also important are civil service requirements. In fact, some analysts suggested during the early 1970s that the existence of civil service and union constraints on employment would severely restrict the employment opportunities blacks could expect from their electoral participation.[19]

A recent study by Peter Eisinger explored the effects of black "political power" on municipal employment of blacks in 40 cities, using analytical methods that allowed for observation of the independent effects of such variables as population size, educational characteristics of the work force, and black political power, particularly the election of black mayors. Eisinger concludes that blacks made substantial gains in both the number and quality of municipal jobs during the decade of the 1970s. Two of the most powerful influences on this development were the percentage of the localities' population that is black and the presence of a black mayor. Eisinger suggests that even in economically distressed cities, black leadership "seems to have created and sustained opportunities for black employment."[20]

The importance of the public employment benefit for blacks goes beyond merely finding additional jobs, for employment in local government provides opportunities for influencing the distribution of benefits. Analysts have long noted that bureaucrats are part of the ruling class: their access to information and elected policymakers and their participation in agenda-setting confers considerable power.

Findings of these studies are generally inconclusive. One recent study of three major cities with black mayors found that black mayors did not seem to spend more than their predecessors and that there were few consistent changes in spending priorities for all three black mayoral administrations.[21] Other studies suggest a tendency for increased spending for social programs and reduced spending for law enforcement or infrastructural items, but the evidence of the effects of a black mayor on public policy is weakest in this area.

CONCLUSION

The evidence from a growing body of research clearly indicates that black electoral participation influences the distribution of public benefits at the local level. It does this by making public officials more attentive and responsive to their needs for basic community services; by increasing the number and quality of municipal jobs held by blacks; and to a lesser extent by inducing shifts in the program priorities of local governments. The employment opportunities seem to be the most prominent and important benefit, since they provide opportunities for upward mobility for the job holders and opportunities to influence both the development and implementation of public policy.

The benefits that accrue to blacks from political participation underscore the high cost of nonvoting by blacks and of the dilution of the black vote. While black voting levels might be increased through special attempts at voter mobilization, the extent of that increase will be limited by both the socioeconomic characteristics of the population and by the remaining barriers to full participation. Eliminating the devices that dilute black voting becomes an especially urgent necessity if American democracy is to provide the same opportunities for blacks that it has for other Americans.

Whatever uncertainties remain about the extent and character of the effects of black political participation on the distribution of benefits, the current level of black voting is the product of a complex array of factors. Some could be remedied in the short run by policy changes such as altered registration requirements and other electoral reforms and by more vigorous educational and mobilization efforts by blacks and by the political parties. However, the socioeconomic and psychological bases of nonvoting cannot be remedied in the short run. Overall improvement in the socioeconomic conditions of blacks and more positive experiences with or perceptions of government will gradually lay the foundation for increased voting.

With respect to elective office, a large part of the problem is the result of discriminatory electoral arrangements. If black electoral power is to be increased substantially, it will be necessary to dismantle the discriminatory mechanisms that now block the path to elective office for many blacks.

NOTES

1. See T. Clark, "The Irish Ethic and the Spirit of Patronage," *Ethnicity* 2 (1975): 305–359; E. Cornwall, "Ethnic Group Representation: The Case of the Portuguese," *Polity* 13 (1975): 5–20.
2. M. L. King, Jr., "The Role of the Behavioral Sciences in the Civil Rights Movement," *Journal of Social Issues* 24 (1968).
3. W. Nelson, Jr., *Black Power in Gary* (Washington, D.C.: Joint Center for Political Studies, 1972).
4. R.E. Wolfinger and S. Rosenstone, *Who Votes?* (New Haven: Yale University Press, 1980).
5. T. E. Cavanagh, "Changes in American Voter Turnout," *Political Science Quarterly* 96 (1981): 53–65.
6. M. D. Morris, *The Politics of Black America* (Washington, D.C.: Harper and Row, 1975).
7. S. Verba and N. Nie, *Participation in America: Political Democracy and Social Equality* (New York: Harper and Row, 1972).
8. U.S. Bureau of the Census, *The Social and Economic Status of the Black Population in the United States, 1790–1978*, p-23, No. 80 (Washington, D.C.: U.S. Bureau of the Census, 1980).
9. See Morris, *The Politics of Black America*, 123–135.
10. Wolfinger and Rosenstone, *Who Votes?*

11. C. V. Hamilton, "The Patron-Recipient Relationship and Minority Politics in New York City," *Political Science Quarterly* 94 (1979): 211–227.

12. T. Pettigrew, "Militant Civil Servants in New York City," in *Politics/America* ed. Herrington Bryce (New York: Praeger, 1976), 14–28.

13. A. Karnig and S. Welch, *Black Representation and Urban Policy* (Chicago: University of Chicago Press, 1980).

14. W. Keech, *The Impact of Negro Voting: The Role of the Vote in the Quest for Equality* (Skokie, Ill.: Rand McNally, 1963).

15. K. R. Mladenka, "The Urban Bureaucracy and the Chicago Political Machine: Who Gets What and the Limits of Political Control," *American Political Science Review* 74 (1980): 993.

16. *Ibid.*, 996.

17. D. Koehler and M. Wrightson, "Inequality in the Delivery of Urban Services, A Reconsideration of the Chicago Parks." Paper prepared for the 1983 Annual Meeting of the American Political Science Association, Chicago, Ill.

18. H. Gosnell, *Negro Politicians: The Rise of Negro Politics in Chicago* (Chicago: University of Chicago Press, 1969).

19. F. Piven, "Militant Civil Servants in New York City," in *Politics/America* ed. W. Burnham (New York: Van Nostrand, Reinhard, 1973).

20. P. Eisinger, *Black Employment in City Government, 1973–1980* (Washington, D.C.: Joint Center for Political Studies, 1983).

21. S. M. Watson, "Do Mayors Matter? The Role of Black Leadership in Urban Policy." Paper prepared for the 1980 Annual Meeting of the American Political Science Association, Washington, D.C.

Editor's Postscript
to the Paperback Edition of
Minority Vote Dilution

When I was asked by the Joint Center for Political Studies to edit this volume of essays, the Supreme Court's 1980 decision, *City of Mobile v. Bolden,* had recently been announced. That decision rendered minority vote dilution very difficult to attack on constitutional grounds, for reasons I explained in chapter 1. *Bolden* was thus a major setback to minority voters — blacks and Hispanics in particular — who had looked to the Constitution to protect their right to elect candidates of their choice.

Civil rights groups across the country quickly rallied behind efforts to persuade Congress to amend Section 2 of the Voting Rights Act of 1965 so as to overcome the effects of *Bolden.* Various conservatives responded by defending the Court's decision and arguing that nothing further need be done to temper its effects. The Joint Center hoped that our book would clarify the issues thus provoked and in so doing help Congress see its way clear to support the amendment, especially in light of the opposition to it that initially had been expressed by President Reagan and his Assistant Attorney General for Civil Rights, William Bradford Reynolds.

Minority Vote Dilution did not appear in time to affect the debate over the 1982 amendment, as we had originally hoped. But it had other, largely unforeseen, consequences. In the summer of 1986 the Supreme Court announced its decision in *Thornburg v. Gingles,* its first interpretation of amended Section 2. The case had originated in North Carolina, where black citizens challenged a 1982 legislative redistricting plan, arguing that one single-member district and six multimember districts impaired black voters' ability to elect candidates of their choice. In the course of its reasoning, the Court in *Gingles* affirmatively cited several articles contained in *Minority Vote Dilution,* as well as other articles by some of the contributors.

The most closely reasoned (and lengthiest) essay in the book was "At-Large Elections and One Person, One Vote," by Alabama attorneys James Blacksher and Larry Menefee. An earlier version of the article had appeared in the *Hastings Law Journal,* which the Court also cited.[1] In *Minority Vote Dilution* I had summarized Blacksher and Menefee's conclusion as an urgent plea for "a much narrower set of evidentiary standards of dilution, which (a) in the name of fairness conform in simplicity to the criteria of proof required in *Reynolds v. Sims,* the major vote dilution case of the 1960s; (b) are easily applied; and (c) accord far less discretion to trial judges."

Blacksher and Menefee's revised standards were contained in the following proposal:

> An at-large election scheme for a state or local multirepresentative body is unconstitutional where jurisdiction-wide elections permit a bloc-voting majority, over a substantial period of time, consistently to defeat candidates publicly identified with the interests of and supported by a politically cohesive, geographically insular racial or ethnic minority group.

The Court in *Gingles* appeared to accept this proposal, holding that the essential questions in a vote dilution claim are whether racial bloc voting by the majority "will regularly defeat the choices of minority voters," and whether the challenged election system "operates to minimize or cancel out [minority voters'] ability to elect their preferred candidates." Proof of dilution requires, first, that the minority group is sufficiently large and geographically compact to constitute a majority in a single-member district; second, that the minority group be politically cohesive; and third, that the white majority sufficiently and ordinarily vote as a bloc to defeat the minority's preferred candidate.

Frank Parker, a prominent voting-rights attorney with the Lawyers' Committee for Civil Rights Under Law and also a contributor to the book, called *Gingles* a "stunning victory for minority voters challenging racially discriminatory electoral systems and a stunning defeat for the Reagan Administration's efforts in conjunction with the voting rights defense bar to restrict and undermine the application of the 1982 amendment to section 2 of the Voting Rights Act."[2]

I do not wish to exaggerate the role that our book may have played in *Gingles,* as several scholars and lawyers in addition to the contributors to this volume were also cited by the Court. The original North Carolina plaintiffs' lawyers — Leslie Winner of Charlotte and Lani Guinier, then with the NAACP Legal Defense Fund — and the plaintiffs' chief expert witness, Professor Bernard Grofman, deserve special mention for their contribution to the decision. Suffice it to say that the justices' argument broadly paralleled the central arguments of *Minority Vote Dilution,* to which they made reference, and the subsequent effects of *Gingles* have, by and large, been those hoped for by the Joint Center. These effects recently have been described by voting-rights attorney Laughlin McDonald of the American Civil Liberties Union.[3]

Yet once the policies one has plumped for become law, they often have some unpalatable consequences, and *Gingles* and its progeny are no exceptions. Pamela Karlan, a law professor at the University of Virginia and formerly with the NAACP Legal Defense Fund, has recently criticized *Gingles* and succeeding lower court decisions for putting too much stress on a "geographical baseline" as the measure of political exclusion of minority voters.[4] By this she means that the courts, by requiring plaintiffs in dilution cases to demonstrate that they are sufficiently numerous and geographically compact to constitute a majority of a single-member district, preclude remedies for minority citizens who may be geographically dispersed across a jurisdiction or not sufficiently numerous to meet what appears to be the *Gingles* test, but nonetheless constitute a sizable population with identifiable interests which has been unable to elect candidates of its choice or otherwise be incorporated into the political system.

Thus, consistent with both the letter and spirit of revised Section 2, Karlan proposes other remedies in addition to single-member districts, including limited and cumulative voting, both capable of overcoming barriers to minorities' election of their preferred candidates. (In this she is expanding on arguments made by Edward Still in the present volume.) She also proposes remedies that would give more influence to already elected minority representatives when legislative rules preclude their effectively representing constituents' interests. The time is at hand, Karlan writes, "for federal courts to be . . . creative in developing a theory of liability under Section 2 that recognizes that minority vote dilution is not always simply a product of at-large as opposed to district-based elections and to develop remedies of equal ingenuity finally to fulfill the promise of civic inclusion."[5]

It is also time, I would add, for voting-rights scholars and lawyers to take the lead yet again in fomenting the creative thinking Karlan advocates. America is still a long way from the goal of civic inclusion of its racial and ethnic minorities, in spite of the gains that have been made.

NOTES

1. James U. Blacksher and Larry T. Menefee, "From *Reynolds v. Sims* to *City of Mobile v. Bolden:* Have the White Suburbs Commandeered the Fifteenth Amendment?" *Hastings Law Journal* 34 (1982), 1–64.
2. Frank R. Parker, "Memorandum to All Attorneys Handling Voting Rights Cases and Other Interested Persons," Joint Center for Political Studies, June 30, 1986.
3. Laughlin McDonald, "The Quiet Revolution in Minority Voting Rights," *Vanderbilt Law Review* 42 (1989), 1249–1297.
4. Pamela S. Karlan, "Maps and Misreadings: The Role of Georgraphic Compactness in Racial Vote Dilution Litigation," *Harvard Civil Rights–Civil Liberties Law Review* 24 (1989), 173–248.
5. Ibid., 248.

Contributors

HOWARD BALL is a professor of political science and dean of the College of Social and Behavioral Science at the University of Utah. He has taught at Rutgers, Hofstra, Mississippi State and Utah universities. He is the author or coauthor of a number of books, including *Compromised Compliance: Implementation of the 1965 Voting Rights Act.* In 1981–82, he was president of the Mississippi Political Science Association.

JAMES BLACKSHER is a civil rights attorney in private practice in Mobile, Alabama. While attending the University of Alabama School of Law, he was a member of *Alabama Law Review* and the founder and student director of the Law School Legal Aid Society. His role as cooperating attorney for the NAACP Legal Defense and Educational Fund in the landmark *Bolden v. City of Mobile* case was designated by *The American Lawyer* as the Outstanding Civil Rights Performance for the year 1982.

CHANDLER DAVIDSON is a professor and past chairperson of the Department of Sociology at Rice University. His research on racial discrimination has been the subject of a book, *Biracial Politics,* and several articles. He has worked as a consultant or expert witness in sixteen lawsuits involving allegations of discrimination, including *Bolden v. City of Mobile.*

DREW S. DAYS III is an associate professor of law at Yale Law School. Previous posts include first assistant counsel for the NAACP Legal Defense and Educational Fund, and assistant attorney general for civil rights in the Carter administration.

ARMAND DERFNER is a lawyer active for many years in vote dilution cases and cases under the Voting Rights Act. He has also been involved in voting rights legislation. Currently he is writing a history of the 1982 extension of the Voting Rights Act.

LUIS FRAGA is an assistant professor of political science at the University of Oklahoma. He received his B.A. degree from Harvard and his M.A. and Ph.D. from Rice University. A student of urban and minority politics, he has contributed research to a number of vote dilution suits. His doctoral dissertation is a study of nonpartisan slating groups.

LANI GUINIER is assistant counsel to the NAACP Legal Defense and Educational Fund. A graduate of Radcliffe College (cum laude) and Yale Law School, she litigates in all areas of civil rights law, but has worked primarily on voting rights cases. During the Carter administration, she was special assistant to Drew S. Days III, assistant attorney general for civil rights.

GEORGE KORBEL was graduated from the University of Minnesota Law School. Presently the litigation coordinator for Texas Rural Legal Aid, he has served as counsel in suits resulting in single-member-district remedies to vote dilution in Houston, San Antonio, Waco, and several other Texas cities and counties. He represented Hispanic interests in *White v. Regester*, a major dilution case decided by the Supreme Court in 1973.

J. MORGAN KOUSSER is the author of *The Shaping of Southern Politics: Suffrage Restriction and the Establishment of the One-Party South, 1880–1910*, as well as over forty-five articles and book reviews. Professor of history and social science at the California Institute of Technology, where he has taught since 1969, he has also been a visiting professor at Michigan and Harvard. He has been appointed Harmsworth Professor of American History at Oxford University for 1984–85.

DALE KRANE is associate professor of political science and coordinator of the public policy and administration program at Mississippi State University. He is a coauthor of *Compromised Compliance: Implementation of the 1965 Voting Rights Act* and the author of articles and essays on program implementation, intergovernmental relations, southern politics, and comparative public policy.

THOMAS P. LAUTH is associate professor of political science and director of the doctor of public administration program at the University of Georgia. His articles on public and state and urban administration have appeared in many journals. He is coauthor of *Compromised Compliance: Implementation of the 1965 Voting Rights Act* (1982).

PEYTON MCCRARY is a professor of history at the University of South Alabama. He was educated at the University of Virginia and Princeton University. He is author of the prize-winning book, *Abraham Lincoln and Reconstruction: The Louisiana Experiment*, and several articles and papers on the Civil War and Reconstruction periods. He is now working on a book-length study of the discriminatory purposes of at-large elections in the South.

LARRY MENEFEE is a civil rights attorney in private practice in Mobile, Alabama. He was educated at Auburn University and the University of Alabama School of Law. After serving as a law clerk for U.S. District Judge Daniel H. Thomas and spending two years in the Peace Corps in Venezuela, he joined the firm of Blacksher, Menefee and Stein, where he has served as counsel for plaintiffs in *Bolden v. City of Mobile* and a number of other vote dilution cases.

MILTON D. MORRIS, director of research and policy analysis for the Joint Center for Political Studies since 1979, was previously a senior fellow at the Brookings Institution. Earlier he had been an associate professor of political science at Southern Illinois University and a research associate with the Joint Center. His books include *The Politics of Black America, Curbing Illegal Immigration*, and *The Administration of Immigration Policy*.

FRANK R. PARKER is director of the Voting Rights Project of the Lawyers' Committee for Civil Rights Under Law in Washington, D.C. He has written extensively on voting rights issues and has litigated more than fifty cases involving congressional and legislative reapportionment, county redistricting, at-large county and municipal elections, and other voting issues.

EDWARD STILL is a civil rights lawyer in private practice in Birmingham, Alabama. He has been one of the lawyers for plaintiffs in reapportionment suits against the city of Mobile, Alabama; the city of Pensacola, Florida; Escambia County, Florida; and the Alabama State Legislature. He is also general counsel to the Alabama Democratic Party.

Index